THE KURDS IN ERDOĞAN'S TURKEY

Edinburgh Studies on Modern Turkey

Series General Editors: **Alpaslan Özerdem**, Dean of the School for Conflict Analysis and Resolution and Professor of Peace and Conflict Studies at George Mason University, VA, and **Ahmet Erdi Öztürk**, Lecturer in International Relations and Politics at London Metropolitan University and an affiliated scholar at the Institute for Research on Migration, Ethnicity and Society (REMESO) at Linköping University, Sweden.

Series Advisory Board: Ayşe Kadıoğlu (Harvard University), Hakan Yavuz (University of Utah), Samim Akgönül (University of Strasbourg), Rebecca Bryant (Utrecht University), Nukhet Ahu Sandal (Ohio University), Mehmet Gurses (Florida Atlantic University), Paul Kubicek (Oakland University), Sinem Akgül Açıkmeşe (Kadir Has University), Gareth Jenkins (Institute for Security and Development Policy), Stephen Karam (World Bank), Peter Mandaville (George Mason University).

Edinburgh Studies on Modern Turkey is an outlet for academic works that examine the domestic and international issues of the Turkish republic from its establishment in the 1920s until the present. This broadly defined frame allows the series to adopt both interdisciplinary and trans-disciplinary approaches, covering research on the country's history and culture as well as political, religious and socio-economic developments. The titles provide wide-ranging discussions of Turkey within its local and global context, utilising an eclectic range of methodological and theoretical approaches that include non-Western political and critical theory. The series is marked by openness and invites both detailed, area-specific case studies as well as broadly construed, interdisciplinary surveys of topics that are appropriately framed by the theme of the series.

Published and forthcoming titles

The Kurds in Erdoğan's Turkey: Balancing Identity, Resistance and Citizenship
William Gourlay

Religion, Identity and Power: Turkey and the Balkans in the Twenty-First Century
Ahmet Erdi Öztürk

edinburghuniversitypress.com/series/esmt

THE KURDS IN ERDOĞAN'S TURKEY

Balancing Identity, Resistance and Citizenship

William Gourlay

EDINBURGH
University Press

Edinburgh University Press is one of the leading university presses in the UK. We publish academic books and journals in our selected subject areas across the humanities and social sciences, combining cutting-edge scholarship with high editorial and production values to produce academic works of lasting importance. For more information visit our website: edinburghuniversitypress.com

© William Gourlay, 2020, 2022

Edinburgh University Press Ltd
The Tun – Holyrood Road
12(2f) Jackson's Entry
Edinburgh EH8 8PJ

First published in hardback by Edinburgh University Press 2020

Typeset in 11/15 Adobe Garamond by
IDSUK (DataConnection) Ltd

A CIP record for this book is available from the British Library

ISBN 978 1 4744 5919 8 (hardback)
ISBN 978 1 4744 5920 4 (paperback)
ISBN 978 1 4744 5922 8 (webready PDF)
ISBN 978 1 4744 5921 1 (epub)

The right of William Gourlay to be identified as the author of this work has been asserted in accordance with the Copyright, Designs and Patents Act 1988, and the Copyright and Related Rights Regulations 2003 (SI No. 2498).

CONTENTS

List of Figures	vi
Acknowledgements	vii
Introduction: Eruption in Diyarbakır	1
1 Identity, ethnicity, politics: from Kemalism to 'New Turkey'	18
2 Talking to Kurds about 'Identity'	43
3 Demarcating Kurdish culture	59
4 The Kurds and Islam: defying hegemony and the 'caliphate'	84
5 Contesting homeland(s): city, soil and landscape	112
6 Kurdayetî: Pan-Kurdish sentiment and solidarity	141
7 Oppression, solidarity, resistance	167
8 Kurds as citizens	193
Conclusion: reconciling ethnic identity, citizenship and the 'ideal' in Erdoğan's Turkey?	221
Bibliography	235
Index	266

FIGURES

I.1	Kurdish boys outside the walls of Diyarbakır, June 2015. © William Gourlay	13
1.1	Dancing during the Gezi Park protests, Istanbul, June 2013. © William Gourlay	34
2.1	Street life in Sur, Diyarbakır, June 2015. © William Gourlay	45
2.2	Kurdish boys in the backstreets of Diyarbakır, October 2014. © William Gourlay	49
4.1	Performance of Kurdish, Turkish, Armenian song, Cathedral of Surp Giragos, Diyarbakır, June 2013. © William Gourlay	103
5.1	The Hasan Paşa Han, Diyarbakır, November 2014. © William Gourlay	118
6.1	Graffiti in Kadıköy, Istanbul, November 2014. It reads, in Kurdish, 'Long live the Kobanî resistance'. © William Gourlay	151
7.1	Crowds gather at the HDP rally, Diyarbakır, 5 June 2015. © William Gourlay	184
8.1	Dancing at HDP rally, Diyarbakır, 5 June 2015. © William Gourlay	204
C.1	Kurds dance the *govend* in Eminönü, Istanbul, following the HDP's electoral success in June 2015. © William Gourlay	226

ACKNOWLEDGEMENTS

While there is only one name in the byline, there are many people who have contributed to the creation of this book, a project that has taken almost a quarter of a century to bear fruit. I must first acknowledge Associate Professors Pete Lentini and Ben MacQueen who supervised the thesis from which the book arises; thanks also to Andrew Singleton who gave shape to the thesis in its early days. During the marathon of thesis creation I shared regular Chocolate Hobnobs and the odd glass of *vin rouge* with many co-tenants in Room H5.57 – I thank them for their support and good cheer. In particular, I note the friendship, advice and encouragement of Dara Conduit, who has travelled a similar research-writing-publishing trajectory. Ahmet, Çemen and Gülen Polat helped demystify Turkish for me on many occasions. Janet McGarry was also extremely helpful in tracking down hard-to-find Turkish texts.

I would also like to acknowledge Shahram Akbarzadeh and Kerry O'Brien, who told me to aim high. Many members of the Kurdish Studies Network have responded to my queries. I thank Istanbul Şehir University for facilitating my research time in Turkey. Tezcan Gümüş has often offered help and translation skills. For several years, Bahar Başer has been a source of encouragement and quintessential Turkish warmth. Custodian of arcane Anatolian knowledge and Turkey-wide contacts, Pat Yale has been a great advocate and friend for decades – one day we will finally catch up in Diyarbakır, Pat!

Thanks also to Wayne Murphy for the wonderful map, and particular thanks to Martin Van Bruinessen for his helpful suggestions, keen eye and kind words.

Adela Rauchova was extremely patient and encouraging in the conceptualisation of this book. I thank Erdi Özturk and Alp Özerdem for allowing me to be a part of their new series. At Edinburgh University Press I have enjoyed working with Nicola Ramsey, Kirsty Woods, Emma Rees, Eliza Wright, Ian Brooke and Bekah Dey. My thanks also to the reviewers whose comments undoubtedly made this a better book. I must also note that I remain responsible for any errors or omissions.

Finally, heartfelt thanks to the countless Turks and Kurds who have offered advice, friendship, occasional directions, numerous cups of *çay*, generosity and spontaneous hospitality over many trips to Turkey. I am especially grateful to the many Kurds, in Diyarbakır, Istanbul and elsewhere, who put up with my questioning, generously giving their time and sharing their experiences to provide the data that made this book possible. My fervent hope is that all of the citizens of Turkey, regardless of ethnicity or religious affiliation, might live in a system that grants them the freedom and democracy that they deserve. *Yaşasın özgürlük/Her bijî azadî*!

Chapter 4 is based on William Gourlay (2018): 'Beyond "brotherhood" and the "caliphate": Kurdish relationships to Islam in an era of AKP authoritarianism and ISIS terror', *British Journal of Middle Eastern Studies*, DOI: 10.1080/13530194.2018.1534679, © 2018 British Society for Middle Eastern Studies, reprinted by permission of Taylor & Francis Ltd, http://www.tandfonline.com on behalf of British Society for Middle Eastern Studies. Parts of Chapters 5 and 7 are from William Gourlay (2018) 'The Kurds and the "Others": Kurdish politics as an inclusive, multi-ethnic vehicle in Turkey', *Journal of Muslim Minority Affairs*, 38(4), pp. 475–92, © Institute of Muslim Minority Affairs, reprinted by permission of Taylor & Francis Ltd, on behalf of Institute of Muslim Minority Affairs. Chapter 6 is derived in part from William Gourlay (2018), '*Kurdayetî*: Pan-Kurdish solidarity and cross-border links in times of war and trauma', *Middle East Critique*, 27(1), pp. 25–42, © Editors of Middle East Critique, reprinted by permission of Taylor & Francis Ltd, on behalf of Editors of Middle East Critique. Chapter 7 is derived in part from William Gourlay (2018) 'Oppression, solidarity, resistance: The forging of Kurdish identity in Turkey', *Ethnopolitics*, 17(2), pp. 130–46, © The Editor of Ethnopolitics, reprinted by permission of Taylor & Francis Ltd, on behalf of The Editor of Ethnopolitics.

For Claire, Bridget and Tommy, my favourite travel companions of all time, and Mum and Dad, who always encouraged every journey, however conceived, and reminded: profunda cernit.

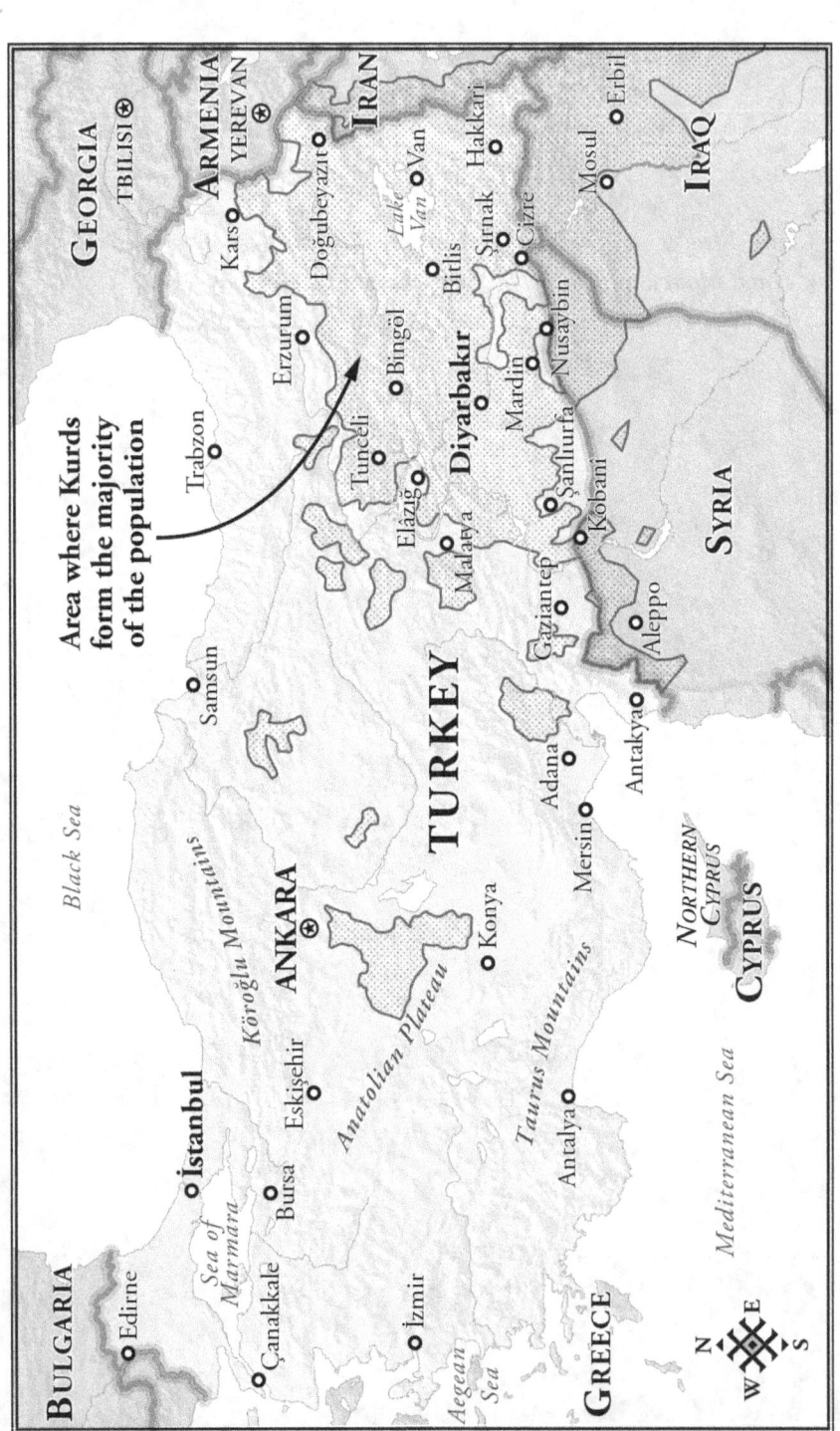

Turkey, and areas of majority Kurdish population. Created by Wayne Murphy using data from naturalearthdata.com, and GeoEPR dataset from Julian Wucherpfennig et al. (2011), 'Politically relevant ethnic groups across space and time: Introducing the GeoEPR dataset', *Conflict Management and Peace Science*, 28(5), pp. 423–37.

INTRODUCTION: ERUPTION IN DIYARBAKIR

In the early evening of 7 June 2015 Diyarbakır erupted. The largest Kurdish-populated city in Turkey's south-east, Diyarbakır sits astride the River Tigris, approximately 1,000 kilometres as the crow flies from Istanbul, a short distance from the borders of Syria and Iraq. For most, if not all, Kurds in Turkey, Diyarbakır looms large as a city of historical significance, a centre for political, cultural and intellectual activity. Some look upon it as a *baş kent*, a capital city, to a putative state that exists only in name: Kurdistan.

Diyarbakır is no stranger to eruptions. Since the establishment of the Republic of Turkey in 1923, the city has often been the scene of political violence and confrontation between Kurds and the instruments of the Turkish state. A Kurdish rebellion led by Sufi Sheikh Said broke out in Diyarbakır province in February 1925, the hapless sheikh being captured within two months and hung from the gallows near one of the grand gates in the old city walls. The uprising that Sheikh Said led was, in large measure, a reaction to the impositions of the newly formed Republic, which, premised on 'unity of language, culture and ideal',[1] sought to deny the very existence of Kurds within its borders. Over fifty years later, amid ongoing disavowal of the Kurds' existence and smothering of their political voices, Diyarbakır again became a flashpoint. Abdullah Öcalan and a cohort of Kurdish nationalists, seeking to carve an independent 'Kurdistan' out of Turkish territory, established the Kurdistan Workers' Party (Partiya Karkerên Kurdistanê, PKK) in Diyarbakır.[2]

The PKK embarked on a military campaign that ravaged Turkey's Kurdish-populated south-east and saw the PKK swiftly branded a terrorist organisation by the state. Diyarbakır became a site of Kurdish civilian protest, routinely met by the heavy hand of Turkey's security apparatus, and its hinterland saw clashes between PKK operatives and the Turkish armed forces continuing intermittently for over thirty years.

On that summer evening in 2015, sitting in a hotel room in Sur, the old walled city of Diyarbakır, I heard, from outside my window, a ripple of bangs and roars. I was familiar with the city's history of political tensions and violence. Such precedents did not reassure me that loud outbursts were of a peaceful nature – but the circumstances now appeared to be different. On that day, Turkey had gone to the polls to vote in a general election for the Grand National Assembly. The pro-Kurdish Halkların Demokratik Partisi (Peoples' Democratic Party; HDP) was making an all-or-nothing tilt at the parliament, seeking to overcome an electoral threshold that stipulated that any party failing to win 10 per cent of the national vote could not claim any seats in the assembly. Diyarbakır, as with much of the surrounding south-eastern region, was HDP heartland. The HDP was taking an enormous risk in competing outright in the election. No pro-Kurdish party had ever succeeded in passing the threshold. Should the HDP also fail to do so, any seats it won were, due to electoral bylaws, most likely to be granted to the ruling Justice and Development Party (Adalet ve Kalkinma Partisi; AKP), thereby increasing its majority and tightening its hold on the political sphere.

Leading up to the election, the mood in Diyarbakır, however, was cautiously optimistic. Over the preceding week, on street corners and in open spaces, I had witnessed spontaneous performances of the *govend*, a Kurdish dance, as people had excitedly come together in anticipation of the vote. Accompanied by bass drum and shrieking *zurna*, they linked hands and moved back and forth in a line dance marked by rhythmic chants, cheers and ululations. Meanwhile, reams of bright purple and green HDP bunting swung from lampposts, in alleyways across Diyarbakır's old town and between apartment buildings and office blocks in the newer neighbourhoods outside the city walls. The faces of HDP co-leaders Selahattin Demirtaş and Figen Yüksekdağ beamed from campaign posters splashed on walls and billboards featuring slogans in Turkish and Kurdish.

I had earlier asked a Kurdish man what he expected of the poll. '*Ya savaş ya barış*,' he shrugged – 'Either war or peace.' It soon became clear, however, that what I was hearing from my hotel room was an eruption of excitement rather than the opening salvoes of any 'war'. The bangs that I could hear in the twilight were fireworks; they were soon augmented by a raucous chorus of bass drums, whistles and car horns. In the weeks before the election, I had been told by cautious Istanbullus to avoid Diyarbakır entirely or, at the very least, to stay in my hotel room when election results were announced. As final voting figures came in it became clear that the HDP had passed the electoral threshold. It would claim 80 seats in the assembly, meaning that the ruling AKP had lost its majority for the first time since 2002. This was a political upheaval.

Despite the warnings, I decided against staying hunkered in my hotel room. I ventured to the lobby, meeting the hotel manager and assorted hangers-on. They were all chatting excitedly. They greeted me with grins, cheers, and slaps on the back. Proceeding outside, I encountered exuberant crowds that grew larger and louder as evening descended. Families and groups of men gathered on street corners or congregated in teahouses. Amid a welter of dust and fumes, in semi-darkness, youths in cars roared along the streets circling the city walls whistling and honking their horns. Others waved flags in the Kurdish *tricoleur* of green, red, yellow (*kesk, sor, zer* in Kurdish). Someone was pounding a bass drum. The Kurds of Diyarbakır were ecstatic. After years lacking representation, years of oppression, years of dismissal as 'terrorists' or 'separatists', Kurds now saw a political avenue opening before them. The HDP had won a place in Turkey's general assembly. Kurdish politics had come of age. Perhaps Turkish politics had come of age, too. The seemingly inexorable rise of the AKP and its leader, Recep Tayyip Erdoğan, had indeed been stopped. It was the dawn of a bright new era.

Or so it seemed.

Why should an election prompt warnings against visiting Kurdish cities such as Diyarbakır? Why might an election result in either 'war or peace'? Why did the HDP's entry into the Grand National Assembly evoke such euphoria among Kurds? What implications did it have for the ruling AKP and Erdoğan, recently directly elected to the presidency? The answers to these questions lie in the political circumstances of the Kurds, their relationship to the Republic of Turkey, the ways in which they define and uphold their identity and their place in – and impact on – Turkey's political milieu. This book seeks to examine each of these as interconnected phenomena. It seeks to analyse the extent to which Kurds are able to reconcile their distinct ethnic identity with their status as citizens in a polity increasingly subject to AKP hegemony. Are these things – ethnic identity and citizenship –entirely incongruent or can there be some overlap between them?

There is no unanimously accepted definition of what constitutes Kurdishness, as Martin Van Bruinessen points out.[3] Broadly outlined, the Kurds constitute peoples who speak several languages of the Iranic family and who since antiquity have inhabited the lands of Mesopotamia across which the modern borders of Iran, Iraq, Syria and Turkey cut. Some Kurds claim descent from the ancient Median civilisation (c. 700 BCE) but the first explicit mentions of the Kurds appear in Arab accounts after the Islamic conquests of the seventh century.[4] Turkic groups first arrived in Anatolia from points further east in the late eleventh century. Both peoples were largely nomadic at the time but this did not preclude overlap and movement both ways across ethnic boundaries. As Turkic empires arose in Anatolia, first the Seljuks centred in Konya, then the Ottomans with a capital eventually at Istanbul, the Kurds retained a degree of semi-autonomy on the marches between Turkish and Persian spheres. While under Ottoman rule (1516–1922),[5] the Kurds were regarded as part of the core Sunni Muslim population of Anatolia, which was not demarcated by ethnic categories, and Kurds fought alongside Turkish nationalist forces headed by Mustafa Kemal Atatürk in the Turkish War of Liberation (Kurtuluş Savaşı), after which the Republic of Turkey was established in 1923.

Thereafter the new nation-state was conceived of as Turkish, the constitution delineating Turkishness as the marker of citizenship.[6] As stated, the premise was on 'unity of language, culture and ideal' – of a Turkish persuasion. Kurds soon reacted to the impositions and restrictions inherent in such circumstances but found the new regime offered little accommodation of their political demands.[7] Since then, the social and political circumstances of the Kurds have been cause for controversy, debate and, at times, violence, as will be further discussed throughout this book.

The Kurds are not the only ethnic minority in Turkey. The most comprehensive study of ethnicity in Turkey, published in 1989, lists a total of forty-seven different groups.[8] It is well understood that the Kurds form the largest ethnic minority, but there are no correct, up-to-date records of the number of Kurds living in Turkey. The last Turkish census that included statistics on mother tongue (and through which ethnic populations figures may be deduced) was undertaken in 1965. That census, the data of which is regarded as questionable, recorded approximately 2.4 million Kurdish speakers, constituting roughly 7.5 per cent of the total population.[9] Since then no official record of ethnicity has been compiled. Estimates of the number of Kurds vary considerably[10] and often arouse controversy.[11] The very fact that there are no official data and that discussions of Kurdish population figures are subject to dispute point to the contested nature of Kurdish identity and the contentious position that Kurds occupy within Turkey's socio-political framework.

If there is dispute over Kurdish population figures, this is also true of the defining elements of Kurdish identity. Delineating the parameters of any ethnic or national identity is a slippery endeavour, the more so in the case of the Kurds, a people split between four Middle Eastern states and, in Turkey, whose very existence was denied for much of the twentieth century. External interference and machinations aside, there has been disagreement among Kurds themselves on what the definitive markers of their ethnicity are, or who qualifies as Kurdish or otherwise.[12] The process of identification was long complicated for the Kurds by the considerable diversity in what Martin Van Bruinessen called in the 1980s the 'secondary symbols' of ethnic distinctiveness – such as 'traditional dress', music and folklore – among Kurdish communities living in different regions across Turkey, as well as often notable similarities with other ethnic groups living in the same regions.[13] Thus, the cuisine, dress and folklore of a Mardinli Kurd may be distinct from that of a Dersimli Kurd but resemble that of an Arab or Assyrian in Mardin, while a Kurd living in one of the cities of western Turkey may have more in common with his Turkish neighbours than with Kurds living in the remote villages of Hakkari. Indeed, Kurds may feel close affiliation with ethnic Turks, or, alternatively, despite assimilation into apparent Turkishness, may still retain a sense of Kurdishness.[14] Yet, as this book seeks to examine, through the pressures of political contestation and conflict, the parameters of Kurdishness in Turkey have begun to crystallise.

It is thus worth noting Engin Isin and Patricia Wood's contention that ethnic categorisation is rarely definitive and is prone to inaccuracy. They cite the example of the 'ethnically Chinese', who live in different countries, speak different languages, adhere to different faiths and pursue manifold practices and customs.[15] Like 'ethnic Chinese', Kurds live across international borders in the Middle East and in diasporic communities worldwide, thereby leading to diversity of lifestyle(s) and conceptualisations of identity. This book in its examination of Kurdish identity and political life in Turkey uses the elements that Anthony Smith sets out as requisite for the categorisation of a group as an *ethnie*, his term for an ethnic community. Smith's elements, each of which may be present to greater or lesser extents in different circumstances and between different *ethnies*, are: 'a collective proper name; a myth of common ancestry; shared historical memories; differentiating elements of common culture; association with a specific homeland; a sense of solidarity held by significant sectors of the population'.[16]

The lack of clearly defined and unanimously agreed-upon aspects of Kurdish identity do not undermine Smith's requisite elements here. Smith notes that such factors as language, religion and skin pigmentation are often regarded as 'objective cultural markers'. They are seen as existing beyond an individual's or group's conscious decision-making about their identity, thereby contributing to the contention that ethnicity is a 'primordial' quality, one that is a 'given'.[17] Despite such commonly held views, Smith argues that the six attributes he uses to define and identify distinct ethnic groups are 'strongly subjective'.[18]

If ethnic identities may be subjective, they must also be subject to change. Stuart Hall argues that identities are 'never stable, fixed or unified', but are 'points of temporary attachment'.[19] Indeed, Martin van Bruinessen recounts Kurdish speakers joining Turkish tribal formations, and vice versa, during centuries of cohabitation between Kurdish and Turkish nomads in Anatolia, and examples of Armenians assuming Kurdish identity in the late nineteenth and early twentieth centuries.[20] More recent examples from Turkey further illustrate the malleable nature of ethnic identity. In 2004, Turkish lawyer Fethiye Çetin published a memoir revealing her discovery that her grandmother was an Armenian who had been rescued by a Turkish official after the genocide of 1915 and raised as a Turk.[21] While Çetin may have previously thought of herself as 'Turkish', it was clear, however, that at least part of her ethnic identity was Armenian.

All of this serves to illustrate that, as Rogers Brubaker argues, ethnic identity is not 'discrete, concrete, tangible, bounded'. Applying this reasoning to the Kurds, this means that the individual and collective attributes that combine to create the category of 'Kurdishness' are sometimes indistinct and open to question or various interpretations; they are not unchangeable in time and circumstance, and are not entirely and irrevocably distinct from the attributes of some Turks, Armenians, Arabs or others. For Brubaker, 'situated actions, cultural idioms, discursive frames . . . political projects and contingent events' act as shapers of identities, be they ethnic, national or otherwise.[22] In other words, individual and collective identities are malleable, assuming different contours and points of attachment depending on the political circumstances and lived experiences of those individuals and collectivities. In this way, the elements that Smith highlights – elements of common culture, sense of solidarity, ideas of homeland – are variously formed and conceived, and contribute to the overall shape of ethnic identity.

Fethiye Çetin's book was published during the early years of the AKP's incumbency. The AKP at this time pursued a programme of political reform, seeking to overturn many of the long-standing Kemalist strictures that had hobbled Turkey's democratic processes and had created an illiberal polity where nationalist rhetoric held sway. Under the AKP's liberalising measures, greater attention was paid to Turkey's multi-ethnic fabric, efforts were made to negotiate a peace with the PKK, and Kurdish political actors were able to operate with increasing freedom. However, with time, as AKP leader Recep Tayyip Erdoğan weathered political challenges and sought to institute a new presidential system, the AKP itself adopted many of the illiberal trappings of its predecessors and grew to a position of hegemony in Turkey's political and public spheres. In these circumstances, the situation of the Kurds was again curtailed. This book, therefore, sets out to analyse the elements of ethnic identity for Kurds and the ways in which the 'contingent events' of Turkey's socio-political arena, particularly during the era of AKP rule, have shaped them.

The seeds of this book have been germinating for some time; indeed, since my first encounter with Kurds in Turkey in 1992. While backpacking, I had boarded a *dolmuş* (minibus) in Malatya bound for the historic site of Nemrut Dağı (Mount Nimrod) in south-east Anatolia. After stopping at a meadow below the summit of the mountain, the *dolmuş* driver casually pointed at a group of women in brightly coloured clothes and sickle-wielding men who were loading forage onto the backs of donkeys. He said, simply, 'Kurdish.' This was a light-bulb moment for me. Vaguely aware of a people known as the Kurds after the fallout of the Iraq War of 1990–1 had brought them to media attention, I had no idea that there were Kurds in Turkey nor, indeed, anyone other than Turks. After proceeding from Nemrut to Diyarbakır, the most important city for Kurds in Turkey, I was initiated into the circumstances of the Kurds. Arriving at a hotel late in the evening, I and several fellow backpackers were directed by the hotel manager to go to the local police station to register our passports. I initially dismissed this as excessive officiousness on the part of the manager and only later learned that this was a necessary precaution for all travellers to the city due to the prevailing security situation. During those first few days in Diyarbakır I observed a heavy military presence and met numerous Kurds who were eager to talk, informing me of the political situation for Kurds in Turkey and their 'struggle'. I was also led by local Kurdish youths around the city to important historical sites such as the Ulu Cami (Great Mosque), several caravanserais and to the churches of Surp Giragos, Meryem Ana and Mar Petyun (Armenian, Syriac and Chaldean respectively, and all in various states of disrepair and neglect). This, alongside later meeting Arabic speakers in Harran and Laz in Trabzon, alerted me to the complex socio-political and multi-ethnic fabric of modern Turkey.

Returning to Turkey in 1994–5, I lived and worked as a teacher in a language school in the west-coast city of İzmir at a time when the state's military campaign against the PKK was peaking. One day I fell into conversation with Cüneyt, a twenty-something student at the school, who was complaining about Kurdish youths speaking Kurdish on local buses. 'We are in Turkey; they should speak Turkish,' he retorted. 'If I come to your country, Australia, I must speak English.' I replied that in Australia people were free to speak and broadcast in any language and that even government publications were offered in several languages. 'Yes, but you don't have separatism,' he replied. His comment was illustrative of a view commonly held in Turkey at that time that equated ethnic diversity, or the fostering of ethnic distinctiveness, with political tumult and fragmentation. Such a view was exacerbated by the PKK and its then agenda – subsequently abandoned[23] – of seeking an independent Kurdish state within Turkish territory. In this way of thinking, widely shared in İzmir, allowing Kurds the right to speak their language, to uphold their ethnic distinctiveness, would eventually lead to the collapse of the nation-state of Turkey. According to this logic, if Kurds wanted to be Kurds, they must, by extension, reject Turkey and desire their own nation-state. The reasoning ran that to avoid ethnic tension and political fragmentation it was necessary to deny ethnic diversity.

It struck me, however, that this thinking was fundamentally flawed; indeed, that Cüneyt's appraisal of the situation with regard to language rules was back-to-front. My experience as an Australian gave me an entirely different perspective. Rather than Australia being able to permit the use of multiple languages due to the absence of any separatist impulses within any ethnic community, my conviction was that ethnic communities in Australia did not harbour separatist aspirations precisely because they were able to use their own language if they desired. Similarly, Australia's recognition of ethnic diversity had not given rise to specific or recurring instances of inter-ethnic tensions. Clearly there are substantially different historical and socio-political parameters determining ethnic relations in Australia as compared to Turkey, but I reasoned that if ethnic communities were able to exist as ethnic communities, upholding aspects of their culture, language and identity – factors that make them distinctive and that they take pride in – within a broader political community, a nation-state, then there should be no need or desire to secede or separate to form their own political community.

In the summer of 1995, as I was preparing to leave İzmir, Turkish academic Doğu Ergil published the findings of an extensive survey conducted among Kurds resident in the Diyarbakır, Batman and Mardin provinces of south-eastern Anatolia. As if to validate my thinking that ethnic identification was not immediately or automatically a signal of separatist intent, Ergil found that although support for the PKK was high among his survey participants, only 11 per cent of them supported the idea of an independent Kurdish state.[24] Ergil likened the PKK's mission to that of a train journey, with party leaders envisioning an independent state as the final destination. The PKK then enjoyed a considerable degree of support among Kurds, as it does today. Ergil's findings revealed, however, that even though individual Kurds were willing to board the PKK train, they did not necessarily harbour separatist inclinations; they did not want to travel the whole distance to an independent Kurdish state. Many were content to alight once they had reached their political goals, whether that be achieving decent livelihoods, incomes, employment, education, health, respect for their identity or more freedom within daily life.[25] As such, they supported the PKK not because, at that time, it pursued a separatist agenda, but because they saw it defending or advancing their political and material interests. Ergil found that a significant majority of Kurds wanted to remain within Turkey, but be respected and treated equally *as Kurds*. As a consequence, he argued that for the vast majority of Kurds there was no inherent contradiction, or clash, between Kurdishness and citizenship within Turkey.[26]

Ergil's survey was groundbreaking in that it highlighted the broader dimensions of the Kurdish question, namely the issues affecting Kurds beyond just those of terrorism and separatism. Even though it was presented as an objective record of Kurdish attitudes, the report received enormous knee-jerk criticism within Turkey. Ümit Cizre Sakallıoğlu noted that Turkey's nationalist press embarked on a relentless campaign to vilify Ergil in the wake of the report.[27] Ergil himself later recalled being accused of complicity with an international conspiracy to partition Turkey.[28] Such overwrought attitudes to Kurds and Kurdishness date back to the very conception of the Republic of Turkey, wherein all citizens were by definition categorised as Turks. The 1980s, during which the PKK embarked on its military campaign, were marked by the militarisation of the Kurdish-populated provinces of southeastern Anatolia and the brutalisation of many of Turkey's Kurdish citizens at the hands of both the PKK and state security forces, as well as state-directed efforts to deny Kurdish identity in its entirety.[29] Inevitably, the trauma of violence, displacement and conflict had major impacts on Kurdish identity and how Kurds viewed politics in the Republic of Turkey.[30]

Meanwhile, until the 1990s, official rhetoric and public discourse held that political unity was paramount and discussion of ethnic distinctiveness was 'divisive'.[31] Cüneyt was echoing this reasoning when he drew a link between Kurds speaking their own language in public and an implicit separatist intent. Official state policy was then to deny the existence of the largest minority in Turkey, thereby denying Kurds space within the public and political spheres to uphold their identity and culture. Sakallıoğlu posited that such a state posture marginalised and disenfranchised that very minority rather than forged a unified national identity.³² It was these parameters – the denial of an identity, the denial of political and cultural rights, the PKK's guerrilla campaign (deemed to be terrorism by many Turks) and the state's equally brutal counter-terror campaign – that defined, and in many ways continue to define, the 'Kurdish issue'. At work here are political grievances and security factors. For a long time, as the state, and much of the public, viewed the issue through a security rather than a political prism, the solution was seen to only be possible through decisive and resolute military action to stamp out the terror threat. Little thought was paid to the socio-political foundations of Kurdish grievances. These were the 'contingent events' that shaped Kurds' political attitudes and the ways they defined – and defended – their ethnic identity.

Circumstances changed in 1999, when Turkish agents captured Abdullah Öcalan, leader of the PKK, who was subsequently imprisoned near Istanbul. A series of ceasefires ensued, none of which endured entirely. After the AKP (Adalet ve Kalkınma Partisi; Justice and Development Party) won government in 2002, the political landscape in Turkey shifted considerably. Although often viewed as an 'Islamist' party, the AKP touted itself as 'conservative democratic', and embarked on a range of political, judicial and human rights reforms with a view to winning membership of the EU.³³ The AKP government in its early years also approached the Kurdish issue in a different manner, shifting from a security lens to one of economic and political development. This resulted in 2009 in the so-called Kurdish Opening, an initiative aiming to address Kurdish grievances through democratic means. This was followed by negotiations with the imprisoned Abdullah Öcalan that led to a PKK ceasefire declaration in March 2013.³⁴ Thereafter the *çözüm süreci* (solution process) began, whereby the government and Öcalan negotiated for peace, a process that continued without any substantive outcomes until July 2015. At that point, amid the political repercussions of the HDP's electoral 'victory' and the AKP's comeuppance, the peace process collapsed comprehensively and the political arena again contracted.

The fieldwork that provides much of the data for this book took place during several periods between June 2013 and June 2015, when negotiations were ongoing, hostilities were at a minimum and a degree of normality had returned to south-eastern Anatolia. The book seeks to take up a question that arose from Doğu Ergil's research twenty years earlier, but that has remained largely unaddressed in the interim – that of everyday Kurds' relationship with the Republic of Turkey. Sakallıoğlu noted at that time that the state's Kurdish policy was likely to have damaged its image in the eyes of its Kurdish citizens. Ergil's survey findings indicated that even if this had been the case, Kurds had not abandoned the state entirely; they still attached some significance to their membership of Turkey, while still wanting recognition of their distinct ethnic identity. It is from here that my research question arises. This book intends to examine how Kurds conceive of, and experience, their Kurdish identity and their status as citizens of Turkey. It seeks to gauge the extent to which they are able to, or willing to, reconcile the two within the context of Turkey's political realm, which for almost two decades has been dominated by the personality of Erdoğan and the AKP. Both initially appeared inclined towards engaging with Kurds' political demands but both have recently tilted towards authoritarianism and a reinvigorated Turkish nationalism.

Diyarbakır – its inhabitants, history and physical presence – is the principal focus of the book. I chose Diyarbakır as the primary site to gather data because it occupies a pivotal place in the Kurdish imagination: for many Kurds in Turkey it is the would-be capital of a 'Kurdistan', and, as noted, it has long been a site of Kurdish mobilisation and of political tensions. The city remained under emergency rule from 1987 until 2002 during the conflict between Turkey's armed forces and the PKK. Its population swelled during this time as Kurdish villages were razed and evacuated by the army.[35] Following the collapse of the government's *çözüm süreçi* (resolution process) and the resumption of hostilities with the PKK in July 2015, it became a site of clashes between the PKK, its affiliates and the Turkish military. In this sense, Diyarbakır has experienced fluctuating fortunes during Erdoğan's time in power, benefiting from the lifting of emergency rule in 2002, a move instigated by the AKP, then experiencing something of a cultural flowering, only to be subjected to intense street-by-street fighting and destruction from late 2015.

Choosing Diyarbakır as a primary site of research also serves another purpose, that of broadening the depth of research undertaken within Turkey. Kimberly Hart contends that Istanbul dominates Turkish life in many regards, a preoccupation that extends to academic research. She notes the aphorism '*Istanbul demek, Türkiye demek*' ('To speak of Istanbul is to

Figure I.1   Kurdish boys outside the walls of Diyarbakır, June 2015. © William Gourlay.

speak of Turkey'). She argues there is an 'Istanbul-centric' assumption that decrees that Istanbul is the automatic first choice and quintessential location for social and political research conducted in Turkey.[36] Hart concedes, and I concur, that Istanbul is of pivotal importance, but restricting research to the city means a less detailed and less comprehensive picture of modern Turkey. This is particularly so regarding Kurdish life and politics, much of which is conducted in the south-east of the country. To this end, my choice of Diyarbakır is intended to raise the analytical gaze from Istanbul, to extend it to the south-east and afford another piece of research that contributes to a broader view of the country as a whole.

That said, while principally focusing on Diyarbakır, this book also takes account of Kurds in Istanbul. As the cultural, financial and spiritual capital – although not the administrative capital, and no longer seat of government – Istanbul is of central importance to virtually all aspects of life in Turkey. It is the largest city in Turkey, and it is often said that it is the largest Kurdish city in the world.[37] Large numbers of Kurds have emigrated here during the life of the Republic of Turkey, most particularly in recent decades, either seeking economic opportunity or escaping the turmoil of the war in the south-east.

Indeed, due to its multi-cultural nature, Istanbul represents a microcosm of Turkey's ethnic diversity, and as the location of significant political developments, it provides a perspective on the 'contingent events' that define Turkey's political terrain.

In examining ideas of Kurdish identity and citizenship in Turkey, this book adopts a bottom-up view, investigating Kurdish ethnicity as it is manifest in everyday situations. As Yael Navaro-Yashin did with her dissection of the secular-Islamist dialectic within modern Turkey,[38] the intention here is to move beyond the boundaries and limitations of analysis of political parties, institutions and movements and their formalised discourses, rather to enter 'public life', engaging and observing the Kurdish residents of Diyarbakır and Istanbul in teahouses, parks, corner shops, mosque courtyards, backstreets, bazaars and street corners, in order to capture the political in its 'fleeting and intangible, transmogrified forms'.[39] Beyond engaging Kurds face-to-face to enquire of their lived experiences in order to construct an image of Kurdish identity, the focus is on urban landscapes and the minutiae of everyday life – graffiti, bill posters, handbills and other such things that may contain political messages or be indicative of political currents, things seemingly as innocuous as street signs and which books, newspapers, CDs, cassettes and souvenir postcards are available for sale – as documentary sources writ small, all of which define Turkey's socio-political terrain and the formation of identities within it. In this sense the book aims to bring to the fore the voices of ordinary Kurds and the apparently mundane elements of their daily lives.

The book proceeds through nine chapters following this introduction. Chapter 1 sets out Turkey's nation-building project, the 'invention' of Turkishness as an ethnic category and nationalism as a forge for unity, and the concurrent development of Kurdish ethnic awareness. It details the AKP's initial attempts to redefine politics to create a more inclusive environment and its recent tilt towards authoritarianism. Providing context for the more thorough analysis of the components of Kurdish identity to come, the chapter examines how the Kurds were affected by these processes and political dynamics. Chapter 2 explains processes of ethnographic data-gathering that contribute to the book's argument, namely how Diyarbakır and Istanbul were chosen as sites of investigation and how Kurds related to the research and researcher. Chapter 3 begins examination of the 'differentiating elements of common culture' that are the building blocks of Kurdish identity. It observes narratives of 'village life' and recourse to 'the mountains' and, in particular, Newroz, the Kurdish new year, and the Kurdish language as totems of Kurdish political and cultural life. It examines the ways in which the AKP have sought to co-opt Newroz and language, and the attempts Kurds have made to assert their distinct ownership of them. Chapter 4 then investigates the role that Islam plays in Turkish and Kurdish life, and how Kurds have for some time been reassessing their relationship to religion(s) as a way to create a distinction between 'their' Islam and that of others, notably the AKP and ISIS. Chapter 5 examines the contested nature of territory and notations of the map in Turkey. In this it observes Kurdish and governmental attitudes to Diyarbakır and the way that alternative designations – Mesopotamia, Anatolia and Kurdistan – feed into broader narratives about Turkey's national identity, and into the AKP's attempts to corral the Kurdish issue for its own benefit. The fact that a putative 'Kurdistan' extends beyond the borders of Turkey, informs the discussion of trans-border Kurdish identity – Kurdayetî – that is the focus of Chapter 6. What impact do Kurds' cross-border connections have? How does the AKP react to them, and how do they affect events in Turkey? Chapter 7 investigates how narratives of oppression and resistance postures that Kurds adopt play into notions of identity. It observes cultural traditions such as Newroz, the use of the Kurdish language, attempts to demarcate a distinct Islam and to re-annotate the maps as instances of 'resistance' that fortify a distinct Kurdish political position and ethnic identity, something that becomes more important as AKP hegemony grows. From the viewpoint of Kurds' enthusiastic participation in Turkey's general and municipal elections, Chapter 8 explores conceptualisations of citizenship in Turkey. It argues that Kurds' political activities constitute engagement in Renan's 'daily plebiscite', that is, they act as affirmation of their place as members of Turkey's body politic, but they are also a mechanism for staking out their own political space in defiance of AKP hegemony. The Conclusion draws together the threads highlighted throughout the book to argue that Kurdish identity in Turkey can be seen at its core as a political identity. Yet such a reality, I argue, is not a threat to Turkey; indeed, when and where Kurds are able to assert such an identity freely and without consequences their sense of engagement and belonging to the body politic of Turkey is enhanced. This much was apparent on that summer evening in 2015, as the Kurds of Diyarbakır took to the streets to celebrate the HDP's victory in winning seats in Turkey's general assembly. However the AKP's hegemonic project and Erdoğan's increasing grip on power make such aspirations harder to achieve. With Erdoğan at the helm, Turkey's political, social and geo-strategic arenas are increasingly tense; this book sets out to examine how Kurds relate and react to these overarching political parameters and how, in turn, they play a role in shaping Turkey's political and social trajectories.

Notes

1. İnce, *Citizenship and Identity in Turkey*, p. 39.
2. Waldman and Calışkan, *The New Turkey and its Discontents*, p. 166.
3. Van Bruinessen, 'The ethnic identity of Kurds in Turkey', pp. 613–21.
4. Jwaideh, *The Kurdish National Movement*, p. 13.
5. The Ottomans ruled over western Anatolia from the early fourteenth century, but only claimed eastern Anatolia under Selim I after 1512.
6. Barkey and Fuller, *Turkey's Kurdish Question*, pp. 6–9.
7. Findley, *Turkey, Islam, Nationalism and Modernity*, pp. 250–1.
8. Andrews (ed.), *Ethnic Groups in the Republic of Turkey*. It is worth noting that several of the larger ethnic groups are divided by religious affiliation or location of origin to reach that total, an example being Turks, who are divided into Sunni, Alevi and Sunni Yörük sub-categories.
9. Mutlu, 'Ethnic Kurds in Turkey', pp. 517–41.
10. Mutlu in 'Ethnic Kurds in Turkey' calculated, on the basis of mother-tongue data gathered in 1990, a Kurdish population of 7 million. Alternatively, Kendal Nezan estimated in 1996 that Kurds made up one-quarter of Turkey's population, which was then 59 million. See Nezan, 'The Kurds', pp. 7–19. Hamit Bozarslan stated in 2008 that the Kurdish population was somewhere between 12 and 15 million. See Bozarslan (2008), 'Kurds and the Turkish state', pp. 333–56.
11. Erdem, 'Türkiye'de Kürtler ne kadardır? (2)', *Radikal*, 25 April 2013.
12. Van Bruinessen, 'The ethnic identity of Kurds in Turkey'.
13. Ibid.
14. Yıldız, *Ne Mutlu Türküm Diyebilene*, p. 43.
15. Isin and Wood, *Citizenship and Identity*, p. 49.
16. Smith, *National Identity*, p. 21.
17. Ibid., pp. 20, 23.

18. Ibid., p. 23.
19. Hall, 'Who needs "Identity"?', pp. 4–6.
20. Van Bruinessen, 'The ethnic identity of Kurds in Turkey'.
21. See Çetin, *My Grandmother: A memoir*.
22. Brubaker, *Ethnicity without Groups*, p. 11. He makes the same claim for 'race' and 'nation' – that they are not tangible and discrete but created and continually shaped by similar processes and dynamic to those that create ethnicity.
23. Yavuz, *Secularism and Muslim Democracy in Turkey*, pp. 176–7.
24. Ergil, *Doğu Sorunu: Teşhisler ve Tesbitler 1995*, p. 68. Ergil's survey was originally conducted and published in July 1995 under the auspices of TOBB (Türkiye Odalar ve Borsalar Birliği; The Turkish Union of Chambers of Commerce). For this study I have used a 2008 reprint.
25. Ibid., pp. 66–7. Ergil's train analogy for the PKK should be seen in light of a 1992 survey that found only 29 per cent of surveyed Kurdish speakers regarded the PKK as best representatives of the Kurds. See Elekdağ, 'Güneydoğu sorununda yeni eğilimler anketi', 6 September 1992, p. 17.
26. Ergil, 'Reframing the problem', p. 149.
27. Sakallıoğlu, 'Historicizing the present and problematizing the future', pp. 1–22.
28. Ergil, 'Reframing the problem', p. 149.
29. See, for instance, McDowall, *The Kurds*, pp. 44–50; Van Bruinessen, *Agha, Shaikh and State*, p. 45.
30. Gurses, *Anatomy of a Civil War*, p. 40.
31. Andrews (ed.), *Ethnic Groups in the Republic of Turkey*, p. 41.
32. Sakallıoğlu, 'Historicizing the present and problematizing the future', p. 9.
33. Taşpınar, 'Turkey: The new model?', pp. 127–36.
34. Yackley, 'Kurd rebel leader orders fighters to halt hostilities', *Reuters*, 21 March.
35. Gurses, *Anatomy of a Civil War*, pp. 18–20.
36. Hart, *And Then We Work for God*, p. 24.
37. A 2008 report estimated the Kurdish population of Istanbul at 1.9 million. See Agirdir, 'Kürtler ve Kürt Sorunu', pp. 4–5.
38. Navaro-Yashin, *Faces of the State*.
39. Ibid., p. 3.

1

IDENTITY, ETHNICITY, POLITICS: FROM KEMALISM TO 'NEW TURKEY'

In late 2005, not long before becoming the first Turk ever to win a Nobel Prize, Orhan Pamuk appeared before an Istanbul court on charges of 'insulting Turkishness'. According to Article 301 of the Turkish Penal Code, it is illegal to 'insult Turkey, the Turkish nation, or Turkish government institutions'. Some months earlier, in a magazine interview, the world-renowned author had made comments about the Armenian genocide of 1915 and the ongoing conflict against Kurdish militants in Turkey. These were deemed by some to have sullied the good name of Turkey and Turks at large.[1] The charges were eventually dropped, but the episode is notable because it demonstrates the sentimental and definitional importance of ethnicity in Turkey. Indeed, Pamuk was heckled by nationalists at his court appearance. The idea of Turkishness is jealously guarded; it is infused with emotion and pride. At the same time, the charges against Pamuk reflect the delicate nature of discussions of ethnic minorities and their places, and plights, in the territory that is now Turkey.

This chapter examines the complexities and dimensions of ethnic identity in the Republic of Turkey. The *Turkish* nature of the Republic was not a fait accompli when it was established in 1923; it required an effort of top-down engineering to forge a sense of ethnic coherence and cohesion. This chapter outlines how the idea of Turkishness crystallised, the impacts this and the state's official discourse and aspiration to ethnic unity had on Kurdish identity, and the ongoing examinations of and controversies surrounding national identity and nationalism in Turkey. The modernising state long denied the very existence of such a thing as Kurdish identity, despite the Kurds constituting the largest non-Turkish community. Amid periodic waves of assimilation and repression, Kurds sought to assert their presence. Within these dynamics the so-called Kurdish Question arose. Over time the contours of the issue have changed, from 1920s denial and attempts at assimilation, to insurgency and discourses of separatism and terrorism in the 1980s and '90s. More recently, political spaces and debates have broadened, only to contract again as the political system succumbs to the authoritarian inclinations and re-appropriated nationalist rhetoric of the AKP and Erdoğan. This chapter thus sets out the dynamics and ongoing debates of Turkish and Kurdish identity formation and the ways they are shaped by political events and processes.

Conceiving Turkishness in the Republic of Turkey

The sensitivities now attached to the idea of Turkishness, demonstrated in the charges brought against Orhan Pamuk, are markedly different to attitudes from a relatively recent past. While it is understood that the ruling elite of the Ottoman Empire that preceded the modern Republic of Turkey spoke Turkish, the term 'Turk' did not retain an ethnic or political meaning as we would understand it today.[2] During the Ottoman era, identity based upon 'language, territory, race' may have been 'of personal, sentimental or social significance', but not of political relevance.[3] Ottoman society was divided into *millets* on the basis of religious affiliation. Muslims, regardless of ethnicity, were lumped together in the *ummah*, while Christians were categorised by denomination: Serbian Orthodox, Maronite, Armenian Apostolic, Greek Orthodox, and the like. Even so, travellers in the Ottoman Balkans in the late nineteenth century recounted encountering villagers who had no concept of their 'ethnicity', but referred to themselves on the basis of their broader religious affiliation, namely Muslim or Christian.[4] Thus Turkish-speaking villagers in what is now Turkey would have regarded themselves first as Muslims rather than as Turks. Indeed, there was a pejorative quality attached to the word 'Turk'. Ottoman grandees used it to describe 'ignorant and uncouth Turkish-speaking peasants',[5] the 'country bumpkins' of backwoods Anatolia.[6] In the 1910s, Young Turk ethnographers, those who first set about instilling a sense of Turkishness among Turkish-speaking populations, found the population in both Istanbul and the provinces singularly reluctant to classify themselves as 'Turks'.[7]

While the idea of Turkishness has undergone a polar shift, from put-down to source of reverence, since the Ottoman demise and emergence of modern Turkey, a further identity shift has also occurred, from status as subjects of a multi-ethnic empire to the citizens of a republic modelled on Western ideas of democracy.[8] Ottoman elites ruled a multi-ethnic subaltern class, but the founders of the Republic of Turkey sought to create a unified national bourgeoisie who could constitute, build and administer a modern society. Thus, in the traumatic years of transition from the early twentieth century until the Republic's establishment in 1923, the Turkish national struggle was multi-faceted: discarding the moribund trappings and social structures of empire, fending off encroaching European powers and creating a united nationalist movement.[9] The first job at hand, however, was the consolidation of the first component of Smith's *ethnie*, a collective proper name: 'Turk'.[10]

Ottoman sultans ruled over a diverse, multi-faith and multi-ethnic population even while the ideas of nationalism and homogenous nation-states took hold in Europe in the late nineteenth century. In the first decade of the twentieth century, minority-language publications and schools teaching in minority languages such as Greek and Armenian were commonplace, but the trauma of receiving Muslim populations expelled from the Balkans and arriving in Anatolia in penury during the Balkan Wars of 1912–13 saw a hardening of attitudes and increasing suspicion of the Other.[11] In fact, this process had been proceeding for decades while Ottoman territories shrank from the Balkan and Caucasus peripheries and rising ethnic nationalism(s) made the Ottoman *millet* system increasingly unworkable.[12] During the First World War it also occurred in the provinces to the south in Mesopotamia. Territorial contraction had two impacts. The first was an influx of a range of ethnicities – Albanians, Bosnians, Greek-speaking Muslims, Pomaks, Circassians, Abkhazians and others – into Istanbul and Anatolia, already home to a plethora of peoples and tongues.[13] The second was the steady development of the notion that only ethnic unity could prevent further fragmentation and ensure survival. That the Greeks, Bulgarians and Serbs, previously *millets*, had peeled off to form their own ethno-political entities in preceding decades only heightened fears of further fragmentation. 'Monoculturalist sense' had to be made of this polyglot community brought together by 'war, deportation, diaspora and immigration'.[14] That required a smooth process of assimilation whereby all could make the transition to being 'Turks'. Ideologue of Turkification, Tekin Alp envisaged Turkishness as an identity in which all Ottoman ethnic and religious diversity would be absorbed.[15] After winning the national struggle against foreign invaders and the Ottoman regime, the elites of the new Republic, dubbed Kemalist after founding President Mustafa Kemal Atatürk, set out to modernise and raise their compatriots from the depths into which they had been forced.[16]

The key to this was unification under the banner of Turkishness. The Kemalist nation-building calculus conceived this in simple terms: all Muslims were automatically deemed to be Turks. The result was the politicisation of language and culture, elements of ethnicity that previously had been only of personal or sentimental importance. In its early years, the Republic put to work all of the apparatus of the modernising state – bureaucracy, media, education system – to instil the message of shared Turkishness. Some traces are still visible. Visiting the primary school of a small village near Diyarbakır I once saw, prominently placed in the central classroom, a wall hanging portraying '*Türk büyükleri*' (Turkish elders), including Atatürk, Ottoman sultans and other Turkish historical figures.[17] These were figures that local schoolchildren should look up to and revere. There were no equivalent displays of notable Kurds, despite this being a village populated entirely by Kurds. Meanwhile, in Diyarbakır, a mural adorning a modern building in Dağkapı Square outside the ancient city walls imparts a message of pervasive Turkishness. Above a multi-storey stylised silhouette of Mustafa Kemal (later Atatürk) is one of his quotes asserting that all those from Istanbul, Thrace, Macedonia, Erzurum or Diyarbakır are 'children of the one race, veins of the same ore' [*hep bir ırkın evlatları, hep aynı cevherin damarlarıdır*]. The mural's placement is no accident. Somewhere in the square is the deliberately obscured grave of Sheikh Said, the leader of the first Kurdish rebellion against the Republic of Turkey. Thus Mustafa Kemal stands guard over the Sheikh in perpetuity and imparts his message of all-encompassing Turkishness.[18]

For many who had arrived in Turkey as refugees, Muslims expelled from the Balkans and Caucasus, such a message rang true. They willingly adopted the cloak of Turkishness.[19] However, the Kemalists would brook little dissent from those who were not willing to do likewise. There was no room for minority status or rights among Anatolia's Muslims. Any recalcitrance that arose on the path to assimilation was viewed as a security issue.[20] For a variety of reasons, including long-standing social structures and their being the largest non-Turkish Muslim population, Kurds proved the least willing to comply with the societal and political impositions of the new Republic.[21] Between the establishment of the Republic in 1923 and 1938 there were eighteen rebellions, sixteen of them in Kurdish-populated south-eastern provinces.[22] Processes of assimilation and alienation appeared to occur simultaneously, some Kurds integrating but others unwilling to knuckle under.[23] Ongoing rebellions heightened official suspicions of ethnic diversity and underscored the imperative to homogenise, by force if necessary.

To substantiate their rhetoric of ethnic unity, the state sought to deny the very existence of the Kurds. Kemalist discourse refused to recognise an ethnic element to Kurdish unrest, instead referring to a need for 'reform of the eastern provinces' ('*şark vilayetlerinin ıslahı*').[24] Broadly speaking, the Turkish populace echoed the narrative of denial. In 1946, even *Son Posta*, a newspaper that did not necessarily adopt the government line, ran an article stating, 'In Turkey no Kurdish minority ever existed, either nomadic or settled, with national consciousness or without it.'[25] Ece Temelkuran records her father, a teacher posted to the south-east in the 1960s, encountering Kurdish students, a people of whose existence he was entirely unaware. When he asked education ministry officials for materials to teach these students, who knew no Turkish, he was told, 'You were deceived. There are no people called Kurds. Kurdish does not exist.'[26] If such statements appear to be instances where Turkish discourse 'doth protest too much', it is notable the lengths that some went to in order to maintain the fiction of the non-existence of Kurds. After the coup of 1980, General Kenan Evren claimed that Kurds were in fact 'mountain Turks', the name 'Kurd' being onomatopoeic, arising from the 'kurt-kart' sound that their boots made while walking through snow.[27]

In the wake of the 1980 coup and the repressive political atmosphere that it spawned, the PKK undertook its first military raids in 1984. Its agenda, calling for an independent Kurdistan, reinforced the idea for Turks that ethnic diversity necessarily led to national fragmentation. Its methods – guerrilla tactics viewed as terrorism by Turkish authorities[28] – saw the securitisation of the very idea of Kurdishness, the widespread adoption of pro-nationalist discourse throughout Turkish society and the entrenchment of the military, guardians of the Kemalist project and, by extension, Turkish identity, called upon to subdue and eliminate the PKK, in Turkish politics and political institutions.[29]

Elise Massicard notes a pervasive 'dogma of unity' in 1990s political discourse. Here terms such as *bütünlük* (integrity), *beraberlik* (solidarity), *bölmek* (to separate), *ayırmak* (to divide) assumed potency, the former two viewed as essential in the political realm, the latter two as threats.[30] I experienced this while teaching in Izmir in the mid-'90s. One of my students, looking at a map of Turkey in class, grew agitated at mentions of Armenian and Kurdish populations. The student, Özcan, tapped his finger forcefully on the desk while repeatedly declaring, 'This is Turkey!' He was immediately discomfited by the very mention of ethnic diversity and equated discussion of the existence of Kurds and Armenians with territorial claims. For Özcan, and many Turks like him, ethnic identity became a zero-sum game. Turkey had to be uniformly Turkish, or its very existence was in jeopardy.

The so-called Kurdish issue may have stemmed from the political grievances of everyday Kurds, economic inequalities, the denial of their identity and the outlawing of their language, but it also came to be associated, for the Turkish public, with the PKK, its tactics and agenda. For many Turks it thus was associated with violence, insurgency, and threats to state institutions, to a normal civil order and to the very idea of Turkey as a sovereign entity. The denial of Kurdish identity and the military measures adopted throughout the 1980s and '90s to counter the PKK, to subdue terrorism and separatism, did nothing to redress those original grievances, but, generally, Turkish society deemed them necessary to maintain the survival of the state, homeland of the Turks and guarantor of the enduring existence of Turkishness.

Kurdishness: Long-suppressed Nationhood, or Otherwise

Some Kurdish nationalists will tell you, on the basis of confidently asserted genealogies, that the Kurds have existed as a primordial, if stateless, 'nation' since the days of the Median Empire around 700 BC.[31] A more sober assessment would recognise that, like 'Turkishness', 'Kurdishness' has assumed potency, definition and political significance only in more recent times. Kurds were included in the Muslim *ummah* during the Ottoman era, and thus did not constitute a distinct *millet* or ethno-religious category, just as Turks did not. Kurdish *emirs* retained a degree of independence on the marches between Ottoman and Persian realms until the nineteenth century. Some note Sheikh Ubeydullah, the leader of a Kurdish uprising against Ottoman and Persian empires in 1880, as making initial claims of Kurdish nationhood,[32] yet any widespread, coherent sense of Kurdish national identity is a recent phenomenon.

Some cite two literary works as evidence of the longevity of a Kurdish national consciousness. The first of these is the *Şerefname*, a history of Kurdish dynasties and principalities, written in 1597 by Şeref Khan, from the Kurdish town of Bitlis, in what is now eastern Turkey. The *Şerefname* came to serve as a potent source of historical detail in later attempts to compile a national genealogy.[33] The second is Ahmad Khani's *Mem û Zîn*, published in 1692 and sometimes referred to as the Kurdish *Romeo and Juliet*. Where the *Şerefname* was written in Persian, Khani wrote in Kurdish. *Mem û Zîn* thus elevated Kurdish to being a literary language; in doing so it became a totem of Kurdish culture and identity. Martin Van Bruinessen notes that *Mem û Zîn* can be read as a demonstration of pride in Kurdish identity and the forceful expression of a desire for a Kurdish state.[34] Indeed, Van Bruinessen observes, many modern Kurdish nationalists recognise these sentiments as familiar and thus view *Mem û Zîn* as the wellspring of a centuries-old Kurdish ethnic and national consciousness.

Important though these two works may be, their influence and significance among broader Kurdish communities must have been limited at a time when the majority of Kurds were illiterate. Furthermore, it is notable that, just as the term 'Turk' has shifted in meaning over time, the same is true of 'Kurd', which once applied only to members of tribal elites and aristocrats, but not 'non-tribal peasantry'.[35] And just as the Young Turks were developing a deeper sense of 'Turkishness' and seeking to disseminate it among the populace in the late-Ottoman era, Kurdish intellectuals similarly formed societies and established journals to elaborate on and disseminate the idea of 'Kurdishness'.[36]

Upon the establishment of the Republic of Turkey in 1923, these two processes of Turkish and Kurdish identity formation continued, albeit in entirely antithetical circumstances. On the one hand, Turkish identity took shape with official imprimatur. Indeed, it was a process that was directed and fostered from above by nationalising elites. On the other hand, the same nationalising elites sought to deny the very existence of Kurdish identity. An increasingly ethno-centric notion of nationalism took hold in Turkey from the 1930s, leading to the disavowal and repudiation of other ethnicities, principally Kurdish.[37] Nation building proceeded towards establishing a mono-ethnic – Turkish – political entity centred on the 'unity of language, culture and ideal'.[38] The fact that a majority of political uprisings in the early years of the Republic were instigated by Kurds only added urgency to this task.

But those seeking to homogenise face a conundrum: marking some as outsiders and attempting to induce them, through violence or discriminatory treatment, to integrate into the whole often serves to single them out. Thus, measures targeting recalcitrant Kurds highlighted their difference from Turks. Kurdish identity formation took place in these circumstances, despite, or in defiance of, the normative order that the state was seeking to impose, under pressure from the 'dominant nationhood' of the Turks.[39]

The pressures imposed by that dominant nationhood weighed heavily, at times, upon Kurds. Travelling through south-eastern Anatolia in 1956, British diplomat Anthony Parsons remarked, 'I did not catch the faintest breath of Kurdish nationalism which the most casual observer in Iraq cannot fail to notice.'[40] Here we must not mistakenly conflate Kurdish nationalism and Kurdish identity, but one may assume that whatever form Kurdish identity took at this time, Parsons did not perceive it as extending to political agitation against the Turkish state. Meanwhile, another British colonial official in Iraq had observed, 'Kurds, like Jews, possess a natural "tenacity" to resist attempts to absorb them.'[41] These observations demonstrate the shifting tides of Kurdish awareness and attitudes in different spaces and times and in light of different political circumstances. The official who remarked on Kurds' 'tenacity' was commenting on the situation in Iraq, but it might equally have applied to Turkey at different times. Through the 1960s and 1970s, Kurdish activists grew increasingly visible within leftist political circles in Turkey. Following the military coup of 1980, which ushered in a period of martial law notable for heavy-handed state and judicial action against groups deemed 'terrorist', the political arena largely shifted from a tussle between left and right ideological persuasions to a field of competing identities, religious, secular and ethnic.[42] In preceding decades, urbanisation had seen the decline of traditional tribal and landholding figures of authority in Kurdish society, the politicisation of Kurdish identity, and the emergence of a Kurdish narrative of national liberation.[43] Amid this tumult of social change and restricted political space the PKK emerged, intent on using military means to pursue a goal of 'national liberation'.

It is clear that 'contingent events', those of Turkey's efforts through legal and military initiatives to prevent Kurds from asserting their distinct ethnic identity, have left an indelible mark on that very identity. In this regard, Turkey's long refusal to countenance the idea of Kurdish identity was largely counterproductive. Efforts to punish those who did herald their Kurdishness had unintended consequences that, rather than forging a cohesive sense of Turkish national identity, have marginalised and excluded segments of the Kurdish population; efforts to punish resulted in some questioning the very legitimacy of the state and others taking up arms against it, while simultaneously granting a new salience to the category of Kurdishness.[44] Between attempts by the state to eradicate it and Kurds' determination to maintain it, Kurdishness has become politicised, adopting a variety of postures, strategies and tactics.[45] Even as the state attempted to extinguish all traces of Kurdishness, Kurds stamped their claims on language, culture and territory, effectively 'Kurdifying' them.[46]

Bearing in mind Turkey's attempts at and goal of assimilation – Turkification – a vital aspect of the assertion of Kurdish identity was the establishment and maintenance, by Kurdish actors, of an ethnic boundary. Fredrik Barth contends that in analysing ethnicity, 'the critical focus of investigation . . . becomes the ethnic boundary that defines the group, not the cultural stuff that it encloses'.[47] This may seem odd. At first glance a distinctive culture would appear to be the central pillar around which ethnicity is constructed. Ernest Gellner, like Barth, downplays the significance of 'culture' and sees a more crucial element: he places greater emphasis on mutual recognition than on 'shared attributes' as the ultimate determinant and adhesive of group formation and cohesion.[48] Similarly, Thomas Hyllel Eriksen highlights a sense of 'we-ness' as an essential aspect of establishing ethnic identity, creating 'group belongingness'. Eriksen argues that social identification relies not only on definition against the Other but also on establishing internal solidarity or cultural commonality.[49] Thus, for Kurds, establishing and recognising affinities with fellow Kurds is important but maintaining differences from the majority Turks has been paramount. These tasks have assumed different degrees of complexity and urgency as the political terrain has shifted in Turkey over recent decades. It is these dynamics that this book intends to explore.

Countenancing Diversity: Re-imagining National Identity

As a foreigner teaching at a Turkish university in the late 1990s, Anna Grabolle-Çeliker recalls being warned against querying the official narrative that deemed any Kurdish political mobilisation to be terrorist and/or *bölücü* (separatist).[50] This chimes with my own experiences teaching in İzmir. In my social circles, when discussions of the Kurdish issue arose, distinct ways of seeing quickly became apparent. Generally, the teachers among whom I worked, all of them expats, were inclined towards some sympathy for the plight of the Kurds, whereas the local İzmirlilar with whom we socialised reduced the issue to one of terrorism and associated threats to the territorial integrity of the nation-state. Such conversations never proceeded far, lest tempers be inflamed, but it was common to hear Turkish students comment that making political concessions to Kurds would be 'giving in to terrorism'.

Nonetheless, through the 1990s, even if there had been any remaining political will to attempt it, the prospect of implementing a programme of 'Turkification' progressively dimmed. Incremental political change became apparent, often in the face of increasing brutality from both the Turkish military and the PKK. Indeed, this was a torrid decade; it was marked by 'terror from below' that was matched by 'terror from above'.[51] Indicative of such dynamics is that over a hundred Kurdish political party members were killed during the '90s,[52] while in 1993, following a declaration to extend its first-ever ceasefire, PKK members killed thirty-three Turkish soldiers in cold blood near Bingöl.[53]

Despite the increasing intensity of the conflict, some Turkish politicians began to adopt a more conciliatory tone. During his presidency, Turgut Özal (1989–93) proposed new approaches to the Kurdish issue and challenged the Kemalist orthodoxy that had thus far held sway.[54] In late 1991, Prime

Minister Süleyman Demirel told a Kurdish gathering in Diyarbakır that Turkey recognised 'the Kurdish reality'. Substantive change was harder to come by, however. Omer Taşpınar highlights the pivotal role that the National Security Council (Milli Güvenlik Kurulu; MGK) played in politics and its conviction that making concessions to Kurds would begin an irreversible process that ultimately led to national and territorial fragmentation. Thus the best intentions of politicians came to nothing due to the military's determination to cut off new approaches to the Kurds.[55]

Discussion of the Kurdish issue eventually did shift beyond such a zero-sum approach following investigations into the broader perspectives of Kurds' circumstances in Turkey, including the survey undertaken by Doğu Ergil mentioned in the introduction. This brought to public attention a range of issues of concern to Kurds. As Ergil himself later noted, the survey, widely reported in the media, highlighted to the Turkish population at large that the Kurdish issue was not solely reducible to terrorism or separatism but arose from a sense among Kurds that they were neither included in nor integrated into Turkish society, and that – tellingly – Kurdish support for the PKK did not necessarily indicate separatist intent but that Kurds viewed the PKK as pursuing and protecting their political goals.[56] At the same time, Kurdish political organisations began to organise and make inroads in the Turkish political arena, albeit amid considerable nationalist backlash and concerted obstructionism from the organs of state.[57]

Various other factors created the political and societal conditions conducive to increased Kurdish activity in politics and broader discussions of identity and ethnicity that saw the 'dogma of unity' losing its potency. Chief among these were Turkish security operatives' capture of PKK leader Abdullah Öcalan in 1999, which led to a PKK ceasefire, and the strengthening of Turkey's relationship and links with the EU. With Öcalan behind bars, the heat in the Kurdish conflict subsided, allowing more space for approaches other than military initiatives. Meanwhile, EU links gave greater impetus and legitimacy to the acknowledgement of ethnic diversity in Turkey.[58]

The ascendancy of the AKP, which won government in 2002, marked a further shift in Turkey's political trajectory and discourse. The AKP adopted a more inclusive conceptualisation of national identity, one that paid heed to the multi-ethnic Ottoman era, and where minorities, such as Kurds, were not automatically viewed as suspect but as an integral part of a cohesive society.[59] Prior to winning government, AKP campaign materials heralded Turkey's diversity in religion, language, sect and ethnicity, and espoused a goal of creating 'harmonious unity bound together through common values and traditions'.[60] In its 2002 election manifesto, the AKP highlighted its acceptance of Turkish society 'with all its colours, its points of commonality and difference'.[61] In this sense, the AKP appeared ready to redefine 'we-ness' at the level of Turkey's national identity, such that 'we-ness' was based not on an exclusionary interpretation of the nation that only allowed room for those identifying as Turks, but rather it countenanced diversity and, to some degree, accepted the reality of Turkey's heterogeneous demographic make-up. Indicative of such a position, Recep Tayyip Erdoğan was later to remark that Turkey was a 'mosaic', an amalgamation of elements drawn from a range of cultural and religious traditions.[62] Changes became apparent in the public and political spheres, too. At the general election of 2011, Erol Dora, a Syriac, won a seat in parliament, the first Christian to do so for several decades,[63] and in 2012 a Syriac weaver was awarded the Woman of the Year in Turkey.[64]

In its recognition and accommodation of diversity, the AKP departed from the nationalism-infused norms and discourses of earlier Kemalist-inclined administrations. Paying heed to the role of Islam in society, thus winning support of Anatolia's observant masses, AKP leaders constituted a 'counter elite'[65] to the Kemalists who had for so long been dominant in Ankara. Indeed, the AKP's early initiatives appeared to upend Turkish politics by curtailing state intervention in the public and economic spheres, as highlighted by Erdoğan who urged his party and administration to adopt a 'trading mentality' (*tüccar zihniyeti*) in their political approach,[66] touting service provision as the primary role of governance. The AKP also pushed through a series of legislative reforms that made the Turkish polity more pluralistic and democratic.[67] These including curtailing military influence in politics. With time, the military, too, assumed more open-minded positions on national identity. In 2009 General İlker Başbuğ, the Chief of General Staff of the Turkish military, an institution known to be infused with a rigid nationalist outlook, emphasised in a speech that the '*Türkiye halkı*' ('people of Turkey'), rather than '*Türk halkı*' ('Turkish people'), had founded the Republic.[68] In this he was apparently broadening the conception of the people from an exclusively Turkish focus and acknowledging the ethnic diversity of Anatolia.

In sum, the changes brought by the AKP amounted to a repudiation of the strictures of Kemalism, which had long adopted a top-down approach that would engineer society, in particular imposing the uniformity and ethnic unity deemed necessary for national cohesion and progress. The AKP approach allowed for diversity – in ethnicity, in attitude to religion – and created the space for societal change to unfurl organically and guided by the ideas of social justice seen as central to the Islamic vision that AKP members and constituents shared. These were the signs of a more confident Turkey, more at ease with its own demographic diversity, and less prone to the defensive world view and suspicions of the Kemalist old guard.

The Kurds and New Political Spaces

Broadening discussions of national identity and making legislative changes, including the lifting of emergency rule (long in place in the south-east of the country and known by its Turkish acronym OHAL) in 2002,[69] had immediate implications for Kurds in Turkey. Furthermore, the AKP appeared to adopt a new approach to the Kurdish issue, reframing it as a political rather than a security issue. In Diyarbakır in 2005, Prime Minister Erdoğan signalled a sea change, declaring that the key to resolving Kurdish discontent was not further repressive measures but the consolidation of democracy.[70]

The Turkish electorate appeared to approve of the AKP government's attempts to pursue new avenues to address the Kurdish issue. The think tank, SETA, surveying constituents across Turkey in 2009, found that a majority felt that military measures had failed and that the job of resolving the Kurdish issue should be the responsibility of the parliament and political parties.[71] The issue was now defined by new dynamics and dimensions. This extended to a degree of soul-searching by the Turkish military, a newly installed police chief in Diyarbakır in 2012 acknowledging faults in the state's earlier actions, which he contended had exacerbated and inflamed the security situation in the region.[72] Erdoğan, too, pushed a conciliatory message, acknowledging the trauma that the state had inflicted in combating terrorism, and declaring that the ascendance to government of the AKP represented a watershed moment, whereupon the 'inhumane acts' that had marked the past would no longer occur.⁷³

A willingness to view the Kurdish issue from alternative perspectives opened the way towards negotiations with the PKK, which further shifted the mood, accelerating the desire for and pace of change. Such was the extent of change that Turkish journalist Yavuz Baydar wrote exultantly that Turkey was shrugging off the 'mass-hypnosis' that had so long allowed the Kurdish presence to be denied. Taboos imposed by the Kemalist ancien régime were shattered, he contended, and a new way forward, to acknowledgement of Turkey's Kurds and to an enhanced democracy, became apparent.⁷⁴ This culminated in PKK leader Öcalan's much-anticipated message delivered on 21 March 2013 in Diyarbakır. Timed to coincide with Newroz, the Kurdish New Year, a letter from the jailed Öcalan read out to an enormous, jubilant crowd announced a ceasefire and called on PKK militants to withdraw from Turkish territory. Öcalan hailed a 'new era' and a 'new Turkey'. He spoke of recapturing the true spirit of 'the notion of "we"', namely the idea of fraternity of Kurds and Turks, claiming it had been trampled on by Kemalist elites.⁷⁵ His message thus complemented Erdoğan's talk of Turkey as a 'mosaic', a Turkey wherein diverse elements could coexist. Here was a previously fractious element pledging to integrate, to play a role in bringing dialogue to replace conflict. Turkey, with Erdoğan at the helm, appeared positioned to resolve one of its most complex and long-standing challenges. Indicative of this, in Mardin in mid-2013 I encountered a group of Kurdish day labourers. Mardin is poised on an escarpment overlooking the plains of northern Syria. Our talk turned to the horrors of the civil war being unleashed in Syria, and the peace process which had recently been instituted in Turkey. When I asked how it was that peace was now taking hold in Turkey one answered with a one-word answer, 'Erdoğan'.

Inevitably, not everyone approved of overtures for peace with the PKK, or with allowing broader contours to the idea of Turkishness. Erdoğan and the AKP's perceived cosying up to the PKK and drive to recognise ethnic diversity unsettled many. Members of the nationalist Milliyetçi Hareket Partisi (Nationalist Action Party; MHP) fell back on shopworn arguments associating engagement with the PKK with territorial fragmentation, one MHP parliamentarian claiming, 'The road is being paved for a federal independent

Kurdish state.'[76] MHP leader Devlet Bahçeli embarked on a series of events in several cities across Turkey touted as 'Protect and Cherish National Values' meetings.[77] These positions were indicative of the rump nationalist attitudes that had earlier brought court action against Orhan Pamuk for his candid discussion of the Kurdish and Armenian issues. Perhaps such a backlash was to be expected given the transformation that was under way; the ground was shifting and the idea of Turkey as a nation-state and a political community was being redefined. In 1980, Kurdish parliamentarian Şerafettin Elçi had been imprisoned for over two years merely for stating, 'There are Kurds in Turkey and I am a Kurd,'[78] but in the new, more open political arena similar declarations no longer incurred such widespread opprobrium or legal consequences.[79]

Changes became apparent on the ground, too. When I first visited Diyarbakır in the 1990s, the city was notable for the stifling presence of the military and for official attempts to stifle anything identifiably Kurdish. Returning during the 2010s, I saw an immediate difference. Travelling by bus into Diyarbakır from Mardin, I saw a sign, erected by the local municipality, welcoming travellers in Turkish, Kurdish and Aramaic. Spending time in the city, I encountered numerous manifestations of Kurdish identity and culture, as well as refurbished Armenian, Chaldean and Assyrian churches. In bookshops, shoppers browsed copies of the *Şerefname* and *Mem û Zîn*, those works held in such esteem by so many Kurds, as well as the works of Kurdish novelists and the nationalist poet Cigerxwîn. In the streets of the old town, travellers and locals alike gathered at the Dengbej Evi-Mala Dengbêjan for performances by *dengbêj* (traditional Kurdish bards), and gift shops offered souvenir tapestries of, among others, Yılmaz Güney, a dissident Kurdish filmmaker, and Sheikh Said, who led the Kurdish insurrection against the Republic of Turkey and was hanged outside the city walls in 1925. None of this would have been possible earlier, before the AKP had broadened discussions of national identity in Turkey allowing space that Kurds and others were able to occupy.

Identity and Difference in Flux: The Gezi Park Protests

Embarking on the peace process appeared to be another significant achievement of the AKP government, building on its steady progress in instituting reforms and in managing the economy through the vagaries of the 2008 financial crisis. In the general election of 2011, the AKP had extended its appeal beyond its initial base, the conservative masses of inner Anatolia, to win over disparate segments of society. It consolidated its control of the parliament, winning 49.8 per cent of the national vote. However, as its popularity peaked its agenda became more conservative and, apparently, more beholden to Islamic impulses. Hakkı Taş documents the AKP's assertive legislative agenda after its 2011 electoral victory as a point at which the government began to centralise power and reshape the political and judicial landscape to its own advantage, while Erdoğan consolidated his position as unassailable leader of the AKP enterprise.[80] Through 2013 Erdoğan, a fixture across all Turkish media, admonished the Turkish electorate to abandon alcohol, railed against co-ed dormitories and counselled families to have more children.[81] In doing so, the AKP was intruding into the private sphere; it was also adopting a top-down approach, seeking to mould society to fit its own ideals, rather than maintaining its previously much-touted, pragmatic 'trading mentality' that allowed society to evolve organically and set its own trajectory.

Soon after the widely heralded announcement of the peace process, the AKP was to receive a sharp rebuke. In late May 2013, environmental activists staged a protest against a government-sponsored development project in Gezi Park in Istanbul's Beyoğlu neighbourhood. When police moved in to clear the protesters' camp it catalysed a public backlash that gradually escalated. Over several weeks, protests spread to all but one of Turkey's provinces; they continued intermittently for months.[82] A notable aspect of the protests was that people from diverse walks of life came to participate and express their displeasure with the political status quo. The Gezi protests grew and spread organically. It is clear that there were diverse catalysts, frustrations and aspirations among protesters, but the underlying factor they all shared was a sense of disenfranchisement in a political arena increasingly dominated by and dictated to by Erdoğan and the AKP.[83]

The Gezi protests appeared to upend many of the existing certainties in Turkey's socio-political sphere. Ece Temelkuran notes that standing out, whether in an ethnic, social or other sense, remains suspect in Turkish politics and society, broadly speaking. It is not only Kurds who are deemed the Other in Turkey, she argues, but also those who commit seemingly innocuous infractions of

Figure 1.1 Dancing during the Gezi Park protests, Istanbul, June 2013. © William Gourlay.

societal norms.[84] This may be seen as the continuation of the notion, stemming from the disruptions and ethnic fragmentation of the late-Ottoman era, that strength is found in unity, and that disunity leaves one open to exploitation, at the mercy of opponents intent on your defeat. But during the Gezi protests the population looked beyond differences, highlighting what they shared in the face of what they saw as the government's unjustifiably heavy-handed responses to initially peaceful protests in Istanbul and beyond. Temelkuran contended that Gezi demonstrated that citizens of Turkey from across the political spectrum could 'co-exist against all odds'.[85] In this sense, a long-standing propensity towards conformism evident in Turkish society was subsumed and, as one journalist observed, 'governing enmities seemed to have been overthrown'.[86] An image widely shared on social media showed two youths holding hands while running from a police water cannon barrage.[87] One of the youths carried a flag depicting Atatürk, an indication of support for the Kemalist-inclined Republican People's Party (CHP); the other carried the banner of the pro-Kurdish Barış ve Demokrasi Partisi (Peace and Democracy Party; BDP). These are two diametrically opposed positions. According to long-standing political orthodoxies, they are not supposed to or assumed to ever hold hands, but here they cooperated in the face of the onslaught of the state security apparatus.

There are direct parallels between the state's treatment of Kurds and the AKP government's response to the peaceful protests of the Gezi event. Both instances exhibited official intolerance of differing opinions, the state's unwillingness to hear constituents' political grievances, violent responses to peaceful protest and political mobilisation, efforts to silence oppositional voices, to undermine their credibility, to portray them as a threat. As Ezgi Başaran observes, the Gezi events demonstrated to mainstream Turkish society that the state could quickly revert to brutal tactics and accusations of terrorism in response to peaceful protest and reasonable political demands, just as the state had long done to Kurds.[88] Such parallels, apparent to many observers, did not necessarily resonate within Turkey between Turks and Kurds, or if they did so only briefly and to limited extent. Some hoped that a new consensus and a more inclusive politics might emerge during Gezi, but any such development proved to be short-lived. For a time hopes were high that concerted, peaceful civil mobilisation might push the AKP and Erdoğan to resume the path that they had originally set out upon, but from which they were steadily, if not intentionally, straying. This was an opportunity for the AKP to rein in its recent authoritarian tendencies and revert to a civil and open politics that engaged constituents from across the spectrum. The groundswell of grassroots involvement created the space for a more liberal and pluralist politics that would continue the process, begun in recent years, of accommodating more diverse and disparate voices.

Abdullah Öcalan was one who hailed the Gezi Park protests as a political turning point.[89] As might be expected, Erdoğan, the target of much of the ire on display, took a dim view of events, initially deriding protesters as '*birkaç tane çapulcu*' ['a few looters'].[90] With events unfurling beyond Istanbul, Erdoğan took an increasingly intransigent line, dismissing dissent as illegitimate and unjustified, despite it being so widespread, on the grounds that, following successive electoral victories, the AKP represented *milli irade* (the national will).[91] Henri Barkey noted that after Gezi Park, the AKP, previously well regarded internationally and viewed by many as an open-minded and liberal political project, came to be seen as echoing the negative traits of its illiberal predecessors.[92] While some AKP figures adopted a conciliatory tone, Gezi laid bare a shift in the party, where Erdoğan was becoming more dominant. In adopting a belligerent tone, he revealed himself to be increasingly intolerant of criticism, opposition and dissent.[93]

The Gezi protests were not intrinsically related to debates about national identity, rather about the ways in which Turkey's citizens wanted to be governed, but in laying bare significant fault lines within society and in provoking a circle-the-wagons response from the government, they effectively brought an end to the inclusive and accommodational politics that the AKP had earlier championed. The AKP's 2002 campaign brochure had pledged to engage Turkey 'with all its colours, its points of commonality and difference', suggesting a new, expansive, all-embracing 'we-ness'. But after Gezi, the AKP's 'we-ness' contracted to those inside the AKP tent, leaving a sizeable proportion of the population outside. Turkish society, broadly speaking, polarised in a similar fashion, with the significant caveat that those outside the AKP tent shared only an opposition to the AKP and agreed on little else.

Instituting 'Yeni Türkiye'

Turkey's political arena only grew more contested and heated following the Gezi Park protests. The optimism that had blossomed through earlier years – as the economy had boomed, as new political spaces had opened up, as an end to the Kurdish conflict appeared to be within reach – progressively dissipated. Erdoğan proposed an executive presidency, a dream he had long harboured, as a remedy to any and all political problems that beset the country. As Yavuz Baydar had earlier noted, Erdoğan's ambition had been to bring about an end to the Kurdish conflict and to update the constitution that had been in place since the coup of 1980.[94] The two were closely linked. To effect the second, he needed to win the Kurdish vote, and to do so he first had to bring an end to the Kurdish conflict. As events unfurled after Gezi it became clear that the task of bringing peace was more complex than Erdoğan realised, hoped or was willing to countenance. The election of June 2015, at which the pro-Kurdish HDP bounded into parliament and deprived the AKP of its majority, demonstrated that while the Kurdish electorate was eager to engage in the political process it would not be easily wooed and would not dance to Erdoğan's tune simply because he had talked into being a peace process. The setback of the June 2015 election offered another chance, just as the Gezi protests had and the subsequent attempted coup of July 2016 did, for the AKP and Erdoğan to recalibrate and adopt a more conciliatory politics that healed divisions and engaged constituents across the spectrum. Instead, in each instance, Erdoğan doubled down, manoeuvring to consolidate control of the AKP, the levers of power and state institutions.

In August 2014, having triumphed in Turkey's first-ever direct vote for the presidency, Erdoğan began talking up a new political project: 'Yeni Türkiye' (New Turkey). He posted on Twitter that a new Turkey had been born, one that 'equated to a new politics, a new sociology, a new economy' ('*Yeni bir siyasete, yeni bir sosyolojiye, yeni bir ekonomiye tekabül ediyor*').[95] This was his pitch for a new executive presidency; he proposed it as the only model that could solve the challenges that Turkey faced. This vision, in which he would be granted extended powers, was offered as an alternative to, and as the only means by which to prevent a return to, the *old* Turkey where the economy was vulnerable and politics was bedevilled by an interfering military and fractious, unworkable coalitions.[96] With this project the last shackles of Kemalism and the lingering hangover of the 1980 coup would be thrown off and, upon assuming the helm, Erdoğan would steer Turkey to a bright new future.

Realising that the Kurdish population would not be co-opted alongside his traditional, conservative voter base into such a project, Erdoğan changed tack and began courting another perennial constituency, the nationalists. His track record and longevity in the corridors of power in Ankara are testament to Erdoğan's political instincts. When he had embarked on the peace process he was undoubtedly aware that this would involve a delicate balance between winning Kurdish favour and limiting nationalist opprobrium. For this reason, some argue that engagement was never made in good faith and that it foundered from the outset due to a lack of commitment from the AKP.[97] This is not to say that the PKK, and other Kurdish political actors, should not bear some responsibility for the collapse of the process, but some academics and many Kurds now contend that the whole process amounted to nothing more than political expediency, a currying of Kurdish favour in the pursuit of Erdoğan's longed-for executive presidency.[98]

This was the 'trading mentality' at work, but from a cynical perspective. Having lost one ancillary constituency – the Kurds – that could boost his vote to the levels he desired, he turned in mid-2015 to another – the nationalists, those who had earlier railed against political engagement with the Kurds. Upon the resumption of hostilities with the PKK, Erdoğan and the AKP abandoned all talk of conciliation and breathed new life into a rhetoric – until recently thought to have been relegated to history – that focused on treason, treachery, separatism and terrorism. The tropes of nationalist discourse re-emerged, as large parts of Diyabakır's Sur neighbourhood, and other Kurdish cities, were destroyed,[99] and those who spoke in favour of peace were howled down or, indeed, arrested.[100] In large measure the Turkish population came along for the ride, concerned at the territorial advances of the Syrian Kurds across the southern border and able to access fewer independent sources of news as Erdoğan tightened his grip on the media. Turkey's politics retained the trappings of democracy, but it now operated largely within parameters created by Erdoğan's machinations, becoming a form of 'personalised rule and unchecked powers legitimised through a crisis-driven narrative and clientelism'.[101]

Analysing Erdoğan's statements over time reveal his fickle approach to the Kurdish issue. In 2005 in Diyarbakır he had declared, 'The Kurdish problem is Turkey's problem, and my problem too.'[102] By early 2015 he had changed his tune, telling a gathering in Ankara, 'There is no longer a Kurdish problem; there are problems of my Kurdish brothers.'[103] In this, Erdoğan appears to be having his cake and eating it too, attempting to retain credibility with nationalist voters while paying lip service to the concerns of Kurds. But there exists an important caveat and departure from his earlier inclusive approach. In evoking his 'Kurdish brothers' he singles out those who adopt his agenda unquestioningly, where previously engagement with Kurdish political actors had involved degrees of compromise, reconciliation and discussion, a meeting between two poles. Erdoğan still appeared to be redefining 'we-ness', but it was to be done on his terms, with an implicit imperative to conform to his particular vision.

Within this configuration of events and discourses, the Kurdish issue assumed new dimensions, as did conceptions of Turkey's national identity and Kurdish ethnic identity. For Kurds, the task at hand was no longer to maintain an identity in the face of official denial, even though nationalist discourse and nationalist political actors again assumed potency. Rather, the job was to maintain the parameters of Kurdish identity as they defined it, to maintain their own political vision and space and discourse of democracy in the 'New Turkey', even as the political arena grew more polarised and the

Erdoğan regime grew more authoritarian. It is this that the following chapters set out to analyse.

Notes

1. *New York Times*, 'Popular Turkish novelist on trial', 16 December 2005.
2. Ergül, 'The Ottoman identity', p. 630.
3. Lewis, *The Emergence of Modern Turkey*, p. 2. It is worth observing that Lewis is widely noted (and often criticised) for his championing of the modernising regime of the new Republic, particularly what he sees as its casting off of Islamic accretions that had prevented the 'emergence' of an authentic Turkish identity. For a critical examination of Lewis' position, see Zürcher, *The Young Turk Legacy and Nation Building*, pp. 43–50.
4. Mazower, *The Balkans: A short history*, pp. 50–2.
5. Lewis, *The Emergence of Modern Turkey*, p. 1.
6. Mardin, 'Playing games with names', p. 118.
7. Üngör, *The Making of Modern Turkey*, pp. 39–40.
8. Mardin, 'Playing games with names', p. 115.
9. Findley, *Turkey, Islam, Nationalism and Modernity*, pp. 204–19.
10. Smith, *National Identity*, p. 21. This problem was not unique to Turkey, as evidenced by the oft-quoted statement of Massimo d'Azeglio after the unification of Italy: 'We have made Italy; now we must make Italians.' See Carter, 'Nation, nationality, nationalism and internationalism in Italy', pp. 545–51.
11. Findley, *Turkey, Islam, Nationalism and Modernity*, pp. 201–2.
12. Yıldız, *Ne Mutlu Türküm Diyebilene*, pp. 58–61.
13. Orhan Pamuk himself is a descendant of Caucasian refugees. He notes that his maternal grandmother was Circassian: Pamuk, *Istanbul: Memories of a city*, p. 11.
14. Navaro-Yashin, *Faces of the State*, p. 65.
15. Soleimani, *Islam and Competing Nationalisms*, pp. 79–80.
16. Kemalists are named after Mustafa Kemal Atatürk, leader of the independence struggle and founding president of the Republic.
17. The boundaries of Turkishness were very widely drawn to incorporate some of those depicted – Attila the Hun, Genghis Khan and eleventh-century polymath Avicenna.
18. Özsoy, 'The missing grave of Sheikh Said', pp. 191–20.
19. Yeğen, *Müstakbel-Türk'ten Sözde-Vatandaş'a.*, pp. 10–11.
20. Yıldız, *Ne Mutlu Türküm Diyebilene*, p. 242.
21. Yeğen, *Müstakbel-Türk'ten Sözde-Vatandaş'a.*, pp. 17–20.

22. Findley, *Turkey, Islam, Nationalism and Modernity*, p. 251; Bozarslan, 'Kurds and the Turkish state', pp. 334–5.
23. Yeğen, *Müstakbel-Türk'ten Sözde-Vatandaş'a*, pp. 15–17.
24. Yıldız, *Ne Mutlu Türküm Diyebilene*, p. 243.
25. Cited in McDowall, *A Modern History of the Kurds*, p. 397.
26. Temelkuran, *Turkey: The insane and the melancholy*, p. 250.
27. *Sabah*, 'Kart-kurt'tan eyalete', 28 February 2007.
28. This book does not engage with discussions about whether the PKK is, or is not, a terrorist group. Definitions of terrorism are notoriously complex. See Hoffman, *Inside Terrorism*, pp. 1–44.
29. Watts, *Activists in Office*, p. 18.
30. Massicard, 'Claiming difference in a unitarist frame', pp. 78–9.
31. Bajalan, 'Şeref Xan's Sharafnama', p. 796.
32. Soleimani, *Islam and Competing Nationalisms*, p. 160.
33. Bajalan, 'Şeref Xan's Sharafnama', p. 797.
34. Van Bruinessen, 'Ehmedî Xanî's *Mem û Zîn*', p. 40.
35. Van Bruinessen, 'Kurdish society, ethnicity, nationalism and refugee problems', pp. 33–67.
36. McDowall, *A Modern History of the Kurds*, pp. 93–4.
37. Çırakman, 'Flags and traitors'.
38. *Cumhuriyet Halk Fırkası Programının İzahı* (Ankara Hakimiyeti Milliye Matbaası, 1931), cited in İnce, *Citizenship and Identity in Turkey*, p. 39.
39. Stansfield, 'Kurds, Persian nationalism and Shi'I rule', pp. 59–84. Stansfield describes Kurds in Iran as surviving within a system of 'dominant nationhood', but the term applies equally effectively to Turkey.
41. Cited in Bengio, *The Kurds of Iraq*, p. 11.
42. Findley, *Turkey, Islam, Nationalism and Modernity*, pp. 352, 364.
43. Ibid., p. 365; Güneş, *The Kurdish National Movement in Turkey*, pp. 81–7.
44. Watts, 'Institutionalising virtual Kurdistan West', p. 129.
45. Yavuz, 'Five stages in the construction of Kurdish nationalism', pp. 1–24.
46. Natali, *The Kurds and the State*, p. 180.
47. Barth, Frederik, *Ethnic Groups and Boundaries*, p. 15. On boundary making among Kurds, see Tezcür, 'Kurdish nationalism and identity in Turkey'.
48. Gellner, *Nations and Nationalism*, pp. 6–7.
49. Eriksen, 'We and us', pp. 427–36.
50. Grabolle-Çeliker, *Kurdish Life in Contemporary Turkey*, p. 3.
51. Ensaroğlu, 'Turkey's Kurdish question', p. 8.
52. Watts, 'Activists in office', p. 4.

53. Ensaroğlu, 'Turkey's Kurdish question', p. 11.
54. On Özal's presidency, see Gunter (2011a), 'Turgut Özal and the Kurdish question', pp. 85–100.
55. Taşpınar, *Kurdish Nationalism and Political Islam*, pp. 104–5.
56. Ergil, 'Knowledge is a potent instrument for change'.
57. On the evolution of Kurdish political parties in 1990s Turkey, see Watts, *Activists in Office*, pp. 51–74.
58. Soner, 'The Justice and Development Party's policies', p. 27.
59. White, *Muslim Nationalism and the New Turks*, p. 50.
60. Cited in Soner, 'The Justice and Development Party's policies', pp. 24–5.
61. Cited in Insel, 'The AKP and normalising democracy', p. 304
62. Cited in White, *Muslim Nationalism and the New Turks*, p. 102.
63. *Hürriyet Daily News*, 'Syriacs send their first deputy to parliament', 14 June 2011.
64. Ziflioğlu, 'Syriac weaver says mutual respect the answer'.
65. Somer, 'Democratization, clashing narratives and "Twin Tolerations"', p. 32.
66. Yavuz, *Secularism and Muslim Democracy*, p. 30.
67. Somer, 'Democratization, clashing narratives and "Twin Tolerations"', p. 41.
68. *Cumhuriyet*, 'Başbuğ'dan 'Türkiye halkı' vurgusu', 14 April 2009; see also Akyol, 'From Turkish people to the people of Turkey'.
69. *Yeni Şafak*, 'Olağanüstü Hal 30 Kasımda Bitiyor', 28 November 2002.
70. Keskin, 'Erdoğan: Kürt sorunu demokrasiyle çözülür'.
71. SETA, *Public Perceptions of the Kurdish Question*, p. 11.
72. *Hürriyet Daily News*, 'All to blame for lost sons', 2012.
73. *Today's Zaman*, 'Erdoğan: Past mistakes in fighting terrorism helped PKK'.
74. Baydar, 'Turkey and the Kurds'.
75. *Hürriyet Daily News*, 'Öcalan calls on Kurdish militants', 21 March 2013.
76. Yackley, 'Kurd rebel leader orders fighters to halt hostilities'.
77. *Hürriyet Daily News*, 'Nationalist party gathers huge crowds', 20 April 2013.
78. *Hürriyet*, '45 Ay Hapis', 11 March 2000. For further discussion of Elçi, see Watts, *Activists in Office*, p. 44.
79. See the example of Fethiye Çetin, mentioned in the previous chapter, who revealed her Armenian roots. A similar example is that of the popular actress Hülya Avşar, who revealed her father's Kurdish background and that to her family she was known as Malakan, a Kurdish name: *Milliyet*, 'Hülya Avşar: Adım Malakan', 26 February 2015.
80. Taş, 'Turkey – from tutelary to delegative democracy', pp. 776–91.

81. Waldman and Calışkan, *The New Turkey*, pp. 71–3.
82. Gençoğlu Onbaşi, 'Gezi Park protests', pp. 272–94.
83. Abbas and Yiğit, 'Scenes from Gezi Park', pp. 61–76.
84. Temelkuran, 'Revolutionary Nice'.
85. Ibid.
86. Christie-Miller, 'Occupy Gezi'.
87. The image can be seen in a story from *Diken*, a Turkish online newspaper: see http://www.diken.com.tr/gezinin-kahramanlari-kimin-ayagina-basarsan-koroglu-olur-baskaldirir/. In the image, an older protester makes the 'grey wolf' symbol, indicative of a hard-line Turkish nationalist position, an indication that a range of political positions were united in their desire to protest against the AKP.
88. Başaran, *Frontline Turkey*, p. 96.
89. *Hürriyet Daily News*, 'PKK leader praises protests', 7 June 2013.
90. *Radikal* (2013a), 'Erdoğan: AKM yıkılacak, Taksim'e cami de yapılacak'.
91. Ulgen, 'Erdoğan's fetishism of the "National Will"'.
92. Barkey, 'Turkish democracy', pp. 75–8.
93. For detailed exploration of this, see Cizre (ed.), *The Turkish AK Party and its Leader*.
94. Baydar, 'Turkey and the Kurds'.
95. See https://twitter.com/rt_erdogan/status/504568554835156992. 'Yeni Türkiye' was also heralded on the presidential website in October 2016. See https://www.tccb.gov.tr/haberler/410/55827/yeni-turkiye-yolunda-verdigimiz-mucadelede-en-buyuk-gucu-millet-olusturuyor.html
96. Waldman and Calışkan, *The New Turkey*, p. 79.
97. Gunter, 'The Turkish–Kurdish peace process', pp. 19–26.
98. See, for example, Ümit Cizre 'Introduction: The politics of redressing grievances', in *The Turkish AK Party and its Leader*.
99. See, for example, *Human Rights Watch*, 'Turkey: Mounting security operation deaths'; *International Crisis Group*, 'Managing Turkey's PKK conflict'.
100. See, for example, Başer et al., '"Academics for Peace" in Turkey', pp. 274–96.
101. Taş, 'Turkey – from tutelary to delegative democracy', p. 777.
102. *Hürriyet*, 'Kürt sorunu benim sorunum', 12 August 2005.
103. Presidency of the Republic of Turkey (2015).

2

TALKING TO KURDS ABOUT 'IDENTITY'

Tensions were heightened during the Gezi protests that began in late May 2013, as I experienced in Istanbul. Arriving soon afterwards in Diyarbakır, I found the situation to which I had become accustomed entirely reversed. In my earlier travels to Turkey, Istanbul had been a city of sunshine and vibrant street life and Diyarbakır one of tensions and an overbearing police and military presence. But in June 2013, the buzz of Istanbul's central Beyoğlu neighbourhood was regularly disrupted by clashes between protesters and police, by water cannon and gas canisters, while in Diyarbakır I found a city basking in the early summer. Streets were crowded with shoppers and families going about their business; the oppressive mood of years past had apparently lifted. Teahouses and restaurants hummed at all hours. Paradoxically, the political temperature was as hot as it had been for a long time in Turkey, but Diyarbakır, historically an epicentre of confrontation and contestation, was uncharacteristically placid. When I remarked at the lack of police presence, someone told me they had all been sent to Istanbul to subdue the protests.

To this end, Istanbul and Diyarbakır serve as useful barometers of the political atmosphere in Turkey, reflecting shifting dynamics in the Kurdish issue as well as nationwide currents of political significance. This was apparent again when I returned in October 2014 and many Kurds were concerned about the emergence of ISIS and its attacks on Syrian Kurdish communities.

The political temperature in Diyarbakır rose accordingly. In May/June 2015 both cities were adorned with the bunting of political parties of all stripes and the citizenry were correspondingly engaged.

Entering 'the field'

In the course of my research I conducted formal interviews with thirty-six Kurds aged from twenty-two to sixty-two, from various localities in Istanbul and Diyarbakır, and from a range of vocations, from 'business men', a film-maker, teachers, café proprietors, journalists and an economist, to shopkeepers, a *kebapçı* (street-side kebab seller), an unemployed gentleman who professed Marxism and several who described themselves as self-employed. Additionally, I documented many conversations, taking notes of spontaneous interactions with a diverse range of individuals and groups (in several instances, with entire families of two generations), including commuters at bus stops, shoppers, passers-by and a *hamal* (porter) who pushed a barrow in the Diyarbakır bazaar.[1]

My primary focus was on Diyarbakır because, as noted earlier, it is of great significance for Turkey's Kurds and, after early trips to Mardin, Urfa and Hilvan, I found it to be the most promising site for research. With the intention of tapping into the geographic, economic and demographic spread of Turkey's Kurdish population, I also conducted research in Istanbul.[2] It is worth noting that Diyarbakır is known as a centre of nationalist, secular Kurdish political activity. Cities such as Bingöl and Dersim (Tunceli) are centres for, respectively, observant Sunni and Alevi Kurds.[3] Accordingly, in the data I gathered, secular rather than religious perspectives predominated. On this note, it is important to underline that in showcasing this research I do not claim to be presenting a comprehensive picture of who 'the Kurds' are, or portraying Kurds as a homogenous, monolithic community. Turkey's Kurdish population is diverse in location, lived experience, economic status and political outlook, and this book only intends to represent a snapshot of Kurdish life based on the places I visited and the individual Kurds I met and interacted with.

My ethnographic activities in Diyarbakır began in the walled city of Sur. This is the historical core of the city, home to both the Ulu Cami (the Grand Mosque) and covered bazaar, and a site of continuous daily activity. Despite

Figure 2.1   Street life in Sur, Diyarbakır, June 2015. © William Gourlay.

some guidebook-worthy sites and some urban regeneration, the narrow, cobbled lanes of Sur retain a ramshackle air and highly visible pockets of poverty. Sur also reveals some of the demographic diversity among Kurds, being meeting place for the well-off, who go for brunch in hip *kahvaltı salonları* (breakfast salons), workplace for municipality staff, shop owners and bazaar stall-holders, as well as home to villagers who fled the conflict in the surrounding countryside in earlier decades.[4] In Sur I moved between a maze of shops and teahouses around the Ulu Cami and nearby neighbourhoods, encountering people from these diverse demographics. In an attempt to diversify the range of views I encountered, I also spent time in the Ofis neighbourhood of Yenşehir (literally 'New City') outside the city walls. This is the city's commercial and administrative centre, a neat grid of streets, with broad footpaths, modern shopfronts, apartment and office buildings. The atmosphere here is noticeably more affluent than in Sur. Those I met here were from the professional classes – teachers, bureaucrats, journalists – and all were tertiary educated.

In Sur, I regularly visited a particular teahouse near the Ulu Cami which was frequented by a range of manual labourers, both those resident nearby and those who dropped in during the course of daily tasks. The owner here acted as something of a 'gatekeeper', introducing me to locals and suggesting others I might contact and interview. With the assistance of other such 'gatekeepers', including contacts from earlier travels to Turkey, I adopted a snowball technique to broaden the pool of interview participants. I relied on this in Istanbul as well, utilising Kurdish contacts from the Gedikpaşa neighbourhood, as well as journalist friends who suggested I visit a Kurdish café near Istanbul University and another popular hangout in Beyoğlu, an area long noted as a congregational spot for Istanbul's leftists, artists and literati. Another time, I was hosted to dinner by a Kurdish family at home in a very well-to-do Bosphorus neighbourhood, evidence that being Kurdish is not an impediment to economic success and acceptance into the upper echelons of Istanbul society and, simultaneously, that such acceptance does not imply assimilation into Turkishness or denial of one's Kurdish identity. Snowballing was an effective way of gathering qualitative data, as a degree of trust was required between myself and my respondents, but I acknowledge that it has its shortcomings, not least that in following contacts within certain social circles an element of 'selection bias' is unavoidable.[5] Notably, all I interviewed were urban dwellers, even though many still retained links to ancestral villages. Similarly, as a consequence of the circles I moved in, and reflecting broader dynamics in Kurdish society, I had many more discussions with men than women. Accordingly, I reiterate that this book does not claim to present a comprehensive or exhaustive portrait of 'the Kurds' in Turkey.

An Australian in Kurdish Neighbourhoods

On my first trip to Diyarbakır I was spotted and followed through the backstreets by a group of children chanting, 'Hello! Hello!' It was immediately apparent to them that I was not a local. Yet, as I have experienced among Kurds, Turks and others in the Middle East, as a visitor one is often an object of curiosity and the recipient of spontaneous welcome and generosity. It can also prompt protective instincts. One woman in a Diyarbakır shop declared that locals ('*Biz Amedliyiz!*' she proudly stated: We are from Amed!) would protect me ('*Biz seni kurtarırız*') if anything happened. What things might actually happen remained unclear. Similarly, several times in the backstreets of Sur I was told to be alert for thieves, a considerable irony because I never once felt threatened.

It must be considered, however, what impact my status as a visitor had on interactions with Kurds and the collection of research data. Ethnographic researchers speak of insider and outsider positions. Insiders are those viewed as having a 'certain level of familiarity and shared attributes' with the communities they are studying.[6] This theoretically creates advantages as the insider's greater familiarity allows better access and more in-depth understanding of societal and political dynamics. Alternatively, some argue that outsiders, arriving with less baggage, may be more neutral or objective in their observations and analysis. That said, some argue that insider–outsider status is not always rigidly drawn,[7] indeed that a researcher's status may vary in different circumstances or from different perspectives.[8] Research among Kurds may present some challenges for some 'insiders', particularly researchers of Turkish ethnicity. One Turkish researcher notes that his ethnic identity and his status as employee of a state-run university raised questions among Kurdish research subjects, many of whom have experienced violence at the hands of the state.[9] Similarly, Bahar Başer notes feeling accused of the 'sins of the Turkish state' by some Kurds, and feeling guilty accordingly.[10] From this perspective, my 'outsiderness' was an advantage in that I was never viewed as a proponent of the Turkish Republic's perspective. Indeed, that I was Australian was viewed positively by many Kurds I met, some of whom remarked on relatives and friends who had emigrated to Australia and related positive accounts of their new lives. More generally, being 'Western' or 'European' also seemed to resonate positively. A man at an HDP rally in Diyarbakır told me that 'Europe supports the Kurds and human rights', while shaking my hand approvingly.

My goal was to conduct research as objectively as possible, and in a manner that would encourage Kurds to participate.[11] There is always the possibility that a community or individuals will be wary of the researcher, viewing them as a 'questionable academic',[12] but this was not something I encountered. My experience is that teachers and academics are generally highly esteemed across Turkey. While living in Izmir I was always called '*hocam*' ('my teacher') by the local shop owner, and the hotel staff where I stayed in Diyarbakır were amused and began calling me '*profesör*' after finding on YouTube a TV interview I had done about the Kurdish defence of Kobanî. This presumably won me some kudos. I would like to think that on three trips to Diyarbakır between 2013 and 2015 I became familiar to a cohort of locals, including those I encountered in daily life – shopkeepers, restaurant owners, *pazarcılar* (bazaar salesmen) and others – and those who I interviewed and conversed with. Certainly, they greeted me with affection each time I returned. Some of them made attempts to teach me Kurdish, to no great effect, although I found the few Kurdish phrases I retained useful in creating a sense of camaraderie whenever I made new acquaintances. In this sense, socialising in informal situations went some way towards creating a degree of 'insiderness' and dispelling any concerns about my intentions. For example, after spending an evening eating sunflower seeds and watching a broadcast football match at my Diyarbakır hotel, one man announced he would like to be interviewed, even though I had not previously asked him.

In my experience, whatever the prevailing political conditions, finding those who identify as Kurdish and who want to talk politics is no great challenge in Turkey. Kurds had volunteered their political viewpoints to me without urging since my earliest visits to Turkey, long before I had ever envisaged undertaking academic research on the issue. In this sense, the work of the ethnographic researcher is straightforward among the Kurds in Turkey. I have discovered that Kurdish people, in the main, are eager to talk about their political circumstances, which inevitably leads to discussion of such topics as identity and citizenship. Some minorities in Turkey are notable for their reticence in talking to outsiders, thus necessitating extended periods of time in the field to win trust as a prelude to data gathering,[13] yet I have encountered no such problem among Kurds. From what I have witnessed among Kurds, political discussions are a mainstay of daily interactions. This may particularly be the case in Diyarbakır, which, compared to other cities, has been noted for high levels of political activism and engagement.[14] In turn, Kurdish political activism appears to be an historical trend, some observing the disproportionately high numbers of Kurds who have served in the Turkish parliament.[15] These circumstances may explain the willingness of Kurds to discuss politics. A further explanation may be frustration with the political process and a desire to have their political opinions heard. Doğu Ergil, discussing his groundbreaking Kurdish social survey of 1995, recalled how eager Kurds were to explain their problems and concerns to the government and the broader population. Up until then they had been voiceless, while being dictated to by the state. An opportunity to have a say was something they took up eagerly.[16] While the situation may have changed considerably since 1995, I still found Kurds eager to engage, to express their grievances and aspirations and their observations of their lives and the political community they lived in.

By the same token, I do not wish to create the impression that this book attempts to speak for all Kurds, or aims to ignore or override the diversity in their outlooks and voices. As has been noted, in recent decades Kurds have found new mechanisms through which to assert and disseminate political positions and new forums in which to represent themselves.[17] This book, therefore, aims to generate new understandings of the political circumstances of Kurds in Turkey and uses, wherever possible, their voices, in the form of recollections of daily life and political events, to do so.

It is notable that at the time of my research trips, between 2013 and 2015, Turkish politics was eventful but less polarised and less on edge than it has been in recent years. While I encountered some people unwilling to

Figure 2.2   Kurdish boys in the backstreets of Diyarbakır, October 2014. © William Gourlay.

participate, the relative state of calm meant that those who did participate could do so without concerns about undue attention from the security services or police. A comparison can be drawn with the experiences of Francis O'Connor and Semih Çelik, who relate conducting research in September 2012, a period of heightened tensions, in Diyarbakır and other Kurdish cities. They had to be cautious in their approaches to participants and found, in turn, that Kurds were hesitant and circumscribed in their engagement with them.[18] In this sense 'contingent events', that is prevailing political incidents, atmosphere and societal interactions, can shape not only the parameters of identity but also the processes of research and the ability to gather data. I was extremely fortunate in that although investigating a topic of considerable political sensitivity I did so at a time of relative calm. This meant I encountered no official restriction to my activities. Despite often passing police and security personnel on Diyarbakır's streets I was never stopped or challenged. It also meant that Kurds, generally, felt free to talk to me without fear of official repercussions.

Conceiving 'identity'

As a starting point for my inquiries, I endeavoured to elicit, without specific reference to ethnicity, how Kurds conceived of their identity in broad terms. This prompted a range of responses that, aside from ethnicity, extended to ideas about citizenship, attachment to place, socio-economic status, legal classification, language, family, religion and gender. Such diversity should not come as a surprise. Charles Taylor describes people as 'self-interpreting animals'.[19] An individual's concept of identity, a core form of self-interpretation, is informed by a multitude of experiences, perspectives and inclinations, resulting in a host of interpretations. Neither should diverse and divergent interpretations and conceptualisations be seen as undermining the validity of claims to Kurdishness. Elise Massicard notes among Turkey's Alevi minority 'the fluctuating and disputed nature of the identity being laid claim to'; but rather than undermining the veracity of these claims, such 'identity confusion' is a result of the political and societal conditions under which identity assumes its (multiple) form(s).[20] Hakan Yavuz, in turn, stresses the 'multiple layers in meaning and substance of Kurdish identity',[21] a concept which, like Alevi identity, has been shaped and buffeted by historical and political events, both at the individual and the collective level.

All citizens of Turkey are issued with an identity card (*nüfus cüzdanı*), which they colloquially refer to as their *kimlik* (literally, 'identity'). Many Kurds I interviewed interpreted questions about their identity literally, referring in their answers to these cards. Identity cards are a mechanism through which to guarantee citizens' rights, but they are also a means by which the state can extend a claim over citizens.[22] This is particularly the case in Turkey, where identity cards bear the Turkish flag. Thus citizens are compelled to carry upon them an emblem of Turkishness, whatever their ethnic affiliation may be. Interview participants who mentioned their identity cards, however, highlighted them as anomalous. The cards categorised them as citizens of Turkey, but they repudiated any implicit claim that the cards make on their ethnicity. Refik commented, 'Even though my identity card has a Turkish flag, and "Turkish" is written on it . . . my real [Kurdish] identity is what is important for me. In other words, my identity card is not valid for me.'[23] Dilek, meanwhile, observed, 'On my ID card, I want to write Kurdish. My ethnicity is Kurdish but I am from Turkey.'[24] Mehmet, similarly, remarked, 'My identity card says "Turkish Republic", I don't have a problem with that . . . [But in] reality my grandfathers are Kurdish, so I can't deny it.'[25]

These comments illustrate some of the ways that Kurds conceive of their membership of the Republic of Turkey. Some accept it implicitly, while for others it is 'not valid'. But in their assertions of Kurdishness, in spite of the Turkish flag emblazoned on their main form of administrative identification, these respondents also demonstrate that their ethnic identity is an entity distinct and separate from, but not always contradictory to, their citizenship (which will be examined later in greater depth). Not all participants mentioned Turkey, or citizenship thereof, within their conceptualisation of identity. However, within diverse interpretations of the concept, all mentioned their Kurdish ethnicity.[26] Indeed, I would argue that many interviewees construed their identity solely in Kurdish terms, while for others being Kurdish was at the top of a hierarchy of identity components. Interviews thus moved swiftly on to discussion of Kurdishness, another concept that was variously conceived.

Ethnicity is commonly equated with membership in a group that shares common descent. Smith lists a myth of common ancestry as the second of his attributes of an ethnic community.[27] Similarly, Donald Horowitz characterises ethnicities as 'a form of greatly extended kinship', highlighting filial ties – mythical or otherwise – as important sources of group cohesion.[28] Eric Hobsbawm notes that since the time of Herodotus the idea of common ancestry has been seen as one means to maintain a unified identity despite political and geographic fragmentation.[29] The Republic of Turkey, aiming to homogenise under the banner of Turkishness, made various attempts to engender a sense of common descent and/or kinship among disparate peoples, such as the Atatürk quote invoking 'children of the one race' mentioned in the previous chapter. But such attempts proved broadly ineffective. Several participants highlighted their ancestry, but did so to demonstrate it as a distinguishing feature of their Kurdish identity. Erdem said, 'I feel like I was . . . you are . . . born with ethnicity first. You aren't born with religion. So I am Kurdish, I am born as Kurdish. Then . . . we are Muslim, which is gained . . . afterwards.'[30]

Erdem saw his Kurdishness as an innate characteristic extending from his birth into a Kurdish family. He applies such a notion universally: '. . . *you* are born with ethnicity first'. Significantly, Erdem's view of religion was entirely the opposite, in that it was not an inherent characteristic but something that was constructed, presumably through practice, example and instruction – something that he 'gained' during his upbringing from parents, elders. Erdem thus outlined his ethnicity as a condition that was present a priori and could not be changed. Others adopted such a position, without specifically mentioning ancestry or 'kinship'. Ali also situated his ethnicity at a level where it could not be altered, '. . . I am Kurdish. I would not say that I am Turkish, because I am not – if I was I would say that . . . When you are Turk, you are proud to say that you are Turk. When you are an Englishman you are proud to say you are English . . . I am Kurdish, so I say I am Kurdish. That's it.'[31] This position is noteworthy, given the antagonistic dialectic between Turkish nationalism and Kurdish nationalism.[32] Ali claims Kurdishness not out of any disdain for Turkish ethnicity; he sees Turkishness as a cause for pride for those to whom it applies, but he does not – cannot – apply it to himself. He sees himself as possessing the criteria for Kurdish ethnicity, so no other categorisation can be countenanced. While there is no hierarchy or intrinsic superiority to being Kurdish for Ali, his ethnicity is not an either/or proposition, it is immutable, inviolable. Refik, who disdains the Turkish flag on his ID card, similarly comments, 'Everyone honours his race. Just like being an Arab, being Suryani [Assyrian], being Armenian, being Turkish, for us being Kurdish [is an honour] – for us as Kurds there is no difference among races.'[33] In Ali's and Refik's responses, one's ethnic identity is something to be upheld but it is not a chauvinistic tool, nor a way of asserting superiority over others. This may be indicative of a theme of tolerance that many Kurds claim, as will be examined later in this book, and also may indicate a degree of flexibility in identification and categorisation that allows for the reconciliation of Kurdish ethnicity with citizenship of Turkey.

Comments such as those by Erdem, asserting that his Kurdishness stemmed from his birth to Kurdish parents, appear to contradict the idea that ethnic identity is malleable. Mert, a café proprietor in Diyarbakır, made a similar observation to Erdem, asserting that 'being Kurdish is not only to be born from Kurdish parents'. He acknowledged that historically 'bloodline' was a standard marker of Kurdishness, but he argued that the notion of being Kurdish had since expanded to assume a political dimension.[34] The political nature of identity was a common theme among participants: one respondent, Mithat, after some equivocation, acknowledged the reason for his identification as Kurdish was '90 per cent political'.[35] Many others noted that their identification varied in different circumstances. This stands to reason if we are to interpret politics at its most basic level as the practice or art of social or public interaction, and to posit that identity emerges at a nexus between social life and self-perception.[36] When asked to define his identity, Ayhan responded, 'This is a hard question because as an individual I have more than one identity,' explaining that he would feel certain aspects of identity more strongly ('*daha çok hissediyorum*') at different times.[37]

As social and – significantly for the Kurds in this study – political settings change, so do the aspects of identity most keenly felt and upheld. Esra commented, 'I first say I am Kurd, then if I am outside the borders [of Turkey] I also say I am a Turkish citizen.'[38] Dilek said, 'It depends on the question. If someone asks, "Where are you from?" I will answer "I am from Turkey." But then I will add "but I am Kurdish, not Turkish."'[39] This raises the issue of legal or statutory interpretations of identity, as opposed to individual or collective identities. Salih, when defining identity, asked, 'Do you mean legally? If you are signing a form you say "Turkish Republic", but this is . . . legal compulsion. But [otherwise] of course we say we are Kurdish.'[40]

These responses confirm Rogers Brubaker's assertion that ethnic identification, and group affiliations generally, are informed and shaped by contingent events, discourses and social circumstances.[41] At different times within living memory, being Kurdish was not automatically a source of pride, or something to be asserted, as Salih's response suggests it is today. Soner related that growing up in late-1970s Diyarbakır, 'being a Kurd was not a kind of identity or nationality or ethnicity. It was like being a kind of . . . peasant.' He recalls being told, 'You are a Kurd . . . so you are nothing.' Soner relates that state officials and police commonly called Kurds '*gundî*', a derogatory Kurdish term for peasant.[42] 'So, I felt a kind of humiliation while I was a kid,' he remarked. Mahmut Altunakar, a Diyarbakır member of parliament in the 1980s, recalled that at a school in western Turkey in the 1940s, other children relentlessly mocked him ('*çocuklar rahat bırakmıyorlardı*') as a Kurd and asked, 'Where is your tail?'[43] If these recollections are evidence that Kurdish identity was once a source of 'humiliation' and mockery, the situation now is enormously different. It would seem that the more Kurds were scorned and the more the Kemalist state attempted to eliminate Kurdishness, the more it became politicised and the more Kurds were determined to grasp it.

Being Different, or How to Spot a Kurd in Turkey

Kurds' recollections of being mocked also highlight the paradox of the Turkish state's position: even as attempts were made to expunge Kurdish identity, various elements in Turkey ridiculed it. Both actions stemmed from a desire to impose uniform Turkishness, but Turkish teachers, students, administrators, police officers who ridiculed Kurds were effectively highlighting Kurdish identity, reifying it, drawing attention to the Kurds as an 'Other'. State policy may have asserted 'unity of language, culture and ideal', but in practice there existed sufficient diversity – and difference – for some Turks to focus on and ridicule. As Kurds sought to defend their identity and culture, they, too, moved to highlight these differences, not as worthy of scorn but of pride.

Serdar, a 'businessman' in Diyarbakır, while discussing identity and Kurdishness in the Republic of Turkey, reeled off a litany of measures of Kurdish distinctiveness: 'The language is different. The culture is different. The sociology is different. The history different.'[44] During our discussion Serdar did not go on to explain *how* these phenomena were different, but in a milieu where state rhetoric has long promoted a message of unity and uniformity, making a claim to difference is an important part of Kurdish identity. Serdar's statement notwithstanding, to the casual observer there are few immediately apparent differences between ethnic Turks and ethnic Kurds. The quotidian flow of life and social interaction in the cities, towns and villages of Turkey where the majority is ethnically Turkish bears striking similarities with that of the Kurdish-majority regions of south-eastern Anatolia. Turks and Kurds are phenotypically indistinguishable. Broadly speaking, in Turkey they subscribe to the same religious affiliations, either Sunni or Alevi Muslim. They share a host of cultural and societal practices, and a great deal of history. Distinct ethnic identities are classified or created through the highlighting of differences and through maintaining a border to ensure those differences in turn are maintained. Martin Van Bruinessen observes that the 'secondary symbols' of cultural practice, such as 'Kurdish' dress, music, folklore and cuisine, show considerable regional variation across Turkey, but they also share similarities with those of other ethnic groups, and thus differences between ethnic groups are not immediately apparent.[45]

Perceptions of difference may confound or arise in unexpected circumstances. Yiğit, a Kurdish university student, told me that when applying to be a volunteer in Istanbul for the pro-Kurdish Halkların Demokratik Partisi (Peoples' Democracy Party; HDP) during the presidential elections of 2014 his ethnic identity had been called into question. Someone asked him, 'What kind of Kurd are you?'[46] Yiğit sports a stereotypical 'hipster' look: with full beard, fashionable glasses and designer T-shirts he would pass unnoticed in the chic neighbourhoods and hang-outs of Istanbul. It seems the HDP staffers deemed his appearance not sufficiently, authentically 'Kurdish', or perhaps too 'Turkish'. Here, it would seem, Yiğit fell short of one particular internally conceived – emic – image of Kurdishness. This highlights the complexity of the issue of Kurdish identity – there is no consensus as to either emic or etic markers.[47] In this case, the staff of the Istanbul HDP, who may see themselves, representatives of the pre-eminent Kurdish political vehicle in Turkey, as quintessentially Kurdish, had preconceived notions of what a Kurdish appearance is, and, one may extrapolate from there, preconceived notions of the constituent elements of Kurdish identity. In this instance, Yiğit didn't make the grade. Van Bruinessen notes that there are disagreements among Kurds themselves about who qualifies – or doesn't – as Kurdish on a range of religious and linguistic grounds across the Middle East.[48] Yiğit's experience reconfirms that Van Bruinessen's 'secondary symbols' – among which physical appearance is included – are not reliable indicators of Kurdish ethnic identity.

Failure to recognise may appear to spell doom for ethnic identification. For Fredrik Barth, an ethnic group is comprised of 'a membership which identities itself, and is identified by others, as constituting a group distinguishable from other categories of the same order'.[49] Thomas Hylland Eriksen similarly contends that identity is created both from within groups and from outside, incorporating elements of 'one's own presentation of and the perceptions of others'.[50] Both Barth and Eriksen stress that in the interplay between internal and external descriptions, ethnicities are negotiated. But that is not to say that internal descriptors are objective, or uniformly held. Barth further argues, 'the features that are taken into account are not the sum of "objective" differences, but only those which the actors themselves regard significant. Not only do ecologic variations mark and exaggerate differences; some cultural features are used by the actors as signals and emblems of differences, others are ignored.'[51] Thus the process of identification is highly subjective and, we may contend, significantly influenced by political circumstances – the 'contingent events' that Brubaker emphasises as enduring shapers of conceptions of ethnicity.

The Turkish-speaking elite that founded the Republic of Turkey in 1923 doubtless aspired to a 'membership that identities itself, and is identified by others' as distinguishably Turkish. As noted earlier, many of the diverse Muslim peoples that had descended upon, or been born within, previously Ottoman territories willingly adopted the cloak of Turkishness, identifying themselves with the Turkish core of the Republic. The state sought to institute a sense of uniformly Turkish 'we-ness', and to play down or eliminate differences through processes of Turkification and assimilation such that a

Turkish national identity could prevail. But not everyone was willing to be moulded in such a way. Leaving aside concerns with the political make-up of the Republic of Turkey, the Kurds have proved the most enduringly resistant to attempts at assimilation, fighting to maintain distinct social and cultural practices and political spaces.

Notes

1. To protect their identities, the names of all participants have been changed throughout the book.
2. Rumelili and Çakmaklı, 'Civic participation and citizenship in Turkey', p. 368.
3. Çiçek, Cuma, *The Kurds of Turkey*, p. 17.
4. Hakyemez, 'Sur'.
5. Atkinson and Flint, 'Accessing hidden and hard-to-reach populations', pp. 1–3.
6. Başer and Toivanen, 'Politicized and depoliticized ethnicities', p. 2070.
7. Halstead, 'Ethnographic encounters', pp. 307–21.
8. Başer and Toivanen, 'Politicized and depoliticized ethnicities'.
9. Alpman, 'Working on communities under political domination', p. 85–100.
10. Başer and Toivanen, 'Politicized and depoliticized ethnicities', p. 2074.
11. Arparcik, 'Feeling solidarity in an estranged city', p. 104.
12. Voloder, 'Introduction', p. 4.
13. Shankland, *The Alevis in Turkey*, pp. 3–4.
14. Rümelili and Çakmaklı, 'Civic participation and citizenship in Turkey', pp. 365–84.
15. Watts, *Activists in Office*, p. 20.
16. Ergil, '"Knowledge is a potent instrument for change"'.
17. Bocheńska, 'Introduction', pp. 1–34.
18. O'Connor and Çelik, 'Outsiders twice over in Kurdistan', pp. 123–44.
19. Taylor, *Human Agency and Language*.
20. Massicard, *The Alevis in Turkey and Europe*, p. 6.
21. Yavuz, Hakan (1998), 'A preamble to the Kurdish question', pp. 9–18.
22. Lyon, *Identifying Citizens*, pp. 22–3.
23. Interview, Diyarbakır, 20 October 2014. Note some quotes have been edited for clarity.
24. Interview, Diyarbakır, 8 June 2015.
25. Interview, Diyarbakır, 9 June 2015.

26. I assume that asked the same question Turks would do the same, particularly given the central place that the idea of Turkishness plays in society and politics in Turkey.
27. Smith, *National Identity*, p. 21. If we are to assume that he orders his attributes in terms of importance, common ancestry is second only to a collective proper name.
28. Horowitz, *Ethnic Groups in Conflict*, pp. 55–7.
29. Hobsbawm, *Nations and Nationalism since 1780*, pp. 58–9. This is of particular relevance to the Kurds, a people spread across international borders.
30. Interview, Diyarbakır, 26 October 2014.
31. Interview, Diyarbakır, 26 October 2014.
32. See Kadıoğlu and Keyman, *Symbiotic Antagonisms*.
33. Interview, Diyarbakır, 20 October 2014.
34. Interview, Diyarbakır, 11 June 2015. Mert saw the political nature of Kurdishness as having (positive) implications for the entire Turkish polity. Significantly, he made this claim just days after the pro-Kurdish HDP had enjoyed considerable success in the general election of 7 June.
35. Interview, Istanbul, 13 June 2015.
36. Poole, *Nation and Identity*, p. 44.
37. Interview, Istanbul, 18 October 2014.
38. Interview, Diyarbakır, 27 October 2014.
39. Interview, Diyarbakır, 8 June 2015.
40. Interview, Diyarbakır, 21 October 2014.
41. Brubaker, *Ethnicity without Groups*.
42. The pejorative use of '*gûndî*' to describe Kurdish peasants may be equated with the Ottoman use of 'Turk' to describe illiterate villagers.
43. Cited in Kahraman, *Kürt Isyanları: Tedip ve Tenkil*. A common schoolyard slur used against Kurds accuses them of having tails.
44. Interview, Diyarbakır, 24 October 2014.
45. Van Bruinessen, 'The ethnic identity of Kurds in Turkey', pp. 613–21.
46. Personal communication, Istanbul, 14 October 2014.
47. This is not unique to issues of Kurdish identity. As noted earlier, identity is a socially constructed phenomenon, and thus identity markers will, in many cases, be subject to debate and disagreement, internally and externally.
48. Van Bruinessen, 'The ethnic identity of Kurds in Turkey'.
49. Barth, *Ethnic Groups and Boundaries*, p. 11.
50. Eriksen, *What is Anthropology?*, p. 161.
51. Barth, *Ethnic Groups and Boundaries*, p. 14.

3

DEMARCATING KURDISH CULTURE

The trajectory that the Republic of Turkey has followed since its establishment has been portrayed as a morality tale in which science, reason and progress have triumphed over the hidebound tradition, superstition and conservatism that were hallmarks of the Ottoman era.[1] Indeed, certain Kemalists explained attempts at assimilation visited upon the Kurds as intended to 'liberate' Kurdish society from retrograde feudal and tribal forces that prevented its advance.[2] Thus assimilation was portrayed as a civilising mission; within the educational system, Kurds were impelled to forget their language and forego their Kurdish identity, even as they were assured that there was no such thing.[3] Stereotypes of Turk and Kurds evolved; these portrayed Turks as forward-looking, intent on modernisation, urbanised, the Kurds as an untamed rural people. A 1926 sketch remarked, 'The typical Kurd is not a city man, but a dweller in stone-built villages snugly nestled in the rugged ravines in which the mountains of this region abound.'[4]

Some of these clichés – that the Kurds are mountain folk with a culture rooted in village life – persist. Like all clichés, they contain elements of truth. Anna Grabolle-Çeliker notes that due to the relative ethnic homogeneity of village life, and shared experiences therein, the village assumes a salience in some evocations of Kurdish identity, particularly after migration to large cities such as Van, Diyarbakır, Ankara and Istanbul.[5] That is not to say that village life is exclusively the domain of Kurds in Turkey, nor that Kurdish village life is peculiarly different to that of villages populated by Turks. Visiting villages in the Aegean littoral in the 1990s and villages near Diyarbakır between 2013 and 2015, I observed similar intra-community and intra-generational dynamics, the same daily rhythms of shepherding, milking, making bread and the like – nothing that immediately marked anything as Turkish or Kurdish. Even within solely Kurdish villages, individual lives vary considerably. On a *dolmuş* heading towards Mardin, I once witnessed an instance of the diversity of Kurds' lived experiences. Beside me sat a well-dressed young couple, holding hands and watching YouTube on their iPhones. On my other side, leaning on the van's sliding door, stood a lad with a weather-beaten complexion and with dusty feet in well-worn flip-flops. He cradled a rattan cage housing a beloved '*keklik*' (partridge) and dismounted at a lonely stretch of road bound for a distant hamlet.

The nexus between the village, the mountains and Kurdishness is apparent in the contention that those Kurds who abandon the mountains for the cities of the plain lose their Kurdish identity.[6] Indeed, the central place of the mountains in Kurdish culture, identity and lore is something that Kurdish authors themselves purvey.[7] Stereotypical images thus have it that village life and association with mountains are important aspects of Kurdish culture. Yet at times these things are overstated. A commonly used proverb states, 'The Kurds have no friend but the mountains.' When I asked an online network of Kurdish scholars how this quote was originally rendered in Kurdish, none were able to provide it. Several told me they had never heard it in Kurdish, concluding that they thought it was conceived by an outsider and had since entered the lexicon of journalists working on Kurdish issues.

Discussing identity with Kurds in Diyarbakır and Istanbul, my questions about village life and the mountains, two phenomena I expected to be central to an emic, idealised Kurdish culture, elicited little response. There may be several reasons why such things did not figure prominently. Firstly, Kurdish life has grown increasingly urbanised in recent decades, in part due to village evacuations during years of conflict, but also due to economic pressures associated with processes of urbanisation experienced worldwide. To some extent this had led to discourses on village life assuming an idyllic quality, but at the same time a paradox where the village is viewed both with nostalgia and contempt.[8] Secondly, those Kurds who I interviewed all lived decidedly urban lives, and while some of them mentioned links to ancestral villages, they all saw the city as the locus of society and politics. As Anthony Smith declares, the attributes of *ethnie* – ethnic identity – that he outlines are strongly subjective,[9] and for various reasons, which I would contend are a result of the highly politicised nature of Kurdish identity in modern Turkey, villages and mountains did not rank highly as markers of Kurdishness. In fact, it was other factors, namely the Kurdish language and the celebration of Newroz, that assumed political weight; as such, the Kurds I met with highlighted them as markers of difference and central pillars of Kurdish identity.

Language: '*ana dil*' or '*zimanê me*'

In 2015, *The Guardian* published a pictorial representation of the tree of Indo-European languages.[10] This was eagerly shared across social media platforms by Kurds, whose language was perched on the Iranian branch that veered away from the European tongues in the mists of time. Turkish social media users, meanwhile, indignantly asked, 'Where is Turkish?' The language map flies in the face of the Kemalist assertion that the Turks are historically inclined towards Europe and that Kurds are Anatolia's untamed 'Oriental' Other. Yet the tree is correct: while Turkish is used in Europe, and while many Turks may see themselves as European, their language is linguistically related to those used in Central Asian states including Uzbekistan and Kirghizstan, among the Uyghurs of far-west China and, indeed, Mongolian, but not to any of Europe. Kurdish, meanwhile, is linguistically related, albeit distantly, to the European languages.

Anthony Smith delineates language, alongside 'religion, custom and pigmentation', among the 'differentiating elements of common culture' that are central to markers of *ethnie*. He notes that these elements are 'are often taken to describe objective markers . . . that persist independently of the will of individuals'.[11] If this were applicable in all instances it would be easy to demarcate Kurdish language, religion, customs and pigmentation (or physical appearance) in contradistinction to the same aspects of Turkish identity. In practice, however, such clear-cut categorisations are not easily drawn. Turks and Kurds exhibit a vast range of physical appearances, none of which are exclusive to one or the other. Thus, as the example of Yiğit volunteering at the HDP office in Istanbul indicates, finding physical criteria that definitively distinguish Kurds from Turks is problematic to say the least. Establishing a clear difference in religious affiliations between Kurds and Turks is similarly complex. As already discussed, finding indisputable markers of difference between Kurds and Turks is challenging, but their languages, which stem from different linguistic families, are clearly distinct. Welat Zeydanlıoğlu thus notes that language carries the burden of being the primary marker of difference for Kurds in Turkey.[12]

The founding elites of the Republic of Turkey were well aware of the role language plays in national identity. More specifically, they were keenly sensitive to the role a single national language played in forging a sense of unity and holding tight the nation-state. Mustafa Kemal (Atatürk) explicitly made the link between language and nationhood, declaring in a speech in 1933, 'One should be quite clear about the fact that the foundation of the Turkish nation will be its national language and its national self.'[13] Thus, a coherent, unified sense of (Turkish) nationhood was to be created through the promulgation of the Turkish language. But here, again, the nation builders of the early Kemalist regime encountered a disconcerting diversity, with a range of languages other than Turkish widely spoken, particularly in the eastern provinces. Indeed, in parts of south-east Anatolia Turkish was 'hardly understood', and again the Kurds posed the greatest challenge, constituting the largest population of the non-Turkish speakers.[14]

The imperative for unification saw the most determined assimilation initiatives directed at the Kurds. The Kurdish language, an immediately apparent marker of difference, was an urgent target. Kemalists recognised it as a vital ethnic marker.[15] Aside from various moves to make its use illegal, it was also demeaned. The state has variously asserted that it was either a primitive language of limited vocabulary, lacking grammatical coherence, merely a mishmash of elements coming from, among others, Turkmen, Persian and Circassian,[16] or, as part of an argument claiming that Kurds were a lost 'Turkish' tribe, in fact was a corrupted form of Turkish that had acquired vocabulary accretions as such purported Kurd-Turks migrated from Central Asia.[17] It was not only in Turkey that claims were made to the lack of authenticity of the Kurds as a distinct, unified ethnicity – some Arab nationalists claim that due to the fact that several Kurdish dialects are mutually incomprehensible, speakers of such distinct dialects do not constitute a single ethnicity. In answer to this, Mahir Aziz contends that despite 'linguistic rifts', these dialects remain identifiably Kurdish and, indeed, serve to distinguish the Kurds from the Others among whom they live, including majority Turks, Persians and Arabs.[18]

As was the case with other assimilationist initiatives, casting aspersions on the Kurdish language did little to dissuade Kurds from upholding it as a central aspect of their ethnic identity. *Ana dil* (Turkish: literally 'mother tongue') consistently recurred as a point of reference for Kurds I spoke with.[19] It is worth underlining that it was a point of *reference* as much as a point of *difference*, in that participants recognised that language was an important marker of Kurdish identity even though, in several cases, they themselves were not conversant in Kurmanji, the main Kurdish dialect used in Turkey. In this sense, even though the Turkish state has not been able to sever the connection between Kurdish language and Kurdish ethnic identity, it has been able to restrict the degree to which the language is actually used. Some Kurds resent what they see as the imposition of the Turkish language through the education system. A Kurdish man in Istanbul related his concern about his three-year-old son who was soon beginning school. His pride in his son making the transition from infant to schoolboy was tempered by his concern that his son once at school, where all classes are in Turkish, would be subject to 'assimilation'.[20] Zehra, in Diyarbakır, lamented for her six-year-old daughter, 'There is no school I can send my daughter to that teaches in *my* language ... She has to learn Turkish and only Turkish. What kind of right is this?'[21]

Manning Nash describes language as a group marker of 'social and psychological weight'. For Nash, 'mastery of language implies learning it from birth, in the context of kinship or primary group'. Will Kymlicka describes language as 'one of the fundamental markers of people's identity'.[22] Yet Peter Alford Andrews notes in the case of Scottish Highlanders, a people like the Kurds subjected to bans on language in an assimilationist drive, retaining even a minor connection to mother tongue was an important means of sustaining ethnic identity.[23] Among respondents interviewed for this research project, opinions varied as to the importance of the language as an identity marker. Many Kurds see language as a point of pride, a hallmark of ethnic authenticity, one that must be maintained and asserted. Berfo declared, 'If there were no language you would not be able to think in Kurdish or even live – the Kurdish culture would disappear. The first foundation is language. Without language there would be no meaning in being Kurdish.'[24] Serdar put the point most forcefully, implying an imperative for Kurds to maintain their language: 'If you forget your language, you should be ashamed . . . Not only you, your kids also.'[25] When I asked if he teaches his own children Kurdish, he replied immediately, 'We do.'

But such assertions of the centrality of language to Kurdish identity were not universally held. Hikmet, an Istanbul journalist, said, thumping his fist to his chest, 'It's not necessary to speak Kurdish to be Kurdish; it's in the heart.'[26] Along similar lines, Esra, a journalist from Diyarbakır, remarked, 'I don't know Kurdish [language], but I know that I am Kurdish and I feel Kurdish . . . Language is very important, but many [Kurdish] people in Turkey don't know the Kurdish language . . . I have many friends who, like me, don't know Kurdish, who grew up in the city centre. A lot of my relatives who grew up in villages, I don't have any contact with them because I don't know Kurdish.'[27]

In fact, those who identify as Kurdish but who do not know the language are more likely to be educated than those who do know it, as Turkish is the only permitted language of education in Turkey.[28] Esra, famous as a Kurdish journalist, is just such an example. She emphasised that her lack of language ability did not detract from her ethnic identity and was a result of governmental policy that prohibited the teaching of Kurdish rather than a dereliction of duty by her or her family: 'This doesn't decrease my Kurdishness. I don't have this connection [with Kurdish speakers] because of policies, not because of myself. I grew up . . . in the centre of Diyarbakır [and] at that time it was forbidden to speak Kurdish . . . At school they gave our generation [the impression] that . . . people who use Kurdish are bad. A lot of children like me, who grew up in the centre of Diyarbakır, were ashamed of their culture.' Such a message, imparted by the state, had considerable impact. Semih, who also grew up in 1980s Diyarbakır, recalls it being considered old-fashioned to speak Kurdish.[29] In Istanbul, Ayşe, a journalist, tells of trying to hide her Kurdishness from her children, who spoke only Turkish and had heard their grandparents speaking another language. Rather than explain that the grandparents were speaking Kurdish, and thus admitting to their Kurdish ethnicity, Ayşe said that they were speaking English. 'We carried it [Kurdish ethnicity] like a secret,' Ayşe remarks.[30]

As well as creating instances where ethnic Kurds had no knowledge of their language, or were ashamed of it, the policy of Turkish-only education created other problems. In major cities and regional centres, such as Diyarbakır, where state control was more pronounced, children, whether ethnically Kurdish or otherwise, were exposed to and taught in Turkish from a young age. Many participants, however, related that they had significant problems beginning school speaking only Kurdish and with no knowledge of Turkish. The situation was exacerbated in rural settlements, villages or *mahalleler* (neighbourhoods) on city outskirts, where the state's reach and educational facilities were limited and where use of Kurdish remained routine. Musa, from a village outside Urfa, received no formal education until his teens. He relates such a situation: 'I learned Turkish around twelve years old; because my friends were Kurdish, they couldn't speak Turkish. [My] family couldn't speak Turkish. We had just one language and that was Kurdish. And [at school] they forced us to speak Turkish . . . My friend was sitting with me but he spoke just Kurdish . . . It was difficult for us. Many teachers hit us. They said you are not learning, but this was not our fault.'[31]

Musa was recalling experiences from the early 2000s, but similar situations persist. In 2014 I spent a day attending classes with a friend who teaches at a primary school on the outskirts of Diyarbakır. I noticed in each class that some children, usually boys, did not participate at all in spoken activities. When I mentioned this, my friend remarked that it was because they did not speak Turkish, but in such large classes he was unable to devote extra attention to them. Lack of ability in Turkish is not restricted to the south-east. I recall seeing a Kurdish boy in a street market in Bayraklı, in İzmir. He led his grandmother to each stall, enquiring of prices and translating for her, as she directed him to haggle.

The imposition of Turkish as the sole means of communication appears to be a case where state policy was counterproductive.[32] It was intended to forge unity, but it created a divide for some and was a source of anxiety and self-denial in others. It may also be argued that the Kurdish language became a factor within the conflict that escalated from the 1980s. Zeydanlıoğlu draws a link between the instigation of the PKK's armed struggle and the revived

'Kemalist spirit' purveyed by the military after the coup of 1980. During their brief rule, the generals severely curtailed perceived political enemies, including the nascent Kurdish movement, and, with the Constitution of 1982, explicitly outlawed the Kurdish language. Zeydanlıoğlu posits this as a 'brutal, linguicidal' policy.[33] Will Kymlicka, highlighting language as a fundamental identity marker, argues that any belittling of a mother tongue will be viewed as an 'assault on identity'.[34] The 1982 banning of Kurdish may well have been viewed in such terms, thus contributing to the radicalisation of Kurds who joined the PKK. David McDowall contends that the virulence of anti-state feeling among many early members of the PKK was due to the fact that they did not know Kurdish, and thus they felt separated by state decree from their Kurdish identity.[35] The vast majority of Kurds never took up arms, but, even among those who did, many saw the language ban as an affront. This was true for many Kurds I met, who resented ongoing restrictions on Kurdish and, consequently, were more determined to learn and use their language.

Even as Kurdish language – or the deprivation thereof – aroused angst among Kurds, in the nationalistic milieu of the 1980s and 1990s, Turkish actors viewed the language as a threat. As conflict with the PKK escalated, the Kurdish language came to be associated with separatism. When then-president Turgut Özal proposed lifting the ban on Kurdish, veteran politician Suleyman Demirel remarked that such a proposal was 'an attempt at dividing the country . . . this is the greatest harm you can inflict on Turkey'.[36] Parliamentarian Alparslan Pehlivanoğlu similarly declared that lifting the ban on Kurdish would amount to having 'admitted that the Kurds are a nation . . . If it passes, there will be cafés where Kurdish folk songs are sung, theatres where Kurdish films shown and coffee houses where Kurdish is spoken. If this is not separatism, what is?'[37]

Despite Cassandra-like comments from Turkish politicians, the ban on using the language in public was repealed in 1991. Those remarks were indicative of popular discourse that held that permitting Kurds to speak their own language, thus acknowledging and condoning ethnic diversity, would destine Turkey to partition along ethnic lines. The political ground has now shifted considerably. Particularly since the rise of the AKP government in 2002, Turkey has seen the broadening of discussions on national identity, such that diversity is not feared as once it was. Nor does the Kurdish language evoke spectres of national calamity. In January 2009, TRT6, a government-sanctioned television channel, began broadcasting in Kurdish, and in 2010 Turkey's first-ever, university-level Kurdish studies course was instituted at Mardin Artuklu University.

Even so, regulation is tight, and official touchiness remains about Kurdish and Kurdish-language education and broadcasting. Zeydanlıoğlu notes that the AKP administration is prone to boasting that language rights for Kurds have never been freer, but he argues that language reforms have been poorly implemented and the linguistic freedoms and rights that most Kurds aspire to have not been realised.[38] Widespread acceptance of the use of Kurdish has not eventuated. Mehmet, a Diyarbakır-born Kurd who grew up in the western city of Izmit, recounts his mother warning him against using Kurdish in public for fear of repercussions.[39] Zoran also told of being warned by his brother while working as a waiter in an Aegean resort town not to use Kurdish. 'It made me very angry. But my brother says we have to be patient.' Such self-censorship was a response to earlier experiences. Zoran recalled instances where he had been harassed by police for speaking Kurdish in Diyarbakır.[40]

Such episodes occur in many forums in Turkey. Ahmet Kaya, upon winning Musician of the Year in Istanbul in 1999, announced that he planned to release an album in Kurdish. This provoked uproar from the chic attendees of the awards ceremony, and widespread ongoing abuse such that he fled Turkey, never to return.[41] On a more mundane level, a Kurdish woman told me of being scolded by a Turkish woman, while queuing in a bank, for speaking to her baby in Kurdish. The Turkish woman remarked, 'Why would you teach a baby such a language?'[42] Meanwhile, in 2009 a ten-year-old girl in Diyarbakır was prosecuted by local officials for giving 'classes' in Kurdish in her home to other children.[43] Naim, a teacher in Diyarbakır, empathised with the efforts of the youthful teacher. He remarked that language is, '*Çok önemli. Vaz geçilmez* [It's very important. We cannot give it up] . . . The most important thing for us is mother-tongue education. The state doesn't give us any [Kurdish] education. I didn't receive any education in my mother tongue. By myself, with my struggle, I tried to learn my mother tongue . . . We make schools in our houses and we learn our language at home by ourselves.'[44]

The banning of the Kurdish language was always impractical. This was made clear to me by Ayhan, an Istanbul-based researcher who was the only one of twelve siblings to have attended school. None of them, nor his parents, could speak Turkish, so Kurdish was their only means of communication. '*Onları görmezden mi geleyim?* [Am I supposed to ignore them?]' he quipped.[45] Indeed, some Kurds argue that the easing of language restrictions was not due to greater societal acceptance of the Kurds but was mere pragmatism – resignation to the fact that Kurdish was still used – rather than actual support for its use. In recent years, however, the AKP government has portrayed itself as a champion of Kurdish-language rights, citing the launch of TRT6 and university language courses. Former Prime Minister Ahmet Davutoğlu even once told a crowd in Diyarbakır, 'I would like to learn our beautiful Kurdish language.'[46] Campaigning for the Istanbul mayoralty in 2019, AKP candidate Binali Yıldırım even made ham-fisted attempts to speak Kurdish in order to garner votes. Yet it remains a point of contention between the state and Kurdish advocates. There are those nationalists, and government officials, who see it as something to be discouraged, or expunged,[47] yet meanwhile the Kurdish political movement continues to pursue broader language rights. Organisations specifically focused on Kurdish-language education, including TZP Kurdî and Kurdî-Der, were established in 2006 and supported by the Diyarbakır municipality. TZP Kurdî's position is that mother-tongue language is an irrevocable right and a measure of a true democracy, while Kurdî-Der promotes the slogan, 'The best language is your mother tongue' and has, in several Kurdish-majority cities, celebrated a self-declared Kurdish-language holiday.[48] Such arguments win widespread support among everyday Kurds, including many I interviewed.

Kimlycka argues that 'language is profoundly important in the construction of democratic political communities'.[49] Since the lifting of the ban on Kurdish in 1991, Kurds have embraced the language, resulting in a plethora of publications, conferences and unofficial language institutes. Yet the number of Kurds who can use the language proficiently remains small due to the fact that it has never been taught in schools or standardised. Kelda Jamison notes even among those who speak Kurdish regularly and claim it as their mother tongue a concern that they are not speaking 'correctly'. Nonetheless, as Jamison observes, even if it is not widely understood it becomes a rallying point for Kurdishness, projecting another point of commonality.[50]

The launch of TRT6 and statements from government figures wanting to learn Kurdish appear to indicate broader acceptance in Turkey's political sphere, but Kurds remain sceptical. Some told me they viewed TRT6 as a government mouthpiece that may broadcast in Kurdish but did not provide any content they enjoyed.[51] Therein lies a conundrum regarding the AKP's position on Kurdish language within a democratic context. The message imparted to me was that Kurds saw the AKP's position on the Kurdish language as a shallow ruse to win Kurdish votes rather than evidence of genuine pluralist impulses to foster diversity and democracy.

The choice of Mardin as the location for the first university-level Kurdish course is instructive. Diyarbakır, the centre of Kurdish cultural and artistic activity in Turkey, and home to the well-regarded Dicle [Tigris] University, would seem a more obvious location for such an initiative.[52] It is tempting to see the choice of Mardin as evidence of an ongoing 'top-down' attitude. The state was allowing Kurdish-language education but only on terms that it decreed acceptable, and this did not extend to allowing the city that most Kurds would have chosen. It may also be seen as a further example of the ongoing wariness of Kurdish self-determination. The government was prepared to allow Kurdish-language education in a gesture towards pluralism but was not willing to give Kurds free rein lest self-determination accumulate a momentum of its own. These are hallmarks of the AKP under Erdoğan: allowing change, and claiming credit for it, but ensuring that such change did not undermine the state agenda. Indeed, the Kurdish-language institute in Mardin was bedevilled by criticisms and official impediments from the outset.[53] Thus, while contrasts can be drawn to the 1980s, when the use of Kurdish was illegal, it was still not the case that Kurds had control over the teaching and study of their language.

When the state's conflict against the PKK reignited in the second half of 2015, the status of the Kurdish language again became fraught. With escalating hostilities in the south-east, the strength-in-unity discourse again gained salience in certain segments of Turkish society, and the previously subsumed narrative that equated Kurdish political activity with terrorism was disinterred. In these circumstances, using Kurdish again became suspect.

In August 2016, an Istanbul labourer was murdered by several workmates, some alleging it was because they objected to his speaking Kurdish.[54] The attempted coup against the AKP in July 2016 ratcheted up tensions in society and defensive postures from government circles which led to a heightened 'terror-alert politics'. This had a ripple effect through Kurdish political and cultural institutions. In late September 2016, a large number of TV and radio stations, among them the Kurdish-language children's channel Zarok TV, were closed down by government decree.[55] Instances of harassment of, and restrictions again being placed on, those using Kurdish also became more widespread. A HDP parliamentarian complained to the parliament about a notice posted in the Kurdish-majority town of Şırnak explicitly directing children against speaking Kurdish,[56] and in Aydın, in western Turkey, several high-school students were interrogated by police for 'disseminating terrorist propaganda' after a teacher reported them for listening to Kurdish music.[57]

Despite this, many Kurds persist with the language both as a means of asserting their identity, but also staking out political territory. During the constitutional referendum of 2017, the HDP broadcast a song entitled *'Bejin Na'* (Kurdish for 'Say no!'), which was duly banned but that signalled ongoing opposition to the designs of Erdoğan,[58] and for the municipal elections of 2019 the HDP broadcast a song in Kurdish to galvanise support for its candidates, replete with footage of rallies and daily life in Diyarbakır and women dancing the *govend* in the Kurdish *tricoleur*.[59] Demet Arparcık observed a pervasive feeling that in the current milieu, state pressure in Istanbul and Diyarbakır has curtailed Kurdish-language activism and she met considerable official resistance to her own research into the topic. Yet she also notes that despite oppression, Kurdish-language activists continue to pursue their agenda.[60] It would seem that Kurds are not prepared to abandon such a central element of their identity.

Celebrating Newroz, or Nevruz

The calendar year in Turkey is punctuated by regular holidays and events. Several of them commemorate episodes from the Turkish war of independence and the establishment of the Republic.[61] Clearly these are intended to engender a sense of common history and, like the Turkish language, forge a unified sense of national identity. These commemorations are instances of Eric

Hobsbawm's 'invention of tradition', whereby ritual or symbolic practices are used to 'inculcate values or norms of behaviour by repetition, which automatically implies continuity with the past'.[62] Manning Nash contends that 'tradition is the past of a culture, as that past is thought to have continuity, a presence and a future. These features of tradition bestow on the past a weight of authority, the very fact of survival, pastness and continuity give an aura of authority, legitimacy and rightness to cultural beliefs and practices . . . Tradition, while chiefly concerned with the past . . . has a forward, future dimension.'[63] The 'invention of tradition' serves as a teleological argument for a nation or group through which it can assert its legitimacy: this is what we have always done, this is evidence of our longevity and validity, and this is a practice we maintain to the present.

The Turkish nation-state justifiably celebrates important events of its founding amid the traumatic years of the early twentieth century. But just as the persistence of the Kurdish language militated against the Kemalists' promotion of the Turkish language as a lightning rod for unification, there exists a day in the calendar that has worked against the narrative of (Turkish) unity. That day is Newroz, the Kurdish New Year, celebrated each year on 21 March. This event, too, clearly falls into the category of an 'invented tradition', but it has allowed the Kurds a point of difference, a means to maintain an ethnic boundary between themselves and the Turks, a means to lay claim to a distinctive cultural tradition. My inquiries among Kurds of the potency of the mountains and village life elicited little response, and my inquiries about 'Kurdish traditions' did not generate anything more than offhand laments to 'slowly vanishing traditions' ('*yavaş yavaş kayboluyor*'). Newroz was the one Kurdish 'tradition' that all participants mentioned. It would seem that this is because Newroz is the centre of potent political narrative. However, like language, it has become contested, increasingly so in the AKP's Turkey.

Celebrated on 21 March and marking the spring equinox, Newroz arises from the Persian tradition, among which, linguistically, the Kurds are included.[64] Newroz comes from the Persian 'Noo rooz' (نوروز, literally 'New Day').[65] Persian and Persianate communities, among whom the Kurds number, have celebrated it as the advent of spring for thousands of years. Indicative of its importance in Kurdish culture, Newroz is the setting where the star-crossed lovers of the seventeenth-century Kurdish epic *Mem û Zîn* first meet each other.⁶⁶ The Iraqi Kurds adopted it as a specifically Kurdish event in the mid-twentieth century, something that Kurds in Turkey took up some time later.⁶⁷ During the Ottoman era, Newroz was a public holiday, but from the Republic of Turkey's early years it was recognised only as an 'Iranian National Day'.⁶⁸ Thus in modern Turkey, it may be argued that Newroz is – or was – a distinctively Kurdish event.

Martin van Bruinessen notes that he encountered little recognition of Newroz among everyday Kurds in Turkey in the 1970s, even though it was known to others, including Bektashi dervishes, some Turkish Alevis and Shi'ite communities. Even so, knowledge of Newroz and its symbolic potency had been increasing in Turkey's Kurdish political movement, and from the mid-'60s certain activists sought to foster it as a tradition worth celebrating and one that was specifically Kurdish.⁶⁹

During the 1980s, the PKK, seeking to promote an agenda of Kurdish awareness, invested it with greater significance. This was boosted after the arrival of Kurdish refugees fleeing Iraq in 1988. Semih recalls meeting, at that time, Iraqi Kurds who celebrated Newroz, but remarks that until then he had been unaware of the tradition. He said his grandmother remembered it, but 'people didn't know it. After the Kurdish movement, it gained another meaning.'⁷⁰ As Hobsbawm notes, invented traditions may be specifically tied to the nation and its associated trappings, nationalism and national symbols, which in turn rest on foundations rooted in social engineering.⁷¹ By the 1980s, Turkey may have moved beyond a programme of social engineering in the name of nation building, but the symbolism of Newroz, invented tradition or otherwise, was becoming plain: it was a festival that was specifically tied to Kurdish identity. And as the PKK's military campaign escalated, the Turkish security forces clamped down on the event as a manifestation of Kurdishness; Newroz celebrations were seen as precursors to separatism.

In fact, it was the PKK who worked to revive the celebration of Newroz and create an explicit connection to Kurdish identity and an ages-old Kurdish foundational myth. PKK discourse highlighted the element of resistance within the myth, which tells of a simple blacksmith, Kawa, who encouraged an oppressed people, the (mythical) ancient forebears of the Kurds, to rise up against evil King Zahhak who enslaved them.⁷² The themes of oppression and uprising within the tale of Kawa and the evil king were potent symbols that could be utilised to mobilise everyday Kurds in Turkey. Significantly, there are several other Kurdish foundational myths, but the PKK overlooked these. One tells of the Kurds descending from a city built at the point where Noah's ark came to rest on Mount Cudi (near modern-day Şırnak in south-east Anatolia), and another claims the Kurds were the progeny of five hundred beautiful women abducted from Europe by King Solomon's henchmen.[73] Such tales may be as poetic as the myth of Kawa, but they do not contain the same element of resistance and victory against evil, and thus did not resonate as strongly.

Thus, the PKK emphasised one particular foundational myth over others, and emphasised a specific reading of the events within the myth in order to create a specifically Kurdish narrative from a tradition which is, in fact, celebrated by many peoples across the Middle East.[74] As well as providing an appealing rallying cry for acts of resistance to the state, the propagation of a specifically Kurdish Newroz myth, a legend that stretches back thousands of years, also added credence to the Kurdish national narrative, an indication that Kurds had operated in unison and as a distinct people since antiquity.[75]

Thus the PKK's Newroz narrative gathered momentum. Soner remarked that until the late 1980s, 'it was not popular, it was not a celebration or a demonstration. You can say Newroz was reshaped in the '90s . . . It has been important since maybe 1990.'[76] As its 'importance' among Kurds grew, and due to its being propagated by the PKK, Turkish security forces and judiciary attempted to stamp it out. Indeed, during the early 1990s Newroz celebrations became fervent pro-Kurdish rallies resulting in clashes with security forces; celebrations in south-eastern cities such as Cizre, Nusaybin and Şırnak in 1992 were marked by violent altercations.[77] Outside south-east Anatolia, those Newroz celebrations that did occur during the 1990s often happened in out-of-the way locations,[78] and generally attracted police attention, resulting in clashes each year on 21 March. Such violence was usually justified by the government, and won approval of the broader Turkish public, on the grounds that Newroz celebrations were 'terrorist' events. But in fact, violence in Cizre, Şırnak and Nusaybin in 1992 all stemmed from the state: security forces fired into crowds of participating Kurds.[79] The fact that in that year ninety-two civilians were killed in Newroz clashes, but not a single soldier, made it hard to maintain the argument that the state was acting to counter 'terrorist' activities.[80] Nonetheless, in the nationalist fervour that prevailed, such arguments were overlooked. In 1999, such was government pressure that Newroz was not celebrated at all in Diyarbakır. A *Hürriyet* report, while conceding that this was made possible by a large number of arrests, depicted this as a 'victory' for the city.[81] But amid the drive to suppress it, the violence involved and the PKK's skilful wielding of the Kawa legend, Newroz became invested with meaning for Kurds.

Musa, a Kurd living in Istanbul's Gedikpaşa neighbourhood, stated, 'Yes, [Newroz is] very important. Maybe you have seen on TV. We always used to have problems . . . In Istanbul and Diyarbakır, just last year the government says, "It's OK, it's legal, you can celebrate." We didn't have any problem with the government, we didn't fight . . . we just celebrated. But before when we wanted to celebrate, they always attacked us.'[82] In Musa's view, it was not the event that was significant, nor were the reasons for the celebration important. Newroz's significance lay in the fact that in the past it had been suppressed and that Kurds had persisted in celebrating it despite the fact that the state 'attacked us'. For Musa, Newroz was not so much a communal celebration, but a communal event of another kind, a means of standing up to government oppression.

Semih, who had attended Newroz celebrations in Kurdish northern Iraq, laughed and quipped, 'In Iraq, it's like a picnic – people go to the countryside and make kebabs.'[83] His laughter was an acknowledgement of the irony that the significance of Newroz could be so different in Turkey. Esra, meanwhile, acknowledged the original reasons for the celebration of Newroz: 'Newroz is certainly important . . . Because Kurdish people used to celebrate Newroz forty or fifty years ago; at that time it was more about . . . the coming of spring.'[84] However, Esra registered that the significance of the event had been transformed by the state's attempts to suppress it, and the violence involved:

> But with the punishment, with the pressure from the state, it becomes another thing. It is something different now. Newroz . . . for many Kurdish people . . . is a celebration that we are here, [despite] everything that you [the state] did . . . For me, it is also a symbol of a lot of people who died during Newroz, so I don't see a lot of things to celebrate. I go to Newroz because I am part of this society . . . but from another perspective, Newroz reminds

me of a lot of bad things. Now Newroz is not [about] culture . . . Now it symbolises: resistance, that we exist, the people who were killed . . . Yes, it's important. I think it's important for every Kurd now.[85]

Berfo was one of few who noted the origins of the tradition, but, echoing the resistance message promulgated by the PKK, he also highlighted the shift in its significance,

> It has actually become a day representing our resistance. Newroz isn't just a day *we* celebrate. It is also a day that many people celebrate in the Middle East. However, it is a very different day for us. We do not just celebrate the coming of spring. Newroz is a day that has been banned for us. In order to celebrate this day many Kurds were killed . . . Just because we want to celebrate spring, many civilians were murdered. This is a day in which we celebrate not only spring but also our resistance.[86]

If, in this instance, Esra and Berfo do not recognise that Newroz is an 'invented' tradition, they at least acknowledge its transformation from an element of Kurdish culture to becoming a part of the Kurds' political make-up, part of the political struggle.[87] This is a message that was shared with me by several Kurds, highlighting that Newroz is now a '*sembol*' (symbol) of Kurdishness.

The death toll at Newroz celebrations in 1992 represented a high-tide mark, both in terms of violence and official disapproval. Thereafter Newroz celebrations generally unfurled without clashes between (Kurdish) protesters and (Turkish) security forces, and eventually came to receive official imprimatur. Such an about-face on the part of Turkish authorities was made possible by a process of recasting the event as a celebration of 'brotherhood', 'cohesion' and 'harmony', which in turn was only possible by emphasising the event's long history and Central Asian origins,[88] rather than the PKK's resistance discourse. A focus on 'harmony' and 'cohesion' may be seen as an attempt to alleviate the tensions associated with the event, but it was accompanied by an attempt at Turkification, the rebranding of it as 'Nevruz' and the highlighting of its purported origins in Turkish history. This involved, each year in March, invitations extended to folkloric groups from Central Asia to dance at official ceremonies, at which government ministers ostentatiously participated, alongside a raft of quasi-scientific publications (re)asserting that the festival had long been celebrated by all Turkic peoples and was rooted in the Turkic Ergenekon legend.[89]

In this sense, rather than extending a hand to the Kurds by recognising the importance of the day for them, the state attempted to dilute, if not entirely eradicate, the Kurdish aspect of the event. In so doing, Turkish politicians and the Ministry of Culture effected a textbook example of Hobsbawm's invention of tradition. Notable in this instance is that the tradition being 'invented' has, at best, tenuous connections to the Turkish folkloric canon, and in effecting their invention the state totally overlooked the event's origins as a Zoroastrian, hence Persian, celebration of spring. The fact that the celebration dates from the Zoroastrian tradition, of course, militates against it being of Turkic origin.[90] As such this may be seen as the co-option of a tradition rather than a retrieval from the recesses of a forgotten history. It is a striking example of the *acquisitive* nature of Turkish nationalism – a nationalism that attempted to eradicate boundaries and in so doing forge a homogenous Turkishness.

The issue here, then, was not whether Newroz/Nevruz is *really* Kurdish or Turkish, but that both sides used it to their own ends: the Turks to homogenise, the Kurds to stand apart. In practice, the state's attempt to co-opt Newroz/Nevruz never gained much traction with the broader Turkish public; the event remains recognised as being Kurdish.[91] Further, recollections of Newroz that Kurds shared with me would suggest that although now state-sanctioned and dressed up as a touchstone for harmony and cohesion, it was anything but a coming together of peoples and an occasion to celebrate brotherhood. Rather, for Kurds, it was a time to recall difference and the state's heavy hand. Esra and Berfo saw Newroz as a time to remember people who had suffered state-backed violence in earlier attempts to celebrate the event; it was also a time to recall the injustice in such responses from the government and the injustice inherent in the state's attitude that the celebration of Newroz should be suppressed; it was a time to assert that Kurdish people had resisted such injustices and that Kurdish people still existed despite them. Nicole Watts argues that pro-Kurdish politicians also used Newroz as a potent symbolic resource in their pursuit of the reclaiming of public spaces from the state and their creation of an alternative politics in the south-east. Thus, even though Kurds enjoy greater cultural freedoms than in recent decades, Newroz remains an important marker of Kurdish distinctiveness.[92]

For a time, while the AKP adopted a more accommodatory approach to the Kurds issue, there was much less political to-and-fro attached to Newroz/Nevruz. Yet it is apparent that the AKP recognised its symbolic value among Kurdish constituents. It must be no coincidence that 21 March was chosen as the date of Abdullah Öcalan's declaration of a PKK ceasefire from his prison cell in 2013.[93] Such an announcement can only have come with official approval, and thus one can imagine that the government allowed such a development with a view to winning support among Kurdish voters. Acknowledging the importance of Newroz as such was a way of tipping a hat to the Kurds. Erdoğan made other such gestures while the resolution process was still in train. In 2015 he tweeted Newroz/Nevruz messages in both Turkish and Kurdish,[94] but even as he did so he pushed the party line of the event being one of 'solidarity and brotherhood', rather than one of particular Kurdish significance.[95]

Following the resumption of hostilities with the PKK and the associated ratcheting up of tensions, Newroz celebrations were banned in several southeastern cities with large Kurdish populations in 2016. In turn, some Kurds chose to celebrate Newroz prior to its official date of 21 March in order to avoid being seen to participate in government-sanctioned events.[96] Here, again, was a Kurdish attempt to stamp the event as something distinctive, something that existed outside the officially constructed narrative, and here again was an official attempt to curtail, or at least manage, participation in the event. In light of the collapsed peace process, and reluctant to be seen closing the space that had recently been opened, government figures continue to acknowledge Newroz, but persist in the narrative that it is an ages-old symbol of solidarity and brotherhood. Meanwhile, Turkish nationalists continue to argue that it is at its core a Turkish celebration, MHP leader Devlet Bahçeli bluntly declaring in 2018, 'Nevruz is Turkish, it is Turanic.' [*Nevruz Türk'tür, Turan'dır.*'] In what perhaps amounts to wishful thinking, he echoed statements from Erdoğan and Prime Minister Binali Yıldırım, adding that it 'secures Turkey's solidarity and brotherhood'.[97]

When I asked Kurds if Newroz was a Turkish festival they scoffed at the idea. They see it as quintessentially Kurdish. Yet its salience did not seem to lie in any associated foundational myth, one that could form a teleological argument that connected the Kurds of modern Turkey with a distant Kurdish past, thus lending legitimacy and historical validity to their claims of ethnic distinctiveness in the present. In the comments recorded above, Musa, Esra and Berfo do not mention, or appear to be aware of, the historical roots of Newroz, or the myth of Kawa rising up against Zahhak. They focus on a time frame that is within living memory, but in so doing they create what might be called a recent tradition, one that – conveniently – echoes the themes at the heart of the Newroz myth. Newroz here is potent due to the fact of resistance, in this instance resistance to attempts at assimilation and the repressive measures of the Turkish state. Zahhak is no longer, but in the narrative he is replaced by the state; and everyday Kurds assume the role of Kawa. In this sense, Newroz continues to play a significant role in defining a distinct Kurdish identity.

Resisting Managed Diversity

In Turkey's widening political environment, issues such as the Kurdish language and the celebration of Newroz have become less contentious than they once were. Participants' responses show that earlier attempts to extinguish Kurdish and impose Turkish only heightened the tenacity with which Kurds have clung to their language. The state's attempt to eliminate a point of difference made that particular point all the more important. Hanging on to Kurdish as a mother tongue has become a rallying point for Kurds and a central pillar of their identity, and the aspiration to be able to teach it in a truly democratic Turkey remains. The state's reaction to Newroz in the 1980s follows a similar trajectory. While Newroz may have been self-consciously reimagined as a tale of Kurdish resistance and uprising by the PKK, the state responded to it in the same way it did to Kurdish language, by attempting to extinguish it in the interests of maintaining, or imposing, homogeneity. As martyrs were created in the clashes that ensued, and as Kurds sought to exercise their right to celebrate, Newroz assumed more potency.

In Erdoğan's Turkey, the Kurdish language and Newroz arouse much less opprobrium. The two are allowed, and even achieve some level of state imprimatur, but really only in a stage-managed way. Erdoğan may pay lip service to both, but only to be able to boast of a free and democratic Turkey. In this sense, the AKP has allowed a more multicultural Turkey than was permissible under earlier governments, but the government keeps a tight hold on proceedings – determining where and how Kurdish language may be studied, allowing Newroz to be celebrated but insisting on a bland message of 'brotherhood' rather than acknowledging any non-Turkish root to the event. In this sense it is allowing a degree of multiculturalism but retaining control of how that multiculturalism manifests itself. This largely excludes Kurdish participation and input. And this is something that Kurds determine to resist, particularly where this relates to elements of their ethnic identity.

Notes

1. Zürcher, *The Young Turk Legacy*, p. 50.
2. Yeğen, 'Turkish nationalism and the Kurdish question', pp. 122–3.
3. Zeydanlioglu, 'Turkey's Kurdish language policy', p. 106
4. Cumberland, 'The Kurds', p. 151.
5. Grabolle-Çeliker, *Kurdish Life in Contemporary Turkey*, pp. 26–50.
6. Entessar, 'The Kurdish mosaic of discord', p. 87.
7. Siaband, 'Mountains, my home', pp. 7–12; Izady, *The Kurds*, p. 188.
8. Grabolle-Çeliker, *Kurdish Life in Contemporary Turkey*, pp. 47, 96–7.
9. Smith, *National Identity*, p. 23.
10. See *Guardian*, 'A language family tree in pictures'.
11. Smith, *National Identity*, p. 23.
12. Zeydanlioğlu, 'Repression or reform?', p. 166.
13. Cited in Mardin, 'Playing games with names', p. 115.
14. Üngör, 'Untying the tongue-tied', pp. 127–50. Servet Mutlu has used Kurdish language ability as a means to calculate Turkey's Kurdish population, although he recognises that there are shortcomings in such a method; see Mutlu, 'Ethnic Kurds in Turkey', pp. 517–41.
15. Andrews (ed.), *Ethnic Groups in the Republic of Turkey*, p. 113.
16. Hassanpour, *Nationalism and Language in Kurdistan*, p. 133.
17. Bayir, 'Representation of the Kurds', pp. 123–4.
18. Aziz, *The Kurds of Iraq*, pp. 51–2.
19. Surveys among Kurds similarly suggest the importance of language. In a 2014 survey, 43 per cent of Kurdish respondents placed having Kurdish as a mother tongue in their top two characteristics of Kurdish identity. See Yılmaz, *Turkiye'de Kimlikler, Kurt Sorunu, ve Cozum Sureci*, p. 17.
20. Personal communication, Istanbul, 3 November 2014.

21. Interview, Diyarbakır, 21 October 2014.
22. Kymlicka, *Politics in the Vernacular*, p. 217.
23. Andrews (ed.), *Ethnic Groups in the Republic of Turkey*, pp. 37–8.
24. Interview, Diyarbakır, 4 June 2015.
25. Interview, Diyarbakır, 24 October 2014.
26. Personal communication, Istanbul, 14 October 2014.
27. Interview, Diyarbakır, 27 October 2014.
28. Yalçın-Heckmann, 'On kinship, tribalism and ethnicity', pp. 622–31.
29. Private conversation, Istanbul, 30 May 2015.
30. Private conversation, Istanbul, 14 October 2014. Years later, after overhearing tourists in a resort *actually* speaking English, her children realised their grandparents had never been conversing in English. It was only then Ayşe admitted that their grandparents spoke Kurdish, thus revealing to her children that they were of Kurdish descent.
31. Interview, Istanbul, 14 October 2014.
32. On the Turkish state's attempts at repressing Kurdishness during the 1980s and '90s, see Van Bruinessen, 'Shifting national and ethnic identities', pp. 39–52. He notes, 'Misguided policies brought about precisely those developments that they had intended to stop.'
33. Zeydanlıoğlu, 'Repression or reform?', p. 167.
34. Kymlicka, *Politics in the Vernacular*, p. 217.
35. McDowall, *A Modern History of the Kurds*, p. 421. The fact that Abdullah Öcalan has only limited command of Kurdish and converses and writes exclusively in Turkish is often used by nationalist Turks as evidence that the PKK is an international conspiracy to break up Turkey. A Turk in Istanbul told me in 2013, 'He is an Armenian. He doesn't even know Kurdish.' This sentiment is widely held.
36. Cited in Gunter, 'Turgut Özal and the Kurdish question', p. 92.
37. Ibid.
38. Zeydanlıoğlu, 'Repression or reform?', pp. 162–85.
39. Interview, Diyarbakır, 9 June 2015.
40. Interview, Diyarbakır, 8 June 2015. Zoran also remarked that Kurdish restaurant owners in Marmaris refrained from playing Kurdish music for fear of attracting unwanted police attention.
41. Kaya was of mixed Turkish-Kurdish descent, but did not speak Kurdish. He died in exile in Paris in 2000. See *BBC*, 'Witness: Kurdish singer Ahmet Kaya'.
42. Interview, Diyarbakır, 29 October 2014.
43. Önderoğlu, 'Mayor defends child', 1 September 2009. Eventually the charges against the girl were dropped.

44. Interview, Diyarbakır, 25 October 2014.
45. Interview, Istanbul, 18 October 2014.
46. *Sabah*, 'More Turks interested in Kurdish', 1 February 2015.
47. In 2002, a member of Turkey's higher education body sought to prosecute Kurdish students advocating for Kurdish-language education. He claimed their campaign was part of an attempt to divide Turkey: Jones, 'Kurdish students accused of undermining Turkey', 22 March 2002. Meanwhile, in 2012, Burhan Kuzu, AKP member for Istanbul, equated allowing education in Kurdish with supporting the devil: see *Radikal*, 'Kuzu: Kürtçe eğitim şeytana uymaktır', 19 October 2012.
48. See *Kurdish Info*, 'Mother tongue education is an indispensable right', 26 August 2013; *Evrensel*, '15 Mayıs Kürt Dil Bayramı: 'En güzel dil ana dili'', 15 May 2015.
49. Kymlicka, *Politics in the Vernacular*, p. 215.
50. Jamison, 'Hefty dictionaries', pp. 31–62.
51. RojTV, a Europe-based PKK-affiliated station, is thought to have a much larger audience: Pope, 'Turkey and the democratic opening for the Kurds', pp. 117–40.
52. Çiçek, 'Kurdish identity and political Islam', pp. 147–63.
53. Taştekin, 'Politics strain Turkey's first Kurdish-language institute', 13 November.
54. *Evrensel*, 'Diyarbakırlı işçi yakılarak öldürüldü', 1 September 2016.
55. *Cumhuriyet*, '12 TV, 11 radyo kanalı kapatıldı', 29 September 2016.
56. *Kurdistan 24*, 'Teacher bans kids from speaking Kurdish', 24 October 2017.
57. *Kurdistan 24*, 'Turkey teacher reports students', 20 February 2017.
58. *Diken*, 'HDP'nin referandum şarkısı 'Bejin Na'ya bir yasak da Diyarbakır'dan', 1 April 2017.
59. See https://www.youtube.com/watch?v=N-o9cyPb-2M.
60. Arparcık, 'Feeling solidarity in an estranged city', p. 106.
61. These include 19 May, remembering Mustafa Kemal's landing at Samsun in 1919, thus beginning the national liberation movement; 30 August (Zafer Bayramı, literally Victory Holiday), recalling the Turkish army's victory over the Greeks at Dumlupınar in 1922; and 29 October (Republic Day), the anniversary of the establishment of the Republic in 1923.
62. Hobsbawm, 'Introduction', pp. 1–14.
63. Nash, *The Cauldron of Ethnicity*, pp. 14–15. Newroz predates the arrival of Islam in Iran/Persia and dates to the Zoroastrian era: see Aykan, 'Whose tradition, whose identity?'.
64. Van Bruinessen, 'The Kurds as objects and subjects of historiography', pp. 51–5.

65. In Turkish, which lacks a 'w', and in the context of the outlawing of the 'q', 'x' and 'w' that are specific to Kurdish, it is rendered 'Nevruz'.
66. See Khani, *Mem and Zin*, pp. 51–9. The Newroz celebration is portrayed as an event in which all of Kurdish society participates.
67. Van Bruinessen, 'The Kurds as objects and subjects of historiography', pp. 52–3.
68. See Yanik, '"Nevruz" or "Newroz"?', p. 287; also Aykan, 'Whose tradition, whose identity?'
69. Van Bruinessen, 'The Kurds as objects and subjects of historiography', pp. 51–5.
70. Private conversation, Istanbul, 30 May 2015.
71. Hobsbawm, 'Introduction', p. 13.
72. Galip, *Imagining Kurdistan*, pp. 18–19.
73. See Bullock and Morris, *No Friends but the Mountains*, pp. 50–1, 57.
74. Aydin, 'Mobilising the Kurds in Turkey', pp. 68–88.
75. Güneş, *The Kurdish National Movement in Turkey*, p. 97.
76. Interview, Istanbul, 13 June 2015.
77. Aydin, 'Mobilising the Kurds in Turkey', pp. 79–80.
78. In 1994, in Izmir, I witnessed a Newroz celebration, replete with bonfire, near a *gecekondu* (shanty) neighbourhood in Salhane, a furtive occasion in a yet-to-be-developed part of the city.
79. Van Bruinessen, 'The Kurds as objects and subjects of historiography', p. 55.
80. Taşpınar, *Kurdish Nationalism and Political Islam in Turkey*, p. 105.
81. The 'victory' is portrayed as that of the people over the PKK. See Berberoğlu, 'Diyarbakır kazandı'.
82. Interview, Istanbul, 14 October 2014.
83. Private communication, Istanbul, 30 May 2015.
84. Interview, Diyarbakır, 27 October 2014.
85. Interview, Diyarbakır, 27 October 2014.
86. Interview, Diyarbakır, 4 June 2015.
87. Parallels about the politicisation of Newroz may be drawn with the Ulster Protestant parades in Northern Ireland.
88. Yanik, '"Nevruz" or "Newroz"?', pp. 288–90.
89. Van Bruinessen, 'The Kurds as objects and subjects of historiography', pp. 58–9; Yanik, '"Nevruz" or "Newroz"?', pp. 291–3.
90. The Turkish argument also ignores any link between Newroz and the legend of Kawa. The Persian epic *Shahnameh* states that the descendants of Kawa were Kurds: Ferdowsi, *Shahnameh*, pp. 13–14.
91. Aydin, 'Mobilising the Kurds in Turkey', p. 81.

92. Watts, 'Activists in office', pp. 125–44.
93. *BBC*, 'Turkey Kurds: PKK chief Ocalan calls for ceasefire', 21 March 2013.
94. See https://twitter.com/RT_Erdogan/status/579219896120303617 and https://twitter.com/RT_Erdogan/status/579232921460072448
95. *Daily Sabah*, 'Turkey's President Erdoğan releases message for Nevruz', 21 March 2015.
96. See *Hürriyet Daily News*, 'Restricted celebrations mark Nevruz day', 20 March 2016.
97. *Sabah*, 'Cumhurbaşkanı Erdoğan'dan "Dünya Nevruz Günü" mesajı.', 21 March 2018.

4

THE KURDS AND ISLAM: DEFYING HEGEMONY AND THE 'CALIPHATE'

Travelling the Istanbul Metro reveals the diversity of Turkish society. I once witnessed a teenage girl, suntanned, with free-flowing hair, sporting tight jeans and fashionable trainers, speaking cheerfully on her mobile phone as the train rattled through the suburbs. Watching her intently all the while was another girl, of similar age, wearing the neat gabardine and headscarf of the religiously observant. This was not a rancorous encounter. The phone correspondent was breezily unaware of being watched, but the conservative girl was clearly fascinated. It struck me that they each represented a very current snapshot of Istanbul, but from entirely different demographics.

Some assume that the gap between the devout and the secular is the most important rift in Turkish society, one that is even more unbridgeable than the ethnic division between Turks and Kurds. Yet creating such clear divisions is simplistic and reductive. The dynamics of ethnic and religious identification are complex and multivalent – and sometimes overlap – in Turkey. From its establishment, the Republic of Turkey kept a tight rein on Islam, adopting a top-down approach, regulating how religion could be practised and disseminated throughout the country. There are analogies here with how the Kemalist state viewed ethnic diversity. It perceived religion and ethnicity as potential threats and sought to manage both lest they became lightning rods for dissent or derailed processes of modernisation and Westernisation. Over time, however, both have retained salience in Turkish society and have had profound impacts on politics and daily life.

Another widely shared assumption is that religion is of only marginal importance in Kurdish politics and negligible as a marker of Kurdish identity.[1] Such an assertion is lent credence by the fact that the major Kurdish political parties in Turkey, Iran, Iraq and Syria all adopt secular agendas. Martin Van Bruinessen documents a saying common in several languages of the Middle East: 'Compared to the unbeliever, the Kurd is a Muslim.'[2] The maxim is probably intended in a pejorative sense, casting aspersions on Kurds' Islamic observance, but Van Bruinessen records it to highlight its imprecision. He acknowledges that there is notable religious heterodoxy among the Kurds, yet he underlines that Islam has long played an important role in the social and political fora of Kurdish life. A Kurdish *kebap* chef in Mardin once complained to me of his wife's piety. 'She is very religious; she is closed up here!' he stated, tapping his head, an indication that different degrees of religiosity are present and can create differences of opinion among Kurds – even within a single family.

In recent decades, Islam has come to play a greater role across many strata of society and politics in Turkey. In the AKP era, Islam is more visible in daily life and political discourse. Thus, as the Kurdish political movement endeavours to participate more fully in the political arena and as individual Kurds strive to assert their ethnic identity, they too have had to define their relationship(s) with religion. Islam-inclined parties in Turkey have often won sizeable portions of the Kurdish vote, to the extent that Recep Tayyip Erdoğan declared in 2007 that the AKP was 'the real representative of the Kurds'.[3] From 2014, the emergence of the so-called Islamic State of Iraq and Syria (ISIS), which pursued violent campaigns against Kurds in Syria and Iraq, further shifted the dynamics of Kurdish ethnicity and Islamic identity. This relationship was further complicated for Kurds in Turkey by consistent allegations and accusations of Turkish complicity with and material support for ISIS.

Anthony Smith notes religion as one of the 'differentiating elements of common culture' that are used to establish ethnic identity.[4] Broadly speaking, the majority of Kurds in Turkey profess Sunni Islam, just as the majority of Turks do.[5] Thus when considering religion, unlike questions of mother tongue, there is no clear-cut distinction between Kurds and Turks. Van Bruinessen notes that boundaries between Kurds and others are ill-defined – the religious one is particularly so. To establish a distinct Kurdish identity requires the highlighting of 'differences in degree rather than differences in kind', Van Bruinessen argues.[6] Thus, if Kurds are to uphold Islam as an element of their identity and at the same time define their own space, whether at an individual or political level, they must establish such 'differences in degree', demonstrating how their relationship to and practice of religion sets them apart from Turks. There is some precedent to this. During the 1880s Sheikh Ubeydullah asserted that Kurdish religiosity was different to that of the Turks, and Ottoman *ulama* looked askance at Kurdish Islamic practice.[7] Yet this imperative has become more compelling as Erdoğan and the AKP have played to Islamic sentiments as a means of winning electoral support and as ISIS, among other jihadist groups in Syria and Iraq, encroached on Kurdish-held territory.

Kurds and Islam

Historical records from the seminal sixteenth-century Kurdish text, *The Şerefname*, to nineteenth-century accounts document Kurdish groups that did not conform to any single religious orthodoxy but straddled traditions and customs.[8] Islam is noted among the Kurds for its heterodox nature rather than its adherence to doctrine and orthodox practice. Van Bruinessen remarks that Islam among Kurds, in their mountainous realm on the fringes of Turkish, Persian and Arabic spheres, thus peripheral and not under the direct control of centres of Islamic learning, evolved organically, without excess deference to or regulation by orthodoxy.[9] Historically, Sufism played an important role in Kurdish communities across the Middle East. It was the Sufi orders that promoted and spread the faith, and until the establishment of the modern education system those Kurds who did receive an education did so largely through the *medrese* of the Sufis. The closure of the orders by Turkey's republican regime in the 1920s thus had a significant negative impact on educational levels in Kurdish-populated regions. With the creation of the Diyanet İşleri Başkanlığı (Religious Affairs Directorate; hereafter Diyanet), the government brought religion within its purview, tightly regulating religious practice across Turkey, thus using it as another mechanism through which to engineer a modern society. The closure of the Sufi orders had the added effect, in the south-east, of curtailing Kurdish religio-social networks and the demise of the Kurdish language as a means of education. Despite the banning of the Sufi orders by the state, they retained a level of importance in Kurdish society.[10] The sarcophagi of several Sufi holy men – painted in garish colours – are on show near the city walls of Diyarbakır. Elsewhere in the south-east, and throughout Turkey, Sufi shrines and mosques remain sites for pilgrimage and prayer.[11]

Noting that religion assumed heterodox forms among Kurds and that religion is not necessarily a mark of distinction between Turks and Kurds is not to say, however, that Kurds themselves do not see their religion as an important component of their identity. Surveys across Turkey reveal that religiosity is widely regarded as a marker of good character.[12] In interviews I conducted with Kurds about ethnic identity, virtually all respondents made at least some mention of Islam, if only to refute it. Many claimed to visit the mosque regularly and to observe the fast during Ramazan.[13]

It is apparent that Islam also plays a role in the structures and rhythms of daily life in Diyarbakır. During repeat visits to the Ulu Cami, the largest and most important mosque in Diyarbakır, I observed that early-evening prayers were a ritual for many locals. This included a stream of arrivals of various ages and appearances, from twenty-something men in Levis and trainers to others of a more pious bearing in 'traditional' attire of baggy *şalvar* trousers and prayer caps. These episodes were notable for a lack of formality or stuffiness. For some it appeared to be a form of conviviality, a group activity, involving the sharing of cigarettes and chatter before or after prayers.

As across the Islamic world, Friday prayers are particularly important for observant Kurds. I noted this one Friday at Diyarbakır's Dengbej Evi/Mala Dengbêjan. When the voice of the *müezzin* (prayer caller) rang out at noon, all those present immediately proceeded to the nearby Behram Paşa Mosque. The *dengbêj* perform lengthy vocal recitations of ballads, often with communal participation, but the *ezan* (call to prayer) brought performances to an abrupt end as all rushed to attend prayers. Another weekly religious event I observed in Diyarbakır was Thursday prayers and pilgrimages to the Mosque of the Prophet Süleyman. This was a focal point for communal activity. On Thursday afternoons pilgrims gather to enter the mosque, while a street market attracts visitors, farmers and traders from *mahalleler* (neighbourhoods) outside the Diyarbakır city walls and from surrounding villages. A young haberdashery seller told me he had never entered the shrine ('Women visit it,' he remarked), but he came to the market to set up his stall every week.[14] While religion was not of particular importance for him, he saw that the shrine played an important part in local public and economic life.

Islam in the Republic of Turkey

Kemalism, the guiding ideology of the Republic of Turkey from its establishment, promulgated secularism and (Turkish) nationalism as the keys to national cohesion and progress. Just as the state sought to deny the Kurdish presence, it endeavoured to maintain top-down control on the practice of religion through the Diyanet, instituting a laicist model that not only separated state and religion but ensured state control of religion. Such impositions placed upon a heterogeneous population, large segments of which were religiously observant, inevitably fomented political tensions. Issues of identity, whether ethnic or religious, remained persistent undercurrents in Turkey's politics. Meanwhile, official discourse held that the secularism undergirding the core of the Kemalist model was as essential as ethnic homogeneity. The eventual emergence of an Islamic political movement was regarded with trepidation because it called into question the very underpinnings of the Kemalist state.[15]

Official attitudes towards Islam began to change after the coup of 1980 and the development of the Turk–Islam thesis, which explicitly incorporated Islam into conceptualisations of national identity. Thereafter Turgut Özal (president 1989–93) oversaw further loosening of Kemalist strictures and greater acknowledgement of ethnicity and religion in the public sphere.[16] In this milieu, pro-Islamic political parties and civil society organisations became more active. The space for Islam in Turkey's socio-political landscape shifted most definitively when the AKP won government in 2002. Although describing itself as a 'social conservative' party, the AKP clearly has Islamic foundations. The AKP's founders were openly pious, proposing Islam not as a political model but a guiding moral code for society, something that attracted many voters.[17] At least initially, the AKP articulated and implemented a political vision in which democracy, personal freedoms and equality became central elements within a polity that also recognised the Islamic underpinnings of Turkish life. The AKP thus worked to alleviate constraints placed on Turkey's political and public spheres by the long-standing Kemalist (political) project. Turkish society under the AKP more openly discussed and debated issues of religion, ethnicity and national identity. Previously emphasis had been placed on uniformity; now political and public spheres became freer and more accepting of diversity.

An Islamic perspective on Turkey's Kurds

The only minorities recognised in Turkey's Constitution are the Jews, Greeks and Armenians, all adherents of faiths other than Islam. In Middle Eastern states, minorities are generally delineated in terms of their religious distinctiveness from the Muslim majority.[18] Concurrently, Middle Eastern regimes have often used the idea of 'religious communalism' as a means to forge solidarity, a mechanism whereby communal identification with a single religion becomes the fulcrum of national solidarity and unity.[19] By both these measures, Kurds in Turkey, the majority of whom are Sunni Muslims, lack the means to distinguish themselves from the majority Turks.[20] In the Constitution they were overlooked for minority status and, on the basis of their faith, co-opted into Turkishness.[21] Meanwhile, the Kemalist model downplayed the role of Islam while insisting on ethnic homogeneity.

Various Islamic thinkers in Turkey have theorised otherwise. Members of the Islamist Refah Party, which emerged in the 1980s and briefly held power under the prime ministership of Necmettin Erbakan (1996–7), contended that ethnic boundaries were artificial boundaries that divided the *ummah*. One Refah MP claimed that the 'disestablishment' of Islam in Turkey was the cause of ethnic conflict, thus suggesting that reinstating Islam in the political realm was to the advantage of Turkey's Kurds.[22] Islamist intellectuals in the 1990s lamented the failure of Turkey's secular framework both to build bridges with Kurdish communities and to outmanoeuvre the 'secular' rallying cry of the PKK.[23] Thus in its policy platform, Refah underlined Islam as a forge for unity, while also counselling the lifting of emergency rule in the south-eastern provinces and proposing the peaceful resolution of the Kurdish issue.[24] In doing so, it won considerable support from Kurdish voters.

The AKP, as successor to Refah, initially approached the Kurdish issue, and Kurdish voters, in a similar manner. From the AKP's viewpoint, the root of the Kurdish problem was that the Republic's imposed secularism had extinguished the Islamic bond and allowed nationalism to create divisions.[25] By this reasoning, if secularism was contained and shared faith acknowledged then Islamic *kardeşlik* (brotherhood) could blossom among Turks and Kurds, defusing military conflict and political tensions.[26] In other words, the Islamic bond would render ethnic divides obsolete, dilute the salience of Kurdish identity and catalyse identification with the ideal of the Republic of Turkey. In this sense, Islam, far from being the regressive force that the founding Republicans feared and sought to jettison, was a means to strengthen the nation-state.

The AKP's positioning of Islam as a national bond meant that ethnic diversity represented less of a threat to the integrity of the nation-state.[27] This allowed the AKP to adopt new approaches to the Kurdish Question. In 2005, then Prime Minister Erdoğan broke new ground in a speech in Diyarbakır when he stated that the key to resolving Kurdish discontent was not further repressive measures but the consolidation of democracy.[28] Several study participants recalled hearing Erdoğan speaking in Diyarbakır and being impressed by his words.[29] At the same time, Islamic themes and motifs came to play a greater role in political discourse throughout Turkey. At rallies prior to the 2011 and 2015 general elections in Diyarbakır and several other Kurdish-populated cities, Erdoğan and other AKP figures evoked the idea of religious fraternity, making it a central theme of their pitch to Kurdish voters. These plays to the Islamic sensibilities of the Kurdish electorate were emphasised by alleging that other parties did not sufficiently respect religion, evoking Jerusalem and alleging the pro-Kurdish HDP was sympathetic to Israel.[30] At one rally, brandishing a Quran published in Kurdish, Erdoğan told an audience, 'They [the HDP] have nothing to do with Islam.'[31] The AKP has often positioned itself as the protector of the common religious values that underpin Turkish society,[32] and here it was doing the same with Kurdish voters, with the intention of steering them away from other political parties.

The AKP and Islam in the Public Sphere

Erdogan's brandishing of the Kurdish Quran is a potent example of the higher visibility of Islam in politics and everyday life. There is some discussion that under the AKP Turkey has diverged from its secular path and that a process of 'Islamification' is under way. The AKP touted itself as a 'conservative democratic' movement when it won government, but it never denied its Islamic underpinnings. With time, those Islamic currents have become more prevalent; religion is now much more visible in Turkey's public sphere, with some arguing that the religious–secular divide is being straddled such that Turkey has become 'post-secular'.[33]

Historically, Turkish politicians of an Islamic inclination did not appeal to voters in the name of implementing Sharia, but of upholding Islamic concepts regarded as central tenets of Turkish life.[34] For the AKP, this meant working to alleviate the impositions that the Kemalist interpretation of secularism had placed on society. In the AKP mindset, Kemalism had corrupted secularism such that it became 'enmity against religion'.[35] Just as some saw secularism as having destroyed a sense of *kardeşlik* that could unite Turks and Kurds, others saw it as having smothered 'authentic' Turkish values and imposed faux Western ones. In championing Islamic values, the AKP thus aimed to redress the wrongdoings of Turkey's ancien régime. A 2004 AKP publication entitled *Muhafazakar Demokrasi* (*Conservative Democracy*) decried earlier governments as *buyurgan* (despotic), *baskıcı* (oppressive) and *tektipci* (homogenising), and set out a new agenda of 'dialogue, forbearance and tolerance'.[36] Thus the AKP saw itself as neatly amalgamating the protection of Islamic values with the buttressing of democracy, circumstances which led to a heightened profile for Islam in public and political spheres as well as the broadening of debates about national identity and the lifting of curbs on Kurdish life.

During the AKP's time in office, aspects of Islam and its conservative social outlook have infiltrated both public and political spheres. The Diyanet now has a much higher profile and receives a greater proportion of government money.[37] And as the AKP's incumbency has grown more entrenched, Erdoğan, since winning the presidential vote in 2014, has increasingly promulgated his conservative views, often informed by Islamic mores, on society. This has included speaking out against abortion, the consumption of alcohol and the cohabitation of unmarried male and female students,[38] as well as his oft-stated desire to raise a 'pious youth'.[39] Further, Islam has become a potent weapon in Turkey's socio-political milieu. During the Gezi events of summer 2013, pro-AKP figures, including Erdoğan, accused protesters of harassing a headscarf-wearing woman in Kabataş and of drinking alcohol in a mosque. Both these accusations implicitly highlighted protesters as trampling on Islamic – thus authentic Turkish – values such as respect for women in headscarves and the sanctity of the mosque.[40] The overall official response to the Gezi protests was heavy-handed, no doubt a measure of the fear that arose in government circles. The AKP thus repudiated its own agenda, as stated in the 2004 campaign publication, of 'dialogue, forbearance and tolerance'. It proved to be as despotic and oppressive as the regimes it had earlier denounced. In the AKP armoury, Islam became a means to undermine and delegitimise the opposition, protest and dissent – the very antithesis of the narrative of 'brotherhood'. That Islam was utilised to discredit the Gezi protests, coupled with Erdoğan's winning the presidency and ongoing consolidation of power, and statements from government figures who muse on removing references to 'secularism' from the constitution,[41] contributes to the image of the AKP evolving into an authoritarian regime of conspicuously Islamic colouring.[42]

The 'jihadi highway'

Alongside the re-emergence of Islam in the public sphere, Ankara has engaged more closely with its Middle Eastern neighbours under the stewardship of the AKP. This was a conscious, strategic decision, a policy intended to ensure 'zero problems with neighbours'[43] and to allow Turkey to assume its purportedly rightful place as a regional leader.[44] The Arab Spring uprisings of 2011, the most important of which for Turkey was Syria, derailed such ambitions. Turkey promptly adopted an anti-Assad position in deference to the Syrian citizens who rose up against him.

As Syria devolved into civil war, Turkey became a base for various elements of the resistance, including affiliates of al-Qaeda and other jihadi offshoots. Turkish officials largely turned a blind eye to such groups, allowing them to transit Turkish territory, while some within Turkey sympathised with and encouraged them in their fight against the Assad regime.[45] ISIS swiftly became the most notorious of these groups, incurring international opprobrium for its widely broadcast brutality. That ISIS members moved openly and won applause from conservative circles in cities such as Istanbul gave rise to arguments that Turkey was supporting or promoting ISIS.[46] Statements from officials and AKP members did little to quell such a contention. When

ISIS first appeared on Turkey's radar in August 2014, then Prime Minister Ahmet Davutoğlu seemed reluctant to criticise the group, arguing that it had emerged as a response to Sunni Arab disenfranchisement in Iraq,[47] a degree of largesse that no Turkish politician would ever extend to PKK members. Later, AKP officials in the border town of Şanlıurfa told a reporter they preferred the presence of ISIS to that of Kurdish militias in northern Syria.[48] Reports of captured ISIS members revealing details of their dealings with the Turkish military only added weight to theories that Turkey was backing ISIS.[49] And as ISIS attacked Kurdish forces in both Syria and Iraq, the situation was to have implications for Turkey and its Kurdish population, as will be examined below.

Shifting Kurdish relationships with Islam

In the general election of 1995, the Refah Party won a considerable proportion of the Kurdish vote, with thirty-five Kurdish deputies being elected to parliament.[50] In the 2007 general election, the AKP claimed six provinces that had previously been won by pro-Kurdish parties, winning 44 per cent of the vote across the Kurdish-populated provinces, outpolling the pro-Kurdish Demokratik Toplum Partisi (Democratic Society Party; DTP).[51] Both these parties stand apart from the centre-right, Kemalist parties that have long prevailed in the Turkish electoral system. In this sense a Kurdish vote for these parties represented a 'protest' vote against the establishment. Abdulbakı Erdoğmuş, a Refah deputy from Diyarbakır, argued that Refah's popularity resulted from being 'the only political party that is outside the system', one that offered the possibility of 'restructuring the system'.[52] In its early years, the AKP, too, represented a new political project, an alternative to the existing order.

The surge in the AKP's vote in the south-east in 2007 was notable because it represented a setback for the pro-Kurdish parties, which had seen their votes steadily increase since 1995. The upward swing in the AKP's electoral fortunes may be attributable to the return of normality and increasing economic prosperity of the region, but also to the publicly apparent 'faces of piety' of party leaders Prime Minister Erdoğan and President Abdullah Gül, among others.[53] This was particularly galling for pro-Kurdish political actors who saw their own support undercut by AKP gains. Whether the AKP's popularity in the Kurdish electorate was due to its Islamic credentials or to positive changes in socio-political dynamics, from 2007 the Kurdish political movement, originally conceived of as staunchly secular, recalibrated their political offering to incorporate more Islamic messages and content.

Van Bruinessen notes that by the late 1990s the PKK had acknowledged the importance of Islam in Kurdish society and began revealing a 'more respectful attitude towards Islam'.[54] Such acknowledgement proceeded apace after 2007 in response to the AKP's emergence as an electoral threat. The pro-Kurdish DTP established relationships with imams and specifically designated a place for Islamic leaders among its delegates. In 2012, Gültan Kışanak, co-leader of the Barış ve Demokrasi Partisi (Peace and Democracy Party, BDP, successor to the DTP), remarked, 'In the BDP, we are open to both secular and religious individuals.'[55] Sebahat Tuncel, another BDP parliamentary deputy, demanded the 'right to pray and learn in our own language.'[56] Similarly, Selahattin Demirtaş, then Kışanak's BDP co-leader, played upon Islamic sensibilities in his rhetoric in 2011, asking of the state, 'Why can't sermons be given in Kurdish in mosques?'[57] Another initiative was PKK leader Abdullah Öcalan's 2013 call to convene a 'Democratic Islam Congress' in Diyarbakır. Öcalan cited the examples of the Prophet Mohammad conducting *shura* (councils) as means of consultation and decision-making.[58]

Meanwhile, religious Kurds became more vocal exponents of Kurdish rights, utilising their Islamic credentials to buttress a pro-Kurdish discourse. In a neat pas de deux, the Kurdish pro-Islamic and the ethno-nationalist movements began to borrow discourses from each other, bolstering their electoral appeal by utilising elements of each other's core messages. Thus the offerings of these two previously distinct Kurdish ideological camps underwent a process of convergence,[59] resulting in Islamic imagery and messaging becoming more involved in and associated with the pursuit of Kurdish political rights. Acknowledgement and incorporation of Islamic ideas and symbols and the sensibilities of observant Kurds were means by which to create a broader Kurdish narrative, reclaiming for the Kurds an Islam that until recently had been monopolised by Turkish Islamic political actors.

Indeed, many conservative Kurds have attitudes towards religion at odds with those of conservative Turks regarding questions of Kurdish rights and identity. Repudiating the AKP's 'Islamic brotherhood' discourse, a leading figure in Mustazaf-Der, a Diyarbakır Kurdish Islamic organisation, used an Islamic perspective to argue, in a 2011 interview, in favour of Kurdish rights. Highlighting Islam's acknowledgement of ethnic and linguistic diversity and noting that, historically, educated Kurds tended to have been schooled in Kurdish at a *medrese* (seminary), he argued that Kurds should be free to use their language and celebrate their culture.[60] Other Kurdish religious actors, such as members of Mustazaf-Der's affiliate organisation Kurdish Hizbullah, who previously upheld a purely Islamic identity, have increasingly emphasised a Kurdish identity within an Islamic context.[61] Similarly, religiously inclined Kurds point to the verse in the Quran exalting the 'diversity of tongues and hues' as reason to uphold a distinctive Kurdish identity and dismiss the idea of 'Islamic brotherhood' on the grounds that it is primarily used to quell Kurdish demands, and thus is assimilationist.[62]

A particularly visible Kurdish assertion of a distinct Islam was the BDP's institution of *sivil Cuma namazı* (literally 'civilian Friday prayers') in the lead-up to the 2011 general election.[63] These were outdoor prayer meetings organised in Kurdish-populated cities on Friday afternoons, the most important time of the week to participate in prayers. Friday gatherings were a way of boycotting 'official' mosques, which, being regulated by the Diyanet, were seen as instruments of state control. Indeed, some saw mosques as being mouthpieces for the AKP.[64] Kurdish mullahs, scholars trained at underground *medreses*, led prayers (in Kurdish) and delivered sermons laced with pro-Kurdish ethno-nationalist messages. In this way, the pro-Kurdish political movement was staking a claim for distinctiveness within the currents of increased religiosity apparent in the public sphere across the country. Tellingly, despite initial misgivings about the PKK's method and agenda, observant Kurds have absorbed nationalist demands propagated by the PKK to create a distinctive Islamic identity.[65] The public gatherings were an element of the BDP's campaign of *sivil itaatsızlık* (civilian disobedience), an attempt to stake out a discrete Kurdish political space.[66] Significantly, in Diyarbakır these prayer gatherings took place in Dağkapı Square, the site of the lost grave of Sheikh Said, who led the Kurdish uprising of 1925.[67]

Erdoğan voiced his disapproval of these gatherings, to which BDP deputy Sebahat Tuncel retorted, 'Beliefs cannot be monopolised by anyone.'[68] Erdoğan's disapproval may have been based on his fear that such events would win widespread support among Kurdish voters. Indeed, whether due to the prayer gatherings or otherwise, pro-Kurdish parties proved dominant in the south-eastern provinces in 2011, and in subsequent elections, despite AKP campaign rallies and Islamic messages. As Kurdish ethno-political actors incorporated Islamic messages into their offerings, Kurdish Islamic actors adopted more ethno-nationalist positions. The result was that Kurdish political groups performed more strongly and outpointed the AKP, its performance in 2007 representing a blip in the Kurdish-populated provinces' voting patterns.[69]

These developments represent the 'differences in degree' that Van Bruinessen notes as necessary to delineate Kurdish ethnicity. Ethnic identity is created both from within and without in a process of self-ascription and external ascription that acknowledges similarities with one's own group and differences from other groups.[70] Self-ascription requires highlighting differences; it is a process of boundary maintenance, one that Fredrik Barth sees as more important than 'cultural stuff' in defining ethnicity.[71] Here Kurdish actors were establishing and maintaining a boundary, which the discourse of Turkish Islamists and the AKP denied, and which the 'stuff' of their religious affiliation as Sunni Muslims would also seem to speak against. Where Turkish political actors put forth Islam as a bridge to unity, Kurdish actors set out to utilise Islam as a form of 'disobedience' and to highlight a specifically Kurdish tradition of Islamic practice and education. Highlighting Quranic verses that speak of diversity added legitimacy to such a stance. These were Kurdish phenomena in defiance of the AKP-sponsored, state-regulated Islam of the Diyanet – they engendered clear assertions of Kurdish identity. They demonstrated a refusal to be absorbed into a homogenous category of Sunni Islam – and by extension Turkishness – that erased their distinct ethnic identity.

Kurdish Attitudes to 'Islamic brotherhood'

In discussions with numerous observant Kurds, Mehmet Gurses encountered considerable scepticism about the efficacy of 'Islamic brotherhood' as a means to solving Kurdish grievance, many Kurds noting that all dominant Muslim ethnicities in the Middle East – Turkish, Persian and Arab – had subjugated Kurds, despite their Islamic faith.[72] Similarly, no Kurds I spoke to looked favourably on the idea of 'Islamic brotherhood'. One respondent dismissed government attempts to foster brotherhood through religion as '*büyük bir palavra*' ('a big lie').[73] A Kurdish journalist in Istanbul told me the AKP, and President Erdoğan in particular, used religion as an '*enstrüman*' (instrument) rather than out of genuine conviction,[74] a sentiment widely echoed by other Kurds. A stallholder in the Diyarbakır bazaar, referring to the AKP, commented, 'You cannot mix culture and tradition and religion. When you mix [them] there is going to be manipulation of the people.'[75] While acknowledging a role for Islam within their identity and their outlook, Kurds I spoke with remained secular in outlook, and suspicious of attempts to bring religion into the political realm, particularly when that took the form of apparently duplicitous attempts to unify. The cohort of Kurds I encountered acknowledged Islam as an aspect of their identity and daily lives but regarded Islam as propagated by the ruling AKP as a mechanism to instil conformity – faith instrumentalised for political ends.

This raises the issue of Kurds' responses to the Kurdish political movement's adoption of Islamic symbols and discourses. Would these also be seen as cynical ploys to garner votes, gestures devoid of authenticity? The answer appears to lie in the relationship between religious and ethnic identities. In the Kurdish villages of Hakkari, Lale Yalçın-Heckmann observed considerable interplay between these two phenomena, which occupy spaces upon a continuum, separating or overlapping according to circumstances.[76] To this end, Sheikh Said, the leader of the 1925 rebellion against the early Turkish republic, is recalled as a religious figure but also as a champion of the Kurdish cause.[77] His status as a Naqshbandi sheikh wins legitimacy but the fact that he fought for Kurds against the Turkish republic elevates him in Kurdish hearts and minds.

Such precedents aside, the Kurdish movement sought to portray their adoption of a more accommodational approach to Islam as a means to reverse the politicisation of religion that had occurred under the AKP. Selahattin Demirtaş, for example, warned against Erdoğan's manipulation of Islam. He remarked, 'The Prime Minister, who uses Islam for his own benefit, is discriminatory [*ayrımcı*]. Our religion is not discriminatory, it is integrative [*bütünleştirici*].'[78] Rahman Dağ noted that the intention of the Democratic Islam Congress proposed by Öcalan was to return Islam to an unadulterated, non-politicised form. He observed that while Islam had been '[elevated] into an instrument of political power', it might also be understood as a mechanism of 'peace, justice and brotherhood'.[79] While these positions may be seen as examples of Kurdish actors attempting to highlight a more 'pure' Islam, they also amount to setting out a position whereby the Islam they offer is not a mechanism for political control or manipulation. As Ömer Tekdemir contends, the 'Islamic reality' that Kurdish actors sought to create was one that was infused with '*eshiri* [tribal] cultural values', one that fostered community rather than political authority.[80] Accordingly many Kurds proved more open to the incorporation of religious elements into the Kurdish political platform than they were to Turkish politicians who wield Islamic symbols.[81] Kurds I spoke with saw Erdoğan's use of Islam as cynical, but did not judge Kurdish actors' statements on Islam the same way.

As if to highlight the clear divide in these competing representations of Islam, AKP figures continued to use religion as a means to discredit their opponents. As noted earlier, this included, while campaigning in 2011 and 2015, casting aspersions on the Islamic credentials of opposition parties. This is part of a broad appropriation of Islam by AKP figures. Prime Minister Ahmet Davutoğlu once claimed that Allah was 'on the AKP's side',[82] and regime-aligned Islamic scholar Hayrettin Karaman implied that voting in favour of the referendum in 2017 that would grant Erdoğan greater executive powers was a religious obligation.[83] Another Islamic figure once claimed that those voting against Erdoğan were non-believers (*imansiz*).[84] When he wielded a Kurdish Quran at a campaign rally in Batman, Erdoğan railed against the HDP, claiming it took direction from the PKK, including classes in Zoroastrianism.[85] What such classes actually entail is unclear, but all of these statements are part of ongoing attempts by the AKP to claim to be the only *true* representatives of Islam in Turkey. In this they are appealing to the (perceived) Islamic sensibilities of the Kurdish electorate. In effect this is a continuation of the 'Islamic brotherhood' narrative by other means, whereby a Kurdish Quran could be used as evidence of the AKP's good will in meeting Kurds halfway in the negotiation of a communal, Islamic identity, but it also reflected concern within the AKP that the Kurdish movement was gaining momentum.

Erdoğan's invocations of Islam cut little ice with Kurdish voters, however. In the election of June 2015, they overwhelmingly opted for the HDP rather than the AKP in south-eastern Anatolia. His 'democracy' speech in Diyarbakır a decade earlier won Kurdish applause, but the threadbare follow-through contributed to widespread dismissal of his utterances as *palavra* (empty talk), and thus the Kurdish Quran was seen as just more cheap electioneering. Erdoğan undercut his own position with his erratic statements on the situation of Kurds. In early 2015 he declared, 'There is no Kurdish problem anymore. What else do you [Kurds] want?'[86] Haluk, a Diyarbakır shopkeeper, remarked, 'People who believed him before, they [now] say, oh, you are playing a dirty game with us. Everyone has their hesitations [now].'[87]

Ultimately, it appears that Kurds in Turkey are not preoccupied with finding measures of 'brotherhood', an idea broadly viewed as another mechanism for homogenisation. This discourse may have been more nuanced than the Kemalist programme of assimilation, but the Kurds I interviewed saw it as an initiative to co-opt them into another hegemonic political project.

The Kurds and ISIS

From mid-2014, the ascendance of an apparently invincible ISIS raised urgent questions about the relationship between Islam, radicalisation and violence. It also gave greater urgency to Kurds' inclinations to articulate a specifically Kurdish interpretation of Islam. ISIS loomed as an existential threat for Kurdish communities in Syria and Iraq as it extended its reach. This particularly came into focus as ISIS besieged the Syrian-Kurdish city of Kobanî. The prospect of ISIS massacring the inhabitants and defenders of Kobanî heightened a sense of kinship and solidarity among Kurds across the Middle East and beyond. ISIS' bloody and remorseless tactics swiftly saw it branded global public enemy number one. For some observers, ISIS, in trumpeting its Islamic foundations and brandishing Islamic symbols, made explicit a link between Islam and violence and intolerance. So while Kurds were worried at ISIS' advance across Syria and Iraq out of concern for their ethnic kin, they were also keen to distance themselves from association with the violent manifestation of Islam that ISIS represented.

ISIS may have claimed to be (re)establishing the 'caliphate', but I met no Kurds who support the group.[88] When the subject of ISIS arose, all Kurds I met decried its methods, tactics, violence and intolerance. Sunni Kurds, in light of their religious affiliation, immediately dissociated themselves from any connection with ISIS. For some this prompted an apologetic stance towards their faith: 'Yes, we are Muslim, but not like that...'[89] In a Diyarbakır teahouse, one Kurdish woman felt impelled to assure me, '*Kürtler fanatik İslamci hiç olmadı*' ('Kurds have never been fanatical Islamists').[90] Indeed, research undertaken in Diyarbakır confirms that the actions of ISIS and other jihadist groups in Syria have accelerated a move away from Islam by many Kurds.[91]

In late 2014, as Kurds sweated on the fate of Kobanî, young Kurdish men rushed to change their appearances to avoid any possibility of being associated with ISIS or other hard-line Islamist groups. Barbers in Diyarbakır reported increasing numbers of young men wanting to have their beards shaved off, in particular after Kurdish nationalists clashed with those sporting full beards and accused them of being 'jihadist'.[92] It is ironic that even as many Kurds decried ISIS for its arbitrary violence and intolerance, Kurdish nationalists demonstrated similar intolerance for those perceived to be pro-ISIS. Nonetheless, the point was that Kurds were desperate to avoid accusations that they were inclined towards ISIS, even down to such superficial characteristics as beards.

Meanwhile, international media attention on ISIS also highlighted the Kurds' resistance and their political plight across the Middle East. Kurds were determined to underline an identity that stood in opposition to ISIS and what it represented. The desperate struggle of the Syrian-Kurdish militia associated with the Partiya Yekîtiya Demokrat (Democratic Union Party; PYD) in pushing back ISIS afforded an opportunity for Kurds to assert their anti-jihadist stance. The PYD is aligned with the PKK, and many Kurds in Turkey claim familial relations with Kurdish communities in Syria. In late 2014, TV screens in the teahouses of Diyarbakır were always tuned for the latest developments in Kobanî; talk on the street similarly was focused on the plight of the PYD's militias. Several Kurds in Diyarbakır told me of friends and acquaintances who had joined the fight against ISIS in Syria. These circumstances added to the narrative that Kurds were Muslim, 'but not like that'.

The advance of ISIS had a further galvanising effect for Kurds. Many Kurds were convinced that Turkey played a role in the rise of ISIS and other jihadi groups in Syria, and that Ankara supported ISIS in its campaigns. Co-chair of the PYD Saleh Muslim once accused Turkey of supplying ISIS directly with the very bullets they used.[93] Appreciative comments for ISIS from some Turks on social media and elsewhere, such as those noted above, fed the idea that ISIS operated with Turkey's connivance. One Kurd told me pro-ISIS social media commentary made Turkey's support for ISIS 'crystal clear'.[94] Another told me he was no longer talking to one of his Turkish friends who called ISIS 'the soldiers of Turkey'.[95] By extension, many Kurds attributed alleged Turkish military complicity with ISIS to the AKP government and Erdoğan specifically. A man in a Diyarbakır teahouse told me, 'Erdoğan is ISIS . . . they are the enemy of God', a statement that prompted nods of agreement from all gathered.[96]

ISIS' three deadliest attacks of 2015 in Turkey – Diyarbakır in June, Suruç in July and Ankara in October – all targeted Kurds and/or oppositional groups, a fact that added to suspicions that the government and security agencies were complicit. The October attack, when suicide bombers struck an opposition protest in Ankara killing over a hundred, was the deadliest terrorist attack ever in Turkey. Erdoğan claimed that ISIS, the PKK, the PYD and Assad's *mukhabarat* (secret police) worked in concert to commit the attack.[97] Coordination between these groups is implausible, to say the least, but this claim was part of an ongoing campaign to discredit the PYD, and ratchet up terrorist rhetoric against the PKK, which until mid-2015 had been negotiating with the government. Erdoğan had recently called the PYD itself a terrorist group;[98] now he was lumping it and the PKK in with other arch-foes. These statements also revealed a deafness – or indifference – to the sensibilities of Turkey's Kurds. Accusing Kurdish militias who were fighting ISIS of terrorism and complicity with jihadists in an attack that killed many Kurds was undoubtedly taken as an affront by many Kurds, but it also marked a shift in the AKP's position from apparently courting the Kurdish vote to appealing to Turkish nationalists.

In these circumstances, Kurdish denunciations of ISIS and celebrations of the PYD militias' resistance in Syria amounted to taking a stand against Turkey, the AKP and Erdoğan. This provided another mechanism for Kurds to define themselves in contradistinction to Turks, the rationale being that Kurds may be Sunni, like Turks, but they would not tolerate ISIS or other jihadists. Similarly, Syrian and Iraqi Kurds fighting against ISIS positioned themselves as standard-bearers for democracy in the struggle against authoritarianism and Islamism in the Middle East.[99] When the PYD triumphed over

ISIS in Kobanî in 2015, Kurds celebrated a victory for progressive secularism against a murderous Islamist foe, while also thumbing their noses at the AKP and Erdoğan.[100] Jihadi ranks had been amassed against Kurdish interests but Kurdish fortitude had won the day even though, according to theories enjoying currency in Kurdish circles, the Turkish state and the AKP machinery lent support – moral if not material – to ISIS. For Sunni Kurds to celebrate this was a way to demonstrate their opposition to and difference from the intolerant brand of Islam that ISIS represented and that the Turkish state had done little to dissuade or prevent. In this way, Kurds marked themselves as Muslims who would not countenance religious violence and intolerance, something that at least some Turks were willing to ignore as ISIS continued its advance.[101] Many Kurds remained cognisant of their identity as Sunni Muslims, but they held themselves apart from those Turks who indulged or overlooked excesses performed in the name of the religion by groups such as ISIS.

Kurds as 'Others'

Leaving aside Anatolia's heterodox Alevi tradition, Turkish ethnicity is explicitly tied to Sunni Islam.[102] It is assumed that those who claim Turkishness are Sunni Muslims. For Kurds, however, there is a much less explicit definitional link between faith and ethnicity. Kurds exhibit much more variety in religious affiliation than Turks – one may still claim Kurdish ethnicity if one is not a Sunni Muslim.

Religious diversity is something that often arose in conversations I had with Kurds. Dilek, a Diyarbakır shop attendant, remarked, 'When you talk about the Kurdish people, you can't only say they are Muslim. Being Kurdish does not [necessarily] mean you are Muslim. You [may be] Christian, or ... Zerdüşt [Zoroastrian], or Yezidi. Kurds in history have [had] many religions.'[103] Following the election of June 2015, several Kurds I spoke with held out as an example Feleknas Uca, a Yezidi Kurd who won a seat as an HDP deputy for Diyarbakır in Turkey's parliament.[104] Martin Van Bruinessen notes that some of the most heterodox religious traditions in the Middle East emerged among the Kurds;[105] historically there have also been communities of Kurdish Jews and Christians. Gelaz, a bookseller who proudly asserted her Kurdishness, declared herself an atheist yet made a point of

Figure 4.1 Performance of Kurdish, Turkish, Armenian song, Cathedral of Surp Giragos, Diyarbakır, June 2013. © William Gourlay.

underlining her respect for Kurdish adherents of Christianity and Judaism.[106] Meanwhile, Mehmet Gurses relates a conversation with an observant Kurd who contended, 'We, Sunni Kurds and Yezidi Kurds, all are part of the same nation regardless of religious differences.'[107]

Acknowledgement of diverse ancestry is not deemed peculiar among Kurds. Zehra, a public servant in Diyarbakır, told me of ancestors on her mother's side who were Yezidi,[108] while Dilek told of Armenian ancestors ('three generations before') who had moved around south-eastern Anatolia and eventually converted to Islam.[109] These historical anomalies were delivered matter-of-factly; notably both of these women declared that they did not consider themselves Muslim but both saw themselves as Kurdish. Acknowledgements of mixed ethnic or religious heritage and history are significant as they distance these Kurds from the Turkish norm. Despite the examples of similar revelations of mixed heritage such as that of Fethiye Çetin outlined earlier, many Turks still cling to notions of cultural 'authenticity' and uniformity, and display an aversion to perceived ethnic or racial 'mixing'.[110] Indeed, Öztürk (roughly translating as 'Pure Turk') is a commonplace surname among Turks, while Özkan ('Pure Blood') is used as both a first name and surname. One can extend this emphasis on ethnic 'purity' to the realm of religious adherence. The idea of straddling faiths or acknowledging religious diversity in the family tree runs counter to commonly held conceptions of Turkishness. In over twenty years of travel to Turkey and friendship with many Turks, I have had no conversations with Turks similar to those of Kurds who shared stories of their forebears' adherence to faiths other than Islam.

Some Kurds also attempt to qualify their commitment to the faith. One man in Istanbul repeated to me a commonly held conviction that Kurds were not entirely willing converts to Islam, remarking, 'At that time . . . we believe they forced us. They hit us to be Muslim, but now we are happy with . . . Muslim culture.'[111] This narrative has long had currency among Kurdish nationalists.[112] Indeed, the process of conversion to Islam among the Kurds was slow, having not occurred on a large scale until the twelfth century and continuing until the fifteenth century.[113] Even then it was not comprehensive. Historical records from the seminal sixteenth-century Kurdish historical text, *The Şerefname*, to nineteenth-century accounts, record Kurdish groups that did not conform to a single religious orthodoxy but straddled traditions and customs.[114] Many seize upon this, as well as the fact that the heterodox traditions of the Yezidis and the Ahl-e Haqq are practised exclusively by Kurds, as a way to define a variegated faith tradition for Kurds that is distinct from that of the monotheism of Turks, Persians and Arabs. In modern Turkey, this allows Kurds another means to assert a posture counter to the AKP, its increasingly entrenched conservative Islamic orthodoxy and the violent jihadism of ISIS.

In further attempts to distance Kurdish identity from Islam, some have claimed that Zoroastrianism is the 'true' religion of the Kurds.[115] In the current milieu where Islam has been tainted by its association with ISIS, there has been a surge in interest in Zoroastrianism among Kurds, particularly in Iraq, some of whom are reinventing it as an intrinsically Kurdish faith.[116] Some even go so far as to say that Zoroaster, the Iranian prophet of the second century BC, was himself of Kurdish ethnicity.[117] I encountered no such inclinations among Kurds in Turkey, but as noted, many were entirely comfortable with the idea that Kurds could be Zoroastrian.

While being Turkish requires identification as a Sunni Muslim, with inherent overtones of AKP-impelled notions of conformity and conservatism, this creates a default position of the 'Other' for those who buck against conforming. As such, adopting a position that advocates broader acceptance of and identification with a variety of religions and faith traditions allows Kurds to define their own political trajectory, one that is ecumenical and liberal and that pursues all-encompassing goals of human rights and democracy. Indeed, Kurdish political movements across the Middle East seek to promote an image as more inclusive and tolerant of ethnic and religious diversity than their Turkish and Arab neighbours.[118]

Contesting Islam and Asserting Difference

Recent decades have seen Islam assume a more prominent role in Turkey's political and public spaces. Politicians and citizens of all stripes have, accordingly, developed different relationships with Islam. When the AKP took power, the nationalist prism through which politics had been viewed was lifted, allowing greater space in politics for Kurds and new approaches to the Kurdish issue. The momentum that the AKP gained among Kurdish voters, alongside more salient Islamic currents in society, have pushed Kurdish individuals and political actors to take account of and articulate new positions on Islam. In so doing they are balancing the various impacts of AKP attempts to assimilate through a narrative of *kardeşlik*, juxtaposed with Erdoğan's wielding of Islamic sensibilities to denigrate and delegitimise political adversaries. Indeed, Erdoğan himself is seeking a position where he can maximise his cachet with Kurds, playing to Islamic sensibilities with his brotherhood discourse and also attempting to portray himself as *more* pious than other political actors. The tussle over seeking definitive Islamic positions has become more complex for all actors with the rise of ISIS and other jihadi actors in Syria, which some Kurds accuse the AKP of supporting and nourishing. The urgency with which Kurds sought to create their own religio-political space has increased in recent years as the AKP has grown more authoritarian and as ISIS emerged as a globally recognised and reviled incarnation of an intolerant and violent Islam. While once the AKP proffered Islam as the fulcrum of unity, it has increasingly wielded religion as a means of delegitimising opponents and critics. Kurds seek to set themselves apart from the government position and to stake out their own definition and practice of Islam that is free of association with either the excesses of ISIS or the conservative, controlling vision of Erdoğan and the AKP.

Ultimately, for many Kurds in Turkey, Islam is an element of their identity, but they are suspicious of the instrumentalisation of their faith and of talk of 'brotherhood' with Turks on the basis of shared Sunni adherence. Rather they are keen to highlight the 'differences in degree' that Van Bruinessen notes as necessary to maintain their own ethnic and political distinctiveness. In this way, just as Turkish nationalism gave impetus to Kurdish nationalism, the Turkification of Islam has seen Kurds redefine their own religious observance.[119]

The practice of *sivil Cuma namaz* was an important element of this. With conflict escalating in 2016, HDP members and a large crowd again gathered for an outdoor prayer service in Diyarbakır, the imam calling for peace and an end to the trauma once again being visited upon the city.[120] But demonstrating that the political ground had again shifted, the prayer leader was later arrested for 'terror propaganda'.[121] At issue here was not the use of religion in the political arena, because many political figures continue to do this. For example, an AKP candidate in the 2019 municipal elections told constituents that electing Erdoğan would give voters the key to heaven.[122] Rather it would seem that using religion as a strategy against the AKP would not be tolerated. Hence, religion remains a site of contestation between Kurds and the ruling AKP.

Notes

1. Leezenberg, 'Political Islam among the Kurds', p. 203; Yavuz (2009), *Secularism and Muslim Democracy in Turkey*, p. 176.
2. Van Bruinessen, *Mullas, Sufis and Heretics*, p. 13.
3. Temelkuran, *Turkey: The insane and the melancholy*, p. 267.
4. Smith, *National Identity*, pp. 21–3.
5. This is not to ignore Alevi minorities among both Turks and Kurds. There are no official figures for the numbers of Alevis but estimates put between 15 and 30 per cent of the total population of Turkey as Alevi. It is estimated that 70 per cent of Kurds are Sunni, the remaining 30 per cent being Alevi or Yezidi: see Çelik, 'Alevis, Kurds and *Hemşehris*', pp. 141–57.
6. Van Bruinessen, 'The ethnic identity of Kurds in Turkey', p. 613.

7. Soleimani, *Islam and Competing Nationalisms in the Middle East*, pp. 161–6.
8. Jwaideh, *The Kurdish National Movement*, pp. 18–21.
9. Van Bruinessen, 'The Kurds and Islam'; Van Bruinessen also notes that two of the more heterodox traditions within the Middle East – the Yezidis and the Ahl-a Haqq – arose among the Kurds.
10. McDowall, *A Modern History of the Kurds*, p. 398; Van Bruinessen, Martin, *Agha, Shaikh and State*, pp. 252–7.
11. In 2008, I unwittingly paid a visit, amid many pilgrims, to the tomb of Veysel Karani in Ziyaret on the Diyarbakır–Bitlis road when the bus I was on stopped there.
12. See, for instance, Çarkoğlu and Toprak, *Turkiye'de Din, Toplum ve Siyaset*, pp. 100–18.
13. In Turkey, the Muslim holy month of Ramadan is known as Ramazan, as it is in Iran (ماه رمضان).
14. Author interview, Diyarbakır, 11 June 2015.
15. Massicard, *The Alevis in Turkey and Europe*, pp. 83–6.
16. Gunter, 'Turgut Özal and the Kurdish question', pp. 85–100.
17. Bahcheli and Noel, 'The Justice and Development Party and the Kurdish question', p. 117.
18. Dawod, 'Ethnicity and power', p. 83.
19. Zubaida, 'Religion and ethnicity as politicized boundaries', p. 95.
20. Similarly, these circumstances allow no acknowledgement of the Alevis in Turkey, among whom there are both Turks and Kurds. On controversies relating to the inherent 'Kurdishness' or 'Turkishness' of the Alevis, see White, 'The debate on the identity of "Alevi Kurds"', pp. 17–29.
21. Such measures can afford a sense of 'belonging' for some minorities: see Voloder, 'Secular citizenship and Muslim belonging in Turkey', pp. 838–56.
22. Cited in Yavuz, *Islamic Political Identity in Turkey*, p. 232.
23. Sakallıoğlu, 'Kurdish nationalism from an Islamist perspective', p. 73.
24. Barkey and Fuller, *Turkey's Kurdish Question*, pp. 101–2.
25. Özcan and Yavuz, 'The Kurdish question and Turkey's Justice and Development Party', p.104.
26. Sarıgil, 'Curbing Kurdish ethnonationalism in Turkey', p. 536.
27. For more on the AKP proposal of Islam as a common bond for Turks and Kurds, see Van Bruinessen, 'Turkey's AKP government and its engagement with the Alevis and Kurds'.
28. See, Keskin, 'Erdoğan: Kürt sorunu demokrasiyle çözülür', 11 August 2005; *Economist*, 'Peace be unto you', 20 August 2005.

29. Interview, Diyarbakır, 11 June 2015.
30. Grigoriadis and Dilek, 'Struggling for the Kurdish vote', pp. 294–7.
31. *Hürriyet*, 'Erdoğan: 'Bunların dinle işi yok", 3 May 2015.
32. Kaya, 'Islamisation of Turkey under the AKP rule', p. 54.
33. Göle, 'Post-secular Turkey', pp. 7–11.
34. Jenkins, *Political Islam in Turkey*, p. 214.
35. Ibid., p. 168.
36. Kaya, *Europeanisation and Tolerance in Turkey*, p. 84.
37. Dayak, 'Turkish secularism revisited', pp. 11–12.
38. Özbudun, 'AKP at the crossroads', p. 157.
39. *Hürriyet*, 'Dindar gençlik yetiştireceğiz', 2 February 2012.
40. Both accusations, incidentally, proved to be unsubstantiated: *Hürriyet Daily News*, 'I did not see anyone consume alcohol', 27 June 2013; *Hürriyet Daily News*, 'Released footage shows no attacks.' 14 February 2014.
41. Yackley, 'Turkish parliament speaker provokes row', 26 April 2016.
42. Kaya, 'Islamisation of Turkey', p. 50.
43. *Ministry of Foreign Affairs*, 'Policy of zero problems with our neighbors'.
44. Uslu, 'Jihadist highway to Jihadist haven', p. 781.
45. Ibid., p. 784.
46. Martin, 'Go inside an ISIS giftshop', 26 February 2015; *Associated Press*, 'Turkey's largest city is rattled', 14 October 2014.
47. *Cumhuriyet*, 'Davutoğlu'ndan cani IŞİD'i meşrulaştıran sözler', 8 August 2014.
48. In this statement the official is conflating the PYD and the PKK, a common stance among Turks: Özyurt, 'Sympathy for the devil that is ISIS', 26 September 2014.
49. Guiton, '"ISIS Sees Turkey as its ally"', 7 November 2014.
50. Yavuz, *Islamic Political Identity in Turkey*, pp. 231–2.
51. Gürbüz, *Rival Kurdish Movements in Turkey*, pp. 60–1.
52. *Milliyet*, 27 November 1994, cited in Yavuz, *Islamic Political Identity in Turkey*, p. 232.
53. *Economist*, 'Peace be unto you', 20 August 2005.
54. Van Bruinessen (1999), 'The Kurds and Islam'. The Kurdish Hizbullah has no connection to the Lebanese Shi'ite organisation. On Kurdish Hizbullah, see Jenkins, *Political Islam in Turkey*, pp. 187–95.
55. Cited in Sarıgil and Fazlıoglu, 'Religion and ethno-nationalism', p. 558.
56. Tuncel, 'Arab Spring, Kurdish Summer', 11 June 2018.
57. *Milliyet*, 'Sivil Itaatsizlike Camide', 6 April 2011.

58. *Hürriyet Daily News*, 'Öcalan calls for democratic Islam congress', 15 October 2013.
59. Gürbüz, *Rival Kurdish Movements in Turkey*, pp. 29, 75–6. See also Çiçek, 'Kurdish identity and political Islam under AKP rule', p. 155.
60. Sarıgil and Fazlıoğlu, 'Religion and ethno-nationalism', p. 554.
61. Gürbüz, *Rival Kurdish Movements in Turkey*, p. 76.
62. Sarıgil and Fazlıoğlu, 'Religion and ethno-nationalism', pp. 555–9.
63. Başer, 'Diyarbakır'da Sivil Cuma', 3 June 2011.
64. Özsöy, 'The missing grave of Sheikh Said', pp. 191–220.
65. Gurses, 'Is Islam a cure for ethnic conflict?', p. 149.
66. Sarıgil and Fazlıoğlu, 'Religion and ethno-nationalism', pp. 556–7.
67. Özsöy, 'The missing grave of Sheikh Said', p. 220.
68. *Bianet*, 'Sivil Cuma Namazı Kılındı', 8 April 2011.
69. Sarıgil and Fazlıoğlu, 'Religion and ethno-nationalism', p. 559.
70. Eriksen, *What is Anthropology?*, pp. 159–61.
71. Barth, *Ethnic Groups and Boundaries*, p. 15. On boundary-making among Kurds, see Tezcür, 'Kurdish nationalism and identity in Turkey'.
72. Gurses, 'Is Islam a cure for ethnic conflict?', p. 146.
73. Author interview, Istanbul, 30 May 2015.
74. Author interview, Istanbul, 14 October 2014.
75. Author interview, Diyarbakır, 26 October 2014.
76. Yalçın-Heckmann, 'Ethnicity, Islam and nationalism among Kurds in Turkey', pp. 114–18.
77. McDowall, *A Modern History of the Kurds*, pp. 197–8; Van Bruinessen, *Agha, Shaikh and State*, p. 298.
78. *Milliyet*, 'Sivil Itaatsizlike Camide', 6 April 2011.
79. Dağ, 'Democratic Islam congress and the Middle East', 13 June 2014.
80. Tekdemir, 'The reappearance of Kurdish Muslims in Turkey'.
81. Accordingly, Kurdish actors were careful to acknowledge Alevis and other communities as well as Sunnis in their political platform. Campaigning in mid-2015, Demirtaş asked why Turkey should not have Alevi members of parliament: *Al Jazeera* (2014), "Neden Alevi bakan olmasın", 4 April.
82. *Yeni Akit*, 'Davutoğlu: Her Müslüman için cihad farz-ı ayndır.', 2 January 2015.
83. Hayrettin Karaman, 'Neyi Oyluyoruz?', *Yeni Safak*, 13 April 2017.
84. https://www.mynet.com/erdogana-oy-vermeyen-imansizdir-110101392250.
85. *Hürriyet*, 'Erdoğan: 'Bunların dinle işi yok', 3 May 2015.

86. *Anadolu Agency*, 'Erdoğan: There is no Kurdish problem in Turkey', 23 March 2015.
87. Author interview, Diyarbakır, 11 June 2014.
88. While my interlocutors dissociated themselves from ISIS, significant numbers of Kurds did join ISIS: see Meleagrou-Hitchens and Alaaldin, 'The Kurds of ISIS'.
89. Author interview, Diyarbakır, 24 October 2014.
90. Interview, Diyarbakır, 10 June 2015.
91. Yanmış and Aktaş, *Kürtlerde Dinî Yaşam*.
92. *Milliyet*, 'IŞİD korkusu imaj değiştiriyor', 13 October 2014.
93. *Zaman*, 'Salih Müslim', 18 September 2013.
94. Author interview, Diyarbakır, 20 October 2014.
95. Author interview, Istanbul, 14 October 2014.
96. Author interview, Diyarbakır, 24 October 2014.
97. Pamuk, 'Turkey's Erdogan sees Syrian and Kurdish hands in Ankara attack', 22 October 2015.
98. *BBC*, 'Erdoğan: PYD de bir terör örgütüdür', 5 October 2015. Turkey continues to insist that the PYD and the PKK are one organisation. In January 2018 and October 2019, Ankara launched campaigns into northern Syria to remove what it deemed to be PKK control of territories bordering Turkey.
99. Kaya and Whiting, 'Sowing division', p. 82.
100. Leezenberg, 'The ambiguities of democratic autonomy', p. 684.
101. By no means all Turks supported ISIS, nor, indeed, support the AKP. In turn, there are some Kurds who joined ISIS or who vote for the AKP. The point here is that many Kurds seek to assert a position that acknowledges Islam but one that is distinct to that of both the AKP and ISIS.
102. Yavuz, *Islamic Political Identity in Turkey*, p. 47.
103. Interview, Diyarbakır, 8 June 2015.
104. The fact that Uca, alongside Ali Atalan, another HDP candidate, won seats as Yezidis, the first to ever do so in Turkey, was a source of pride for some Kurds. Discussing this with a Kurdish woman, I remarked that Uca's electoral victory was '*Hayret bir şey*' ('A surprise'). She promptly responded, '*Hayret değil güzel bir şey*' ('It's not surprising, it's wonderful'). Interview, 8 June 2015.
105. Van Bruinessen, 'The Kurds and Islam'.
106. Interview, Diyarbakır, 10 June 2015. Jewish Kurds are few in number and tend not to be found in Turkey. Izady notes that Judaism was well established among Kurds by the second century: Izady, *The Kurds*, p. 162. It has also been noted that Christianity was accepted among many Kurds by the third century and that vestigial practices remain in some parts: see Jwaideh, *The Kurdish National Movement*, pp. 18–19.

107. Gurses, *Anatomy of a Civil War*, p. 89.
108. Interview, Diyarbakır, 21 October 2014.
109. Interview, Diyarbakır, 8 June 2015.
110. White, *Muslim Nationalism and the New Turks*, pp. 102–6.
111. Interview, Istanbul, 14 October 2014.
112. Leezenberg, 'The ambiguities of democratic autonomy', p. 203.
113. Izady, *The Kurds*, p. 135.
114. Jwaideh, *The Kurdish National Movement*, pp. 18–21.
115. Izady, *The Kurds*, p. 136.
116. Latif, 'Thanks to extremism', 28 May 2015.
117. Szanto, '"Zoroaster was a Kurd!"', pp. 96–110.
118. Bengio (ed.). 'The Kurdish momentum', pp. 269–81.
119. Gurses, 'Is Islam a cure for ethnic conflict?', p. 137.
120. *Oda TV*, 'HDP'nin Cuma namazı buluşmasında neler yaşandı', 4 March 2016.
121. *Cumhuriyet*, 'Demirtaş da katılmıştı', 7 December 2016.
122. *Diken*, 'AKP'li Göktaş'tan 'ilahi' vaat', 16 March 2019.

5

CONTESTING HOMELAND(S): CITY, SOIL AND LANDSCAPE

According to a Kurdish proverb, 'Damascus is all sugar, but one's homeland is sweeter.'[1] Attachment to land is a powerful element of identity and source of legitimation. Readily apparent in discussion and debate among Kurds is an insistence on highlighting the historical continuity of the Kurdish presence in and connection to the lands they live in (which extend beyond Turkey into Iran, Iraq and northern Syria). Christopher Houston links this to Kurdish attempts at nation building, albeit in circumstances where the Kurds lack a state of their own. Houston remarks that such brandishing of historical validation narratives is standard practice across the Middle East, a way of using the past as a 'key political resource in the present'.[2] Anthony Smith notes 'an association with a specific "homeland"' as one of his attributes of *ethnie*.[3] Many Kurds demonstrate a strong connection to a home town, even among those who have migrated to larger cities due to disruption or to seek economic opportunities.[4] This may be seen as an 'objective' aspect of identity, in that these sites relate to something 'tangible', the places where Kurds currently live and have done so throughout history.

Yet the delineation of a homeland or claiming of a territory must also be subjective. Different peoples may construe landscapes in different ways, and may, indeed, make competing claims over territory. The Republic of Turkey sees Diyarbakır and Anatolia's south-east as intrinsic parts of its sovereign territory even though relatively few ethnic Turks would look upon these as homeland/home town.⁵ Kurds, on the other hand, can point to the south-eastern provinces and demonstrate long-standing family ties. Thus, establishing a link to a specific territory – inherently immutable – can act as an 'anchor' for Kurdish ethnic identity, but it also becomes a point of contention between Kurds and the state.

'*Toprak*': Naming, Claiming and Relating to the Landscape

Ümit Cizre describes the territory of modern Turkey as an 'ethnic mosaic of the Anatolian rectangle inherited from the Ottoman Empire'.⁶ Such a situation was an unpalatable reality for the founders of the Republic who sought to call into being a homogenous political entity. They attempted to stamp out the Kurdish language, which flew in the face of claims of homogeneity. The map also did so – it revealed, alongside Turkish nomenclature, place names in a litany of other languages. To solve this conundrum the state embarked on a project of 'toponymical engineering', whereby, in a parallel to social engineering, the map was re-annotated to remove topographical features that testified to Anatolia's multi-ethnic history.⁷

In south-east Anatolia the re-annotation of the map assumed more urgency because the Turkish footprint on the landscape and proportion of the population was particularly limited. The population of Diyarbakır province in the early twentieth century was indicative; aside from Turks, it included Kurds, Arabs, Armenians, Assyrians (of various denominations), Jews, Kızılbaş (Alevis) and Zazas. As a result, the map featured a preponderance of villages with Arab, Armenian, Assyrian and Kurdish names.⁸ These place names testified to the ethnic diversity of the region; a further uncomfortable truth was that these peoples' presence in Anatolia predated that of the Turks, thus calling into question the notion of the Turkish homeland. Until 1980, according to Senem Aslan, the cartographic re-categorisation of south-east and eastern Turkey resulted in the renaming of two-thirds of the subdistricts and over 60 per cent of villages.⁹ Diyarbakır itself came in for reclassification, being so named by Atatürk in 1937, a Turkish rendering of 'the Land of Copper' to replace the Ottoman name of Diyarbekir (from the Arabic, 'Land of Bekir').¹⁰

The renaming of places was a means of asserting control, of enforcing uniformity in the name of national cohesion. James C. Scott posits this as standard practice among 'high modernist' states that act to make societies 'legible', or manageable in the pursuit of a vision of modernity. In Scott's estimation, such attempts to bring about a 'fixed social order' rarely succeed, as they fail to recognise 'local knowledge' or local political sensibilities that may help or hinder them.[11] The Turkish imperative was to recalibrate the concept of 'Turkey', shifting from an ethnic nation to a territorial or civic nation, amalgamating – or assimilating – the diverse peoples of Anatolia into a single national identity. In this it, too, paid no heed to local voices or demands. Anthony Smith contends such circumstances often result in ethnic dissent[12] – the persistence of the so-called Kurdish issue is an example of this. The intention to recast the map, and landscape, as uniformly Turkish was not an attempt to sever Kurds' connection to the land, but to re-categorise the land that they were attached to and them with it. Ultimately many Kurds refused to be absorbed into Turkishness; indeed, they did not even accede to the re-annotation of the map. Many Kurds still refer to locations by their 'old' names, including attaching the Kurdish name Amed to Diyarbakır.

For Harold Isaacs, 'the place, the land, the soil' to which a group is 'attached' forms a 'physical element' of that identity. Isaacs argued that the peoples' interactions with the land were seminal: the 'environment itself powerfully shapes the history, mores and character of the group and the life patterns of its individual members'.[13] This may be less so in a modern, largely urbanised polity, where the *political*, rather than physical, environment has more powerful impacts on the 'mores and character' of any group, and indeed how the group conceives and asserts its identity.[14] But that is not to say that attachment to the land does not remain an important element of identity.

Walker Connor highlights the 'spiritual bond' between nation and territory as enunciated by the German couplet, '*Blut und Boden*' ('blood and soil').[15] Some Kurds I spoke with made equivalent links between ethnic identity and *toprak* (Turkish: earth, soil). Zehra saw it as key to her Kurdishness, 'First of all, I am a Kurd because I grew up on this land (*bu topraklarda*). I identify myself first as a Kurd, not a Muslim. This is because I first identify myself with my language, my family, my environment, the earth (*toprak*), water, air. All amount to being a Kurd . . . The language, culture and land (*toprak*) they come from are very important for shaping someone's identity.'[16] Musa saw *toprak* as an essential component of identity, equivalent in weight to language, stating, 'Earth (*toprak*) is very important for you because if you don't have earth you are nothing.'[17] For Osman, a teacher in Diyarbakır, his Kurdishness was not defined by the modern classifications of nation-states, but on his presence in south-east Anatolia: 'I also define myself as a Kurd. I am not Turkish ("*Türkiyeli*"), but I see myself as a Kurd living on Kurdish land. This could be interpreted or perceived differently by others, saying I am "Turkish" or "Iranian", but I see myself as a Kurd who has been living on this land since the history of Kurds began.'[18]

Other Diyarbakır natives highlighted the pull that *toprak* retains. Dilek, who was born in Diyarbakır but whose family had fled the political tensions of the 1990s to live in Malatya, explained her recent return to Diyarbakır after graduating from university. 'When I left here I was so small, so I always wanted to come back to Diyarbakır and live here. Now I am here. And I am happy. It's my *toprak*. *Toprak* always calls you.'[19] Mehmet's family was from Diyarbakır but moved to Iznik, where he grew up, to seek economic opportunities. Now returned to Diyarbakır, he recalled his parents' desire to return to live near his grandparents, who had been unwilling to leave the city: 'My [parents] missed their family too. We came back. Of course it's important for us . . . for my family, my grandfather, they are old people, you know. They . . . love [their] *toprak*.'[20] For both Dilek and Mehmet, *toprak* – in this case the soil, or earth, of Diyarbakır – is of central importance to them and their families. We might argue that, for them, there is an intrinsic link between family and *toprak*. Location feeds into their sense of identity, such that it 'called' them when they were not there. These are very personal attachments, ties to the land contributing to individual identities.

Ties to location are an important marker of authenticity in Turkey. Jenny White recalls a discussion in Istanbul with someone who impugned a politician he saw as lacking any specific locational affiliation. White argues this is evidence of a Turkish mentality that prioritises being 'rooted to location'; being so positioned grants 'loyalty, honour and recognisable sociable identity'.[21] Echoing this, Behram, a Diyarbakır teahouse owner, once told me, 'We are Kurdish; real Kurdish.' When I asked him what he meant, he explained that his family had lived in Diyarbakır for over three hundred years. In Behram's eyes, his family's long association with Diyarbakır, the pre-eminent Kurdish city in Turkey, lent authenticity to their identity as Kurds.[22]

Association with location may not only serve as a marker of ethnic authenticity but has also been disputed in other contexts in Turkey's contested political arena. Yael Navaro-Yashin documents how the Turkish term *yerellik* (literally: native-ness) assumed currency in the 1990s dialectic between proponents of secular and Islamic lifestyles. Debate raged as to whether wearing the headscarf – or not wearing it – were examples of *yerellik*, that is, whether it was something that was the norm in Anatolia and thus was authentically Turkish.[23] *Yerellik* stems from the Turkish word for 'place' (*yer*), but it also demarcates 'local culture', the implication being that something that can be tied to a location (*yer*) or associated with the land has more legitimacy, a more authentic identity.

Yerellik became an element of the political armoury of the AKP when, after the inconclusive election of 7 June 2015, President Recep Tayyip Erdoğan appealed to constituents to vote into parliament 'local and national' ('*yerli ve milli*') deputies in the follow-up election of November.[24] This may be seen as a thinly disguised appeal to the nationalist impulses of the electorate to vote against HDP candidates. The evocation of '*yerli and milli*' representatives would seem to imply that HDP candidates, many of whom are Kurdish, should not be considered truly '*yerli*' (which translates literally as 'of the place'). Alternatively, this call may be seen as exhorting the electorate to be wary of external intervention or manipulation of the vote, a pitfall that can only be avoided by voting for the AKP.[25] In 2018, Erdoğan was to appeal to the main opposition party, the CHP, as 'local and national' friends to support the invasion of Kurdish-controlled Afrin in northern Syria, at the same time calling into question the loyalty of the HDP and warning it against protesting the military campaign.[26] Later the same year, while rationalising the AKP's alliance with the hard-line nationalist MHP for the forthcoming general election, Erdoğan argued that the CHP did not, in fact, maintain a 'local and national' outlook.[27] In all of these instances, Erdoğan is putting forth himself – and his political allies – as the sole defenders of 'local and national' interests, and thus the only ones who are authentic representatives of the '*yer*', of Turkey's *toprak*. In this way, as he has done with religion, Erdoğan has politicised the idea of place, of soil, claiming a monopoly on political legitimacy, and thus repudiating the claims to such of the HDP, or Kurds, or anyone else who opposes him.

Diyarbakır: symbolic city

If landscape or soil can be an element of identity, can urban locations also be so? Behram's claim, cited earlier, suggests such a position. He declared that his family were 'real Kurdish' due to their centuries-long residence in Diyarbakır.[28] Mehlika, an office worker who had been raised in Izmir, explained to me that she had moved to Diyarbakır to affirm and fortify her Kurdishness, particularly through the language. 'I haven't been able to connect with the language much. That is why I chose to come here, so I can learn,' she said.[29] Muna Güvenç recounts a similar link being made between Kurdish identity and Diyarbakır. In 2007 she met a university student who had moved from a village to the city and thereupon learned of her Kurdishness. 'Before, I didn't know that I was a Kurd,' the student remarked. 'As I have lived here, now I know that I am a Kurd. Kurd is my identity.'[30] These examples demonstrate different ways in which Diyarbakır features within Kurdish identity.

Diyarbakır certainly looms large in the Kurdish imagination. It is widely touted as the capital of any putative Kurdistan; on repeat trips to the city I have been told by Kurds that it is their *baş kent* (Turkish: 'capital city'). In quotes too many to relate here, Kurds have explained to me this status on the basis of many different factors: its large population, historical significance, architectural heritage, its economic, political and social importance, its city walls and the eleventh-century Ulu Cami (Great Mosque).[31] One Kurdish man in Istanbul's Gedikpaşa neighbourhood even referred to it as 'the Paris of Kurdistan'.[32] Whatever the justification, Kurds I met with intoned a constant refrain of Diyarbakır's importance.

This symbolic attachment to the city echoes Anna Grabolle-Çeliker's record of sometimes wistful evocations of village life among Kurdish communities in Istanbul. She notes that tales of village life were tinged with nostalgia, noting that attachment to the village was a 'way of belonging', or adhering to a Kurdish identity amid the rush of modern life in Istanbul.[33] Notably, only a handful of participants in this study made any mention of village life as being significant to them personally. Rather, interviewees, including those in Istanbul, embraced Diyarbakır as a pole of Kurdish identity. In this sense, perhaps the city, rather than village life, now constitutes a 'way of belonging' for Kurdish communities that are largely urbanised.

Figure 5.1 The Hasan Paşa Han, Diyarbakır, November 2014. © William Gourlay.

Diyarbakır is also internationally recognised as a node in the Kurdish struggle broadly defined and is often referred to as a Kurdish – rather than Turkish – city. It has been a touchstone for international journalists and for the US military since the 1990–1 Gulf War. Lokman is one of several fifty-something Kurdish men I have met on trips to Diyarbakır who have repertoires of stories working as fixers for journalists and military personnel dating back to this period. In October 2014, when ISIS was active in northern Syria, I regularly encountered journalists, film-makers and Kurdish fixers (some of whom were of Syrian origin) in the hotel lobbies and cafes of Diyarbakır. They gathered here before crossing into Syria or Iraq to cover the campaign – largely conducted by Kurdish forces – against ISIS. International observers know that Diyarbakır is the place to find Kurdish contacts and ensure an entry into a Kurdish community that stretches across borders. The itinerary of EU delegations discussing Turkey's accession process routinely included Diyarbakır, alongside Istanbul and Ankara, a recognition of its pivotal importance in Kurdish politics (and by extension its importance to the democratisation process in Turkey). These visits also lend credence to its 'status as informal Kurdish capital'.[34]

Capital or otherwise, Zeynep Gambetti argues the city was long subject to Turkish colonisation but then began throwing off its colonialist baggage.[35] This proceeded apace during the 2000s, following the election of the pro-Kurdish HADEP to the municipality (People's Democracy Party, an earlier incarnation of the HDP), which, according to Nicole Watts, instilled a new 'public-spiritedness as disaffected locals threw their weight behind individuals perceived as "one of their own"'.[36] In this new milieu, a departure from the 1990s when an oppressive military presence weighed upon the city, Diyarbakır's public sphere blossomed to incorporate new 'political and intellectual networks'.[37] Occurring simultaneously was the refurbishment of – and celebration of – the city's architectural legacy, not only sites of Kurdish, or Islamic, significance, but also the churches of the Armenian, Syriac and Chaldean communities. Reflecting on this in 2008, Osman Baydemir, mayor of Greater Diyarbakır, enthused that 'Diyarbakır has become the brand city of art and culture' for the entire Middle East.[38] The reclaiming of Diyarbakır's urban spaces built a heightened sense of Kurdish pride – and nationalism[39] – further evidence of the important role that the city plays in the constitution of Kurdish identity.

If recent positive political developments in Diyarbakır foster a sense of Kurdishness, traumatic historical events also earmark the city as significant for Kurds, and contribute to its role in the constitution of Kurdish identity. Refik commented, 'Diyarbakır is the geography where Kurds lived through the most suffering ("*en çok acı yasadiği bir coğrafiya*"). This region has witnessed grief since Ottoman times. Because of this, [and for] political and cultural reasons, it is a very important city.'[40] I would argue that a history of 'suffering' adds to its historical importance. But of course, while Kurdish history is replete with incidents of suffering it is also the case that most of these spurred resistance from Kurdish populations. Thus, Diyarbakır becomes a city of pain and loss but also a city where resistance and solidarity are forged, and in so doing it becomes a beacon of Kurdishness. Grabolle-Çeliker recorded among Kurds from Van a lament that they had become 'assimilated' and were thus less authentically Kurdish than those from Diyarbakır.[41]

Many Kurds I spoke with touted Diyarbakır as a centre of Kurdish mobilisation and struggle against state impositions. For Ali, 'It's . . . important that in this city the resistance was first raised. It makes Diyarbakır very important [historically]. So, anybody . . . if they are Kurdish, if they know . . . the reality of this country, they would say Diyarbakır – Amed – is very important for Kurds. Because the problems started [laughs] here.' There is a rueful aspect to Ali's response, who later explained how he had 'grown up under the shadow of weapons'.[42] His laughter when mentioning the 'problems' starting was not flippant, but a recognition of the irony that Diyarbakır's traumatic past contributed to its importance in the present. Musa similarly noted that many PKK operations occurred in and operatives came from the city and province, commenting, '. . . And Diyarbakır had too many, y'know, Turkish people say "terrorists", but we say "heroes".'[43]

The city's traumatic history extends to the founding of the Republic of Turkey. The Sheikh Said Rebellion of 1925, the first major Kurdish rebellion against the Republic of Turkey, was conducted mostly in Diyarbakır province,[44] something that often arose in my conversations with Kurds. As the first major challenge to state policies of centralisation and ethnic homogenisation, the Sheikh Said Rebellion had a formative effect on Turkey's Kurdish policy and subsequent measures aimed at quelling Kurdish identity and culture.[45] By the same token, the rebellion set a precedent for Kurdish assertiveness and resistance to state initiatives, something that resonates for Kurds – and Turks – to this day. Thus, Diyarbakır has been a central locus of contention for almost a century.

Diyarbakır's significance also extends to its status as a centre of Kurdish thought and political mobilisation. Diyarbakır residents assured me that it remained a beacon for all Kurds. Lokman commented, 'All [cities] are important . . . but one can always be a guide to others. It is Amed. Why? If a movement starts from Diyarbakır, other people follow . . . So we are . . . their guide, the other cities' guide.'[46] Gelaz similarly remarked, 'Thoughts, ideas and our pulse beat here. Here is the town centre for intellectual thoughts.' Esra, a journalist who travels regularly among Kurdish populations, corroborates this: 'If you go to . . . Turkish Kurdistan, you will see that a lot of people look at what Diyarbakır is saying politically . . . and what they are discussing here. And even in the municipalities, those municipalities look at what the municipality here is doing. So [for] Kurdish people politically, culturally, the heart is here.'[47] This extends to Syria and Iraq, according to Esra: 'I was in Erbil, in Zakho and Dohuk, and when I say I am from Amed everybody helps me, because it is like someone came from the capital.' Semih recounts similar resonances from his travels in Iran and Iraq: 'Diyarbakır is important for Kurds in Iran and Iraq. People see Diyarbakır as being engaged in politics. Diyarbakır is a symbol, it has a symbolic importance.'

Contesting Diyarbakır/Amed

Diyarbakır's symbolic importance is not lost on anyone, neither Turk nor Kurd. Many Kurds seek to further 'Kurdify' the city, referring to it by its Kurdish name, Amed.[48] This comes from Amida, a name dating to at least the Byzantine era.[49] The official labelling of the city as Diyarbakır dates only to the 1930s, when Atatürk dubbed the city as such, thus Kurdish insistence on labelling the city Amed is a pushback against Turkish encroachment. Turks during the Seljuk and Ottoman eras had used the name Hamid or Kara Hamid,[50] but in modern Turkey speaking of Amed leaves one open to angry or dismissive responses. On a TV broadcast in late 2015, Erdoğan retorted, '*Amed ne ya?*' ('What is Amed?'), upon hearing that then Prime Minister Ahmet Davutoğlu had used that name on a campaign billboard.[51]

Turkish officialdom's wariness of alternative names for the city runs deep because, by dint of their historical use by Arab, Armenian and Assyrian communities, they further testify to the faint Turkish imprint on the city and the province. From the early years of the Republic, Turkish elites made a concerted effort to implant Turkish culture into the landscape of the southeast, with Diyarbakır, the city and province, intended to become a showcase of Turkishness.[52] The process of propagating Turkishness was accompanied by revisionist initiatives that often went to absurd lengths, such as purportedly academic works that made unsupported assertions about the Turkish provenance of the city and certain historical landmarks, including the Ulu Camii, which had, in fact, been built during the Byzantine era and began life as a cathedral.[53]

Conversely, I argue that Kurdish attempts to reclaim the city are, at times, not only a matter of 'Kurdification' but also of acknowledging the city's diverse historical make-up. This has been underway since Kurdish-run parties claimed the mayoralty in 1999 and is apparent in Diyarbakır's fabric. Travelling by bus on the D950 Highway in 2014, I was greeted, as all are, on the city outskirts by a large road sign welcoming visitors in Kurdish, Turkish and Syriac. In the Sülüklü Han, a refurbished seventeenth-century caravanserai in Sur, the walled old city, a wall panel outlines a brief history of the building in six languages (and four scripts): Turkish, Syriac, Armenian, Arabic, and Kurdish dialects of Kurmanji and Zazaki. That such signs could be erected in Diyarbakır demonstrates the different political milieu that prevails compared to earlier decades. Travelling to the city in the 1990s I observed that officials did not tolerate manifestations of Kurdish or other identities. Multilingual signs that have been erected outside and within the city were not an AKP undertaking, but were the initiative of the Kurdish mayor of Sur, Abdullah Demirbaş. The municipality also undertook from 2006 to provide *çok dilli belediyecilik* (multilingual governance), offering information in Turkish, Kurdish, Armenian and Syriac, to highlight the city's diversity and to promote mutual respect and understanding.[54] Demirbaş was outspoken in his advocacy for his constituents, regardless of their ethnicity. He remarked in a 2013 interview, 'I'm not just fighting for Kurds but for the diversity of this region. Assyrian Christians, the Armenians, the Arabs – for the last 85 years we've been told there are only Turks and only one religion.'[55] Through these and other measures, the Diyarbakır municipality worked to assert an alternative identity on the city, reversing the homogenisation of earlier eras and recognising the city's multi-ethnic past.[56] In so doing they were repudiating Turkish claims to and co-option of Diyarbakır.

Individual Kurds I met with also readily highlighted their city's multi-ethnic and multi-confessional history. A stallholder in the Diyarbakır bazaar assured me that only thirty years ago there had been Christians, Jews, Assyrians and many Armenians ('*en çok Ermeni*') still resident in the city, but commented that they had left for Europe 'for political reasons'.[57] During my visits to Diyarbakır, the café alongside the recently restored Armenian Surp Giragos Cathedral was a popular hangout, while the church itself accepted a steady stream of visitors. In June 2013 I attended a packed concert at the cathedral featuring a programme of Kurdish, Armenian and Turkish music and poetry. Mehdi, a Diyarbakır-born Kurd resident in Istanbul, told me, 'Before the Armenian genocide, before the Yezidi genocide, before the coups, we usually lived together – it's our reality.'[58] Zehra contended, 'Diyarbakır is a place where different ethnic groups can come together . . . allowing them to make something great. This has always happened in Diyarbakır.'[59] As with the acknowledgement of religious diversity among Kurds, the diverse multi-confessional legacy of the city was cited proudly and was sometimes brandished as a distinguishing feature between Kurds and Turks. Şahin commented, 'There are many ethnicities living here, and in history too . . . They all live together, therefore the city is very important.'⁶⁰ Gelaz noted, 'This city is important for Armenians, Syriacs and Kurds. The Turks never liked the people in Diyarbakır. That's why there are no other Turks besides . . . police and soldiers. The Turks have no historical significance with Diyarbakır.'⁶¹

Acknowledgement of ethnic diversity in the city is not confined to historical recollections. Incidents I witnessed suggest that the residents of Sur neighbourhood hold members of the small Assyrian community in high regard. In 2013, when I was seeking out the Assyrian Meryemana Church, a local offered me directions and then asked that I send his warm regards to the *papaz* (priest). Another time, a porter in the Diyarbakır bazaar proudly told me that the priest was his *komşi* (Diyarbakır dialect for 'neighbour') whose children played with his own. At the general election in June 2015, I saw the priest entering a polling booth. A Kurdish bystander assured me that the priest – and all Assyrians – would vote for the pro-Kurdish HDP.⁶² '*Hepimiz HDP'liyiz* [We are all with the HDP]' he said. Whether or not this is true, in so doing he was implicitly counting the Assyrians as constituent elements of the 'we' who were facing off against Erdoğan and the AKP.

Acceptance of the Assyrian community mirrors that of the Armenians. Kurds have warmly embraced Mıgırdiç Margosyan, an Armenian writer who grew up in Diyarbakır's Hançepek quarter in the 1940s, and championed him as a native son.⁶³ Several Kurdish politicians have also made attempts to come to terms with the traumas of the Armenian genocide of 1915. In Diyarbakır the municipality supported the refurbishment of the Surp Giragos Cathedral, another measure that reversed the Turkification of the city. Here it is possible to draw parallels between the Kurds' struggle for recognition and rights in Turkey with that of the Armenians. A local Armenian woman was reported as saying that given the Kurds' own efforts to assert their rights, they could not 'deny the same rights for us [Armenians]'.⁶⁴ Shared history and status as disenfranchised minorities have in fact fostered a sense of kinship for some Kurds and Armenians. Diyarbakır-born ethnic Armenian Aram Tigran was one of the best-loved proponents of Kurdish music. He famously remarked, 'There is no distinction between Turk, Kurd, Arab and Armenian.

We are brothers.'⁶⁵ Meanwhile, American journalist Meline Toumani, upon having her Armenian heritage revealed to a group of Kurdish students, was promptly told, 'You are our brother!'⁶⁶ Similarly, a Kurdish schoolteacher in a village outside Diyarbakır told me, 'We are just like the Armenians; the only difference is that we are Muslim.'⁶⁷ As Toumani notes, such declarations may be expressions of equality and open-mindedness, but they also conveniently serve as repudiations of the Turkish status quo. In Diyarbakır, Kurds' acknowledgement of the ongoing, albeit much diminished, presence of the Assyrians and Armenians, does the same thing.

The early Republic's efforts to recast Diyarbakır as entirely Turkish amounted to little, meanwhile. Indeed, an influx of ethnic Turks into the Diyarbakır region after the 1930s had the opposite effect to that intended: Turkish settlers gradually became Kurdified rather than Turkifying the locals.⁶⁸ In the Turkish imagination the city and the broader south-east region remained Turkey's 'Inner Orient', with predictably dire associations, from lawlessness to backwardness, to ethnic 'Otherness' – but not Turkishness.⁶⁹ Such associations were inflamed by the PKK insurgency that began in the mid-1980s. In 1992, when I first travelled in Turkey as a backpacker and I mentioned to a Turkish hotelier in Cappadocia that I planned to visit Diyarbakır he was aghast, warning me that it was a den of murderers. Two decades later, when conducting research for this book and staying in Istanbul's Üsküdar neighbourhood, my comments that I had visited Diyarbakır many times continued to raise eyebrows.

In Turkey's political and social milieu, Diyarbakır remains a Kurdish city. Therein lies its potency and importance, and the reasons why it remains contested in Erdoğan's Turkey. Its pivotal role in the PKK insurgency means that for many it is the 'city of the Kurdish intifada',⁷⁰ hence the warning I received before first visiting. By the same token, its role as a political and symbolic capital make it crucial in the Turkish state's approach to the Kurdish issue, whether that involves military campaigns or political overtures. This paradox is captured in descriptions of the city as both 'gateway to democracy and fortress'.⁷¹ If the Republic of Turkey is to bring an end to the Kurdish issue it must either undermine Diyarbakır's value as a political symbol, while simultaneously crushing the PKK, or it must win the city over amid processes of negotiation and democratisation. The government has long been aware of this. In 1999, then Prime Minister Mesut Yılmaz remarked that 'the road to the EU passes through Diyarbakır',[72] an acknowledgement that solving the grievances of Kurds with respect to human rights violations and lack of democracy would speed Turkey's EU approval process. Turkish politicians have also historically chosen Diyarbakır as a favourite location to make official pronouncements, and thus to win favour with the Kurdish electorate. It was during a 2005 speech in Diyarbakır that Erdoğan made his famous declaration that the Kurds required greater democracy rather than more repression.[73] In 2015, then Prime Minister Davutoğlu told a Diyarbakır gathering of his vision of a new Middle East that Turks, Kurds and Arabs would build in concert.[74] Meanwhile, it must be no coincidence that Diyarbakır was the scene for the announcement of Öcalan's PKK ceasefire on Newroz in 2013,[75] a declaration – and location – that can only have happened with government approval.

It would seem that to win kudos in Diyarbakır is to win Kurdish hearts and minds. But at the same time, the government has tried to undercut the importance of the city. This is apparent in the 2010 selection of Artuklu University in Mardin, rather than Diyarbakır's Dicle University, as the institution to house the first-ever Kurdish-language institute in a Turkish tertiary institution. Notably, this was dubbed the Yasayan Diller Enstitutusu (The Living Languages Institute). The intention here would appear to be threefold: firstly, to lump Kurdish in with other 'living' languages, thus rendering it in need of state 'protection' rather than recognising it as the second most-used language;[76] secondly, to ensure governmental oversight of how Kurdish-language studies proceed in Turkey; and thirdly, to elevate Mardin in the Kurdish imaginary, thus denting Diyarbakır's standing as primary centre of political and cultural activity.[77] In effect, Kurds are being allowed to have their cake, but the government is eating it. That is, the government appears to concede to Kurdish aspirations but at the same time it interferes in or attempts to manipulate the Kurdish status quo.

In late 2015, following the reignition of conflict with the PKK, official prevarication over Diyarbakır's status as either a key to resolving Kurdish tensions or a conflict zone fell decisively towards the latter. For the first time ever, PKK operatives brought their military campaigns into the urban centres of Diyarbakır, Cizre, Şırnak and other cities. The Turkish military struck forcefully in response to PKK encroachment, resulting in multiple casualties, displacement of populations and visiting unprecedented levels of destruction on these cities. Large sections of Sur neighbourhood, within the walls of Diyarbakır, were destroyed and later razed by government bulldozers.[78] Such was the destruction that, when looking at photos in early 2017, Mıgırdıç Margosyan, who claimed to know the city 'stone by stone', was unable to recognise his street or house.[79] Demet Arparcık found people hunkered down at this time too traumatised to leave their homes.[80] The government subsequently expropriated much of the area, including the historic churches of the neighbourhood.[81] The reappropriation of Sur offered an opportunity to reverse the Kurdish reclamation of the city. Prime Minister Davutoğlu remarked in early 2016 that the government would rebuild Sur from the ground up, as had happened to Toledo following the Spanish Civil War.[82] This suggestion received a scathing response from Kurds.[83] A state-directed rebuilding programme would allow unprecedented government control over the city, while also undercutting the authority of Kurdish administrators in Sur. Adding insult to injury, in late 2016 the government removed democratically elected mayors, the majority of them HDP, from Diyarbakır and a number of other municipalities on grounds of 'support for terrorism', replacing them with 'trustees'.[84] Some claim that the AKP allocated 'trustees' extra funds in order to provide expanded services and thus win popular approval;[85] other reports document moves by trustees to remove monuments to Kurdish figures from cities across the south-east.[86] In effect, these measures are attempts to reassert top-down control of daily life and urban fabric in Diyarbakır and other cities. Trustees did not move to directly deny the existence of Kurds, as had happened in earlier eras, but removed or demolished monuments commemorating civilians killed by Turkish forces and Ahmed Khani, the poet, that thus did not accord with the trustees' vision for Turkey. In this sense, the AKP may have maintained a version of multiculturalism, one that tolerated a Kurdish presence, but only on terms that it dictated.

Diyarbakır resonates in different symbolic ways – as a centre of thought, for its historical significance, as a 'capital city', as a site of Kurdification and of rejection of assimilation. However, as locus for political and cultural activity and a pole to which Kurds turn, a beacon of Kurdish identity, it remains contested, more so as Erdoğan moves to assert his hegemony over the Turkish polity. Yet, as Arparcık notes, despite residents of Diyarbakır feeling fearful in their traumatised city, their sense of Kurdish solidarity remains rock solid.[87]

Alternative Labels

Many Kurds relate to earth (*toprak*) and the city of Diyarbakır at a personal level; both play into conceptualisations of Kurdish identity. Such attachments can ascend to broader categorisations: to a collective identity and to the notion of a homeland. Anthony Smith notes the strategic use of 'landscapes or poetic spaces' in attempts to define and demarcate national identities.[88] The land is often portrayed as the 'cradle' of a people, 'where terrain and people have exerted mutual and beneficial influence over several generations'.[89] Walker Connor lists multiple examples, among them Kurdistan, where a national idea is reinforced when something 'mundanely tangible' (namely, the landscape where a people lives) is re-conceived, becoming the 'emotion-laden' homeland or motherland.[90] The bureaucrats and cartographers of the Republic of Turkey were aware of this – in their re-annotation of the map they were attempting to expunge any sense of a Kurdish (or Armenian, Arab or Assyrian) homeland, and present a clean – Turkified – slate, one that implied a Turkish homeland.

National territory carries 'baggage' with it, as T. K. Oomen highlights. This can encompass 'history, heritage, language, religion and race'. All of these linked aspects play into each other. For Oomen, a clearly defined homeland is an 'irreducible minimum' in the emergence of a nation.[91] I would contend that if an ethnic group is to be defined as something other than a diasporic or immigrant community then a homeland, however conceived, is similarly essential. In India, Oomen observes, 'attachment to the nation is primarily an attachment to the homeland', Mother India, rather than any sense of affiliation to the polity or community of peoples. He further notes that not just any piece of territory can be a homeland, citing the case of the Jews, who insisted on a return to their ancient homeland.[92] Enough of the constituent elements mentioned above – history, heritage, etc. – must be present to make a case for 'homeland' status. For Kurds, in constituting an ethnic identity distinct from that of the Turks, specifying a homeland is required, one to which Kurdish communities can demonstrate a physical link.

Mesopotamia and Anatolia

One way of highlighting a physical link is to evoke historical or alternative labels and establish a Kurdish presence at the time such labels were in use. In my discussions with Kurds some reached back into history to evoke a Mesopotamian identity and connection. Doing so serves several purposes. It firstly repudiates the state's reclassification of the map and establishes a long-standing Kurdish link with the land. In an indicative comment, Refik asserted, 'Mesopotamia belongs to the Kurds, it is our homeland, our *toprak* . . . this is my native land (*burası benim toprağıdır*).'[93] Claims to a Mesopotamian heritage by Kurds are also claims to prior occupancy, to legitimacy and, for some Kurdish nationalists, to ownership. There was no Turkish presence in Anatolia until the eleventh century, so in claiming a link that extends back to 'Mesopotamia', a term that dates to the era of Alexander the Great (c. 330 BC), Kurds were drawing attention to the fact that the Kurdish presence preceded that of the Turkish. This current recurred in interviews. Refik argued, 'We have existed in these lands for years. We are a nation, a single community that existed since the time of Mesopotamia. Later, Turks came from Central Asia and called us citizens of this country, which is not acceptable. Because we were here [before them] in these lands.'[94] Zehra argued the Kurdish presence predated and thus invalidated Turkish claims: 'From history, we have lived on these lands, these lands are ours. This is where we live but people invaded from Central Asia and conquered these lands and took them from us. Then they told us that they are going to manage us and that we are their citizens. Is there anything more ridiculous than this? This is Cengiz Han's [Genghis Khan's] dream, but I don't want him to be happy.'[95] Some Kurds drew a link between this long presence and status as 'natives', but clearly not in a way in which Turkish nationalists who evoke '*yerellik*' would approve. Lokman commented, 'Living in Mesopotamia . . . we are native people. Turks came later on. We are the original people . . . So I don't consider myself as an ethnic [minority] here. I believe I am a native.'[96]

This emphasis on prior residence is an important way for Kurds to distinguish themselves from Turks and to fend off attempts to be absorbed into the catch-all category of Turkishness. Donald Horowitz notes that it is commonplace to underline indigenousness or prior occupation in the case of large-scale immigration of another ethnic group.⁹⁷ Horowitz refers to cases involving contemporary local populations fearing subjugation or loss of position to itinerant workers. The situation is different in Turkey, where the Turkish presence is almost a thousand years old, but the principle is the same. To assert their existence and difference, Kurds call upon their long-standing presence in south-eastern Anatolia. Alev Çınar writes that a nation may 'declare[s] itself into being through the writing of history', by asserting its 'eternal presence that is validated by its historicity'.⁹⁸ This would particularly be so where the 'nation', or the ethnic group, has been written out of the history books, as happened with the Kurds in Turkey. However, in their evocations of Mesopotamia and other ancient links to the land, Kurds are not necessarily making a claim to the territory itself, in the sense of creating their own independent polity. They are claiming prior occupancy as a point of distinction from the Turkishness that the state decrees.

Referring to Mesopotamia is also a way of calling into question the legitimacy of the Republic of Turkey and, by extension, its political claim over the Kurds. To that end, the Kurdish political movement has appropriated Mesopotamia as a label, attaching it to radio and TV stations, arts organisations and cultural centres.⁹⁹ The Mesopotamia Social Forum, a civil society event organised in Diyarbakır in 2009 and 2011, is one such example. As Marlies Casier notes, it can be seen as an attempt to create 'an alternative political imaginary and consequent political project in answer to the socio-political realities it holds responsible for existing inequalities'.¹⁰⁰ Those particular 'socio-political realities' are the international borders that divide Kurdish populations and the constraints that are placed upon these populations by national regimes that have agendas that do not extend to the protection of Kurdish rights, and, historically, have often led to their repression. Thus, the use of the Mesopotamia label, and associated imagery, is a mechanism in Turkey and beyond to 'signify a Kurdish identity, the Kurdist cause'.¹⁰¹ It is a conscious effort to situate Kurdish identity within an indisputable history that allots them a legitimate space among the peoples of the region. That many Kurds I spoke to readily referred to Mesopotamia within discussions of identity and perspectives on their political circumstances in Turkey is a measure of the influence of the Kurdish nationalist movement's broader political discourses on the world views of Kurds at street level.

Yet during my discussions it was noticeable that within this appropriation of Mesopotamia terminology many Kurds claim themselves as one people among many, not the only Mesopotamian people. Soner, interviewed in Istanbul, remarked on the historicity of Mesopotamia and emphasised that, 'It's like a pot of mixed cultures since the early stages of history . . . It's the same for Anatolia, too. It doesn't belong to one identity. So . . . I like to describe myself like I'm from Mesopotamia.'[102] For Mesut, claiming a Mesopotamian heritage was a point of pride: 'To be born in this geography is very important. Because you [are familiar with] different cultures. Kurds are one of the very old nations here and one of the native nations of Mesopotamia. We are not . . . [opposed to] Turkish identity. We think that Turks, Armenians, Suriyani, [Assyrians] different nations can live together. For that you should have [a] democratic regime, you should have peace with other nations.'[103] In this way, Mesopotamia is a label that allows scope for broader accommodation of ethnicities, while also being clearly distinct from Turkey, which carries its own ethnic overtones. So here, again, Kurds are marking themselves as distinct from the Turks, who, in the Kurdish imagination, emphasise – and impose – ethnic uniformity. Kurdish evocations of Mesopotamia do not stamp an exclusively Kurdish claim on the area, but, as was the case with their acknowledgement of diversity within religious observance and of the historical diversity of Diyarbakır's population, they herald acceptance of ethnic and cultural diversity, of pluralism, as a marker of Kurdishness in contradistinction to Turkish visions, either Kemalist ethnic conformity or AKP hegemony. These are acknowledgements of themselves among many peoples who have lived in the region. They define their identity as part of a canvas broader than a monocultural vision; they take pride in the acceptance of diversity, and take a stand against the Turkish status quo.

Another label applied to the Asian land mass of Turkey is that of Anatolia. Ayhan, a researcher in Istanbul, described himself as Anatolian as a way of incorporating disparate elements of his identity and upbringing. 'I am a Kurd. I received my education in Turkish. Officially I am a Turkish citizen. Or I could say I am Anatolian because I have visited many places there, I was educated there, I worked there. I have friends from every region, we have similar foods, we dance similar dances and we have similar songs.'[104]

Anatolia is a neutral descriptor: it carries no apparent ethnic implication, in contrast to 'Turkey' and 'Kurdistan'.[105] The concept of Anadoluculuk (literally 'Anatolianness') was even proposed as a shared identity, an alternative to Islamic, pan-Turkish and ill-defined pluralist Ottoman ideologies, in the late-Ottoman era.[106] One man I met in Istanbul refused to specify whether he was Turkish or Kurdish, rather calling himself 'Anatolian'.[107] However, evocations of Anatolia by Kurds are relatively few, perhaps because during the Republic's nation-building period Anatolia was often portrayed as the cultural repository of Turkish identity. Kemalist ideologues 'imaginatively reconstructed' Anatolia, rather than other previously Ottoman-held territories in the Levant, the Balkans or the Caucasus, as a quintessentially 'Turkish' space.[108] In 1925, an article in the Kemalist periodical *Anadolu Mecmuası* (*Anatolian Journal*) stated categorically, 'Anatolia is only Anatolia, Anatolia is a strictly Turkish land.'[109] More recently, the term Anatolia has been used to obscure ethnic diversity. Meline Toumani notes that official publications at the 2007 reopening of the Armenian cathedral of Akdamar/Aghtamar blandly described the building as 'Anatolian', rather than acknowledging its Armenian provenance.[110] Thus Anatolia acts as a double-edged sword, quelling Turkish nationalists' qualms about acknowledging the country's ethnic diversity, but at the same time being used to obfuscate that very history. Perhaps for these reasons, Anatolia did not retain the currency that Mesopotamia did among Kurds as a historical label for the lands they and their predecessors occupied.

Kurdistan

The incorporation of Mesopotamia into PKK discourse echoes a broadening of its political agenda, moving beyond an initial goal of forging a 'Kurdistan'. Casier sees this as a continuation of PKK initiatives to 'rethink the spatial order of current politics', an initiative that does not aim to create a nation-state – Kurdistan – but is 'a project for autonomy, within its philosophy of a democratic society'.[111] Central to the assertion of Anatolia's innate Turkishness in the *Anadolu Mecmuası* article mentioned above was its repudiation of any mooted 'Kurdistan'. 'Kurdistan is a fabricated, imagined part of the map of Anatolia', the article continued. As should be understood from the re-annotation of the map, alternative topographies that bore witness to other ethnic identities were deemed a threat to the uniformity that Kemalists sought. By prime ministerial decree, in 1939 and 1940 German-language and French-language atlases and maps were outlawed, confiscated and destroyed because they contained the term 'Kurdistan'.[112]

It is not unusual to find Turks arguing on social media that there has never been a country called Kurdistan. One might respond that there was no country officially called Turkey until 1923 and that even if not demarcating a nation or country, 'Kurdistan' has been in long usage. It is found in Armenian sources that predate the arrival of Turks in Anatolia.[113] In the 1520s, under the rule of Ottoman Sultan Süleyman, one of the eight Ottoman provinces was called 'Kurdistan'[114] and by imperial decree the Kurdish provinces were autonomous.[115] It would appear that Turkish efforts here are, again, examples where they 'doth protest too much'. Kurds in response latch onto the long history of 'Kurdistan' as a cartographical term. Refik remarked, 'During the Ottoman time, Kurdistan was present. During the Seljuk time, Kurdistan existed. Kurdistan was geographically locatable and it was where Kurds lived. The ground, the soil, the houses all belonged to the Kurds.'[116]

In contention, then, is the political significance of 'Kurdistan'. It is, of course, a key symbolic resource and rallying cry of the Kurdish political movement and, I would argue, a central tenet of Kurdish identity. Maria O'Shea depicts 'Kurdistan' in the Kurdish imagination as a potent mélange of facts, myths and wishful thinking that persists despite divisions among Kurds and political circumstances that militate against such an idea.[117] Many Kurdish nationalists draw an explicit link between the ancient Medes and 'Kurdistan' as a means to highlight homogeneity among modern-day Kurds in spite of the political and territorial divisions which are apparent in the present.[118] In discussions, I encountered evocations of the historical Kurdish presence and the validity of the label 'Kurdistan'. Osman, a Diyarbakır teacher, argued, 'Yes, right now we are considered citizens of Turkey, but we have been living on this land (*topraklarda biz eskiden beri yaşıyoruz*) for years. We still consider it to be Kurdistan. Maybe formally and politically it is known as Turkey, but I never felt that.'[119] Osman's colleague, Fehim, remarked, 'We are from Kurdistan. These lands' (*toprakların*) name is Kurdistan no matter what anyone says.

Geographically this is Kurdistan, . . . but under the circumstances in Turkey I am considered a Turk . . . However, I would love to have a free Kurdistan. I see myself as a Kurd.'[120] It is from here that Turkish concern at the term arises – that it is intrinsically linked to separatist intent.

Yet applying an alternative toponomy does not automatically amount to a claim for independence, even if that new label may be 'Kurdistan'.[121] Michael Gunter opines that 'almost all Kurds dream of a united Kurdistan'. But in view of traumatic events responding to attempts during the twentieth century to establish – or even demand – independence, many Kurds take a pragmatic view of their political circumstances, resigning themselves to living within the boundaries of existing states, states that reacted swiftly and often brutally to Kurdish tilts at independence. Thus the signature cry of most Kurdish political organisations in the latter years of the twentieth century became 'Democracy for Turkey/Iraq/Iran and autonomy for the Kurds'.[122]

In the early 2000s, Bahar Başer found that diaspora Turkish communities in Sweden and Germany generally responded negatively to the term 'Kurdistan', some dismissing it as 'offensive' or 'pathetic'. Başer argues that it evoked a 'spectre of division' for these Turks.[123] No study has investigated public responses to 'Kurdistan' in Turkey, but, as indicated by earlier official blacklisting of atlases and maps that used the term, for many years even uttering it invited official and public reproach and censure.

The situation changed, however, during the years that the AKP engaged with the PKK on the peace process. In 2013 in Diyarbakır, at an event with Kurdish singer Şivan Perwer and Iraqi Kurdish leader Massoud Barzani, Erdoğan was recorded mentioning 'Kurdistan' for the first time. His statement incurred criticism from nationalist circles, but in a sign of the shifting political milieu and national discourse, he defended his position. He later remarked that Mustafa Kemal (Atatürk) had used the term, and that he could hardly be accused of being separatist,[124] thereby demonstrating that enunciating 'Kurdistan' should be possible in the Turkish polity and did not represent a threat to it. Here was another example of a more confident Turkey, a mature political arena, more pluralist, more open to diversity and debate.

As with so many apparent advances towards a political solution to the Kurdish issue, the pendulum was to swing back again following the political upheavals of 2015 and 2016. When HDP deputy Osman Baydemir remarked in parliament in 2017 that he represented 'Kurdistan within Turkey' he was roundly rebuked and later fined and temporarily excluded from parliament.[125] Thereafter official tolerance for the use of 'Kurdistan' declined. In early 2019, prosecutors brought proceedings against political organisations that had 'Kurdistan' in their names,[126] and board members of a Diyarbakır business council faced prosecution for using 'Kurdistan' in the association's name and articles of its charter.[127] While campaigning for municipal elections in February 2019, several HDP candidates mentioned representing 'Kurdistan'. Erdoğan reacted indignantly, retorting, 'If you really want a Kurdistan, there is one in northern Iraq. Goodbye to you.'[128] This would appear to be backtracking on his earlier tolerant position on the mentioning of Kurdistan, but here he stressed that there was no such region in Turkey, and played on latent fears of separatism by declaring that no one could divide Turkey. In response, HDP members in Istanbul came together to repudiate Erdoğan's ostracising language. HDP press officer Azad Barış underlined a commitment to the land and political system that prevailed, stating, 'Our homes, stories, loved ones, graves are all on this soil.'[129]

Kurdistan is undoubtedly controversial terminology in Turkey, but it may be variously interpreted. While it was once unutterable in any context, the Turkish state has been forced by circumstance to admit it as a reality, albeit one that must be confined to northern Iraq, hence outside of Turkey's borders. Simultaneously, Kurdistan may be used as a bogeyman in modern politics. Erdoğan's riposte to HDP members was likely intended as a put-down but it also played to the nationalist base in Turkey and played on underlying fears that the nation-state is threatened by Kurdish mobilisation. Conversely, many Kurds see the naming of territory as Kurdistan as a simple statement of fact, one that does not necessarily imply any separatist ambition.

Spatial Contestations: Identity and Politics

In drawing attention to their long presence in the lands that are now the south-eastern provinces of Turkey (and across borders in Syria, Iran and Iraq), in attaching alternative labels to the territory that dilute or repudiate official Turkish labels, Kurds are contesting the spatial order of modern Turkey. The claims they are making are explicitly political, but they are not necessarily territorial claims; rather they are claims in the realm of identity, a form of political capital. Asserting a link with the soil (*toprak*) or with Diyarbakır, in all of its guises whether as a capital city or centre of protest or politics or culture and intellectual activity, establishing the historical depth of the Kurds' presence in the region and re-conceiving that region as Mesopotamia or Anatolia or Kurdistan, are yet more mechanisms of Kurdish identification. They become means of forging internal cohesion – rallying points around which Kurds can coalesce – but also means of asserting difference from the Turkish uniformity that Kemalists, and more recently the AKP government, tried to impose.

Kurds in Turkey have greater freedom than in earlier decades to assert their presence in and connection to the landscape, yet contestations over labels and the very idea of 'localness' remain heated. Kurds may try to reclaim territory they see as colonised and may attach alternative labels to the landscape as a means of consolidating Kurdish identity, but in Erdoğan's Turkey implications remain. There are strict limits to what is tolerated. Repercussions may be profound, as the destruction and appropriation of Sur demonstrates, and in the current environment, where nationalist currents are resurgent and evocations of '*yerellik*' remain potent, Kurdish attitudes to and labels for the landscape may actually be used by Erdoğan as political ammunition to win favour from Turkish voters.

Notes

1. Anonymous, 'Proverbs of Kurdistan', p. 72.
2. Houston, *Kurdistan*, p. 2.
3. Smith, *National Identity*, p. 21.
4. Grabolle-Çeliker, *Kurdish Life in Contemporary Turkey*. It should be noted that an attachment to hometown is similarly held by Turks.
5. Mehrdad Irady claims that ethnic Turks have been 'streaming out of' Anatolia's south-east for western provinces since the 1960s. See Izady, *The Kurds*, p. 127.
6. Cizre, 'Turkey's Kurdish problem', p. 244.
7. Öktem, 'The nation's imprint'.
8. Üngör, *The Making of Modern Turkey*, pp. 12–13, 40, 243.
9. Aslan, 'Incoherent state'. On the multi-ethnic imprint on the Anatolian landscape, see the interactive map created by the Hrant Dink Foundation detailing Armenian, Syriac, Greek and Jewish sites: http://turkiyekulturvarliklari.hrantdink.org/en/.

10. Üngör, *The Making of Modern Turkey*, p. 244. This parallels Arabisation programmes in Iraq under Saddam Hussein.
11. Scott, *Seeing like a State*, pp. 91–3, 311–16.
12. Smith, *National Identity*, p. 134.
13. Isaacs, 'Basic group identity', pp. 44–5.
14. Indeed, Anna Grabolle-Çeliker notes that Kurdish identity is often more politicised among those from regions where the state's hand was more repressive: see Grabolle-Çeliker, *Kurdish Life in Contemporary Turkey*, p. 89.
15. Connor, *Ethnonationalism*, p. 205.
16. Interview, Diyarbakır, 21 October 2014.
17. Interview, Istanbul, 14 October 2014. *Toprak* is a concept that retains currency among Turks too. A well-loved song by twentieth-century minstrel Âşık Veysel Şatıroğlu is a paean to the Anatolian soil: 'Benim sâdık yârim kara topraktır' (My faithful beloved is the black earth).
18. Interview, Diyarbakır, 29 October 2014.
19. Interview, Diyarbakır, 8 June 2015.
20. Interview, Diyarbakır, 9 June 2015.
21. White, *Muslim Nationalism and the New Turks*, p. 106.
22. Interview, Diyarbakır, 22 October 2014. Behram was to repeat this claim when I visited again the following year, also declaring as 'real Kurdish', on the basis of long residence in the city, a local elder who often hovered in the street.
23. Navaro-Yashin, *Faces of the State*, p .20.
24. *Hürriyet*, 'Cumhurbaşkanı Erdoğan: '1 Kasım'da 550 tane yerli ve milli milletvekili istiyorum'', 21 September 2015.
25. Onuş, 'Erdoğan'ın kastettiği, "yerli ve milli" vekiller kim?', 21 September 2015.
26. *T24*, 'Erdoğan: Ey HDP, sokağa çıkarsanız biliniz ki güvenlik güçlerimiz sizin boynunuzdadır!', 21 January 2018.
27. *Posta*, 'Cumhurbaşkanı Erdoğan: CHP'nin bakışı yerli ve milli değil', 21 April 2018.
28. Interview, Diyarbakır, 22 October 2014. Behram also claimed that this long association with Diyarbakır meant that he spoke 'real Kurdish'. There is also a dialect of Turkish specific to Diyarbakır that is distinct from 'standard Turkish' and related to Azeri dialects of early Turkic settlers in Anatolia. See Dorleijn, 'Turkish–Kurdish language contact', pp. 79–80.
29. Interview, Diyarbakır, 29 October 2014.
30. Güvenç, 'Constructing narratives of Kurdish nationalism', pp. 25–40.

31. Home to important shrines, churches, monasteries and pilgrimage sites, the province of Diyarbakır is also of significance to other ethnic and religious groups: see Üngör, *The Making of Modern Turkey*, p. 14.
32. Private conversation, Istanbul, 4 November 2014.
33. Grabolle-Çeliker, *Kurdish Life in Contemporary Turkey*, p. 46.
34. Gambetti, 'Decolonizing Diyarbakır', p. 101.
35. Ibid.
36. Watts, 'Activists in office', pp. 135–6.
37. Yüksel, 'Rescaled localities and redefined class relations', pp. 433–55.
38. Cited in Yüksel, 'Rescaled localities and redefined class relations'.
39. Güvenç, 'Constructing narratives of Kurdish nationalism'.
40. Interview, Diyarbakır, 20 October 2014.
41. As well as other locations such as Hakkari and Şirnak, see Grabolle-Çeliker, *Kurdish Life in Contemporary Turkey*, p. 87.
42. Interview, Diyarbakır, 26 October 2014.
43. Interview, Istanbul, 14 October 2014.
44. Van Bruinessen, *Agha, Shaikh and State*, pp. 265–305.
45. Belge, 'State building and the limits of legibility', p. 99.
46. Interview, Diyarbakır, 11 June 2015.
47. Interview, Diyarbakır, 27 October 2014.
48. This extends to other realms, for example the changing of name of the Diyarbakır football team to become Amed Spor: see *Bianet*, 'Diyarbakır municipality FC adopts a Kurdish name', 29 October 2014. The move incurred the wrath of Turkish nationalists and the Turkish Football Federation.
49. Norwich, *A Short History of Byzantium*, p. 27.
50. See, for example, *Book of Dede Korkut*, p. 195. *Kara* (Turkish for 'black') refers to the city's signature basalt walls.
51. *Diken*, 'Erdoğan'ın 'Amed ne ya?' sorusuna yanıt Davutoğlu'nun 'Amed'li seçim afişinden', 30 October 2015.
52. Üngör, *The Making of Modern Turkey*, p. 170.
53. Ibid., pp. 234–5.
54. Güneş, *The Kurdish National Movement in Turkey*, p. 168.
55. Jones, 'Jail is occupational hazard for Kurdish mayor', 16 January 2013.
56. Gambetti, 'Decolonizing Diyarbakır', p. 99.
57. Author interview, Diyarbakır, 1 November 2014. A significant proportion of the non-Muslim population departed in the 1950s: see Yanmış and Aktaş, *Kürtlerde Dinî Yaşam*, p. 9.

58. Interview, Istanbul, 13 June 2015. For insight into Armenian life in mid-twentieth-century Diyarbakır, see Margosyan, *Gâvur Mahallesi*.
59. Interview, Diyarbakır, 21 October 2014.
60. Interview, Diyarbakır, 24 October 2014. Indeed, I was often assured by locals of the city's welcoming (*misafirperver*) nature. One woman in a shop told me that 'biz Amedliyiz' ('we Diyarbakır locals' – she used the Kurdish name, Amed) would protect me if I had any troubles.
61. Interview, Diyarbakır, 10 June 2015.
62. Author interview, 7 June 2015.
63. Margosyan's memoir of growing up in Diyarbakır, *Gâvur Mahallesi* [Infidel Quarter], first published in 1992, was translated into Kurdish in 1999.
64. Jones, 'Turkey'.
65. *Radikal*, 'Hani farklılıklar zenginliğimizdi', 12 August 2009.
66. Toumani, *There Was and There Was Not*, pp. 126–7.
67. Private communication, 23 October 2014.
68. Üngör, *The Making of Modern Turkey*, p. 168.
69. Marilungo, 'The city of terrorism or a city for breakfast', pp. 276–9.
70. Şengül, 'Qırıx: An "Inverted Rhapsody"', p. 35.
71. Hakyemez, 'Sur'.
72. *Hürriyet Daily News*, 'Yilmaz', 17 December 1999.
73. Keskin, 'Erdoğan: Kürt sorunu demokrasiyle çözülür', 11 August 2005.
74. *Hürriyet Daily News*, 'PM Davutoğlu wants a new Middle East for Turks, Kurds, Arabs', 25 January 2015.
75. Yackley, 'Kurd rebel leader orders fighters to halt hostilities', 21 March 2013.
76. Gurses, *Anatomy of a Civil War*, p. 130.
77. Çiçek, 'Kurdish identity and political Islam under AKP rule', p. 159.
78. Jacinto, 'Destruction of Kurdish sites continues', 20 July 2016; Assénat, 'Diyarbakır: aperçu de l'après-guerre', 3 May 2016; *Hürriyet Daily News*, 'Pictures released by the armed forces'; *Bianet*, 'Mıgırdıç Margosyan couldn't recognize his street amidst ruins', 25 April 2017.
79. Ibid.
80. Arparcık, 'Feeling solidarity in an estranged city', pp. 108–9.
81. *Agos*, 'Expropriation means closing down of Surp Giragos', 28 April 2016.
82. *Hürriyet Daily News*, 'Diyarbakır's ruined Sur to be rebuilt', 1 February 2016.
83. *Rudaw*, 'Why is Spanish Toledo not good enough for Diyarbakır?', 9 April 2016.
84. *Reuters*, 'Turkey removes two dozen elected mayors', 11 September 2016.
85. *Bozarslan*, 'Erdoğan's threats to replace elected mayors could backfire', 1 March 2019.

86. *Stockholm Center for Freedom*, 'Monument of Kurdish philosopher and poet Ahmad-i Khani demolished by Turkish government', 28 June 2017.
87. Arparcık, 'Feeling solidarity in an estranged city', pp. 108–9.
88. Smith, *National Identity*, p. 78.
89. Ibid., p. 9.
90. Connor, *Ethnonationalism*, p. 205.
91. Oomen, *Citizenship, Nationality and Ethnicity*, pp. 185–6.
92. Ibid., p. 186.
93. Interview, Diyarbakir, 20 October 2014.
94. Interview, Diyarbakir, 20 October 2014.
95. Interview, Diyarbakir, 21 October 2014. Genghis Khan is generally regarded in a positive light among Turkic peoples, and Cengiz is a common boy's name in Turkey.
96. Interview, Diyarbakir, 11 June 2015.
97. Horowitz, *Ethnic Groups in Conflict*, pp. 57–8.
98. Çınar, 'National history as a contested site', pp. 364–91.
99. Casier, 'Beyond Kurdistan?', pp. 417–32. For more on the events of the MSF, see http://www.transform-network.net/blog/blog-2009/news/detail/Blog/mesopotamia-social-forum-msf-in-diyarbakir.html.
100. Casier, 'Beyond Kurdistan?', p. 417.
101. Ibid., p. 422.
102. Interview, Istanbul, 13 June 2015.
103. Interview, Diyarbakır, 21 October 2014.
104. Interview, Istanbul, 18 October 2014.
105. Anatolia arises from the Greek Ανατολή, meaning 'east' or 'Orient'.
106. Sofos and Özkirimli, *Tormented by History*, p. 134.
107. Interview, Istanbul, May 2013. Notably, he was from Malatya. A Kurdish woman in Diyarbakır told me the population of Malatya was mostly Kurdish, 'But they think they are Turks.'
108. Navaro-Yashin, *Faces of the State*, p. 47.
109. Cited in Üngör, *The Making of Modern Turkey*, pp. 241–2.
110. Toumani, *There Was and There Was Not*, p. 146.
111. Casier, 'Beyond Kurdistan?', p. 417.
112. Üngör, *The Making of Modern Turkey*, p. 242.
113. Asatrian, 'Prolegomena to the study of the Kurds', pp. 1–57.
114. Imber, *The Ottoman Empire*, p. 179.
115. Houston, *Kurdistan*, pp. 39–40.
116. Interview, Diyarbakır, 20 October 2014.

117. O'Shea, *Trapped Between the Map and Reality*.
118. Güneş, *The Kurdish National Movement in Turkey*, pp. 33–4.
119. Interview, Diyarbakır, 29 October 2014.
120. Interview, Diyarbakır, 29 October 2014.
121. Indeed, one of the provinces in Iran is officially called Kurdistan (Persian: کردستان استان). This does not amount to de facto independent status, nor is it evidence of any separatist intent.
122. Gunter, 'The Kurdish minority identity in Iraq', pp. 263–82.
123. Başer, *Diasporas and Homeland Conflicts*, pp. 173–4.
124. *Haberler*, 'Erdoğan: Mustafa Kemal de Kürdistan Dedi Oda mı Bölücüydü', 19 November 2013.
125. *Hurriyet*, 'TBMM'de bir ilk . . . HDP'li Osman Baydemir'e 'Kürdistan' cezası', 13 December 2017.
126. *Bianet*, 'Closure case for parties', 11 February 2019.
127. Bozarslan, 'Turkish judiciary toughens stance', 22 February 2019.
128. *Daily Sabah*, 'Every citizen regardless of ethnic roots part of nation', 12 March 2019.
129. *Bianet*, 'We are the own children of this country', 15 March 2019.

6

KURDAYETÎ: PAN-KURDISH SENTIMENT AND SOLIDARITY

The Kurds have a reputation as a divided people. Writing in the late seventeenth century, the narrator of the Kurdish literary epic *Mem û Zîn* laments the Kurds' 'disunited, always rebellious and divided' nature and their plight, despite their bravery and resilience, as vassals of others.[1] The narrator might well have been prophesying the Kurdish future. After the apportioning of territory that occurred in the Middle East following the First World War, the Kurds remained divided and were rendered minorities in the newly formalised Turkish, Persian and Arab (in Syria and Iraq) states. Thereafter, as David McDowall notes, modern Kurdish history became marked by two distinct struggles, the first *against* the governments of the nation-states in which Kurdish peoples live, the second to forge a coherent sense of community and nationhood *among* themselves.[2] New state boundaries formalised divisions between Kurdish communities. Hakan Yavuz argues that regional, religious and linguistic cleavages prevent the emergence of what he calls a 'full-fledged Kurdish identity'.[3]

In contrast, Kendal Nezan observed, at a pan-Kurdish conference in 1990, affinities among Kurds despite a 'total lack of contact, in spite of huge distances that separated their homelands'. He argues that 'being a Kurd means to share the same basic cultural identity forged by centuries of history'.[4] Nezan is not alone in his conceptualisation of a shared Kurdish cultural identity. I have encountered the idea of pan-Kurdish identity and solidarity among

Kurds in Turkey, Syria, Iran, Australia and Europe – in Iraqi Kurdish terminology this is known as Kurdayetî. Kurdayetî is sometimes regarded as a form of Kurdish nationalism that amounts to a desire for an independent Kurdish homeland.[5] It is not a term that is commonly used by Kurds in Turkey. However, I use it here to describe a shared political identity that extends across borders and does not necessarily prefigure territorial claims but is a form of social and political capital used to protect Kurdish interests. In recent years, with the spread of modern communication technologies and alongside geopolitical developments, Kurdayetî has become more pronounced. It thus becomes a more potent force in Kurdish politics, which in turn has a bearing on politics in Turkey. This chapter examines the extent to which Kurdayetî is manifest in Turkey and the impacts it has in and for Turkey in the political and social arenas.

Kurdayetî and associated flow-on effects in regional politics have become all the more salient in light of the rise and fall of the Islamic State of Iraq and Syria (ISIS) since mid-2014. Kurdayetî grew significantly as Kurdish communities from across Turkey, Syria and Iraq cooperated to protect themselves from the ISIS threat. A sense of cross-border solidarity hardened as Kurds felt that the nation-states in which they live were unwilling to protect them physically and were disdainful of Kurdish interests. Kurdish solidarity, and hopes for the lasting recalibration of the regional political order, blossomed as Kurdish actors were able to extend control and implement administrative models across territory reclaimed from ISIS. In Turkey, this meant that Kurds watched with trepidation as ISIS encroached upon Kurdish populations in Syria, and then rejoiced as the Kurdish-led Syrian Democratic Forces (SDF) rolled back ISIS and extended Abdullah Öcalan's model of 'democratic confederalism' in the north-east corner of Syria,[6] abutting the Turkish border. Kurds were similarly excited as the *peshmerga* of northern Iraq secured the contested city of Kirkuk and Iraqi-Kurdish leader Massoud Barzani asked constituents, in a September 2017 referendum, if they desired independence. Turkey, for its part, stood by apparently indifferent as ISIS initially extended its control along the Turkey–Syria and Turkey–Iraq borders in late 2014, but began to take an active interest as Kurdish control was consolidated in these areas after ISIS was expelled.

The fears and hopes that Kurds in Turkey experienced at observing the plight of their cross-border ethnic kin illustrate the importance of Kurdayetî as a central pole of Kurdish identity. At the same time, Turkey's reactions to these developments are illuminating. Its unresponsiveness to the threat ISIS posed to Kurdish lives is viewed by some as evidence of an inherent anti-Kurdish bias, as is Ankara's apparent opposition to advances for Kurdish actors outside of its borders. The situation here is considerably complicated by the relationship between the Syrian Kurds and the PKK. Turkey claims that the Syrian PYD (Democratic Unity Party) is merely an extension of the PKK, and thus it views the consolidation of PYD control as a direct threat. Whether or not this is true, these circumstances mean that Kurdish cross-border cooperation and solidarity have considerable flow-on effects in Turkey.

Kurdayetî: Both 'we' and 'us'

The formation of Kurdish national consciousness is sometimes traced back to Ahmad Khani's seventeenth-century epic, *Mem û Zîn*,[7] but Kurdayetî was not specifically articulated as a concept until the mid-twentieth century. It appeared as the title of a poem written by Kemal Gir in Iraq. Translated as 'Kurdishness', the idea gradually became politicised in Iraq, a means of asserting Kurdish ethnic and ideological positions in contradistinction to those of then widely propagated Arab nationalism and socialism.[8] Originally conceived of and debated by the intellectual classes, with time, Kurdayetî, and the associated notion of Kurdish distinctiveness, came to resonate more broadly among Kurds at all levels as populations became urbanised and societal dynamics like tribalism, feudalism and religious authority, which had previously entrenched divisions, began to collapse.

Just as the markers of Kurdish identity are subjective and open to debate, Kurdayetî, a form of collective identity, is not automatically immutable or universally understood.[9] Like ethnicity, nation and nationalism, Kurdayetî is influenced and shaped by discourses, political forces and 'contingent events'.[10] Kurds I have met from Iran, Iraq and Syria acknowledge differences between their communities but proudly assert their Kurdishness as a common identity shared across borders. Indeed, Denise Natali argues that Kurdayetî has become one among a 'repertoire of identities' that are a result of individual social and political circumstances within each state.[11]

Popular consensus often portrays blood ties as integral to ethnic and national identities.[12] These are at work within Kurdayetî, but I argue that the cultural affinities that Kendal Nezan observed at the pan-Kurdish conference are just as potent. As outlined earlier, Thomas Hyllel Eriksen contends that a sense of 'we-ness', the establishment of internal solidarity and cultural commonality, is an essential element of identity formation.[13] A sense of 'we' forms through interdependence and internal cohesion: what we do and share defines who 'we' are as a people. The idea of 'we-ness' plays a pivotal role in Anthony Smith's definitional elements of an ethnic group: a collective proper name, myth of common ancestry, historical memories, common culture, homeland and, most relevant to this chapter, a sense of solidarity.[14] All of these are shared by significant segments of the designated population, commonalities that define who 'we' are.

The establishment of new Middle Eastern states in the 1920s would appear to militate against a sense of 'we-ness' enduring among Kurds. The arbitrary drawing of new borders divided Kurdish tribes, families and communities; governments saw their borders as sovereign boundaries not to be transgressed. In response, however, trans-border movement became a matter of course for many divided Kurdish communities, a fact aided by the remote nature and inaccessibility to government officials of much of the border regions.[15] As such, cross-border contact, while heightened with the advent of globalisation and mass communication since the 1990s, is not a new phenomenon for some Kurds. One Kurd from Doğubeyazit, near the Turkey–Iran border, told me that when he was a child during the 1980s it was routine to cross into Iran and goods were regularly smuggled both ways across the border.[16]

Among Kurds I met with in Turkey, cross-border encounters were common. Zehra, a sociologist in Diyarbakır, was married to a Kurd from Syria, had lived in Kurdish northern Iraq for seven years and, although having never travelled to 'Iranian Kurdistan', stayed in contact with Kurdish friends living there.[17] Refik, who had lived and studied in Iran, noted in a matter-of-fact way the cultural similarities he shared with Iranian Kurds.[18] Ayhan, a Kurdish researcher in Istanbul, recalled, 'I have met an Iranian Kurd. His accent was very similar to my family's. I really liked this . . . We laughed and talked about the same things, we had the same responses . . . I have also met a few [Kurds] from Syria. We share many commonalities with them as well.'[19]

Borders, as such, are not insurmountable barriers. Aykut remarked, 'We have brotherhood. We were always brothers and sisters. Countries might have split us up but our bond with other Kurds has never been broken. In order for these boundaries to be removed, Kurds must resist and they will resist and are resisting. No problem there.'[20] For Fehim, borders were 'only symbolic'. He argued that even across international borders Kurds 'never separated [from] each other. We saw each other as brothers and sisters and as family. They are Kurds and we are Kurds.'[21] Osman acknowledged different political experiences in each country where Kurdish communities resided but stated, 'this will not be an obstacle . . . Separation is out of the question.'[22]

Cross-border traffic was not limited to material goods, either. Political thought and ideologies were also disseminated.[23] Aside from contraband, smuggling between Syria and Turkey in the 1940s carried information, ideas and nationalist thought.[24] Thus, Kurdayetî also spread after its conception in Iraq. Another medium that defied borders was the broadcast of Kurdish-language programmes on Radio Yerevan from the mid-1950s. These had a rallying effect for Kurds in Turkey, forbidden from broadcasting and publishing in Kurdish, who tuned in clandestinely to hear their mother tongue. Radio Yerevan broadcasts helped foster a collective consciousness, a sense of 'we-ness', among Kurds wherever they listened, whether in Turkey, Syria, Iran or Iraq.[25]

That Kurds had to listen to Radio Yerevan to hear the Kurdish language highlighted the repressive circumstances they were living in. Experiences of repression, in turn, catalysed a second and complementary element that Eriksen posits as essential in identity formation, namely a sense of 'us-ness'. The sense of 'us' forms in contradistinction to the Other,[26] where the Other looks upon 'us' as different to them, and, if detecting a threat or rival, attempts to subdue or attack 'us'. In this case, the Other (the Turkish state) saw the Kurds as a threat to the ideal of ethnic unity and tried to extinguish, or deny, Kurdish identity, in so doing heightening the sense of 'us' among Kurdish populations. This did not only happen in Turkey. I would argue that marginalisation and disenfranchisement at the hands of Turkish, Persian and Arab nationalising governments after the 1920s impelled the transgression of borders and increased the salience of Kurdayetî, contributing to a sense of shared identity and reinforcing Kurdish solidarity.

One might further argue that marginalised Kurds in Turkey are able to draw parallels between their plight at the hands of Turkish authorities and the sufferings of Kurds under Saddam Hussein's regime in Iraq or Syrian Kurds attacked by ISIS. They are all likely to feel that they have been singled out because of their Kurdish identity, for their 'us-ness', and to view their individual misfortunes as an element of common experience, of 'we-ness'.

A salient example was Saddam Hussein's assault in 1988 on the inhabitants of the Kurdish city of Halabja in northern Iraq, when thousands were killed in a chemical weapons attack. Selahattin Demirtaş, the leader of the pro-Kurdish Halkların Demokratik Partisi (HDP) in Turkey, recalled hearing of the events in Halabja as a high school student. He recounted in a 2015 interview, 'On that day I discovered the meaning of Kurdishness. I realised what a heavy responsibility it is to be Kurdish. I recognised my identity.'[27] A trauma experienced by Kurds in Iraq prompted Demirtaş to fully recognise his Kurdish identity, which immediately and inherently transcended borders. He rallied to his ethnic identity due to the oppression of his ethnic kin by a dominant group, the Iraqi military. Domination, of course, may occur across borders and be enacted by different groups. The fact that the Iraqi regime, not the Turkish government under which Demirtaş lived, were perpetrators of the Halabja massacre did not prevent him from feeling solidarity with the victims of the gas attack. A sense of commonality arises through experiences of oppression, despite being subject to it by various Others, thus heightening Kurdish distinctiveness against all of those Others and cementing the bonds between Kurds despite international boundaries.

The idea of Kurdish distinctiveness, and the fact that it has so often been galvanised by repressive state actions, results in Kurds identifying more closely with their ethnic kin than with other citizens of the nation-states they live in. Rohat, a Kurd in Diyarbakır, told me his affinity with Kurds was greater than any connection he could envisage with a Turk: 'I am closer to a Kurd from Rojava than a Turk from Izmir. Even though there is a border, we [Kurds] are brothers.'[28] His friend, Berfo, shared similar sentiments, underlining the sense of kinship he felt with Kurds regardless of borders and other divisions.[29] Research conducted by Bahar Başer among diaspora groups in Germany and Sweden revealed that Kurds from Turkey feel greater affinity with the Kurdish groups from Iraq, Syria and Iran than to the Turkish groups.[30] Similarly, a study of Iranian Kurds found greater identification with fellow Kurds than with Iranian citizens.[31]

That is not to say that Kurdish identity is uniform and uniformly understood, nor that it is solely a result of the Kurds' passivity and helplessness in the face of state oppression. Kurds have been proactive in responding and adapting to the diverse political circumstances within which they work in different countries.[32] The borders imposed on Kurds act as 'systems of domination', and thus present immediate targets for Kurdish political movements in all four countries to challenge.[33] In each case, the Kurds' political trajectory is portrayed as a struggle against the impositions and depravations of the dominant order, and thus a common narrative emerges of Kurdishness entwined with struggle. Parallel experiences and chronicles of injustice and repression help to forge a collective identity – Kurdayetî – and a sense that Kurds must rely on themselves rather than national governments to protect and promote their political ambitions.

Crises, Cross-border Movement and Consolidating Solidarity

Anthony Smith recognises that his hallmarks of ethnic identity vary in potency across times and places. Similarly, Rogers Brubaker argues that 'groupness', or communal identification, is 'variable and contingent rather than fixed and given'. Thus 'groupness' can be understood as 'phases of extraordinary cohesion and moments of intensely felt collective solidarity ... It allows us to treat groupness as an "event", something that happens.'[34] That is, intense communal identification is intermittent, emerging or being prompted only at certain times. Inverting this, we might argue that 'groupness' is as much catalysed by events as it is an event in itself: there must be events that trigger this 'extraordinary cohesion' and 'intensely felt collective solidarity'. Such events take myriad forms: military or sporting victories, cultural celebrations and achievements, religious ceremonies, responses to threats or disasters. Simmel's rule states that pressures placed upon a group by external forces impel internal identification, thus forging the sensation of 'groupness'. I argue that this is true in the case of Kurdayetî, as state repression not only forged a sense of Kurdish distinctiveness but also often forced Kurdish populations to seek sanctuary across borders, where they encountered fellow Kurdish populations and awakened to their affinities and shared experiences.

Escaping Saddam Hussein's murderous al-Anfal campaign in 1988, large numbers of Iraqi Kurds fled north to seek safety, gathering at the border with Turkey and eventually being allowed to cross.[35] Similar scenes ensued on the Iraq–Turkey border after the First Gulf War of 1991. These were pivotal moments for Kurds internationally. First, they brought the plight of the Kurds onto the international stage, and, second, they had a galvanising effect on Kurds as refugees arrived in the cities of south-east Turkey and in Istanbul. Soner, in 1988 a teenager in Diyarbakır, explained that prior to the arrival of refugees from Iraq he did not know there were Kurds living outside Turkey. He told me this was a revelatory moment. Learning that he had ethnic kin living in Iraq immediately created a sense of cross-border solidarity and boosted a sense of Kurdish identity for him and his cohorts. As Soner noted, while previously Kurdish identity was something discussed in intellectual circles, now it became a topic of interest to 'ordinary people'.[36]

The arrival of Iraqi Kurds in Turkey also made it untenable for the Turkish state to maintain its denial of Kurdish identity. Martin van Bruinessen records his surprise at seeing during the 1980s in the neighbourhoods of Istanbul, Iraqi Kurds, who had fled Saddam's regime, wearing traditional dress, which had hitherto been outlawed.[37] Here was incontrovertible evidence that Kurds were not merely 'mountain Turks'. Turkish authorities were never particularly welcoming of or pleased at the arrival of these Kurds. Sheri Laizer recalls seeing Turkish security agents in 1991 trailing Iraqi Kurds in Diyarbakır's backstreets and notes that Kurdish villagers rather than local authorities provided supplies for the Kurdish refugees.[38] Most significantly, these Iraqi Kurdish arrivals interacted with local Kurds, thus boosting awareness of each other's political circumstances.[39] In these circumstances the milieu of Kurdish cross-border fixers, mentioned in the previous chapter, arose. These men spoke to me matter-of-factly about their experiences guiding journalists and military personnel among traumatised Kurdish communities; in the process it became apparent that they paid little heed to international borders and regarded themselves as working within a pan-Kurdish space, something within which they felt an integral part.

The cross-border solidarity created by the Iraqi Kurds' flight from Halabja and Saddam's wrath in 1991 are salient examples of 'groupness as an event'. These triggered intense responses from Kurds, a solidarity that extended across borders and that was reinforced by physical contact when previously divided populations encountered each other, sharing their stories and rediscovering the things they had in common. For Soner, Halabja created a sense of Kurdayetî, an understanding that his status as a Kurd was not an anomaly but was part of a collectivity that extended beyond Turkey. It further prompted discussions of Kurdish identity to spread. Kurdishness expanded beyond a topic of discussion for an intellectual cohort to become something discussed as a collective identity among the masses in everyday contexts. These events facilitated a burgeoning sense of 'we-ness' among Kurds.

Traumatic events such as Halabja also catalysed migration further afield. Kurds began seeking economic opportunities in Europe in the 1970s. This accelerated after successive political crises, including Turkey's 1980 coup; increasing numbers of Kurds sought asylum in European states and elsewhere.[40] The establishment and consolidation of Kurdish diaspora communities in Europe led to the trans-nationalisation of the Kurdish movement. Escaping the political restrictions that circumscribed them at home, Kurdish activists, civil society organisations, media and academics in Europe have freely interacted, communicated and collaborated since the early 1990s.[41] Unrestricted interaction did not necessarily mean consensus on political agendas and aspirations but it allowed the protection of Kurdish culture and traditions and a growing sense of political agency among Kurds as they embarked on political projects without hindrance.[42] This saw further broadening of Kurdish activism to include the masses, and a recalibration of the Kurdish struggle to focus on human rights and free political participation in the existing nation-states of Turkey and Iran, in particular, rather than the pursuit of an independent Kurdish state.[43]

In 1999, Turkish security forces captured Kurdistan Workers Party (PKK) leader Abdullah Öcalan, another event that brought the trans-national nature and mass appeal of the Kurdish cause into greater focus. Öcalan's arrest precipitated an outburst of protests in Turkey, Europe and beyond. This extended to hunger strikes, self-immolations, and demonstrations by almost 150 Kurdish associations worldwide.[44] Kurds from all walks of life, despite dislocation across continents and territorial divisions, 'closed ranks'.[45] Here was another 'groupness' event where intense collective identification negated and papered over, however fleetingly, differences in location, circumstance and ideology among Kurds. The trauma of Öcalan's capture sharpened Kurdish solidarity. It also demonstrated that in Europe, Kurds were mobilised and engaged in politics and in contact with their kin in the homelands. Kurdayetî, like the Kurdish political movement, was no longer restricted to the nation-states where Kurds originated, but had gone trans-national, the diaspora allowing Kurdish identity to cross-pollinate and reconstitute itself.[46]

Kurdayetî confronts ISIS

The advance of ISIS into Kurdish-controlled and populated territory in Syria and Iraq from mid-2014 spurred another outpouring of Kurdayetî, simultaneously demonstrating its vitality and trans-national reach. The Syrian city of Kobanî, besieged by ISIS in late 2014, became a focal point. Capital of one of the autonomous Rojava cantons declared by the Kurdish-run Partiya Yekîtiya Demokrat (PYD) in 2012, Kobanî was little known, even among Kurds, until the threat posed by ISIS propelled it to prominence in the international media. ISIS forces seized surrounding villages through September 2014, Kurdish (and other) civilians fled into Turkey, and the Kurdish YPG and YPJ militias maintained a rearguard action but looked to be fighting against overwhelming odds. A massacre of the scale of Halabja, albeit by different perpetrators, and the snuffing out of a symbol of the Syrian Kurds' new-found autonomy, appeared imminent.

Kurds I met in late 2014 in Turkey were, in equal measure, distressed, indignant and agitated at events unfurling in Kobanî. ISIS' earlier massacres of Yezidis and Shiites meant all were aware of the fate awaiting the city's defenders should it fall. That some Kurds had crossed the border to participate made the fight all the more personal. Esra, a journalist in Diyarbakır, noted that Kurds from Turkey were falling in the conflict – it was not just cross-border affinities that inspired sympathy and grief but actual familial relations. She retorted, 'They say, "It's outside of [Turkey's] borders, why are you doing this for Kobanî?" What do they mean by this? It's [our] children. The people, YPG guerrillas, who died in Kobanî, their funerals are coming [home] here . . . Just yesterday three people, three bodies came to Diyarbakır. Whose children are they?'[47]

These connections were potent, but the Kurdish struggle in Kobanî was important in other ways. Kenan, a teacher in Diyarbakır, told me, 'Kobanî is our *namus*,' using the Turkish word for 'honour'.[48] Kenan, told me that the defence of Kobanî was the first time that 'all Kurdish hearts are together'.[49] In Kenan's estimation, Kurds, through a history he claimed to be thousands of years old, had always been divided, but Kobanî acted as a trigger for unity.[50] His sentiments were echoed by many I spoke with in late 2014. Ali remarked, 'The Rojava resistance brings all Kurds together . . . Kurdish people suddenly realise . . . where they are and who they are and what they need to do.'[51] As Janroj Yilmaz Keles argues, televised images of the horrors ISIS had visited upon other communities and the desperation of Kobanî's defenders served to collapse physical and political distances and bring together Kurdish communities as one. Keles calls this a 'deterritorialised solidarity'.[52] The defence of Kobanî was something that all Kurds were observing, and its salvation something they all wished for. This was Kurdayetî realised, a 'deterritorialised solidarity' that had unified 'Kurdish hearts'.

Kobanî therefore constituted an event that catalysed 'groupness', an instance where solidarity was magnified – as Simmel's rule dictates – by external pressure. In this era of global communication and media coverage, Kobanî

Figure 6.1　Graffiti in Kadıköy, Istanbul, November 2014. It reads, in Kurdish, 'Long live the Kobanî resistance'. © William Gourlay.

was front and centre, receiving worldwide attention. For many Kurds it was emblematic of a history of oppression at the hands of regional states. Mithat, a Kurdish student in Istanbul, highlighted the parallels between Halabja and Kobanî. 'The genocide of . . . Halabja became a [catalyst for] national consciousness . . . it is on a level with Kobanî. For all Kurds . . . [Kobanî] creates national unity.'[53] Like the arrest of Öcalan, Kobanî provoked protests across the globe, this time accompanied by social media campaigns.[54] It also spurred Kurds, and others, to mobilise. A Kurdish waiter in Istanbul told me, 'Right now they are fighting in Kobani, . . . fighting for [the] four parts of Kurdistan, not just for [the] Syrian part . . . because we are brothers. They can be from other countries but they are our brothers, [the] same people.'[55]

In late October 2014, a column of Kurdish *peshmerga* vehicles and heavy weaponry crossed from Kurdish-controlled northern Iraq into Turkey, passing through the Kurdish-populated south-east and into northern Syria. Here was a potent symbol of Kurdayetî, a highly visible instance of Kurdish cross-border cooperation. Iraqi *peshmerga* units were mobilised to relieve the beleaguered defenders of Kobanî, the desperate plight of their ethnic kin transcending borders and compelling their participation. This was significant given the acrimonious relations and divergent political goals of the Kurdistan Democratic Party (KDP) administration of Iraqi Kurdistan and the PYD in Syria.[56] However, in these dire circumstances Kurdish actors realised that compromise was necessary to avert disaster.[57]

The jubilant reception the *peshmerga* received in south-east Turkey was yet more evidence of the potency of Kurdayetî. Cheering crowds lined the *peshmerga* convoy's route.[58] Kurds were ecstatic at the arrival of their well-armed kin from Iraq, symbols of Kurdish strength and self-reliance. The convoy did not pass through Diyarbakır, but I witnessed much chatter on the street and enormous excitement at the mission of the *peshmerga*. All talk was of Kurdish brotherhood. Here Kurds from Iraq, Syria and Turkey were coming together to fight together, alongside their 'brothers', to see off a fearful adversary.[59] Even so, the prospect that Kobanî might fall remained a galvanising factor for Kurds. The Minister of Self-Defence for the Kobanî Canton remarked that the city had become 'the castle of resistance for the four parts of Kurdistan'.[60] Among those I spoke to in Diyarbakır, many remarked that Kobanî was the most important city for Kurds outside of

Turkey. Tellingly, they deemed a city under threat more important than even Erbil, capital of Kurdish Northern-Iraq.

Kurdayetî intensifies in these circumstances because the oppression that Kurds endure underlines their distinctiveness from those around them, whether they be Turk, Arab or Persian. As Martin van Bruinessen notes, repression in Turkey, Syria, Iran and Iraq, coupled with increased intra-Kurdish communication, has long acted to entrench perceived disparities between Kurds and non-Kurds in those nation-states.[61] That the Kurds of Kobanî became the targets of ISIS fighters because of their very Kurdishness had the same effect, sentiment snowballing as global Kurdish communities shared images and information about ongoing events. This feeds disaffection, mobilisation and sometimes radicalisation among Kurds in Turkey, Syria, Iran and Iraq when considered in the context of commonly held Kurdish perceptions of discrimination, political mismanagement and corruption.[62] In turn, the notion among Kurds that nation-states are incapable of acting or unwilling to act in their interests gains traction. Consequently, Kurds perceive that they can only rely on their fellow Kurds. Kobanî therefore fitted into the historical Kurdish narrative of tragic yet noble fights against overwhelming odds. It provided yet another example of Kurdish 'we-ness', their common hopes and collaboration to defend the city, and Kurdish 'us-ness', their distinctiveness from both ISIS attackers and Turks who remained, at best, indifferent to the city's plight. It became a symbol of Kurdishness. To defend it became all the more important. Kobanî became a lightning rod for Kurdayetî, a sense of solidarity, a sense of common political identity, an understanding of the necessity of self-reliance.

Simultaneously, and paradoxically, ISIS acted as a unifier. It represented a threat to Kurds in Syria and Iraq (a threat amplified, many Kurds allege, by Turkey's complicity), and thus it aroused a sense of shared fate and highlighted the need to act in concert. Despite instances of cross-border interaction outlined earlier, Kurdish ethno-nationalist narratives and political objectives in Turkey, Syria, Iran and Iraq have evolved separately within the prevailing political constraints of each country.[63] Different Kurdish political organisations seek to protect their own positions and agendas, and thus cross-border tensions and competition remain at an organisational level. Indeed, cross-border military cooperation between competing groups is virtually unheard of. However, the pan-national threat that ISIS posed prompted Kurdish leaders to reassess priorities. Kurds were beset by a force that saw them as all alike, that cast them as godless enemies. Thus, not only civilian Kurds but also Kurdish political leaders previously noted for bickering and divergent political goals saw themselves as sharing the same plight, placed in a position whereby they had to fight to see off the existential threat that ISIS presented. In this shared narrative, a threat presented itself in different circumstances in Syria, Iraq and Turkey, yet it was a threat that could be seen as uniform, a common enemy, by Kurds in each of those countries. In fighting a common enemy, solidarity was precipitated and the Kurds' sense of shared identity was aroused and protected.

Kurdish Suspicions and Disappointments

ISIS may have been a new oppressor, but many Kurds claimed a familiar hand was working to undermine Kurdish interests, alleging that Turkey was supporting ISIS. As noted earlier, one Kurdish student, observing pro-ISIS commentary on Turkish social media, told me it was 'crystal-clear' that ISIS was a Turkish proxy.[64] Kurdish suspicions of Turkish complicity and anxiety at the fate of Kobanî were exacerbated when Erdoğan glibly remarked that the city was about to fall.[65] Some weeks after Erdoğan's statement, Refik told me, 'The fact that the Turkish government did not open its gates for Kobanî clearly helped out ISIS with their plan of destroying the Kurds.'[66]

Kurdish suspicions do not amount to incontrovertible evidence that Turkey was supporting ISIS, but Erdoğan's indifference demonstrated to Kurds that, in their hour of need, they could not rely on Turkey, despite its powerful military and its – theoretical – opposition to ISIS. Erdoğan's comment also reflects how Turkey misplayed its hand as regards ISIS and the Kurds. Mesut Yeğen observed that Kobanî was of vital interest to Kurds in Turkey, and to the then-ongoing peace process with the PKK, but he notes that the AKP 'failed' to recognise the importance of Kobanî'.[67] Ankara had an opportunity to win favour with Turkey's Kurds and the PKK, with which it was then negotiating, by interceding on the side of the besieged Kurdish fighters. Turkey might have offered a helping hand to Kurds when their backs were against the wall. Here was an opportunity for inter-ethnic 'groupness'. Had Turkey stood by Kurds in the fight against ISIS it would have won great kudos and forged a sense of common purpose between Turks and Kurds.

At one point, Prime Minister Davutoğlu stated that Turkey would do all within its power to prevent Kobanî falling,[68] which would have opened an entirely new era of Turkish–Kurdish cooperation. But Davutoğlu's words amounted to nothing. Turkey adopted a passive-aggressive stance, stationing military units on its border within view of Kobanî, closing the border and refusing to intervene when the city appeared doomed.[69] Henri Barkey remarked that Turkey's response to Kobanî was a miscalculation. He described the episode as 'a stepping stone for [Kurdish] national mobilization and nation-building. . . . Even if Kobanî falls, it will strengthen Kurdishness.'[70] It seems plausible that Ankara hoped Kurdish forces might get their comeuppance in Kobanî, which would then strengthen its hand as it negotiated with a chastened PKK. As it turned out, Turkey's posture only served to antagonise Kurdish populations. Anger at Turkey's position was plainly apparent among Kurds I mixed with in late 2014. In such circumstances, Kurds sought refuge in their Kurdish identity, distancing themselves from a nation-state that they considered dismissive of and indifferent to their interests. Indicative of such a position, one Kurd interviewed in 2014 remarked, 'I used to call myself a Turkish Kurd, but I no longer want to be called that. I am a human being and a Kurd. I am nothing Turkish.'[71] With empathy from Turkish observers and support from the powerful Turkish military unforthcoming, any coherence created during the siege of Kobanî was not an anti-ISIS solidarity connecting Turks and Kurds, rather it was pan-Kurdish sentiment.

Victory over ISIS and its Aftermath

Recent Kurdish history is replete with events that have rallied solidarity and nationalist sentiment. For Iraqi Kurds there was Halabja, in Turkey there were the Sheikh Said and Dersim uprisings and in Iran there was the short-lived Mahabad republic. Kobanî is the latest addition to this list. In one crucial aspect, however, Kobanî proves different to the others. In the telling, these events are all portrayed as heroic struggles, but Kobanî is the only one that did not end in defeat. With bolstered firepower courtesy of the Iraqi *peshmerga* and aided by allied air strikes, the defenders in Kobanî gradually pushed back the ISIS siege, ultimately lifting it in January 2015. This was something unprecedented for the Kurds – a victory.

When the Iraqi Kurdish forces left Kobanî and returned home, a *peshmerga* commander remarked, 'We fought against the occupiers with our brothers and sisters in Kobanî . . . The resistance and victory in Kobanî was an important stage for national unity.'[72] His comments underscored the important role that Kurdayetî played in the victory, the importance that fighting alongside 'brothers and sisters' played in strengthening Kurdish lines in the face of the onslaught, the role that a sense of fraternity played in inspiring the defence. He also underlined the role that Kurdayetî, in the form of 'national unity', would play in shoring up defensive lines while military threats remained present.

A victory, Kobanî thus immediately entered the canon of Kurdish myth, as a theatre where Kurds had come together from all corners to fight together. The victory had an impact well beyond the borders of Syria. Significantly, it demonstrated the value of cooperation. One Kurd in Diyarbakır presciently told me as the siege of Kobanî was ongoing, 'When you resist as a unity, see how strong you are.'[73] Kobanî was evidence that when Kurdish groups come together shoulder-to-shoulder, great outcomes can be achieved despite overwhelming odds. Until then, ISIS had not been defeated in battle. Its withdrawal from the outskirts of Kobanî brought an end to its reputation as invincible. The threat posed by ISIS had impelled diverse Kurdish groups to put aside their differences, and the resulting victory revealed the benefits of doing so.

As a global audience watched ISIS emerge, expand and threaten Western interests, Kurds won attention and plaudits for their role in the international campaign to stop that expansion. Kobanî's Defence Minister remarked in November 2014, 'Our two-month resistance has shown the whole world who the Kurds are.'[74] Kurds I spoke with in Turkey in 2014 and 2015 were very aware of the international attention focused on Kurdish militaries fighting ISIS, and were equally aware that Kurdish forces were seen as 'the good guys'. They extolled the virtues of Kurdish forces as acting honourably and promoting secularism and pluralism, qualities in short supply in the Syrian and anti-ISIS conflicts, and they portrayed the territories they capture as being 'liberated'. In fighting and winning a reputation as a reliable ally against a widely reviled enemy, the Kurds won considerable international legitimacy. This in turn further entrenches Kurdayetî. Cross-border solidarity and common action produced important military successes, winning Kurds international recognition and praise, and territorial advances, which many Kurds viewed as righting historical wrongs. These developments gave Kurds reason to take pride in their Kurdishness; it afforded them agency in a troubled geopolitical terrain. Historical tables were turned and Kurds demonstrated their political clout. It would seem that Kurds also expected to accrue international goodwill that in the longer term could be utilised to support and protect Kurdish claims and interests.

Indeed, never before have Kurdish players enjoyed so much military and political support from the West.[75] The PYD, previously little known, was able to rapidly establish working relations with international powers. Similarly, it has become routine for high-ranking western delegations to visit Erbil to discuss regional developments. Through these mechanisms, Kurdish actors became more visible and assertive on the international stage and, with the benefit of international military support, were able to expand Kurdish-controlled territory in northern Syria and consolidate control in the disputed territories in northern Iraq.

Turkey's Response

Such changes did not go unnoticed within the region, however. As early as 2012, commentators noted Turkey's disquiet at developments in the Kurds' favour in northern Syria. Ihsan Dağı contends that this reflects a commonly held Turkish view, a zero-sum approach whereby any political advance for Kurds is viewed as a setback for Turks.[76]

Such a contention would explain increasing alarm in Ankara as, after Kobanî, Kurdish-led militias advanced across northern Syria, defeating ISIS and allowing the PYD to institute its own rule. Attributing Turkey's agitation to a single cause, however, is oversimplifying a complex situation. Ankara has long contended that the PYD is nothing more than the Syrian extension of the PKK,[77] and as such is a 'terrorist' organisation that represents a threat to Turkey. After the collapse of the peace process with the PKK in mid-2015, Turkey ramped up its accusations of 'terrorism' at the PYD. Davutoğlu argued that the YPG's role in fighting ISIS did not absolve them of the 'terrorist' label.[78] Erdoğan went to the length of equating the PYD with ISIS, against which both it and the PKK were fighting.[79] In October 2015, after the deadliest terrorist attack ever in Turkey, when ISIS suicide bombers struck in Ankara killing over a hundred, Erdoğan accused the PYD and PKK of conspiring with ISIS and Assad's *mukhabarat* (secret police) to carry out the attack.[80] Such allegations contributed to an increasingly nationalist rhetoric in Turkey's politics, and may have struck a chord with Erdoğan's base, but they further reveal insensitivity to the Kurdish electorate. Erdoğan cannot have been unaware that Kurds were greatly concerned at the fate of their ethnic kin in Syria and saw ISIS as an evil adversary, so to accuse Syrian Kurds of operating in tandem with ISIS was unthinking at the very least – to say nothing of the implausibility of such a claim.

Turkey's bad-mouthing of the PYD, however, found no significant international audience. US officials have long maintained that they do not view the PYD as terrorists.[81] Indeed, the US and other powers continued to cooperate with the PYD, under the umbrella of the Syrian Democratic Forces (SDF) created in mid-2015 throughout the campaign against ISIS, allowing the consolidation of Kurdish control across north-east Syria and further creating consternation in Ankara. Here, the very same factors that contributed to a growing sense of Kurdayetî and Kurdish assertiveness unsettled Turkey, another demonstration of the potency of Kurdish identity as a factor shaping Turkey's politics. While Kurds were celebrating and taking pride in the appearance of Kurdish actors on the world stage, Erdoğan and the Turkish establishment were fretting at the purported threat that such circumstances posed to Turkey.

Turkey eventually responded. Its first commitment of ground troops to the war in Syria, in Operation Euphrates Shield (*Fırat Kalkanı Harekâtı*) of August 2016, was aimed at reclaiming al Bab from ISIS, but it is clear that Ankara's motivation was as much intended to outflank Syrian Kurdish forces. Defence Minister Fikri Işık stated that Turkey's goal was to prevent the YPG linking cantons along the Turkey–Syria border.[82] Thus a Turkish strike at ISIS was used as a pretext to stymie further advances for the Kurds.[83] Indeed, Turkish fears at the Kurds' intentions in Syria ran deep. Erdoğan and other Turkish figures consistently accused the Syrian Kurds of planning to create a new state in northern Syria,[84] a precedent considered entirely unpalatable as it was assumed it would catalyse further Kurdish agitation in Turkey. The PYD's consistent denial of such intentions did nothing to assuage Ankara's fears; Turkey reserved the right to act unilaterally to prevent such an eventuality.

Turkey struck again in January 2018, this time forgoing any pretence that it was targeting ISIS, invading the north-west Syrian canton of Afrin in a campaign dubbed Operation Olive Branch. Ankara's justification was that as the (Kurdish-majority) region was controlled by the PYD it was a springboard for terrorist attacks into Turkey, and thus a real and present danger. Erdoğan, playing on Turks' nationalist impulses and latent geopolitical fears, accused the Syrian Kurds of collaborating with 'postmodern Crusaders'.[85] As noted, there are clear links between the PYD and the PKK. These arise through complex organisational relationships and a shared political vision. An element of Kurdayetî is also apparent: pan-Kurdish solidarity means the fortunes of both organisations give heart to Kurds on both sides of the Turkey–Syria border. Despite this, Turkey, for some time, had abided the existence of the PYD, and regularly held meetings with its leader, Saleh Muslim. But in the fevered political atmosphere following the resumption of hostilities with the PKK, the coup attempt of mid-2016 and the Syrian Kurds' increasing political clout and territorial reach, Ankara viewed the PYD as an increasing threat. Allied with various anti-Assad Syrian militias, Turkish armed forces, boasting overwhelming firepower, routed SDF militias in Afrin and took control of the province after a two-month campaign.

Further demonstrating the potency of Kurdayetî, the invasion of Afrin prompted outpourings of Kurdish anger and dismay around the globe.[86] In Turkey, HDP deputies in parliament decried the military campaign, one of them, Mahmut Toğrul, citing an Amnesty International report that noted increasing numbers of civilian casualties. Indicative of the nationalist fervour then prevailing, AKP sitting members accused the HDP of being the 'mouthpiece of the PKK', after which fisticuffs broke out between AKP and HDP sitting members.[87] Subsequently, several hundred HDP members, journalists, activists, academics and ordinary citizens were arrested for speaking out against the Afrin offensive.[88] From the state's perspective, voicing concerns about the offensive equated to support for terrorism.[89]

Significantly, many who made criticisms, such as the Turkish Medical Association, were not necessarily Kurdish, but were expressing concerns on humanitarian grounds. All were roundly condemned, however, and accused of terror propaganda. In this sense, Turkey's politics had come full circle, rekindling the ethos of earlier decades when official rhetoric – widely supported by the public – equated any criticism or questioning of government policy or military action with terrorism, even if that criticism raised humanitarian issues and did not specifically mention Kurds.

Ankara dismissed humanitarian concerns by declaring its campaign into Afrin was solely aimed at 'terrorists'. Turkey was at pains to explain that it did not target Syrian Kurds, only the PKK. Yet such claims rang hollow when victorious forces in Afrin city immediately toppled a statue of the mythical Kurdish hero Kawa.[90] Meanwhile, reports emerged of widespread looting across Afrin, the expulsion of 300,000 Kurds and the commandeering of Afrin's famed olive harvest.[91] Thus, while Turkey may have argued that it was undertaking justifiable measures in response to a terrorist threat, its actions looked much more like deliberate strikes at Afrin's Kurdish population at large.

A similar course of events unfurled in October 2019 when Turkey invaded Kurdish-administered Rojava in north-east Syria, using the same pretext, that of removing the purported threat of the SDF militia from the Turkey–Syria border. Ankara again argued it was solely targeting 'terrorists', a claim put to the lie by war crimes committed by Turkish-backed forces, including the murder of Kurdish politician Hevrin Khalef, who had no connection to the SDF, and the displacement of numerous civilians, of Kurdish and other ethnicities.[92] Turkey's invasion was met with international opprobrium due to widespread support for the Kurdish-led SDF's role in defeating ISIS and disgust at the depredations of the invading forces.[93] This led to a doubling down by the Turkish public, who parroted Erdoğan's 'anti-terror' narrative. Indeed, despite recently growing misgivings about Erdoğan, the president enjoyed a surge of popularity at home as nationalist fervour skyrocketed.[94] Conversely, as some observed, the invasion is likely to have led to 'an emotional fracture' for Kurds in Turkey, who, unconvinced by claims of 'anti-terrorist' intent likely viewed it as part of an anti-Kurdish policy.[95]

Here were echoes of Turkey's response to the Iraqi Kurds' referendum in September 2017. When an overwhelming majority of Iraqi Kurds voted in favour of independence, Ankara, in concert with Baghdad and Tehran, ensured the blockade of Iraqi Kurdistan. Few situations spur cooperation between the governments of these three neighbours, but a Kurdish attempt to alter the regional status quo is apparently sufficient. In this instance, Ankara could not claim to be moving against 'terrorists', because the referendum, while controversial, was an attempt at changing the political situation through a democratic mechanism. Rather, Erdoğan claimed to be concerned with upholding international law and protecting Iraq's sovereignty.[96] Kurdish commentary on social media proposed an alternative view – that Turkey's knee-jerk reaction to the referendum and its invasion of Afrin demonstrated its ongoing anti-Kurdish posture. Kurds in Turkey expressed excitement at the outcome of the referendum, in marked contrast to Ankara, but were vocal in their criticism of Ankara's forceful response.[97] From a geopolitical perspective, these events demonstrate both the potency of Kurdayetî and Ankara's understanding of that potency. Turkey acted so decisively because it understands – or fears – that political developments for Syrian and Iraqi Kurds have important flow-on effects among Kurds in Turkey. Whether or not there is innate anti-Kurdish prejudice in Turkish government circles, the ruses of acting against 'terrorists' or in favour of Iraq's territorial integrity are used to justify actions that will circumvent the momentum of Kurdish political movements – inside or outside of Turkey – and thus maintain the political status quo. That Kurdish advances in Syria and Iraq coincided with political turmoil in Turkey only added urgency to the task of quelling Kurdayetî.

Cross-border Currents

Despite their reputation as a divided people, Kurds have always retained a sense of solidarity that extends across borders. In a globalised world, communication and connection is easier than ever before, and as a result of geopolitical developments since the 1990s, in particular, the upheavals of conflicts in the Middle East, Kurdayetî, the sense of pan-Kurdish identity, has blossomed. Kurds in Turkey fretted at the fate of their ethnic kin as Saddam Hussein gassed Halabja and as ISIS encroached on Kobanî threatening annihilation, and watched excitedly as Syrian Kurds extended their control along the Turkey–Syria border and as Iraqi Kurds voted for independence. Kurdish responses to these developments always appeared to be the diametric opposite of reactions from the broader Turkish population and the state apparatus. Erdoğan downplayed the threat to Kobanî, railed against the Iraqi Kurds' referendum and sent the army against Afrin. This entrenches divisions between Kurds and the Turks among whom they live and a government that has proven unwilling to act in their interests. Trans-national Kurdish links have assumed urgency and pan-Kurdish identification has crystallised. External threats fomented the Simmel effect of stronger internal cohesion, even across borders, and a feeling that Kurds must rely on their own kin.

Ironically, ISIS created opportunities for the Kurds, despite the horrors inflicted and tribulations endured. A powerful narrative of self-reliance and strength in unity has emerged, a counterweight to ages-old Kurdish narratives of oppression and injustice. Kurdayetî thus remains an undeniable aspect of Kurdish identity, one that is increasingly prominent and one from which Kurds in Turkey draw strength.

It also has an impact in Turkey's political arena. Ankara has felt compelled to respond to the geopolitical advances of Syrian and Iraqi Kurds, as have other regional capitals. Turkey is at pains to argue that its actions against the Iraqi Kurdistan referendum and adventures into Afrin and Rojava are not anti-Kurdish moves, but are motivated by other considerations. Yet Kurdish discontent is palpable. And Turkey's hair-trigger responses to such events are acknowledgement of the strength and significance of bonds that exist between Kurds across borders. Like all identities, a pan-Kurdish identity is shaped by 'contingent events'; these are experienced differently according to individual and political circumstances, but where it is conceived as a form of kinship and solidarity that extends across borders, it plays a powerful role in the legitimation and affirmation of Kurdishness for many Kurds in Turkey. The comments of Kurds I spoke with testify to that.

Notes

1. Khani, *Mem and Zin*, pp. 30–2.
2. McDowall, *A Modern History of the Kurds*, p. 1.
3. Yavuz, 'Kurdish nationalism in Turkey', p. 232.
4. Nezan, 'The Kurds', pp. 7–19.

5. Gunter, *Historical Dictionary of the Kurds*, p. 170.
6. The principal military elements of the SDF are the YPG (Yekîneyên Parastina Gel; People's Protection Units) and YPJ (Yekîneyên Parastina Jin; Women's Protection Units) militia of the Partiya Yekîtiya Demokrat (PYD; Democratic Unity Party), which is affiliated with the PKK.
7. Van Bruinessen, 'Ehmedî Xanî's Mem û Zîn', pp. 40–57.
8. Natali, 'Manufacturing identity and managing Kurds in Iraq', pp. 253–88.
9. Hall, 'Who needs "Identity"?', pp. 1–17.
10. Brubaker, *Ethnicity without Groups*, pp. 11–12.
11. Natali, *The Kurds and the State*, pp. xvii, 75.
12. Connor, *Ethnonationalism*, pp. 197–202.
13. Eriksen, 'We and us', pp. 427–36.
14. Smith, *National Identity*, p. 21.
15. Bozarslan, 'Kurds and the Turkish state', pp. 333–56.
16. Private communication, London, July 2016.
17. Interview, Diyarbakır, 21 October 2014.
18. Interview, Diyarbakır, 20 October 2014.
19. Interview, Istanbul, 18 October 2014.
20. Interview, Diyarbakır, 29 October 2014.
21. Interview, Diyarbakır, 29 October 2014.
22. Interview, Diyarbakır, 29 October 2014.
23. Hashimoto and Bezci, 'Do the Kurds have "No Friends but the Mountains"?', pp. 640–55.
24. Özen, 'Latent dynamics of movement formation', pp. 57–74.
25. Yeğen, 'Armed struggle to peace negotiations', pp. 365–83. See also Ghazaryan, 'The Kurdish voice of Radio Yerevan', 24 January 2019.
26. Eriksen, 'We and us'.
27. Sarıkaya, 'Demirtaş'ın Bilinmeyenleri!', 8 February 2015.
28. Private communication, Diyarbakır, 4 June 2015.
29. Private communication, Diyarbakır, 4 June 2015.
30. Başer, *Diasporas and Homeland Conflicts*, p. 185.
31. Akbarzadeh et al., 'The Iranian Kurds' transnational links'.
32. Natali, *The Kurds and the State*, p. 181.
33. Cizre, 'Turkey's Kurdish problem', pp. 222–52.
34. Brubaker, *Ethnicity without Groups*, p. 12.
35. *Human Rights Watch*, 'Whatever happened to the Iraqi Kurds?', 11 March 1991.
36. Interview, Istanbul, 13 June 2015.

37. Van Bruinessen, 'Shifting national and ethnic identities', p. 42.
38. Laiser, *Martyrs, Traitors and Patriots*, pp. 1, 21–6.
39. In 1991, similar events occurred in Iran, when Iraqi Kurdish refugees were received by Kurdish populations: see Van Bruinessen, 'Shifting national and ethnic identities', p. 43.
40. Başer, *Diasporas and Homeland Conflicts*, pp. 56–70.
41. Watts, 'Institutionalising virtual Kurdistan West', pp. 121–47.
42. Casier, 'The politics of solidarity', pp. 197–217.
43. Watts, 'Institutionalising virtual Kurdistan West'.
44. Gürbüz, *Rival Kurdish Movements in Turkey*, pp. 49–50.
45. Akkaya and Jongerden, 'The PKK in the 2000s', pp. 143–62.
46. Başer, *Diasporas and Homeland Conflicts*, pp. 69–75.
47. Interview, Diyarbakır, 27 October 2014.
48. In fact, *namûs* is a common term across the Middle East. It also appears in Arabic. It is said to derive from the Greek *nomos* (νόμος) meaning 'custom': Bocheńska, 'Introduction', p. 6.
49. Interview, Diyarbakır, 28 October 2014.
50. This position overlooks those Kurds who actually joined ISIS: see Meleagrou-Hitchens and Alaaldin, 'The Kurds of ISIS', 8 August 2016.
51. Interview, Diyarbakır, 26 October 2014.
52. Keles, 'The European Kurds rallying to fight IS', 10 December 2014.
53. Interview, Istanbul, 13 June 2015.
54. For an example of a pro-YPG/Kobanî social media campaign, see Twitter: https://twitter.com/hashtag/ShowYourV4YPG?src=hash, accessed 2 December 2016.
55. Interview, Istanbul, 14 October 2014.
56. Bezci and Borroz, 'ISIS helps forge the Kurdish nation', 5 February 2016.
57. Paasche, 'Syrian and Iraqi Kurds', pp. 77–88. The *peshmergas*' movement through Turkey can only have been possible with Ankara's approval – evidently Iraqi Kurdish leaders convinced Turkey to let this happen.
58. *Reuters*, 'Iraqi Peshmerga fighters approach Kobani', 29 October 2014.
59. Kurds from Iran as well as diaspora Kurds from Europe also came to defend Kobanî and participate in other campaigns against ISIS: see, for example, Aghajanian, 'Copenhagen to Kobani, Berlin to Erbil'.
60. *E-Kurd Daily*, 'Syrian Kurdistan's Kobani defense minister', 15 November 2014.
61. Van Bruinessen (1998), 'Shifting national and ethnic identities', pp. 39–52.
62. Unver, 'Schrödinger's Kurds', pp. 65–98.

63. Lowe, 'The Serhildan and the Kurdish national story in Syria', pp. 161–79.
64. Interview, Diyarbakır, 20 October 2014.
65. *Cumhuriyet*, 'Erdoğan: Şu an Kobani düştü düşüyor', 7 October 2014.
66. Interview, Diyarbakır, 20 October 2014.
67. Ashdown, 'This is what being a Kurd is about', 10 January 2015.
68. *Reuters*, 'Turkey vows support for besieged Syrian town', 3 October 2014.
69. *BBC*, 'Turkey clamps down on Syria border', 22 September 2014.
70. See Krajeski, 'What Kobani means for Turkey's Kurds', 8 November 2014.
71. Chudacoff and Blaser, 'I do not want to be called a Turkish Kurd', 12 October 2014.
72. *Firat News Agency*, 'YPG/YPJ fighters at the border to Jarablus', 11 February 2015.
73. Interview, Diyarbakır, 21 October 2014.
74. *E-Kurd Daily*, 'Syrian Kurdistan's Kobani defense minister'.
75. Abdulla, 'How ISIL advanced Kurdish nationalism', pp. 89–97.
76. Dağı, 'Good for the Kurds, bad for the Turks?', 29 July 2012.
77. On the complexities of this issue, see Kaya and Lowe, 'The curious question of the PYD–PKK relationship', pp. 275–88.
78. *Daily Sabah*, 'Fighting ISIS does not legitimize YPG terrorists', 27 September 2015.
79. *BBC*, 'Erdoğan: PYD de bir terör örgütüdür', 5 October 2015.
80. Pamuk, 'Turkey's Erdogan sees Syrian and Kurdish hands', 22 October 2015.
81. *Hürriyet Daily News*, 'YPG not a terrorist organisation for US', 22 September 2015.
82. *Al Jazeera*, 'Turkey deploys tanks in Syria', 26 August 2016.
83. Similarly, when Turkey had earlier – and reluctantly, it must be added – joined the international campaign against ISIS, it also took the opportunity to strike PKK positions in northern Iraq: see *Milliyet*, 'Türkiye'nin IŞİD ile PKK çatışması', 27 July 2015.
84. *Hürriyet Daily News*, 'Turkey won't allow establishment of a state', 24 June 2017.
85. *Yeni Şafak*, 'Postmodern Haçlı Seferi', 25 January 2018.
86. ANF News, 'Thousands of Kurds protest Afrin invasion', 11 March 2018. See also Crabapple, 'How Turkey's campaign in Afrin is stoking Syrian hatreds', 11 April 2018.
87. *Hürriyet Daily News*, 'Deputies brawl in Turkish parliament', 8 March 2018.
88. *BBC*, 'Turkey arrests hundreds', 29 January 2018.
89. *Index on Censorship*, 'War abroad, repression at home', 10 April 2018.

90. *Reuters*, 'Turkey-backed forces pull down Kurdish statue', 18 March 2018.
91. *BBC*, 'Afrin looted by Turkish-backed rebels', 19 March 2018. See also *Syrian Observatory for Human Rights*, http://www.syriahr.com/en/?p=102951 20 September 2018.
92. *CNN*, 'Kurdish politician and 10 others killed', 13 October 2019.
93. *Syrian Observatory for Human Rights*, 13 October 2019.
94. Gauthier-Villars, 'Turkish leader's political star rebounds', 29 October 2019.
95. Butler, 'Syria offensive feeds disenchantment', 23 October 2019.
96. *Reuters*, 'Erdoğan calls Kurdish referendum illegitimate', 29 September 2017.
97. *Kurdistan 24*, 'Ankara's rejection of Kurdistan referendum unites Iraq and Turkey Kurds', 26 September 2017.

7

OPPRESSION, SOLIDARITY, RESISTANCE

Early one evening in October 2014, in the backstreets of the old city of Diyarbakır, I wandered past a group of four Kurdish boys aged between ten and twelve. Fingers raised in the V-for-victory sign, with steadfast looks on their faces, they were chanting, '*Bijî serok Apo.*' Translated from Kurdish their chant means, 'Long live leader Apo.' They were brandishing the name of Abdullah Öcalan, the leader of the Kurdistan Workers' Party (PKK), imprisoned near Istanbul since 1999. Returning home from work, or running errands, local residents smiled and nodded as they passed. Although delivered in everyday surroundings, the boys' gesture was undeniably political.

As I continued on my way, their cries rang out in the dusk. I pondered what would drive small boys to do such a thing. Why would they want to evoke the name of a jailed political leader in a nameless backstreet? Their posture and attitude were of defiance. It occurred to me that I recognised elements of resistance in the aspects of Kurdish identity that I was investigating – using the Kurdish tongue, Kurds' stance on religion, the celebration of Newroz – and that those I spoke with consistently imparted a message of resistance. This is not something that I had come looking for, or expected, but it was apparent that resistance – to the state, to assimilation, to political circumstances, to Erdoğan's message – was an element of the Kurdish experience and posture. The PKK's confrontation with the Turkish military is well documented, but Kurdish resistance assumes myriad other forms, to the extent that it becomes a marker of identity.

During my time in Turkey, my eye became attuned to the numerous, minor, seemingly innocuous forms of resistance that occur within everyday life. On several occasions in Diyarbakır I was offered *kaçak çay* (literally 'escaped tea') that had been smuggled across the border from Iraqi Kurdistan. Locals assured me that this 'Kurdish' tea was far superior to Turkish brews. Drinking tea hardly amounts to a political activity, and assurances of its superiority were offered jokingly, but the fact of its provenance and the illicit means by which it reached the Kurdish cities of south-eastern Anatolia added a frisson of excitement to its consumption. Products for sale in shops and bazaar stalls were also – to varying degrees – subversive: 'Kurdistan' T-shirts emblazoned with the Iraqi Kurdish flag; books including *Şerefname*, a Kurdish history periodical *Kürt Tarihi*, Ahmad Khani's literary epic *Mem û Zîn* (in Kurdish) and works by previously outlawed authors Musa Anter, Mehmed Uzun, Ismail Beşikçi and the poet Cigerxwîn; souvenir carpets embroidered with notable figures from leader of the 1925 rebellion Sheikh Said, to outlawed film-maker Yılmaz Güney, Islamic philosopher Said Nursi, Iraqi Kurdish leader Mustafa Barzani, 1960s revolutionary Deniz Gezmiş and Che Guevara. All of these were notable oppositional or nonconformist figures and all, aside from Che and Gezmiş, were Kurdish. None of these items would have been available for sale during the 1990s, or at least not above the counter. They would have been condemned as contravening and threatening the unity of the Republic of Turkey. That these could now be sold freely testifies to the degree that Turkey has changed to allow more visible manifestations of Kurdish and other ethnic identities.

Nonetheless, the imperative to conform remains strong in a political sphere dominated by the AKP and the personality of Erdoğan. Political spaces have expanded and contracted over time, but state pressure, in one form or other, has been a constant. From the 1980s, repressive measures on the Kurds, ostensibly directed towards the PKK, had the effect of rallying Kurdish political sentiment such that resistance to state hegemony expanded beyond the PKK's military campaign to encompass a much broader 'popular resistance', known in Kurdish as '*serhildan*'. The political realm is now freer, yet in Erdoğan's Turkey, nationalist rhetoric is resurgent and political opposition, particularly from Kurds, is suspect.

This chapter examines the intersection of oppression and Kurdish resistance to the state and the impacts these have on the formation of Kurdish identity. The Kurdish issue is no longer solely framed as a quest for a Kurdish state and Kurdish identity is no longer deemed an existential threat. However, the scope for Kurdish political activity has narrowed amid a deteriorating security environment since late 2015. In these circumstances, the notion of '*serhildan*' retains potency and remains a pole of Kurdish identity. The chapter examines ways in which a history of oppression by the Turkish state has forged solidarity among Kurds and thereby conceptualisations of Kurdishness. Despite a broadening of national dialogue about ethnicity and identity in recent years, Kurds continue to subscribe to a narrative of oppression and see the need to maintain a posture of resistance.

As well as through the markers of *ethnie* already discussed, identity comes into focus 'through social situations and encounters, and through people's ways of coping with the demands and challenges of life'.[1] Thus public and political spaces are of crucial importance to ethnic identification. When individuals express grievances about their political circumstances in public spaces, solidarities and collective identities are forged.[2] The airing of grievances can take myriad forms, from public protest to 'everyday resistance' to violent insurgency.[3] These activities in turn may themselves constitute a form of identity making. In Lebanon, Hizbullah conceives of society, in all of its manifestations and all of its participants, as the embodiment of resistance itself. Resistance, seen in these terms, is a vital marker of identity.[4] In coming together in public spaces to resist military occupation, oppressive regimes or government agendas, individuals broaden their circles to make known their discontents and assert their presence; in so doing they proclaim their identities as individuals and collectivities. Kurds have done this in many ways, from joining the PKK to selling 'Kurdistan' T-shirts. Kurdish acts of resistance to oppression, both that of state security agencies and more recent hegemonic imperatives of the AKP's instrumentalisation of the 'national will', have become important markers of Kurdish identity that allow them to call attention both to who they are and to how they are different from others.

Kurds in Turkey: A History of Oppression?

The Republic of Turkey was established in 1923; by 1938 there had been eighteen insurrections, sixteen of them Kurdish.[5] The Turkish military put them all down brutally. This occurred alongside state-sponsored assimilation programmes. Salih, a municipal employee in Diyarbakır, cited an acquaintance whose surname was Öztürk, as well as the well-known Kurdish politician Ahmet Türk.[6] 'It shows how we are oppressed. It's a kind of pressure, a kind of insult on your Kurdishness to give surnames like Türk, Özturk.'[7] Kurdish nationalists use this history to construct a narrative of ongoing state oppression and heroic resistance by Kurds. Some allege the narrative has been manipulated to portray all conflicts involving Kurds as being attacks targeting Kurdish ethnic or cultural identity.[8] Whether or not one agrees, the narrative of state oppression clearly retains currency among Kurds in Turkey, many of whom feel they have been marginalised and treated unjustly by the state apparatus due to their ethnic identity. When asked what it means to be a Kurd, Salih told me, 'To be a Kurd is to be oppressed. To be isolated from your culture, your language, your nation ... We have lived under the oppression of the state for years.'[9] Another interviewee, Refik, told me, 'Most Kurds have been trampled on (*Kürtlerin coğu ezilmiştir*).'[10]

Salih and Refik, both in their twenties, attained adulthood in a time of relative calm in Turkey's south-east. Earlier decades had been more traumatic. The emergency rule imposed on the Kurdish-populated provinces in 1987, as conflict with the PKK grew more intense, saw repressive measures peak. Kurdish children in some districts were so used to police intimidation that if a policeman came to their house they would 'immediately put their hands on their heads in a gesture of surrender'.[11] Recalling life in 1980s Diyarbakır, Ali remarked, 'I am fifty years old, but I remember problems started when I was sixteen ... I grew up under the shadow of weapons. Every day ... there was an uneasy atmosphere.'[12] On my first visit to Diyarbakır in 1992, tensions were immediately apparent. I noted a pervasive military presence and the resentment with which locals looked upon security agencies.

Hakan Yavuz argues that a generation of Kurds had their self-images shaped as a result of growing up under emergency rule, claiming that the PKK terror campaign exacted a 'human cost' upon Kurds.[13] One might alternatively attribute such a cost to the actions of the Turkish security agencies and the government that condoned the hard-line measures undertaken. Here the restrictions of emergency law are the 'contingent events' that mould identities.[14] Socio-political dynamics resulted in an 'uneasy atmosphere', restricted opportunities, lack of development and strained state–society interactions, all of which had an impact on Kurdish identity. Just what impacts these dynamics had on identities depends on how Kurds, individually or collectively, perceived and reacted to them.

During the interviews I conducted, respondents immediately blamed the state for repression they had experienced – none of them mentioned the PKK. Interviewees recounted diverse experiences of brutality, mistreatment and discrimination. One stallholder in Diyarbakır's bazaar quipped, 'Who can say "I didn't have a problem with the state, or police, or soldiers"? Everyone has.'[15] Specific examples reported to me included forced evacuations from homes and villages, street harassment by police, and arbitrary arrests. Dilek, a shop attendant, recalled that when she was a twelve-year-old in the 1990s, the 'secret police' came to her family's home every night at 1 am, thumping on the door, then rifling through personal items and threatening her parents.[16] This led to negative associations with the state for Dilek. She recounted her shock, after her family fled to Malatya, seeing locals willingly approaching police to ask for directions, something that she could not reconcile with her experiences of the Diyarbakır police.

Zoran, also a child in 1990s Diyarbakır, told of the arbitrary arrest of his father, who later returned home severely beaten.[17] State action sometimes assumed an even more violent turn. Counterterrorist strategies devolved into state-sponsored terror such that some accuse Ankara of conducting a 'dirty war', something that even Erdoğan conceded when peace attempts were ongoing in 2013.[18] Mesut lamented the Kurds' experience of such events: 'We know that the people just saying that we are Kurds or wanting to . . . live as Kurds, lots of people [were] disappeared and killed. And so many . . . villages, maybe two thousand villages, [were] burned and maybe two million people [were] moved from their native land . . . So many people lived under this pressure . . .'[19]

Experiences of oppression and violence have been channelled by the Kurdish nationalist movement into a convincing narrative that finds wide support among the Kurdish masses.[20] The legend of Kawa, the youth who instigated the rebellion against the tyrannical king in the tale of Newroz, played a pivotal role here, an instance where rising up against oppression instils unity and begins the march towards freedom.[21] Newroz was one of several symbols used to inspire a counter-hegemonic identity and movement, a way of striking back against injustice. Within the associated discourse, ideas such as 'oppressed nation' and 'popular resistance' gained currency.[22] Collective action, whether that entailed funeral marches or street protests, became the standard response to state oppression, during which a process of 'education' occurred whereby Kurds increasingly became aware of their distinct identity.[23]

Testimonies gathered in my research suggest that a narrative of oppression found a willing audience because experiences of ill treatment and discrimination were common, from tales of harassment at schools and workplaces to repressive measures from state bodies endured either personally or by friends, family and acquaintances. Many Kurds accepted the narrative because they had lived it themselves. Consequently, Kurds blame the state and associated Turkish nationalist ideology, not the PKK, for the 'human cost' that Yavuz says was imposed on Kurdish society. Further, I argue that through experiences of ill treatment at the hands of the state, the 'self-image', or identity, of respondents was shaped.

Oppression Catalysing a Collective Identity

While relating the story of his father being beaten up by the police, Zoran remarked, 'It makes me . . . protect my [Kurdish] identity.'[24] The experiences of Salih, who lamented the imposition of Turkish names, and Dilek, whose family was harassed by police, also drove them to more forcefully assert their Kurdishness. Just as experiences of oppression are well documented and widespread, it is also recognised that such oppression played a role in catalysing Kurdish nationalism.[25] This again is Simmel's rule at work, which states that the internal cohesion of any group depends on the degree of external pressure placed upon it.[26] Oppression by the state apparatus made significant numbers of Kurds less likely to identify with the (Turkish) state and pushed them to seek recourse in an alternative (Kurdish) identity.

Refik complained of state policies '... restricting our language, destroying our culture or putting it under a shroud (*bir örtü altına alınması*)'. He equated it to 'top-down oppression (*tepeden baskılması*)'.²⁷ This widely shared historical narrative made Refik more determined to defend his Kurdish identity even though he lived in an era when Kurdish culture was less likely to be put 'under a shroud'. Historically, the south-eastern provinces have also routinely received fewer state resources, schools and medical facilities such that Kurdish-populated regions have been the most underdeveloped in the country.²⁸ Such circumstances had a cumulative effect on burgeoning Kurdish awareness from the 1980s. Yavuz notes that the 'lack of democratisation and worsening economic conditions consolidated ethnic and regional loyalties. People gradually became more aware of their "Kurdish-being".'²⁹ Ece Temelkuran relates a tale of a Kurdish elder who automatically pulled out his identity papers whenever he saw a policeman because he knew they would be demanded. The elder quipped that the situation was the same as that of a donkey at a market who always smiled at strangers because he was so used to having his teeth examined by prospective buyers.³⁰

Associated narratives of marginalisation and neglect from the state and being singled out by security services are broadly accepted by many Kurds. A study in mid-2014 found that among various segments of society in Turkey, including Kurds, Turks, 'secularists' and 'religious', it was Kurds who recorded feeling the highest levels of 'ill treatment' (*kötü muamele*) in a range of public settings such as shops, universities, hospitals and state offices.³¹ Another 2014 study of 2,100 Kurds in three south-eastern provinces, including Diyarbakır, found high levels of exposure to violence.³²

Encapsulating such circumstances, Esra, a journalist in Diyarbakır, told me, 'If one part of your body is hurting you emphasise that part ... My hurting part is Kurdish ... So we firstly emphasise that we are Kurdish.'³³ As Esra explained, the actions of the state and Turkey's political milieu meant that it was the Kurdish component of her identity that was 'hurting', thus she was more determined to assert her Kurdishness. Applied to Turkey's Kurdish population en masse, this is a reiteration of Simmel's rule. As Eriksen underlines, Simmel's rule does not merely explain the relative strength of group identification, it also highlights what *kind* of group will be formed in the face of that pressure. The nature of the 'group depends on where the pressure is perceived as coming from, e.g. class, nationality, gender'.[34] This accords with Esra's comments about which aspect of her identity is 'hurting': she mentioned that aside from her ethnicity it could equally have been her gender or her religion. But in everyday life in the Republic of Turkey she saw her Kurdishness as most under pressure. She saw the need to defend that most vigorously; she saw Kurdishness as her primary identity.[35]

Esra did not consider her own experiences as isolated but placed herself within the context of the collective experience of Kurds; this in turn contributed to their cohesiveness, their distinctiveness: 'Why [do] we still insist that we are Kurdish? Because we experience the same thing.' Further, she highlights that because shared experiences were negative they reinforced a sense of identity and solidarity: 'We had the same nightmare . . . All the people who had the nightmare share a link . . . This makes the meaning of Kurdishness, I think.'[36] Sharing 'the same nightmare', as Esra frames it, plays a role in Kurdish conceptualisations of themselves as a people who have suffered throughout history, creating a 'victim tradition', similar to discourses among Armenians and Jews.[37] This is another measure of authenticity and a catalyst for ethnic solidarity. Identity is generally more politicised among Kurds who have been subjected to repressive state measures; Anna Grabolle-Çeliker records Kurds from Van lamenting they were more 'assimilated', thus less authentically Kurdish, than those from Diyarbakır and places where state oppression – and resistance to it – was more pronounced.[38]

Further highlighting how experiences of war and oppression catalyse a sense of group identity, Ramazan Aras, in interviews with Kurdish villagers, notes how respondents used 'I' in their testimonies when telling tales of village life, but when recounting episodes of violence they used 'we' or 'the Kurds'. Aras contends that framing their memories as being part of a collective was a way of protecting themselves from individual repercussions from the state,[39] but it may also be argued that while everyday life is recalled as an individual experience, oppressive measures have the effect of creating a bond between those who endure them, hence forging a stronger sense of collective identity. Singled out by security forces for their Kurdishness, these Kurds were alerted to their own distinctiveness, their own shared identity.

The murder in 1991 of Vedat Aydın is an example of oppression having a catalysing effect on Kurdish identity and solidarity. Aydın, a non-violent activist and member of the pro-Kurdish Halkın Emek Partisi (HEP), was taken from his home in Diyarbakır by police officers in July 1991 and later found dead.[40] Aydın's murder has never been solved, but it is widely believed to have been carried out by state agents, another minor episode in the 'dirty war'. His funeral in Diyarbakır drew a huge crowd. Semih, a teenager at the time, attended the funeral and recalls it as a pivotal event. He recounted the enormity of the crowd, aged 'from seven to seventy', and the pervasive 'sense of humiliation' among locals. Standing in the crowd, Semih recalled, he felt an intense solidarity, 'after years of shame'.[41] A sense of injustice strengthened his resolve to uphold his Kurdish identity, and camaraderie drew him closer to other Kurds. Asef Bayat notes the streets as locations where individuals may air grievances; by doing so in public places they also 'enlarge solidarities and extend their protests . . . by recognising their mutual interests and shared sentiments'.[42] In such circumstances, those subjected to violence or oppression may discover a sense of agency and the crystallisation of group identity.[43] For Semih, amid the funeral crowd, this was just such a moment. He noted that 'everything changed', in the sense that he was individually more conscious of his ethnic identity, but also that those gathered in Diyarbakır felt a greater sense of collective resentment and common purpose.

Berxwedan Jiyane: 'Resistance is Life'

Following the uprisings of the Arab Spring, state oppression is seen, paradoxically, as an important generator of unity among political oppositions: a more brutal regime is more likely to see people mobilising against it.[44] Clearly, this is not always the case. There are countless incidents throughout history, including that relating to the Kurds, where extreme repression has quelled social mobilisation.[45] It is important to note, thus, that *awareness of* oppression is not the same as *resistance to* oppression.[46]

Indeed, resistance is not passive but is a conscious activity.[47] Charles Tripp defines resistance as 'activities aimed at contesting and resisting systems of power that people in different places have found increasingly intolerable for a wide variety of reasons'.[48] Alongside its narrative of oppression, the PKK also promoted a narrative of resistance; from 1982 until 1995 it published a magazine entitled *Berxwedan* ('*Resistance*').[49] In contrast, the Turkish state long framed Kurdish resistance as illegitimate, seeking to justify its harsh responses to Kurdish agitation.[50] Martin van Bruinessen argues, however, that repressive measures intended to subdue Kurdish identity and to stamp out radicalism backfired. 'Misguided policies brought about precisely those developments that they had intended to stop,' he states.[51] Even Erdoğan conceded this in 2013, remarking that 'inhumane treatment' had given the PKK 'opportunity' and 'excuse' to conduct its terror campaign.[52] Erdoğan was attempting to explain the impact of state measures on support for the PKK rather than as a catalyst for Kurdish identity formation. Nonetheless his comments are an acknowledgement that the misdeeds of the state played a role in mobilisation.

The PKK

No discussion of Kurdish resistance, indeed of the Kurds in Turkey, is complete without consideration of the PKK. My research did not focus on the PKK or its struggle, but it is worthy of brief examination here. No one I interviewed explicitly espoused membership of the PKK, but it is apparent that the organisation enjoys the moral support of many Kurds. Some interviewees adopted a deferential tone to the PKK leader, calling him 'Mr Öcalan'. Many spoke of 'the Movement'. It did not need to be named on the assumption I knew what they were referring to. Pro-PKK graffiti was visible in parts of Diyarbakır during my time in the city. In the old town, I saw the slogan '*PKK halktır*' ('The PKK is the people') written on a wall. Yet I heard no one mention its violent tactics or its original goal of independence. This appears to corroborate the findings of Doğu Erğil in 1995, namely that the PKK is seen by a majority of Kurds as a vehicle that pursues and protects Kurdish interests, rather than as solely a mechanism for separatism. Indeed, the PKK wins support across various segments of Kurdish society.[53]

Yet the association of the PKK with the Kurdish cause can have negative implications. Erdem recalled, 'Until I was a teenager, I didn't know I was Kurdish. When the word Kurdish was pronounced it meant "fear" and "scary" because there was ongoing conflict between the Turkish state and the PKK. Therefore being Kurdish was a "terrorist".'[54] Broadly speaking, Turks do not equate Kurdishness with terrorism, despite what Erdem states, but few Turks are able to consider the PKK as anything other than a terrorist organisation. In popular parlance, the PKK are deemed 'baby killers'.[55]

In this sense, Turks and Kurds view the PKK from diametrically opposite perspectives. Turks consider it through the prism of its more bloodthirsty acts as an offensive and predatory force, while Kurds see it as a defensive and resistant force. Kurds tend to accentuate the circumstances that led the PKK to take up arms. Mesut commented, 'Some . . . criticise Kurds [for pursuing] their rights with guns . . . They are not fetishists of the gun or fetishists of violence, but if there is not a democratic way . . .'[56] In other words, Mesut saw the PKK's tactics as a last resort, because no legal avenues were available for Kurds to participate in politics or protect their rights and identity. Indeed, while Turks decry the PKK, its agenda and tactics, one might argue that the activities of the Turkish state spurred its existence and ensured its longevity. Ezgi Başaran, meeting a group of young PKK militants in 2013 and discussing their lived experiences, noted that all had been at the receiving end of discrimination, and often much worse, due to their Kurdishness. 'They were hurt; and this was their reality,' she noted.[57] It was these circumstances that pushed some to 'go to the mountains', as joining the PKK is referred to, and that pushed many others to sympathise with it and view it as a champion of Kurdish rights. I have encountered praise for the PKK in various quarters, including among Kurds in Melbourne, Australia, in the 1990s. They stressed to me that they didn't necessarily support the goal of a separate state (which the PKK still then espoused), but said that the PKK's campaign for Kurdish rights 'made them proud to be Kurdish again'. Denise Natali notes a 'sense of outrage among the Kurdish masses' that is the lifeblood of the PKK, 'even if they don't support [it] openly'.[58] Despite self-evident shortcomings, the PKK and its leader Öcalan act as a 'symbol of unity and resistance' for Kurds at large.[59]

Indeed, the violent trajectory that the PKK pursued highlighted the plight of the Kurds in Turkey. Şerafettin Elçi, the parliamentarian jailed for twenty-seven months for making a simple statement of Kurdish identity in 1979, argues, 'If it were not for the armed struggle, it would not have been possible for the Kurds to be on Turkey's agenda, or for Kurdishness to be a topic for discussion.'[60] Significantly, the PKK's military campaign also brought the so-called Kurdish issue into focus for the broader Turkish population. In a 2003 interview, celebrated Turkish journalist Hasan Cemal remarked that the PKK's emergence had enlightened him to the struggles of the Kurdish people. He conceded that even with a university degree in political science he had been unaware of the situation until then.[61] In this sense, acts of resistance – on the part of the PKK – catalysed an awareness of Kurdish identity in the Turkish population as well. In the nationalist milieu of Turkey at the time, this would not have been a positive conceptualisation. Nonetheless, this played a part in the gradual opening of Turkish discourse to broader discussions of ethnic identity.

The prism through which the Turkish population and government viewed the PKK has shifted over time. In the lead-up to the June 2015 election I saw a Kurdish youth riding a moped through Diyarbakır's Yenişehir wearing the combat fatigues of a PKK guerrilla. Such a thing would have been anathema to Turkish society prior to the 'resolution process' beginning. A Kurdish friend told me that while once the state struck immediately at any suspicion of PKK activity, or even of support for the organisation, such sensitivity appeared to be waning. 'Anyway, there are too many supporters of "the movement" now for the police to arrest everybody!' he quipped.[62] But things were to change again from mid-2015, as will be examined later.

The Serhildan

Of course, a relatively small number of Kurds have followed the PKK path and 'gone to the mountains'. Yet Kurds have mobilised against the state in myriad ways without resorting to violent insurgency. From early 1990, the funerals of PKK members attracted large crowds, as had the one for the politician Vedat Aydın, such that for the first time 'civil resistance' outweighed PKK activities.[63] While previously the 'Kurdish struggle' had been carried out principally by PKK operatives, now a broader cross-section of Kurdish society began to participate in individual, localised and largely uncoordinated activities that fall within Tripp's definition of resistance. This marked a broadening from a Gramscian 'war of manoeuvre', solely comprised of the PKK's military campaign of guerrilla attacks, to a 'war of position' consisting of (non-violent) confrontations in the public sphere[64] that included many more Kurds than just those who were members of the PKK. In 2006, children in Diyarbakır, protesting at Turkish security forces attacks on the PKK, brought the city to a halt for two days. This set off a spate of demonstrations across Kurdish cities, an indication that Kurdish political activity had assumed a different shape, one that encompassed multiple segments of society.[65]

A slogan popularised by the PKK states '*berxwedan jiyane*' (literally, 'resistance is life'). For many Kurds, perennially suffering oppression, resistance is seen as part of the fabric of the everyday. In Kurdish this public mobilisation became known as the '*serhildan*', from '*ser*' (head) and '*hildan*' (to raise). This nomenclature illustrates vital emic aspects of its conceptualisation, first as a symbol of resistance, raising one's head in defiance of an oppressor, and second as an assertion of identity, raising one's head to demonstrate one's presence. This is an instance of the 'art of presence', making oneself 'heard, seen, felt and realised', in spite of political constraints or unjust strictures.[66] It is *symbolic* resistance, a demonstration, through gestures and actions, of the Kurdish cause.[67] The *serhildan*, then, while consisting of acts of resistance, also constitutes a clear statement of collective identity. This posture has a long history among the Kurds. Ahmad Khani wrote in the seventeenth century, 'Resolution, bravery and generosity, courage, princeliness and endurance, this is the mettle of the Kurds, shown by sword and equitable fervour.'[68] One interviewee lamented that Kurds lack a flag, homeland and other 'normal' markers of nationhood, but he saw the *serhildan* as a substitute. 'We can [claim] . . . solidarity . . . because we have this . . . *serhildan*.'[69] He saw it as a rallying point, something that all could participate in, but also a hallmark of Kurdish identity where other 'normal' national markers were absent.

In contrast, the Kurdish language may be regarded as a 'normal' national marker, yet that too may be utilised in an act of resistance. A Kurdish youth I knew in Izmir in the 1990s told me he would casually slip Kurdish swear words, while maintaining an affable demeanour, into conversations with officials, teachers or the general public as an act of subversion. Mithat, a Kurdish university student in Istanbul, related in 2015 an episode when he was prosecuted, alongside others, for his political activities. During court proceedings, he and his colleagues refused to address the court in Turkish, responding only in Kurdish although all speak fluent Turkish. They demanded a Kurdish interpreter. 'The court didn't accept our request. And we protested . . . we turned our backs . . . ,' Mithat explained.[70] After some time, the court relented, finding an interpreter. Mithat revealed, however, that since the court case – over two years previously – he had not spoken Kurdish at all.

The Kurdish language that Mithat and his colleagues insisted they had the right to speak was thus a way of redrawing the power dynamic of the court, resisting its authority, but it was simultaneously a forceful demonstration of their Kurdish identity. The very fact that Mithat had neither inclination nor need to speak Kurdish in the course of normal life since the court case amplifies the political nature of his demand to use the language and to utilise his ethnic identity as an act of resistance.

The nature of the *serhildan* is that it occurs in workaday circumstances. If, as the proverb states, 'resistance is life', it must be allowed to occur simply and without planning. Scott argues that 'everyday' resistance is as important as that of major rebellions (which receive more attention but rarely bring benefits to those rebelling). Resistance in the everyday is what must be done by the disempowered in order to maintain their interests as best they can, Scott contends.[71] One correspondent related to me that Kurdish children playing soccer often shout '*Bîjî Apo*' ('Long live Apo') when they score a goal.[72] The implication here is that by kicking a goal one is scoring a small victory for the Kurdish cause, striking back against the Turkish state – it is something even children can accomplish. The boys I encountered in the Diyarbakır backstreets, related at the beginning of this chapter, were mimicking this activity, albeit without a soccer ball. The message of resistance is imparted from a young age and widely among Kurds, and it resonates even with children such that the act of kicking a goal in a game of street football has become politicised. These 'Apo' chants are resistance at its most ephemeral – no authority is even present to be challenged – but they build camaraderie and thereby solidarity, which creates political capital with which to maintain Kurdish interests. As in the case of Hizbullah, resistance 'goes beyond combat and becomes an individual process, carried out through daily practices related to body, sound, signs and space'.[73] It is an activity that everybody from schoolchildren to grandmothers can participate in. Everyday acts of resistance constitute ways to downplay or revoke the imperatives of dominant forces in political situations.[74] These acts impart agency to those who are overlooked or downtrodden, giving them a voice and a means of asserting their presence. In this way, the violence traditionally associated with resistance is made secondary and resistance itself demarcates peoples, creating a distinction between those who resist and those who oppress; in so doing, resistance becomes a central marker of identity.

It is recognised that conflict, and people's responses to it, can have major impacts on behaviours and identities.[75] For many Kurds in Turkey, political circumstances – tensions, oppressive measures – spur specific reactions, forms of resistance, a desire to challenge societal norms in a political space where Turkish nationalist discourse is dominant; it can be as simple as asserting one's Kurdishness.[76] Esra remarked, 'For many years we have lived under pressure. So we emphasise that we are Kurdish.'[77] Many Kurds repeated this attitude, lending credence to Van Bruinessen's argument that oppressive circumstances, whether due to state policy or nationalist intolerance and rhetoric, resulted in a hardening of Kurdish identification. When asked about his ethnicity, Soner, a researcher in Istanbul, said, 'It's a . . . reaction . . . When I describe myself as a Kurd it is . . . a kind of protest . . . Sometimes I feel that Kurdish identity is not welcomed and I try to emphasise it.'[78] Thus Soner and Esra are marking a political space in circumstances where they feel pressured to conform to a homogenous Turkish ideal; upholding – or flaunting – their Kurdish identity is a way of resisting this ideal. They are enacting a symbolic resistance, a gesture of the endurance of the Kurdish cause, as are the children playing soccer and Mithat speaking Kurdish in the courtroom.

These actions should be seen in the context of the AKP's domination of the political sphere and Erdoğan's claims to being the sole representative of the 'national will' (*milli irade*). For some time, Erdoğan had made this claim on the basis of the AKP's electoral majorities. He evokes the 'national will' in order to validate any and all AKP initiatives, but also to vilify and delegitimise oppositional voices or those who don't conform.[79] Erdoğan's 'national will' discourse is thus a homogenising project akin to the assimilation projects directed at Kurds in earlier decades. Here again, Kurdish distinctiveness is frowned upon, not due to the state's aspiration to ethnic uniformity but due to the AKP's goal of ideational uniformity, or universal subscription to Erdoğan's political vision.

These instances are episodes of the Kurds' 'war of position' writ small. They are more than attempts by Kurds to maintain their interests, more than a holding pattern against an overwhelming status quo, rather they are a pushing of boundaries. Mithat conceded that his identity as Kurdish was '90 per cent political'. As such it is a conscious reaction to societal condition. All of these are proactive attempts to redefine the political milieu in circumstances where the state no longer denies the existence of Kurds, nor makes overt attempts to assimilate them into a homogenous 'Turkish' national identity, but where many Kurds still feel the need to define and defend their own political space. These episodes of 'everyday resistance' are loud declarations of Kurdish identity.

Resistance through Electoral Mechanisms

'Everyday resistance' may be a 'war of position' writ small, but a 'war of position' is more generally understood as an engagement in politics; it is an attempt to gradually win over civil institutions and the public sphere through the exercise of 'moral and intellectual leadership'.[80] This provides a platform for resistance to be exercised through the mechanisms of the state, or through the ballot box. It is 'constructive resistance', a means of challenging the existing order by using the very machinery of that order to further a model that offers a political alternative.[81]

Kurds and pro-Kurdish parties have long participated in electoral politics in Turkey, but the general election of 7 June 2015 marked a turning point. For the first time the pro-Kurdish HDP was contesting on a party basis. Kurdish candidates had previously run as independents to circumvent a rule that dictates that only parties passing a threshold of 10 per cent of the national vote can assume seats in parliament. No Kurdish party had ever succeeded in passing the threshold. The election was also significant because President Erdoğan campaigned vigorously for the AKP in pursuit of a sufficient majority to facilitate the creation of a 'Turkish-style' presidency that would grant him expanded executive powers. Consequently, the election was viewed as a referendum on Erdoğan's presidential ambitions. Early in the campaign, Selahattin Demirtaş, leader of the HDP, marking out a resistance posture, stated baldly, 'We will not allow you to be president.'[82] The HDP thus offered itself as the conduit of alternative values and political aspirations. Voting for the HDP became an act of resistance to Erdoğan and his designs.[83]

It may appear counterintuitive to illustrate participation in an official activity, such as a general election, as an example of resistance. I would respond by arguing that Kurdish resistance is not resistance for resistance's sake, nor necessarily resistance to the system or the state broadly defined.

Rather it is resistance to the system's inherent injustices and inequalities, as Kurds perceive them. It is important to stress that even in repressive circumstances there are spaces for resistance, or at least opposition. As Dick Hebdige notes, 'commodities can be symbolically "repossessed" in everyday life, and endowed with implicitly oppositional meanings'.[84] In this instance, Kurds were 'repossessing' the 'commodity' of the election to impart their message of resistance to Turkish – or the AKP's – hegemony, using the tools of the dominant culture to defend their own. There was a dual nature to Kurdish participation in the election – compliance in a dialectic with resistance. Kurdish resistance is not automatically against the political framework of the state, but against the way it operates. Broadly, Kurds recognise the legitimacy of the state (as will be examined in the next chapter), but if seeing its functioning as unjust, or not representative of their interests, they resist, even through sanctioned activities, as a means of delimiting their own space, to ensure justice and representation within the political system.

The tone set by Demirtaş' statement of intent to derail Erdoğan's aspirations spurred Kurdish mobilisation. Kurds found many ways of signalling their opposition as Erdoğan criss-crossed the country to campaign. This included turning their backs, whistling and making the V-for-victory peace sign as his motorcade passed in Kurdish-majority cities such as Mardin and Muş.[85] In Diyarbakır streets were abuzz with election chatter and festooned with HDP banners, bunting, posters and graffiti. The HDP campaign culminated in a major rally near Diyarbakır railway station two days before the election. At the rally a festival atmosphere reigned. Of the many people I spoke to, all were convinced that the HDP would pass the threshold. One man told me, 'We will win.' He viewed victory not as winning government but as seeing HDP candidates in parliament. This was a step towards a Kurdish 'war of position', an opportunity for Kurds, through their HDP representatives, to bring 'moral and intellectual leadership' to a 'civil institution', the parliament of Turkey, not necessarily as a precursor to usurping power, but as a means to promoting a Kurdish political agenda through the officially sanctioned mechanisms of elections and the parliament. It was also a way of defining a political space, resisting the status quo and AKP hegemony, through legitimate means.

Figure 7.1 Crowds gather at the HDP rally, Diyarbakır, 5 June 2015. © William Gourlay.

Reflecting Turkey's tense geopolitical circumstances, two explosions – bombs planted by ISIS – disrupted the HDP rally, dispelling the carnival atmosphere. The rally was abruptly called off. The crowd fled in panic and rushed the wounded to hospitals. Four people were killed. Returning days later to the site of the blasts, I saw that locals had created a makeshift shrine decorated with balloons, flowers and handwritten notes. While I was present, pedestrians gathered and cars slowed to observe. The traffic ground to a halt and car horns sounded. Initially I thought this was the frustration of commuters being held up, but then I realised that bystanders at the makeshift shrine were facing the traffic and making the peace sign; those in cars were doing the same. Amid a growing chorus of horns, people faced each other, holding each other's gaze, raising their heads proudly. This was not a traffic jam, but a powerful gesture of solidarity and defiance on a gritty street corner where Kurdish lives had been taken. It was *serhildan* in action: people raising their heads in defiance and in a statement of presence.

These events contributed further to discourses of oppression and resistance. They only heightened the desire of the Kurds of Diyarbakır to participate in the electoral process. Asserting one's right to vote was now, more than ever, imperative; it was a way to resist the forces arrayed against Kurdish political ambitions. Polling booths were lively on election day. Images of those wounded in the bombings in Diyarbakır casting their votes circulated widely on social media.[86] As if to vindicate Kurdish determination, the HDP polled impressively, gaining 13 per cent of the vote, winning the third-largest number of seats and denying the AKP a parliamentary majority for the first time since 2002. I was told by many that the election was a way to deliver a message to Erdoğan. These Kurdish voters, and many others, had thus embarked on a 'war of position', participating in the political life of the Republic of Turkey, but at the same time performing an act of *constructive* resistance against the government, and Erdoğan specifically. This was somehow brazen: Kurds used legal political mechanisms to define themselves *against* the status quo and *against* what they saw as the AKP's and Erdoğan's hegemonic ambitions. The HDP, and many Kurds, maintained this resistance posture through a succession of elections that followed, from a repeat election in November 2015 that Erdoğan invoked to overcome a hung parliament, to a constitutional referendum on Erdoğan's presidential model in 2017 and further general and local elections in 2018 and 2019.

Maintaining Resistance in 'New Turkey'?

In some regards, the June 2015 general election represented the high-water mark for the HDP. It has not since achieved such a large share of the vote. June 2015 also marked a significant shift in Turkey's politics. The AKP won the follow-up election in November among a profoundly polarised electorate where nationalist rhetoric had re-emerged, conflict with the PKK had reignited and discourses of 'terror' and 'treachery' again assumed currency.

Through the political turbulence that followed, Erdoğan won the executive presidency that he had long coveted after 52 per cent of the electorate voted in the affirmative in a constitutional referendum in April 2017. Yet even with extended powers, Erdoğan made no concerted attempt to bridge divides that were widening within society. It might be argued that a polarised electorate worked to Erdoğan's advantage. Just as Simmel's rule explains Kurdish solidarity, it can be equally effectively applied to Erdoğan and the AKP. Having failed to win the Kurdish vote to consolidate his political position, Erdoğan evoked the spectres of terrorism and unnamed, malevolent external forces to rally the nationalist constituency and forge an alliance with the MHP.

The political temperature increased across the board, but Kurds appeared to be most affected. Conflict laid waste to some neighbourhoods in Kurdish cities, including Diyarbakır. In a 2016 interview, just prior to his arrest on 'terrorism' charges, HDP leader Demirtaş remarked, 'We are Kurds. Spending time in jail is our folklore.'[87] This echoed comments related to me about how regularly Kurds had been imprisoned in the 1980s. The atmosphere of openness and tolerance apparent to me in Diyarbakır between 2013 and 2015 was no longer. A group of youths was detained by police in Istanbul for 'terrorist propaganda', after they flashed 'the victory sign used by the PKK terror group'.[88] Yet, as was apparent in the 1990s, oppressive measures do not necessarily lead to quiescence but can heighten tensions and harden political resolve. Demet Arparcık relates being stopped by Turkish security forces travelling on a minibus near Diyarbakır in 2017. Despite passengers being compliant, soldiers were menacing and the situation tense. When a Kurdish grandmother muttered a curse at the soldiers in Kurdish, Arparcık said she and her fellow passengers felt a moment of intense solidarity.[89] An external threat transformed a group of travellers into a community: Turkish aggression consolidating Kurdish resistance and identity.

These measures were part of an increasingly authoritarian AKP's broad crackdown on 'terror'. In circumstances when the downtrodden rise up they are often dismissed as 'mobs' or 'rabble' by the authorities against whose interests they act.[90] With broad brushstrokes, peoples or groups may be negatively (mis)characterised. This had already happened during the Gezi protests of 2013 when Erdoğan had dismissed protesters as '*birkaç çapulcular*' ('a few looters').[91] Now the broadest brushstrokes were applied to the HDP, manifestly the most important political representative of Kurds in Turkey, as the government, with Erdoğan leading the charge, made a concerted effort to equate the HDP with the PKK, thereby undermining its legitimacy as a political entity and besmirching it in the eye of the electorate. There is some irony in claiming the HDP is a terrorist entity considering it was the target of over 120 violent attacks on electoral activity during the June 2015 election.[92] Nonetheless, this is the line consistently pushed by the AKP. Erdoğan emphatically equates the HDP with the PKK, sometimes, reflecting concerns with geopolitical shifts and external threats mentioned in the previous chapter, throwing in the Syrian Kurdish PYD and its military arm the YPG for good measure.⁹³ It may also reflect concerns that because the HDP wins a far greater proportion of the vote than any earlier pro-Kurdish parties it constitutes an ongoing challenge to the AKP.

Claims that the HDP is complicit with the PKK have flow-on effects in society. A Turkish professor once remarked that each time a Turkish soldier falls victim to the PKK, a HDP parliamentarian should be eliminated.⁹⁴ Such extreme sentiments are not commonly held, yet many within the AKP architecture see the marginalisation of the HDP as a political goal, party officials remarking prior to municipal elections in early 2019 that while the military focuses on subduing the PKK, the AKP should do the same to the HDP.⁹⁵

Therein arises a dilemma for Erdoğan and the AKP. In attempting to smother the HDP on grounds of its purported links to the PKK, Erdoğan wins the support of nationalist Turks and is able to maintain an alliance with the hard-line MHP, but he also risks losing the Kurdish vote, a sizeable constituency. Simultaneously he galvanises many Kurds in their opposition to him. Erdoğan goes to great lengths to emphasise that he is not anti-Kurdish, just anti-PKK; he consistently refers to 'my Kurdish brothers' in his speeches and continues to assert that the AKP is a protector of Kurds not only in Turkey but also Syria.⁹⁶ His approach is top-down and paternalistic. Whether he genuinely regards himself as protector of the Kurds is impossible to say, but it appears that few Kurds buy it. A sense of resentment and resistance remains. Amid the destruction of Kurdish cities during the escalating conflict against the PKK in early 2016, supporters of Amedspor, Diyarbakır's totemic football team, chanted, 'Everywhere is Sur, everywhere is resistance.'⁹⁷ Indeed, Amedspor has a fan group known as '*Direniş*' (Turkish for 'resistance'). In response to a prevailing atmosphere of intimidation and 'racism', a member of '*Direniş*' related a common sentiment among club members: 'We will win by resisting.'⁹⁸ And for all Erdoğan's protestations that his gripe is only with terrorists and his talk of 'Kurdish brothers', there is still a sentiment among Kurds that they are targets of 'assimilation'. Imam Taşcier, an HDP deputy from Diyarbakır, remarked in a 2019 interview on the government's 'hardened policy' towards Kurds, adding that 'it can't solve the problem by marginalizing and terrorizing Kurds'.⁹⁹

The narrative of oppression and the desire to register one's resistance retain currency for many Kurds. The narrative was fed by the fact that so many Kurds endured repression and injustices at the hands of the state. As Esra noted, they 'shared the same nightmare'. This in turn forged a sense of solidarity, as Simmel's rule predicts. That Kurds suffered as a result of their ethnicity – their Kurdishness – precipitated strong identification with their ethnic kin, and in contradistinction to the homogenous Turkish identity that the founding elites of the Republic of Turkey imagined. That particular nightmare may have ended. In Turkey's current political landscape the aspiration to ethnic homogeneity is no longer so rigidly pursued and debates about national identity are broader and more open. Yet the narrative of oppression survives, fed by a desire for acknowledgement of historical wrongs but also from a conviction that there is still insufficient political space for Kurds in Turkey. This often manifests as opposition to the AKP government, which is seen as intent on hegemony over the Turkish political space, and to President Erdoğan, who is similarly perceived, by some, as being despotic and, despite evocation of his 'Kurdish brothers', as working in concert with Turkish nationalists and thus intrinsically anti-Kurdish. In such circumstances, voting against the government becomes an act of constructive resistance, albeit within a government-sanctioned forum. Beyond just recognising the oppression they are subjected to, many Kurds in Turkey have actively responded to 'contesting and resisting systems of power' that they find intolerable. Through various everyday activities, Kurds are adopting a resistance posture as a way of upholding their identity, from drinking smuggled tea, to wearing a Kurdistan T-shirt or buying an embroidery of Sheikh Said. Doing so provides both a means of rallying internal (Kurdish) cohesion and of delineating themselves against the (Turkish) Other. Within Turkey's current political dynamics, where divergence from government-sanctioned norms are 'Otherised', a Kurdish-resistance continuum develops: significant numbers of Kurds resist and in so doing highlight their difference as Kurds, which in turn incurs official opprobrium, which further impels Kurds to resist. The cycle is endless, until a new politics arises. Nonetheless, that Kurdish resistance occurs in everyday, legal contexts indicates that these assertions of Kurdishness are not statements of separatist intent but are strikes at the status quo in order to define a new Kurdish way of belonging within Turkey's body politic. The *serhildan* continues – lifting the head as a gesture of presence and of resistance.

Notes

1. Eriksen, *Ethnicity and Nationalism*, p. 1.
2. Bayat, *Life as Politics*.
3. Scott, *Weapons of the Weak*.
4. Harb and Leenders, 'Know thy enemy', pp. 173–97.
5. Findley, *Turkey, Islam, Nationalism and Modernity*, p. 251.
6. Öztürk is a relatively common surname. It translates, roughly, as 'Pure Turk'. On the naming issue, see, for instance, Aslan, 'Incoherent state'.
7. Interview, Diyarbakır, 21 October 2014.
8. Kaya, *Europeanisation and Tolerance in Turkey*, p. 115.
9. Interview, Diyarbakır, 21 October 2014.
10. Interview, Diyarbakır, 20 October 2014.
11. Cited in McDowall, *The Kurds*, p. 61.
12. Interview, Diyarbakır, 26 October 2014.
13. Yavuz, 'Kurdish nationalism in Turkey', p. 247.
14. Brubaker, *Ethnicity without Groups*, p. 11.
15. Interview, Diyarbakır, 11 June 2015.
16. Interview, Diyarbakır, 8 June 2015.
17. Interview, Diyarbakır, 8 June 2015.
18. *Hürriyet Daily News*, 'No winner in dirty war', 1 May 2013.
19. Interview, Diyarbakır, 21 October 2014.
20. Güneş, 'Explaining the PKK's mobilization of the Kurds in Turkey', pp. 247–67.
21. Ibid.
22. Aydın, 'Mobilising the Kurds in Turkey', pp. 68–88.
23. Westrheim, 'Taking to the streets!', pp. 137–61.
24. Interview, Diyarbakır, 8 June 2015.
25. Gunter, 'The modern origins of Kurdish nationalism', pp. 2–17.
26. Eriksen, *What is Anthropology?*, p. 163.
27. Interview, Diyarbakır, 20 October 2014.
28. Bozarslan, 'Kurds and the Turkish state', pp. 334–5.
29. Yavuz, 'Kurdish nationalism in Turkey', pp. 243–4.
30. Temelkuran, *Turkey: The insane and the melancholy*, p. 255.
31. Yılmaz, 'Turkiye'de Kimlikler, Kurt Sorunu, ve Cozum Sureci', p. 10.
32. Gurses, *Anatomy of a Civil War*, pp. 12–13.

33. Interview, Diyarbakır, 27 October 2014.
34. Eriksen, *What is Anthropology?*, pp. 163–4.
35. Echoing this sentiment, Garo Paylan, an Armenian HDP parliamentarian, was quoted on social media saying in September 2016 that the HDP identified most with whoever was suffering most. On this basis he remarked, 'I'm more Kurd these days.' See https://twitter.com/MiddleEastInst/status/781854838078529536; http://www.mei.edu/events/7th-annual-turkey-conference.
36. Interview, Diyarbakır, 27 October 2014.
37. Grabolle-Çeliker, *Kurdish Life in Contemporary Turkey*, p. 102.
38. Ibid., pp. 87–9.
39. Aras, *The Formation of Kurdishness in Turkey*, p. 197.
40. *Amnesty International*, 'Vedat Aydin, President of People's Labour Party in Diyarbakir'.
41. Interview, Istanbul, 30 May 2015.
42. Bayat, *Life as Politics*, p. 12.
43. Gurses, *Anatomy of a Civil War*, pp. 41–3.
44. Hosseinioun, 'Reconceptualising resistance and reform in the Middle East', p. 68.
45. Van Bruinessen, 'Genocide in Kurdistan?', pp. 141–70.
46. Bayat, *Life as Politics*, p. 53.
47. Scott, *Weapons of the Weak*.
48. Tripp, *The Power and the People*, p. 8.
49. Güneş, *The Kurdish National Movement in Turkey*, p. 46.
50. Yavuz, 'Five stages in the construction of Kurdish nationalism in Turkey', p. 8.
51. Van Bruinessen, 'Shifting national and ethnic identities', p. 44.
52. *Today's Zaman*, 'Erdoğan: "Past mistakes in fighting terrorism helped PKK"', 22 January 2013.
53. Karakoç and Sarıgil, 'Why religious people support ethnic insurgency?'.
54. Interview, Diyarbakır, 26 October 2014.
55. Saraçoğlu, *Kurds of Modern Turkey*, p. 149. The 'baby killer' terminology retains popularity among Turkish nationalists on social media.
56. Interview, Diyarbakır, 21 October 2014.
57. Başaran, *Frontline Turkey*, p. 89.
58. Natali, *The Kurds and the State*, p. 112.
59. Temelkuran, *Turkey: The insane and the melancholy*, p. 255.

60. Başaran, 'Çözüm için Kürtleri tatmin, Türkleri de ikna etmek lazım', 6 February 2012.
61. Düzel, 'Basın General Emri Dinlememeli,' 26 May 2003.
62. Interview, Istanbul, 13 June 2015.
63. McDowall, *A Modern History of the Kurds*, p. 427.
64. Gramsci, *Selections from the Prison Notebooks*, p. 238.
65. Darıcı, '"Adults See Politics as a Game"', pp. 775–90.
66. Bayat, *Life as Politics*, p. 69.
67. Darweish and Rigby, *Popular Protest in Palestine*, p. 7.
68. Khani, *Mem and Zin*, p. 31.
69. Interview, Diyarbakır, 26 October 2014.
70. Interview, Istanbul, 13 June 2015.
71. Scott, *Weapons of the Weak*, p. 29.
72. Interview, Diyarbakır, 27 October 2014.
73. Harb and Leenders, 'Know thy enemy', pp. 186–9.
74. Scott, *Weapons of the Weak*, p. 32.
75. Gurses, *Anatomy of a Civil War*, p. 40.
76. Grabolle-Çeliker, *Kurdish Life in Contemporary Turkey*, pp. 96–7.
77. Interview, Diyarbakır, 27 October 2014.
78. Interview, Istanbul, 13 June 2015.
79. Ulgen, 'Erdoğan's fetishism of the "National Will"', 6 June 2013.
80. Bayat, *Making Islam Democratic*, pp. 20–1.
81. Darweish and Rigby, *Popular Protest in Palestine*, p. 8.
82. *Hürriyet Daily News*, 'We will not make you the president', 17 March 2015.
83. Ibid.
84. Hebdige, *Subculture*, p. 19.
85. See, for example, *DIHA*, 'Halk Mardin'de Erdoğan'a sırtını döndü', 7 May 2015. The V-for-victory sign has long been a symbol of Kurdish resistance: Temelkuran, *Turkey: The Insane and the Melancholy*, pp. 247–8.
86. See, for example, https://twitter.com/ferhatttunc/status/607511294216912897?.
87. Başaran, *Frontline Turkey*, p. 10.
88. *Hürriyet Daily News*, 'Police detain five for making victory sign,' 24 July 2017.
89. Arparcık, 'Feeling solidarity in an estranged city', p. 108.
90. Scott, *Weapons of the Weak*, p. 46.
91. *Radikal*, 'Biz birkaç çapulcunun yaptıklarını yapmayız', 9 June 2013.

92. Kemahlıoğlu, 'Winds of change?', p. 453.
93. *Hürriyet*, 'Erdoğan'dan manifesto sonrası bir ilk . . .', 3 February 2019.
94. *Diken*, 'Ak Trol' değil profesör',10 August 2015.
95. Demirtaş, 'No Kurdish opening likely after local polls', 9 February 2019.
96. Erdoğan, 'Trump is right on Syria', 7 January 2019.
97. *Hürriyet Daily News*, 'Amedspor holds Fenerbahce to draw', 9 February 2016.
98. Kasapoğlu, 'Turkey Kurds', 15 May 2019.
99. Taştekin, 'Kurds in Turkey unite', 15 January 2019.

8

KURDS AS CITIZENS

Mark Twain once famously remarked, 'Citizenship is what makes a republic; monarchies can get along without it.'[1] The distinction appears salient in considering the Republic of Turkey and the Ottoman Empire that preceded it. The Ottoman model of governance and authority rested on a complex system of socio-ethnic and religious balances, where primary identities were religious and allegiance was to the sultan. New ideas of state–society relationships, including republicanism, the nation-state and the citizen, sweeping in from Europe in the nineteenth century imperilled the Ottoman model, ultimately leading to its collapse and fragmentation along ethnic lines.[2] The Republic's founders in 1923 eagerly disposed of the moribund sultanate and reimagined the population as citizens, highlighting 'unity of language, culture and ideal'[3] to cement the new polity.

Twain continued: 'What keeps a republic on its legs is good citizenship.' By this he meant that an active citizenry will ensure the proper functioning of the republic. This is not necessarily how things panned out in Turkey, where emphasis has always been on ensuring the authority of the state and outlining citizens' duties rather than encouraging them to pursue their rights and liberties. From the outset, the parameters of citizenship were imposed, not negotiated. The Republic expected obedience and sought to entrench loyalty through ethnic unity. Article 88 of the first constitution (1924) decreed, 'The people of Turkey regardless of religion and race would, in terms of citizenship, be considered Turkish.'[4] More carefully worded, but imparting essentially the same message, Article 66 of the 1982 constitution, written after the 1980 coup and still in place, states, 'everyone connected to the Turkish state with ties of citizenship is a Turk'.[5] This formulation, theoretically, is inclusive, granting citizenship of the nation-state to all, whether they be ethnically Turkish or otherwise. But in practice it has been understood – and enforced – as the co-option of all into Turkishness, thus citizenship is conflated with uniform subscription to Turkishness and no divergence will be countenanced. Turkish citizenship, as is the case with Turkish nationalism noted earlier, was acquisitive but simultaneously exclusive – it attempted to claim all for Turkishness, but it fiercely denounced those who refused to accept such a nomenclature.[6]

The constitutional articles discussed above outline but one interpretation of citizenship. Yet citizenship is a multifaceted entity, and like ethnicity, the other concern of this book, is open to myriad interpretations. It is comprised of political rights as well as socio-economic rights.[7] It may be viewed from a cultural perspective, encompassing the right to 'unhindered and dignified representation, as well as to the maintenance and propagation of distinct cultural identities and lifestyles'.[8] Similarly, citizenship bestows membership of a political community, and can be taken to be a practice in the sense that individuals participate in the political life of that community.[9] Viewed this way, the delineation of the parameters of citizenship is a two-way process, a dialogue between the individuals (who make up society) and the state.

Ahmet İçduygu and Özlem Kaygusuz note, however, that Turkish citizenship is seen as a 'civic-territorial ... duty-based, passive identity' that has been defined 'against the outside world, and against the Other'.[10] In other words, citizens must observe their duty to the state, rather than the state having any obligations to the citizen. The citizen owes loyalty but is not encouraged or expected to participate in society or community. While conformity is expected and loyalty is expected (rather than earned), participation in the political process and the public sphere, those qualities that encompass active citizenship, are not. The passive and duty-based nature of citizenship among Turks is indeed echoed in a 2015 study that found that Turks' participation in political activity is particularly low.[11] Surveying participants across Turkey, the study found that 96 per cent of Turks regarded voting in elections as a key indicator of being a 'good citizen', but also found that only small numbers had ever taken part in campaign rallies or demonstrations, joined a political party or made contact with political officials for any reason. This focus on elections as the principal marker and responsibility of citizenship demonstrates a limited conceptualisation of the idea among Turks. Even so, rates of civic engagement and ideas of citizenship vary across Turkey.[12]

Where does this leave Kurds? Regarding the 'unity of language, culture and ideal' conceived as the core of the Republic, issues arise immediately, regarding language and culture. But what of the 'ideal'? As earlier chapters have outlined, a central aspect of Kurdishness is asserting one's difference, or maintaining a boundary, from broader Turkish society. Thus the idea of citizenship, conceived as passive and duty-bound to the state, must be problematic for Kurds. Research suggests that years of conflict and political tension have spurred greater civic engagement in cities like Diyarbakır.[13] Further complicating the matter is the notion that citizenship and identity are incompatible entities. As Engin Isin and Patricia Wood note, the idea that there is an inherent conflict between the two arises because citizenship is often understood to be universal, whereas identity is seen to be particular.[14] The circumstances of the Kurds in Turkey appear to be a salient case in that their particular ethnic identity (Kurdish) appears to be incompatible with the universal citizenship (Turkish) within which they are categorised. Yet, as Doğu Ergil's study in 1995 found, many Kurds accept their status as members of the Turkish polity.[15] This has also been my observation. Broadly speaking, Kurds are able to reconcile membership of Turkey's political community with their self-definition as Kurds. That said, Kurds may well be willing to identify with Turkey, the political entity, but many would never countenance identifying with Turkishness, the ethnic identity. This point was made clear to me when one participant, Aykut, a teacher in Diyarbakır, bristled at the suggestion he should be classified as a 'Turkish citizen' but was happy to be seen as a 'citizen of Turkey'. Here he drew a distinction between the ethnic category ('Turkish') and the state ('Turkey') – he could envision himself as a member of the political community, but not the ethnic group.[16]

This chapter seeks to examine this notion and the mechanisms by which this is possible. It may be tempting to assume that Kurds conceive of citizenship in Turkey as a categorisation that is inherently 'Turkish', but it is entirely possible that they have given the concept little thought. Kurdish identity has been highly politicised, but discussion of Kurdish citizenship in the Republic of Turkey has been very little discussed. Christian Joppke argues for a definition of citizenship at its most basic, as membership in a nation-state, but he highlights that even then it assumes two meanings, one as articulated by the people, the other as propagated by the state. He further notes that the greatest gap in the literature is in the former, what they perceive or understand as amounting to citizenship.[17] This chapter, then, will examine how Kurds in Turkey view and enact their citizenship and, in turn, the impacts this has in Turkey's political arena.

Citizenship as Obligation, Imposition, Resignation

If the Turks in the survey mentioned above had only a limited understanding of citizenship, the Kurds interviewed for this study did not prove to have ready answers on the subject either. My question, 'How do you define citizenship?' generally drew blank looks. Offering further prompts such as 'paying taxes' or 'voting in elections' often did little to help. Rather than being able to define the constituent parts of citizenship, or what it meant to them, several interviewees immediately remarked that it was something that had been imposed upon them. Zehra said that in Turkey one is 'imprisoned into citizenship and identity' ('*hapis ederek bir vatandaşlık ve kimlik olusturuyor*').[18] Salih said, while laughing ruefully, 'It's a compulsory thing.'[19] Soner observed, 'It's a kind of obligation. I didn't choose it.'[20]

Taken at its broadest interpretation – membership of political community – there is never a voluntary element to citizenship, notwithstanding a situation when someone chooses citizenship of a second country. In one definition, citizenship 'explicitly ties populations to unique, territorially defined polities'.[21] One becomes a citizen of a nation-state by virtue of being born there, so in this sense my Australian citizenship is 'compulsory' and 'an obligation' too. What is significant in the negative connotations in the comments above is that the speakers take the idea of citizenship to implicitly mean membership in a Turkish, rather than Kurdish, political entity.

It must be noted, however, that any disconnect in the embrace of citizenship by Kurds is not solely due to their own intransigence. Many also argue that the state does not recognise them as Kurds – as they would like to be recognised – and this contributes to their ambivalence about claiming, or valuing, membership of the state. Mert, a café proprietor, observed begrudgingly, 'I would say I am a citizen. But we feel like second-class citizens here.'[22] Ayhan similarly remarked, 'OK, I am a citizen, but I cannot speak my own language and live my own culture. Yes, citizenship is a system, it is the relationship with our government. But the problem is that this [government] does not [accept] different cultures and languages.'[23] Here, the model of 'cultural citizenship' is not being implemented. 'Rights to unhindered and dignified representation, as well as to the maintenance and propagation of distinct cultural identities' are not upheld.[24]

That these concerns arise reflects the top-down nature of politics and the long-term nation-building project in Turkey whereby politics, policy and political status are not negotiated but imposed. They also result from the dominance that Turkish nationalism has maintained in definitions of national identity. Despite the wording of the constitutional definition of citizenship, nationalist discourse has, in practice, allowed little scope for variation, and Turkishness is assumed – and vigorously asserted – to be the norm. A popular mantra, recited by politicians particularly while the PKK's separatist agenda peaked in the 1990s, is '*tek dil, tek bayrak, tek millet*' (Turkish: 'one language, one flag, one nation'). When I mentioned it to Kurds they greeted it, universally, with scorn. Yet the one-language-one-flag discourse retains currency and still largely dictates societal dynamics and pervades official thought, or so Kurds perceive. Research undertaken in Diyarbakır in 2014 revealed that some view the state as being in opposition to the citizenry.[25] Ayhan lamented, 'Currently being a Turkish citizen resembles a very bad illustration comprised of racism and nationalism . . . Those who live in Turkey gain admission [only] as a Turk. Something this simplistic should not be acceptable.'[26] Those Kurds who perceive a Turk-centric definition of citizenship – of membership in the nation-state – to be dominant are reluctant to fully invest in such membership.

Yet, as discussions unfurled, respondents revealed degrees of acceptance to ideas of citizenship. Kurds appeared at the very least resigned to citizenship, or willing to accommodate it, as an administrative status. Zehra declared that her citizenship was a bureaucratic category that allowed her to go about her work,[27] and several noted that if travelling overseas they were deemed

Turkish due to their passports.[28] Mithat, who complained of having 'no link with the government', acknowledged, however, that he had access to government services such as universities and hospitals.[29] In fact, government service provision to the Kurdish-populated south-east is markedly improved on earlier decades. In part this is a result of the AKP in its early years recasting governance as the provision of services to constituents, part of what Erdoğan espoused as a 'trading mentality' (*tüccaret zihniyeti*) in the party and government, whereby a transaction involving delivery of services to constituents would be rewarded with winning the loyalty of those constituents.[30] It is well documented that the poverty and lack of economic development in the south-east played a role in the Kurds reinforcing their ethnic identity, their 'Kurdish-being'.[31] Erdoğan's initial aspiration appears to have been to address economic shortcomings as a pathway to better governance and, as a result, electoral popularity for the AKP. This is a form of 'eudaemonic legitimation', whereby satisfying the economic demands of citizens buttresses regime legitimacy.[32] During visits to Diyarbakır over many years, I have observed the material improvements in infrastructure in the city, and the shift in political mood from neglected Diyarbakır in 1992 to optimistic Diyarbakır in mid-2015 was all but palpable.

Yet even here many Kurds saw themselves as second-class citizens. They acknowledged that improvements had occurred but they perceived economic development and investment as still being skewed towards the western, non-Kurdish, regions of the country. Zehra remarked, 'Our expectations, if we live together, are that we need to be part of this country too ... They make many investments in Istanbul. Therefore, they need to do the same to the cities where Kurds live. By doing so, we might be able to trust the Government more.'[33] This was a common refrain. I have often heard comments that the government should invest in factories in the south-east in order to create jobs for Kurds and stimulate the economy. In fact, Turkish politicians have regularly observed the chronic underdevelopment of the south-east and used it as an all-encompassing explanation for Kurdish unrest.[34] Kurds may agree with them that it is a source of grievance but many would further argue that any economic divide is a result of anti-Kurdish prejudice.[35] Many of them also commented that better service provision would, if not addressing all Kurdish concerns, at least foster a sense of loyalty to the Turkish political system – a neat example of 'eudaemonic legitimation'. Indeed, Zeynep Gambetti observes that discourses of both 'imposed' poverty and of the state's obligation to provide employment are common in Diyarbakır. Notably, Rümelili and Çakmaklı's research in Diyarbakır found a greater emphasis on rights, rather than obligations, inherent in citizenship compared to other cities.[36] This demonstrates the ambiguity of Kurds' perceptions of the state: it has long been regarded as an oppressive hegemon but it is also seen as a potential 'purveyor of goods and services'.[37] When asked if he would feel a stronger bond with the state if it provided better services, Mert remarked, 'You mean like in America? Sure, why not? I would say that I am a Turkish citizen.'[38]

This raises an important point. Although many Kurds reveal ambivalence about their relationship with the Republic of Turkey, many also appear to harbour an idea of *provisional* citizenship: they do not reject the idea outright, but they would more fully embrace their status as citizens if the state did more for them. Kurds, generally, do not subscribe to the passive model of citizenship that İçduygu and Kaygusuz discuss and which many Turks appear to practice. Rather they expect citizenship to be a transaction, a form of social contract. In order to grant their loyalty to the state they expect the government to offer them something in return. I describe this as *provisional* citizenship because, as Kurds explained to me, they would feel a stronger link with the state if they felt it did more to meet their demands and their needs. In the examples above these amounted to cultural demands, the 'claims to dignifying representation, normative accommodation, and active cultivation of . . . [distinct ethnic] identities' that are the hallmarks of 'cultural citizenship'.[39] This also included material needs – jobs, factories, welfare, public services – but they further extend to political and democratic rights and demands.

Weight of Circumstances: Belonging, Friends, Relatives

When I switched questioning to address the idea of 'belonging' in Turkey, interviewees had different and more ready responses than to the question of citizenship. Even some who had seemed bemused by or antagonistic to the idea of citizenship were more positive about the prospect of belonging in Turkey.

In many cases, respondents offered experiences of growing up and going through schooling as exemplifying their belonging in Turkey. 'I kind of do [belong], because I have a Turkish passport [laughs] and I was educated in Turkish,' said Soner.[40] For Mithat, speaking Turkish and being educated similarly created a bond: 'Because of this we became members of the Turkish community.'[41] For Ayhan, his very presence in Turkey for the entirety of his life engendered an identification with the nation-state: 'Of course I feel that I belong in Turkey, whether it be the community structure, political status or any other topic. I am thirty years old and I have never been overseas . . . I do not have any other experiences to compare my life to. In one way or another I feel as though I belong here, because I have done things that people in this country do. I live like them.' Thus, despite negative experiences that some had experienced at the hands of the state (Mithat, for one, had been arrested for his political activities), the sheer weight of experience, the comings and goings of everyday life, created some form of bond. Esra noted, despite her being proud of her Kurdish identity, that when the Turkish national football team played international matches she felt a sense of pride and patriotism.[42] Notable in many responses was the importance that many gave to the Turkish language. Despite the tenacity with which many Kurds upheld the Kurdish language as a marker of their identity, they still highlighted Turkish as something that they 'shared' with Turks. The fact that they had been schooled and grew up reading, writing and listening to Turkish created a sense of belonging and a connection.

In my observation, despite criticism of the state, many Kurds have a sense that they share a social trajectory with Turks. Indeed, Kurds who live in Turkey tend to look to the large cities of Turkey's west, rather than to Kurdish-majority cities in Syria, Iran or Kurdish-administered northern Iraq, as cities of economic or educational opportunity.[43] Highlighting this point is the fact that some Kurds baulk at the idea of an independent Kurdish state if it means they would need a passport to travel to Istanbul.[44] Several Kurds whom I met in Diyarbakır and who styled themselves as 'businessmen' regularly travelled to resort towns in Turkey's west to partake in the tourism industry. Thus many Kurds understand that their citizenship in Turkey offers tangible benefits; this makes them willing to identify as members of Turkey's political community. They have been conditioned to the socio-political and economic conditions within Turkey.

A connection to Turkey manifests in other ways. Esra mentioned her distress at hearing of the Soma mining disaster, in Manisa, in May 2014, when over three hundred Turkish miners were killed.⁴⁵ She identified those killed as compatriots, despite their living on the opposite side of the country. 'We have a past together so I feel like they are my people. I don't see them as another people because we have a fate in this country together,' she remarked.⁴⁶ Her grief intensified her sense of connection with others, even if they might be ethnically Turkish, and with it her sense of belonging in the nation-state. Similarly, the intertwined history of Turks and Kurds in Anatolia creates a degree of affinity. Salih noted, 'Yes, if you live together nearly a thousand years, I mean from the time of Malazgirt⁴⁷ . . . of course we share many cultural, folkloric figures, peculiarities. For example, our folk dances resemble each other, our clothing styles resemble each other . . .' He saw Turks and Kurds as 'cousins' who are more alike than different.⁴⁸ This is the point that Martin van Bruinessen makes when he notes the considerable diversity in the 'primary markers' of identity among Kurds and, indeed, overlap with such markers for Turks.⁴⁹

Many Kurds also note a connection with Turks at the day-to-day level. All but one interviewee readily remarked that they have friends who are Turks. Fehim, a teacher in Diyarbakır, observed, 'It is a forced [political] relationship. However, we have willingly made many Turkish friends.'⁵⁰ He was referring to Kurds' status as citizens of Turkey as a forced relationship, but he conceded that despite this imposition Kurds were able to develop companionship with Turks. Fehim was the most begrudging on this point; all others seemed to regard it as a natural thing to develop friendships with people they lived alongside, regardless of ethnicity. A conversation I had with two Kurdish men in a Diyarbakır shop elicited cries of '*tabiki*' ('of course') when I asked if they had friendships or other connections with Turks.⁵¹ Both of them rubbed their index fingers together, a widely recognised Turkish gesture for friendship and warm relations.

Many also cited examples of marriage between Turks and Kurds as an example of amicable relations. Even Mert, who espoused one of the more politically radical philosophies among those I interviewed, remarked casually that he had Turkish relatives. He said, 'My sister she is married to a Turkish man. And I know he is from different ideology, but we have no problem. Why would we?'⁵² A study in 2010 found that in fact Turkish–Kurdish intermarriage is not particularly common, with such marriages occurring in less than 6 per cent of cases.⁵³ Nonetheless, Kurds mentioned these marriages in a matter-of-fact manner, clearly regarding them as a normal part of life. As Ümit Cizre notes, Turks and Kurds have not been insulated from each other, and long coexistence as part of Anatolia's 'ethnic mosaic' has determined that neither peoples' history can be entirely extricated from the other's. Indeed, she argues, 'A Turkish factor has remained integral to the Kurdish sense of self, be it in the form of resentment and resistance, or affection and affinity.'⁵⁴ This is apparent in friendships and the fact that Kurds see themselves as able to be absorbed through marriage into the fabric of broader Turkish society. To marry someone who is Turkish, thus indisputably a citizen, is considered nothing out of the ordinary. The weight of circumstance, and lived experience, contribute to a form of identification, some sense of allegiance – personal, situational, familial – with Turks and Turkey as a home and place where they had grown up.

Nevertheless, several respondents highlighted that while they enjoy friendships with Turks or have Turkish relatives, they knew, through experience, to avoid political conversations, specifically those that touched on ethnicity, with their Turkish friends. Here the idea of resentment that Cizre mentions is apparent. Mert's comment, noted above, is a case in point. He described his brother-in-law as having a 'different ideology', by which he meant that he voted for the AKP, and thus he chose not to discuss politics with him. Musa said he had many Turkish friends but he 'never' spoke about politics or issues of ethnicity with them. He remarked, 'Turkish people are kind; they have good hearts and good personalities. But when you talk about Turk and Kurd they don't like it. They say we are brothers. But when you ask why the police is killing or attacking Kurdish people, they say the Kurds force police to do that. That's why if we have Turkish friend we never talk about this.'⁵⁵ Many Kurds shared this attitude: political discussions with Turks were best avoided. It is apparently simple enough for Turks and Kurds to find common ground, indeed 'affection and affinity' as Cizre notes, in public life but the political becomes problematic. Zehra remarked, 'We actually don't have any problems with Turks. We have a problem with Turkey's system.'⁵⁶ Displeasure with the political system and their place within the political hierarchy acts to dilute the strength of bonds that Kurds feel for Turkey. This suggests that the Kurdish issue at its core is not one of ethnicity – there is no intrinsic enmity between Kurds and Turks – but of political circumstance. As has been noted, 'identity politics is more about politics than identity'.[57]

Indeed, Turkey has no significant history of intercommunal violence; the violence that has bedevilled the south-east has essentially been between the state security apparatus and the PKK.[58] This, in turn, suggests that should the political conditions be conducive, Kurds will more closely identify with the Turkish body politic and be more likely to embrace their positions as citizens within it.

Participating in Politics: Citizenship made Manifest

Ernst Renan conceives of the nation as a 'daily plebiscite', a 'large-scale solidarity ... summarized by a tangible fact, namely, consent, the clearly expressed desire to continue a common life'.[59] If elections may be taken as a literal example of a 'daily plebiscite', then the Kurds' enthusiastic participation in Turkey's electoral processes must also be construed as 'consent' to the idea of citizenship in Turkey and of a 'desire to continue a common life' in the body politic.

Through May and June 2015, election fever raged across Turkey, as I observed. Campaign materials – bunting, posters, billboards, flags, as well as buses broadcasting campaign slogans – of all parties were clearly in evidence in Istanbul and Diyarbakır.[60] In Istanbul's Beyoğlu and Kadıköy neighbourhoods, quarters frequented by Kurds and leftists of all persuasions, HDP campaign activity was plain to see. In Diyarbakır, I noted palpable anticipation and excitement in the lead-up to the election. HDP leader Selahattin Demirtaş' decision to contest the election on a party basis with the aim of passing the 10 per cent national vote threshold raised the stakes considerably for Kurdish voters. Rather than being concerned that the HDP might have overreached, Kurds I spoke with were confident that the HDP would clear the threshold and take up seats in the parliament. On multiple occasions I witnessed groups spontaneously gathering in the streets to dance the *govend*,[61] often brandishing HDP banners and chanting '*Bizler HDP, bizler meclise*' – 'We are the HDP, we are [coming] into parliament.'

It must be reiterated that the HDP is not solely intended as a political vehicle for Kurds,[62] but it is also clear that the bulk of its supporters are Kurdish and that Kurds I spoke to saw the HDP as representing their interests *as Kurds*.

Figure 8.1   Dancing at HDP rally, Diyarbakır, 5 June 2015. © William Gourlay.

That the HDP was participating confidently – and freely – in the electoral process, all the while voicing an alternative and inclusive political vision, boosted Kurds' enthusiasm for the party and the elections, and in so doing for the political process. James Kellas notes a similar phenomenon in Scotland, where the idea of dual nationality (voters' willingness to profess Britishness and Scottishness simultaneously) rises considerably during electoral campaigns.[63] Kellas' findings suggest that identification with the political community – the sense of citizenship – is affected, just as ethnic identity is, by contingent events and that electoral periods have the effect of making citizenship a more appealing, or more broadly interpreted, prospect in situations where there are different ethnic or national categories.

Politicians of all stripes in June 2015 promoted their agendas at rallies and on TV broadcasts. In Diyarbakır, excitement had been building for some time in anticipation of Selahattin Demirtaş' appearance at a final rally two days before polling day. In the morning, everyone – the staff at the hotel where I stayed, people sitting in teahouses, those on the street – spoke eagerly of the '*miting*'. Many urged me to attend. By the middle of the day, crowds gathered in the centre of the old town and began progressing towards the square in Yenişehir where the rally would be held. A raucous parade of humanity snaked through the streets carrying banners and chanting pro-HDP slogans. I saw several people I knew joining the procession, including a very timid man who cleaned rooms in my hotel. Amid the crowd he was completely transformed. Caught up in the moment, he raucously joined in chants, and flashed the V-for-victory sign.

Meanwhile, shops were closed and the centre of the city was quiet but for the chants that rang out as people progressed towards Yenişehir. The most consistent slogan was '*Önce baraj, sonra saray*' ('First the threshold, then the palace'). The message here was that the HDP would first pass the 10 per cent voting threshold to win seats in the national assembly and thereafter, at some later date, win the presidency. In combination with the many examples of Kurdish traditional dress and flags in the Kurdish *tricoleur*, explicit statements of Kurdish nationalist identity, a claim to take the presidential palace may be seen as a threat to the political system. But it should also be considered in the context of the equally popular '*bizler meclise*' ('we are coming into parliament') slogan. Both slogans, I argue, demonstrate the palpable excitement that Kurds experienced at the prospect of the HDP entering parliament, winning political legitimacy for and conveying the voices of Kurds – and others – as citizens in ongoing political debates. They were an affirmation of Turkey's political system, in that Kurds were demonstrating it was possible to be visibly Kurdish while participating in a Turkish election. With these slogans, HDP supporters were demonstrating their acceptance of their position as citizens *as Kurds* within Turkey.

A festival atmosphere reigned at the campaign rally in Yenişehir. Numerous people welcomed me, clearly an outsider. I encountered people of all ages and backgrounds, from university students with guitars to conservative elders with moustaches and cloth caps. Of the many I spoke to, all were convinced that the HDP would pass the threshold. Crowds sang Kurdish songs or joined hands to dance the *govend*. The event amounted to a clear demonstration of Kurdish identity: in this context the HDP, despite its multicultural agenda, was presented by the crowd as a manifestation of their Kurdishness.

Despite the fact that ISIS struck, disrupting the rally, as was detailed previously, the excitement continued until the election. Polling stations were busy and lively on election day. A refrain I regularly heard was that '*herşeye rağmen*' ('despite everything') they would enact their right to vote. One young Kurdish man told me outside a polling booth on the day, '*Biz toplanmış, biz katılmış*' ('We joined in, we participated').[64] Following the bombs at the rally I was hesitant about spending time at electoral locations, but the day passed without incident. After the poll booths closed in the late afternoon the city fell silent, but in the early evening as preliminary voting figures were released it became apparent that the HDP would pass the electoral threshold. As if to vindicate the Kurds' enthusiasm, the HDP polled impressively, gaining 13 per cent of the vote, winning the third-largest number of seats in parliament and denying the AKP a parliamentary majority for the first time since it emerged in 2002.[65] As evening arrived, Diyarbakır erupted in a cacophony of cheers, whistles, firecrackers and car horns. The streets throbbed with crowds of people waving flags, promenading with family, cruising in their cars. The HDP had made a way into parliament and Diyarbakır was ecstatic. Here was Rénan's 'daily plebiscite' made manifest. This was not a daily event, but a specific and pivotal episode. Kurds willingly and enthusiastically participated, casting their votes in order to have their say in how the country should be governed.

Broadly speaking, the Kurdish vote in Turkey is a two-horse race between the AKP and HDP.[66] The emphatic showing of the HDP, leaping over the threshold, demonstrated that Kurdish support had swung behind the pro-Kurdish party and away from the AKP. Pro-Kurdish parties had previously only ever polled around 6 per cent, and thus the June 2015 election marked a watershed moment for Kurdish politics. Despite the travails that the party has endured, including renewed conflict in the south-east and concerted government and judicial pressure, it has maintained its vote above the threshold ever since. This is another example whereby, as Dick Hebdige observes, a 'commodity', in this case the electoral process, has been 'repossessed' and 'endowed with implicitly oppositional meanings'.[67] Kurds demonstrated their enthusiasm for voting and their loss of enthusiasm for Erdoğan. If considering these developments from the perspective of Kurdish citizenship, one might argue that in voting Kurds were signalling their approval of their status as citizens and simultaneously signalling their disapproval of the AKP. Thus Kurds' votes against the government should be seen as an exercise of rights that indicates an acceptance of *membership* of the political system if not acceptance of the actual day-to-day practices of governance by that system. By this I mean Kurdish votes in the election, even those delivered as protest votes against the government, are an active assertion by Kurds of their rights as citizens. Hypothetically, if Kurds are members of the body politic then they should be able to voice their opinions to signal their displeasure with the policy direction of the nation-state or with the specific actions of state agencies, bureaucracy, educational system or security apparatus. Elise Massicard argues that Kurdish politics is not solely about recognition but is also a means of 'voicing alternative projects for politics and society'.[68] As in the case of any group, political party or segment of society, protests, in many political contexts, and votes against the government that Kurds cast, may be seen as demonstrations of a desire to participate in the political life of the polity, a demonstration of their desire for a better or more just polity. This is not a rejection of the political system, but an implicit acceptance of it as a means to building a better society.

Following the election of 7 June 2015, one might argue that Kurds were embarking further on a 'war of position'.[69] Dilek, in conversation the day after the election, remarked that Kurds would 'take their war into parliament now'.[70] By this she meant that the Kurdish struggle could now take place within the confines of the national assembly, to be fought through the legitimate political mechanisms of parliamentary debate and negotiation, rather than a physical 'war of manoeuvre'. A war of position, alternatively, is an initiative to change the political status quo, but at the same time it is, implicitly, an acceptance of membership of the body politic. It represents joining-the-system-in-order-to-change-it, but it is simultaneously an acknowledgement that the system is redeemable, worthy of merit and membership. In that sense, Kurds' enthusiastic support for the HDP, a party that had an agenda to redefine the political status quo, may be seen as a challenge to existing political currents or the overarching conservative dynamic of what remains an essentially nationalism-infused politics, but it is comprised of a vision for change from within to instil a more democratic, pluralist model for all of Turkey. Several Kurds I spoke to relished this prospect; some saw in it an opportunity to reverse their status as 'second-class citizens'.[71] While the parliamentary prospects of the HDP looked rosy, Kurds displayed an optimism about their political circumstances; their citizenship within what appeared a smoothly functioning democracy was more valuable to them and they identified more strongly with Turkey as a nation-state, a political entity, even a homeland, that could be pluralist.

Struggling for Democracy?

In taking their 'war into parliament now', as Dilek remarked, Kurds were adopting a Gramscian 'war of position', but in fact this process had been under way for some time. Asef Bayat depicts such an undertaking as an effort at 'exerting moral and intellectual leadership over civil institutions and processes'.[72] In many respects, the Kurdish struggle is a measure of the health of democracy in Turkey.[73] Thus it may be argued that if Kurds are to undertake a 'war of position' and exert said 'moral and intellectual leadership' then their struggle must transcend a focus on issues of interest solely to Kurds and embrace a broader struggle for democracy across ethnic boundaries. This is something that interviewees' acknowledgement of the multicultural history of Anatolia and Diyarbakır touches on. They argue that minorities other than just the Kurds have been wronged politically and they therefore identify with them as others who fall outside the Turkish mainstream. But a broader acknowledgement of a wider struggle is also apparent. In 2008, the then mayor of the Sur neighbourhood of Diyarbakır, Abdullah Demirbaş, remarked in an interview, 'I am not working for the Kurds; I am working for all people. Democracy means that when you want something for yourself, you also want it for others.'[74]

Demirbaş was furthering a general Kurdish discourse that had, during the 1990s, swung from 'national liberation' to political and human rights as a result of the interaction of various organisations that were not exclusively Kurdish. Kurdish actors realised a political agenda that highlighted democracy and human rights could appeal to a wider audience within the Turkish electorate while also gaining legitimacy for the Kurdish cause internationally.[75] Against the fractious timbre of politics in Turkey, the DTP (precursor to the HDP) argued that 'the principle of pluralism based upon multiculturalism and the equal, free and balanced development of differences and distinctions ... must be accepted'.[76] To some degree, it may be argued, this approach arose out of the conflict conditions Kurdish political actors had found themselves in, leading to a desire for greater democratic engagement, underpinned by the 'logic of equality'.[77] In turn, this spurred a repositioning of the Kurdish agenda within the demands of a broad variety of Turkey's societal segments – workers, women, other minority groups – for equality and democracy.[78] In this way, the Kurdish political movement came to represent more than an exclusively Kurdish politics and positioned itself as a vehicle for multiculturalism and democracy. Selahattin Demirtaş echoed these sentiments while campaigning in 2015, telling an audience the HDP's goal was to win a victory for all the 'oppressed of Turkey'.[79]

When I repeated such comments to study participants, they broadly concurred. Many agreed that what was at issue was not just Kurdish rights but also the lack of an open political landscape where all could participate without fear or favour. Several pointed to the candidate lists of the HDP, which campaigned in 2015 with candidates from across ethnic divides, as evidence of a more inclusive politics. As with their acknowledgement of other minorities in discussions of religion, most I interviewed argued for a greater role for other minorities in politics. Within this, many saw the Kurds as taking a primary role, for instance Gelaz remarked, 'Yes it is everyone's struggle. It is the Kurdish movement but it was undertaken for all peoples.'[80] Others pointed to earlier successes the Kurdish movement had achieved, such as the establishment of TRT6, the state-run Kurdish broadcaster, and argued that these had had flow-on effects such that other minority languages, including Arabic and Bosnian, were also broadcast on state-run media. For Semih, the initiatives of the Kurdish movement had resulted in an 'end of the politics of assimilation', and thus a more inclusive and democratic polity. 'Now [even] the Circassians are demanding their rights,' he noted.[81] Refik similarly remarked, 'Thanks to the Kurdish movement, Arabs, without any bloodshed or destruction, were able to rise and own a TV channel.'[82] They made these remarks without any bitterness that Kurds had suffered in order for other ethnicities to win gains, but rather with a sense of pride that Kurds, as they saw it, had been able to open avenues for others.

Ralf Dahrendorf contends that the true test of citizenship is its ability to accommodate heterogeneity.[83] Thus it can be argued that in espousing a more pluralist politics, Kurds are working for a more robust model of citizenship, and are implicitly asserting their status as citizens in Turkey. Thus, to some degree the Kurdish struggle has come to transcend the issue of Kurdishness –

it is not even a struggle against 'Turkishness', per se, but it becomes one of democracy. As evidence of this, HDP leader Demirtaş while campaigning pledged to abandon 'ethnic politics' after the 7 June election.[84] Campaign materials that I collected in Diyarbakır highlighted the HDP position, stating, '[*T*]üm ınançların özgürce yaşanması gerektiğini savunuyoruz' ('We advocate that all beliefs should live freely').[85] The HDP includes Kurds, Turks, Armenians, Yezidis, Assyrians, Circassians and Alevis as electoral candidates.[86] An HDP campaign video in late 2015 spoke of a Turkey that was '*hem çok renkli hem çok dilli*' ('both multi-coloured and multilingual'), while also being '*inadına adil eşit ve özgür, inadına beraber*' ('determinedly just, equal and free, determinedly together').[87] A Kurdish HDP supporter I met in Istanbul assured me, 'The HDP is different. It's not a Kurdish party, it's a Kurdish-dominant party.'[88] Underlining this statement, when I had earlier approached an HDP campaign stand in central Istanbul saying that I was researching Kurdish politics, the HDP activists present immediately retorted, 'But we are Turks.'[89] The HDP thus represented a liberal, ecumenical political vehicle, one that sought to pursue the interests of and win the support of citizens from across Turkey's ethnic and religious spectrum. In this way, the HDP set itself apart from the evermore autocratic AKP, which increasingly resorts to rump nationalist slogans that emphasise unity of language, nation and flag and an authoritarian appropriation of Islamic mores.

Dahrendorf continues that citizenship commands 'common respect for basic entitlements among people who are different in origin, culture and creed'.[90] As Mithat noted, 'We are not fighting against the Turkish community, or the Armenian, or others ... We struggle with the Turkish government or Turkish state with their policies, and *jandarma* [police]. We are struggling with their ideology and security apparatus.'[91] Mithat, and many others I spoke to, see their struggle as one for democracy, one in which there was still much work to do. Salih remarked, 'The country is a symbolic thing. You have borders, you live together, but if there is no democracy, no fundamental human rights, no equality ... it doesn't make any sense.'[92] It has become commonly accepted that allowing minorities a place in the political framework is no longer seen 'as a matter of discretionary policies or pragmatic compromises but rather as a matter of fundamental justice'.[93] Accordingly, minority participation is a key indicator of a fully functioning democracy.

The idea that Kurds believe they have a role to play in furthering democracy further demonstrates their acceptance of the status of 'citizen' within Turkey. One would not work towards the betterment of a political community if one did not feel a sense of membership within it. In this regard, the Kurds' struggle should not be seen as a struggle *against* Turkey, as Mithat's comment above attests to, but should be seen as a struggle *within* Turkey, or even a struggle *on behalf of* Turkey. Here, again, the notion of *provisional* citizenship arises. Earlier, I argued that Kurds would more wholeheartedly embrace their citizenship if certain economic measures were implemented; it is also the case the political changes would accelerate such a process. Erdem remarked, 'If you actually start giving people their rights, without conditions ... then if people realise that they have lived with Turks for a thousand years, and they have so much in common, and [if] they are convinced that Turkey no longer looks at them as an enemy, then it's possible [they will view] Turkey as their own country.'[94] Ali expressed similar sentiments, saying that in a more democratic environment, 'Of course [we] will feel we can trust this government, or we can trust Turkey. Turkey is also our state.'[95] Esra, too, remarked, 'At the end, the [Kurdish] dream depends on ... freedom. It can be inside Turkey, [if] you can live freely and talk freely. It can be outside Turkey. It depends totally [on] the politics of Turkey ... If it becomes ... a more democratic country, and I feel that freely as a Kurdish woman I can live in this country, why not?'[96] Many Kurds expressed similar views: were the political situation improved, from a point of view of democracy and human rights, then they would more fully value their status as citizens. Accordingly, in mobilising, in voicing their opposition to Erdoğan, in airing their grievances, Kurds are – just as Doğu Ergil found in 1995 – not demonstrating that they 'want out', but in fact that they 'want to come in'.[97]

Turning Up – again – at the Ballot Box

The HDP's success in the election of June 2015 had ongoing implications for Turkey. It upset the AKP apple cart, leading to a hardening of resolve from Erdoğan, which in turn catalysed a series of political shocks, few of which were positive for Kurds. Erdoğan then used the coup attempt of July 2016 to tighten his grip on the political arena. A particular focus, despite it having no connection to the coup attempt, was the Kurdish political movement.

In November 2016, the government moved to install 'trustees' to the mayoralty of Diyarbakır, among other south-eastern cities, removing the HDP incumbents on charges of 'insulting the president'.[98] Several days later, HDP co-leaders Selahattin Demirtaş and Figen Yüksekdağ were arrested on charges of heading an organisation that was an extension of the PKK.

Despite these setbacks, and resurgent conflict across the south-east, the HDP remained a dogged presence in parliament and at the ballot box, a measure of the ongoing mobilisation of Kurds across Turkey. These developments, among others, call into question just how free and fair Turkey's electoral and political processes are, and might have reasonably been expected to undermine Kurdish confidence in the political system. Yet, if electoral participation is any indication, this did not happen. In the wake of the June 2015 general election, Turkey entered an unprecedented cycle of electoral activity: a follow-up election in November 2015, the constitutional referendum of April 2017, which narrowly saw the approval of Erdoğan's executive presidency, a snap general election in June 2018, the municipal elections of March 2019, and a 'do-over' Istanbul municipal election three months later. This cycle of elections clearly demonstrates Erdoğan's overwhelming influence in the political sphere. The follow-up election of 2015 resulted from his obstruction of coalition talks following the inconclusive June election, the general election of 2018 was dragged forward, ahead of a scheduled poll in November 2019, at Erdoğan's behest as the economy faltered, and the municipal poll in Istanbul was rerun after Erdoğan called into question the March result and pressured the Supreme Electoral Board to nullify it.

At each of these, the HDP played a crucial role, shaping up as a thorn in the side of the AKP and Erdoğan. Meanwhile, it is apparent that attempts were made to shift the ground from under the HDP in order to clear a path for AKP dominance.[99] Following the Turkish invasion of Syria's Kurdish-run Afrin in early 2018, and the AKP forming the *Cumhur İttifakı* (National Alliance) with the MHP, nationalist sentiment was surging, which translated into highly charged rhetoric during campaigning for the 2018 general election. The *Millet İttifakı* (People's Alliance) formed by four opposition parties, including the CHP, did not include the HDP, most probably in order to avoid being tarred by the accusations of 'terrorism' directed at the pro-Kurdish party. Nonetheless, HDP co-leader Demirtaş ran for president from his prison cell.

And despite pressures brought to bear on the HDP, it attracted enough votes to again surpass the threshold, thereby preventing the AKP making advances in the Kurdish provinces and meaning it could only maintain its hold on power due to the support of its alliance partner the MHP.

Given the fractious nature of politics at the time, the Kurds were touted as 'kingmakers' in the June 2018 election.[100] Ultimately this was not the case. Opposition parties did not fare as well as expected, and neither Demirtaş nor CHP presidential candidate Muharrem İnce seriously dented Erdoğan's appeal, who won over 52 per cent in the presidential poll. Nonetheless, the dynamics of the Kurdish issue were very much a consideration in campaigning. Revealing a new appreciation of the importance of the Kurdish vote, İnce took his campaign to Diyarbakır pledging to address Kurdish grievances and also visited Demirtaş in prison.[101] Meanwhile, Erdoğan attempted to have his Kurdish cake and eat it too, campaigning in Kurdish cities with a message of conciliation, while also playing on the Turkish national vote elsewhere, telling audiences in Turkey's west that after the success of the Afrin campaign, the military was poised to hit the PKK in Iraqi Kurdistan.[102] In the end it was the nationalist vote that carried the day for Erdoğan and the AKP, while the HDP won around 11.7 per cent of the vote. Some analysts explained the decline in the HDP's vote in 2018 as a result of the earlier upsurge in PKK activity, which rendered the HDP irrelevant, and argued that the AKP had effectively countered the electoral challenge that the HDP posed.[103] An alternative view would argue that disruption across the south-east and concerted efforts to marginalise the HDP had predictable results.

If the 2018 election results were underwhelming for Kurds and others opposed to Erdoğan, the municipal elections of March 2019 offered another chance to rally and send a message to Ankara. Overwhelmingly the elections were viewed as a referendum on Erdoğan, even though he was not a candidate. Having previously presided over a booming economy, and now with expanded presidential powers, his popularity appeared in free fall as the economy stalled. The polls also offered an opportunity for Kurds and the HDP to reclaim those municipalities across the south-east they had won in the previous municipal vote but where the AKP had installed 'trustees' in 2016. As a measure of Kurdish enthusiasm for the political wrestling match, six pro-Kurdish parties formed an alliance to maximise their impact at the ballot.[104] Further, the HDP made the tactical decision not to position candidates in major cities, including Istanbul, Ankara and Izmir, and to encourage its followers there to back candidates opposed to the AKP. From prison, Demirtaş urged a strategic approach to voting, with a view to tipping the balance against the AKP.[105] In not fielding candidates in those cities, the HDP aimed to undermine the AKP's dominance by avoiding splintering the opposition vote.

The call to vote for candidates other than their own suggests heightened engagement in the political system on the part of Kurdish political actors. Party survival requires garnering votes to ensure one's own electoral success, but here Demirtaş and other HDP figures adopted a position to ensure supporters directed their votes elsewhere. In this sense, they were signalling their disapproval of the ruling AKP. Yet, again, this was not an indication of wanting out of the political system, rather it was a demonstration of wanting in, or at least wanting non-AKP candidates to win, even if they were not Kurdish. So here Kurdish voters were urged to be active citizens, but to do so not on an ethnic basis but on the basis of opposition to the ruling party.

In the event, opposition candidates took the major cities of Adana, Ankara and Mersin, while the HDP reclaimed much of the south-east in a major blow to Erdoğan and the AKP. High turnouts across the south-east suggest that Kurds remain engaged in the political process,[106] and in combination with the outcomes of strategic voting elsewhere demonstrate that the Kurdish factor remains significant.

The major controversy arising out of the March polls was the eventual annulment of the Istanbul result at the behest of Erdoğan, who alleged electoral fraud after CHP candidate Ekrem İmamoğlu claimed a narrow victory. This led to a 'do-over' election on 30 June. Yet here again, the Kurdish vote was significant. Signalling awareness of this, the AKP sent its candidate for Istanbul, Binali Yıldırım, to Diyarbakır in an attempt to win Kurdish hearts and minds, greeting a rally in Kurdish and furthering well-tried tropes of Kurdish-brotherhood discourse.[107] Meanwhile, the state-run Anadolu Agency purveyed a message purportedly from PKK leader Abdullah Öcalan saying that HDP supporters should remain neutral ('*tarafsız*') in the 'do-over' election.[108] This can be seen as an attempt by the government to dissuade, or disrupt, the Kurdish vote in order to protect Yıldırım's chances. Meanwhile,

Demirtaş again urged Kurdish voters to support Imamoğlu, who had promised to bridge divides in Turkey's troubled society. Recently installed Kurdish mayor of Diyarbakır Adnan Selcuk Mizrakli also signalled his support for Imamoğlu, stating that his victory would be a 'boost for democratic forces in Turkey'.[109]

At the polls, Istanbul's Kurdish voters appeared to ignore Öcalan; they rallied behind Imamoğlu, helping him claim a convincing victory. This changed the complexion of Turkey's politics considerably, apparently signalling an end to Erdogan's electoral dominance. There were echoes in these municipal elections of the HDP's electoral emergence in 2015. The Kurdish vote had significant repercussions for the ruling AKP and hence for the country as a whole. In Istanbul, at least, they did appear to play the role of 'kingmakers'. From the perspective of citizenship, Kurds again eagerly executed their right to vote, putting their trust in the system, clearly demonstrating their desire to be a part of the political community. The Kurds on many measures were thus central and important participants in the 'daily plebiscite', and it is notable that Imamoğlu maintained an inclusive approach to Kurdish voters, travelling to Diyarbakır after his victory, thus marking a politics entirely different to Erdoğan's polarising approach.

The 'Ideal': Retaining Currency?

Without exception, when asked about identity or ethnicity, Kurds I interviewed readily gave detailed responses and related experiences that informed their understandings of these concepts. Clearly, these are questions of immediate import for Kurds, ideas that they grapple with frequently. Despite the importance they placed on their Kurdish ethnicity, no participants explicitly argued for 'independence' or 'liberation' or the creation of a Kurdish state.[110] I take from this that they implicitly accept their circumstances – if not their status – as citizens, members of the body politic of Turkey. As those I spoke to relate, this is to a degree a result of circumstance. Kurds have been schooled in Turkish, married into Turkish families, and lived – for centuries – alongside Turks, which for many has created a sense of belonging. In contrast, some saw it as an imposition with which they were forced to abide, others saw it only valuable as it allowed them to work, others still regarded themselves as 'second-class citizens'.

By the same token, the very circumstances that make Kurds feel this way often spur them into greater political engagement and a more active citizenship than their Turkish compatriots. This has led to some broadening of vision from Kurdish political actors, calling for a more inclusive politics. Such a stance demonstrates a desire to change the political system but, simultaneously, an acceptance of membership within it. The time when citizenship is most apparent across the ethnic divide is during electoral events, of which there have been many in the last six years. At the June 2015 election, I witnessed palpable excitement at the success of the pro-Kurdish HDP, the great optimism that Kurds shared at the prospect of their elected members representing them in the national assembly. In the elections that have followed, despite a deteriorating security environment and increased state pressure, Kurds have continued to participate, playing a pivotal role in electoral outcomes, something that the AKP clearly realises, and that Kurds themselves increasingly recognise as they seek to stake out their political territory. Recognising oneself as a political player requires essential acceptance of one's place in Turkey. If, as Twain argues, citizenship makes a republic, Kurds are enacting their rights as citizens in order to make, or reshape, the republic as they see fit. So it may be that Kurds chafe against the Turkish evocation of the 'unity of language, culture and ideal' that was once trumpeted as the foundation of the Republic of Turkey, but I argue that Kurds do subscribe to an element of that 'ideal', that is, to be active, participating members of the political community.

Notes

1. Twain, *Mark Twain's Speeches*, p. 136.
2. Karpat, 'The transformation of the Ottoman state', pp. 243–81.
3. *Cumhuriyet Halk Fırkası Programının İzahı* (Ankara Hakimiyeti Milliye Matbaası, 1931), cited in İnce, *Citizenship and Identity in Turkey*, p. 39.
4. Cited in İnce, *Citizenship and Identity in Turkey*, p. 12.
5. Ibid.
6. Kadıoğlu, 'Denationalization of citizenship?', pp. 283–99.
7. Barbalet, *Citizenship*, pp. 31–43.
8. Pakulski, 'Cultural citizenship', pp. 73–86.
9. İnce, *Citizenship and Identity in Turkey*, p. 29.

10. İçduygu and Kaygusuz, 'The politics of citizenship by drawing borders', pp. 26–50.
11. Çarkoğlu and Kalaycıoğlu, *Türkiye'de ve Dünya'da Milliyetçilik*.
12. Rümelili and Çakmaklı, 'Civic participation and citizenship in Turkey', pp. 365–84.
13. Ibid., p. 376.
14. Isin and Wood, *Citizenship and Identity*, p. 3.
15. Ergil, '"Knowledge is a potent instrument for change"'.
16. Interview, Diyarbakır, 29 October 2014. Similarly, many Kurds object to being classified as 'Turkish Kurds' but prefer to be called 'Kurds from Turkey'. By the same reasoning, I do not refer to the 'Turkish Republic', but use 'Republic of Turkey'.
17. Joppke, 'Transformation of citizenship', pp. 37–48.
18. Interview, Diyarbakır, 21 October 2014.
19. Interview, Diyarbakır, 21 October 2014.
20. Interview, Istanbul, 13 June 2015.
21. Herbst, *States and Power in Africa*, p. 231.
22. Interview, Istanbul, 11 June 2015.
23. Interview, Istanbul, 18 October 2014.
24. Pakulski, 'Cultural citizenship', p. 79.
25. Rümelili and Çakmakli, 'Civic participation and citizenship in Turkey', p. 377.
26. Interview, Istanbul, 18 October 2014.
27. Interview, Diyarbakır, 21 October 2014.
28. Interviewees revealed a range of attitudes to the idea that their passports denoted them as Turkish; this is similar to the case of Turkish identity cards, as discussed in chapter 2.
29. Interview, Istanbul, 13 June 2015.
30. Yavuz, *Secularism and Muslim Democracy in Turkey*, p. 30.
31. Bozarslan, 'Kurds and the Turkish state', pp. 334–5; Yavuz, 'Kurdish nationalism in Turkey', pp. 243–4.
32. Holmes, 'On Communism, Post-Communism, Modernity and Post-Modernity', pp. 21–44.
33. Interview, Diyarbakır, 21 October 2014.
34. Bozarslan, 'Kurds and the Turkish state', pp. 334–5.
35. İçduygu et al., 'The ethnic question in an environment of insecurity', pp. 991–1010.
36. Rümelili and Çakmakli, 'Civic participation and citizenship in Turkey', p. 377.

37. Gambetti, 'Decolonizing Diyarbakır', pp. 95–127.
38. Interview, Diyarbakır, 11 June 2015.
39. Pakulski, 'Cultural citizenship', p. 79.
40. Interview, Istanbul, 13 June 2016.
41. Interview, Istanbul, 13 June 2016.
42. Interview, Diyarbakır, 27 October 2014.
43. *International Crisis Group*, 'Turkey: Ending the PKK insurgency'. See also Sönmez, 'Kurds still migrating to western Turkish cities', 4 May 2013.
44. Poyrazlar, 'What do Turkey's Kurds really want?', 27 December 2013.
45. Akkoyunlu, 'Opinion: Soma disaster threatens Turkey's fragile social contract', 16 May 2014. The official response to the tragedy may also have forged a connection. Then Prime Minister Erdoğan appeared unmoved by the fate of those killed, drawing comparisons with nineteenth-century mining disasters in Britain. This is another example of AKP hegemony. The owners of the mine were linked to the AKP, and the miners who were affected received little support. See *Hürriyet Daily News*, 'Turkish PM cites 19th-century Britain', 14 May 2014.
46. Interview, Diyarbakır, 27 October 2014.
47. The battle of Manzikert (Malazgirt in Turkish) in 1071 marks the first victory of the Seljuk Turks over the Byzantines, and is seen as the precursor to the conquest of Anatolia by the Turks.
48. Interview, Diyarbakır, 21 October 2014.
49. Van Bruinessen, 'The ethnic identity of Kurds in Turkey', pp. 613–21.
50. Interview, Diyarbakır, 29 October 2014.
51. Conversation, Diyarbakır, 5 June 2013.
52. Interview, Diyarbakır, 11 June 2015.
53. Koç and Eryut, 'Demographic integration through intermarriage'.
54. Cizre, 'Turkey's Kurdish problem', p. 241.
55. Interview, Istanbul, 14 October 2014.
56. Interview, Diyarbakır, 21 October 2014.
57. King and Neil Melvin, 'Diaspora politics', pp. 108–38.
58. Saraçoğlu, *Kurds of Modern Turkey*, pp. 150–81.
59. Rénan, 'What is a nation?', pp. 52, 54.
60. Of course, such manifestations of electoral participation were not limited to the HDP, or Diyarbakır. In various Istanbul neighbourhoods I saw posters, bunting and campaign buses (broadcasting campaign slogans) for all four major parties and several minor ones.

61. The *govend* is a dance performed by a group, which links hands to form a circle. It is similar to dances performed by Turks, Greeks and others.
62. Celep, 'Can the Kurdish left contribute to Turkey's democratization?', pp. 165–80.
63. Kellas records similar sentiments among Catalans in Spain: Kellas, *The Politics of Nationalism and Ethnicity*, pp. 21–3.
64. Private conversation, Diyarbakır, 7 June 2015.
65. Letsch, 'Turkey election', 8 June 2015.
66. Cağaptay, *The New Sultan*, p. 148.
67. Hebdige, *Subculture*, p. 19.
68. Massicard, *The Alevis in Turkey and Europe*, pp. 85–6.
69. Gramsci, *Selections from the Prison Notebooks*, p. 238.
70. Interview, Diyarbakır, 8 June 2015.
71. Interviews, Diyarbakır, 8, 10 and 11 June 2015.
72. Bayat, *Making Islam Democratic*, p. 21.
73. Ergil, Doğu, 'The Kurdish question in Turkey', pp. 122–35.
74. Toumani, 'Minority rules', 17 February 2008.
75. Güneş, 'Kurdish politics in Turkey', pp. 27–8.
76. Güneş, *The Kurdish National Movement in Turkey*, p. 170.
77. Gurses, *Anatomy of a Civil War*, pp. 73–4.
78. Güneş, *The Kurdish National Movement in Turkey*, p. 154.
79. *Firat News Agency*, 'Demirtaş: We will present the oppressed of Turkey with a great victory', 19 March 2015.
80. Interview, Diyarbakır, 10 June 2015.
81. Interview, Istanbul, 30 May 2015.
82. Interview, Diyarbakır, 20 October 2014.
83. Dahrendorf, 'The changing quality of citizenship', p. 17.
84. Demirtaş, 'HDP not to return "ethnic politics" after polls', 1 June 2015.
85. 'Biz'ler, hayatın farklı inanç ve düşüncerlerle zenginleştiğine inanıyoruz. Ve biz'ler ayrım yapmaksızın ve hic bir baksıya maruz kalmadan, tüm ınançların özgürce yasanması gerektiğini savunuyoruz.' (We believe diverse beliefs and philosophies enrich life. And, without exception or in the face of pressure, we argue that all beliefs should live freely.) HDP campaign brochure, Diyarbakır, June 2015. (My translation.)
86. *Hürriyet Daily News*, 'Inclusive HDP candidate list aspires to pass 10 pct election threshold', 7 April 2015.
87. *Diken*, 'HDP'nin Seçim Videosu Yayında', 16 October 2015.

88. Author interview, Istanbul, 13 June 2015.
89. Author interview, Istanbul, 1 June 2015.
90. Dahrendorf, 'The changing quality of citizenship'.
91. Interview, Istanbul, 13 June 2015.
92. Interview, Diyarbakır, 21 October 2014.
93. Kymlicka, *Politics in the Vernacular*, p. 6.
94. Interview, Diyarbakır, 26 October 2014.
95. Interview, Diyarbakır, 26 October 2014.
96. Interview, Diyarbakır, 27 October 2014.
97. Ergil, 'Knowledge is a potent instrument for change'.
98. *BBC*, 'Diyarbakır Büyükşehir Belediyesi'ne kayyum atandı', 1 November 2016.
99. Zaman, 'Electoral noose tightens', 4 June 2018.
100. *International Crisis Group*, 'Turkey's election reinvigorates debate over Kurdish demands', 5 June 2018.
101. *Habertürk*, 'Muharrem İnce'den Diyarbakır'da Kürt sorunu mesajı', 11 June 2018.
102. *CNN Türk*, 'Cumhurbaşkanı Erdoğan', 5 June 2018.
103. Alptekin, 'Kurdish votes in the June 24, 2018 elections', pp. 211–30.
104. Tastekin, 'Kurds in Turkey unite', 15 January 2019.
105. *Rudaw*, 'Jailed Demirtas calls for strategic voting', 29 March 2019.
106. Blaser, 'Why Turkey's PKK conflict looms larger than ever', 9 April 2019.
107. *Rudaw*, 'Yıldırım: Kürdistan mebusu da vardı', 6 June 2019.
108. Yackley, 'Jailed militant leader enters Istanbul election fray', 21 June 2019.
109. *Al Monitor*, 'New Diyarbakir mayor backs opposition candidate', 4 June 2019.
110. It is possible that some participants were self-censoring in this regard, i.e. choosing not to reveal any inclination towards separatism for fear of repercussions should my data be procured by authorities. The possibility remains that some participants may have harboured separatist views but chose to conceal them.

CONCLUSION: RECONCILING ETHNIC IDENTITY, CITIZENSHIP AND THE 'IDEAL' IN ERDOĞAN'S TURKEY?

To the casual observer the daily hubbub in the Hasan Paşa Han in the old city of Diyarbakır is little different to that found in the warren of streets around Istiklal Caddesi in Istanbul's Beyoğlu neighbourhood. Shops buzz with locals from early morning until late at night. Traders set out their wares and send deliveries via teenaged shop assistants wearing football shirts. In the teahouses, chatter is intense and lively over the clatter of teaspoons and backgammon pieces. Copious amounts of tea are drunk and cigarettes smoked.[1] The distant call of the muezzin punctuates the day. In these instances of street life at the two ends of Turkey there is a degree of homogeneity that would please the founders of the Republic.

But closer examination exposes differences. In Diyarbakır you are likely – but not guaranteed – to hear snatches of Kurdish conversation. And the issues of import discussed at the teahouses are different. A Kurdish teacher in Diyarbakır once told me that all Kurds are instinctively politically engaged but if I went to central Anatolia I'd find that 'they only talk about cows and potatoes'. The implication here was that Kurds, due to their political environment, must grapple with weighty issues, but Turks, living freely, are engaged only with workaday concerns. Such an approach clearly oversimplifies the complex circumstances of modern Turkey but it points to the threads of politics running through Kurdish life as I encountered it in Diyarbakır and Istanbul.

In my discussions with Kurds, the 'cultural stuff'[2] that is often thought to be the essence of ethnic identity rarely arose. No one focused on music, folklore or traditional dress as important emblems of Kurdish identity. Indeed, as noted, Martin van Bruinessen records such 'secondary symbols' as unreliable identity markers to distinguish the Kurds from other peoples living in Anatolia.[3] The points that assumed importance in the conversations I had with Kurds were not inherently exclusive to their ethnicity but were relationships they had to specific ideas, concepts and entities: their practice and relationship to Islam, among other religions; relationships to adherents of other religions; relationship to the *toprak* (soil) of the landscape, whether defined as Anatolia, Mesopotamia or Kurdistan; relationship to the city of Diyarbakır as a purported capital city; relationships with Kurds living in neighbouring states; relationship with the Republic of Turkey, something that often manifests as resistance to state initiatives. In this sense, the Kurdish identity that was revealed to me can be seen at its core as a political identity. Mithat in Istanbul revealed as much, stating that choosing to identify as Kurdish was '90 per cent political'.

This is not to say that elements of culture are not important to Kurds or that there are no distinctively Kurdish cultural entities in Turkey. Newroz, the New Year event celebrated each year at the spring equinox of 21 March, is one. Emerging from the Persian tradition, and attached to a Kurdish foundational myth of great antiquity, Newroz *could* be construed as a specifically Kurdish event in the context of modern Turkey. Tellingly, many Kurds I met with remarked on it as an important event, yet they generally overlooked its cultural specificity as a marker of identity. What was more important was the fact that in years past Kurds had attempted to celebrate Newroz in spite of Turkey's efforts to forbid it; in so doing many had been arrested, wounded or killed at the hands of state security forces. These events helped to to redefine Newroz as a symbol of resistance. One fellow told me that Newroz in northern Iraq was a day of picnicking in the countryside, but it was a different phenomenon of different significance in Turkey. Those I spoke to saw Newroz as an important Kurdish event but they attached significance to it as a political struggle in the present rather than an ages-old cultural tradition. In this way, what was once a symbol of Kurdish culture had become a symbol of the Kurds' political struggle, but it remained no less potent for this transformation. That the state now accepted the event, having attempted to redefine it as a celebration of brotherhood, made the fact of those struggles and its portrayal as an act of resistance all the more important.

The Kurdish language assumed a similar position and trajectory to that of Newroz as a constituent element of identity. It too could be framed as a central pillar of Kurdish *culture*, an objective marker of Kurdishness, but of concern to most Kurds I spoke with was the *political* struggle that surrounded it. They highlighted the restrictions that had been placed on the use of the language and the hurdles, legislative and societal, still imposed that restricted its use in public and in education. Various restrictions had been placed on the use of Kurdish since the establishment of the Republic of Turkey, including an outright ban on its use in the wake of the 1980 coup. These moves had been intended to forge a sense of unity that would help Turkey cohere as a homogenous (mono-ethnic, Turkish) nation-state. However, the state's attempt to deny a point of difference drew more attention to that very point of difference, and lent to it a political potency. Yet even now, when official bans on the language had been lifted, Kurds held tight to their language as something that belonged to them, arguing their right to be able to speak it freely, to teach, broadcast and publish in it, while looking askance at Turkish politicians who used Kurdish as a means to court the Kurdish vote.

These examples point to the significance of political events, encounters and interactions in the shaping of the parameters of identity. The political constraints under which Kurds were living in Turkey heightened the potency of language and Newroz as markers of Kurdishness and as a consequence increased the tenacity with which Kurds clung to them. In this sense, language and Newroz were effectively transmuted into causes. To be free to speak, teach and broadcast in Kurdish and to celebrate Newroz without hindrance were political goals for which to agitate. They became rallying points, poles around which Kurds could coalesce. And in rallying, Kurds were highlighting their distinctiveness within Turkey's political terrain.

Asserting difference is an essential mechanism for identification. Throughout the interviews and conversations that I conducted, a consistent, implicit theme was that Kurds latched onto various identity markers, diverse, contested and disparate though they may have been, as mechanisms to create distinctions between themselves and the dominant Other, in this case, the

Turks. This was noticeable in Kurdish attitudes to religion and, by extension, religious and ethnic minorities. While there is no immediately apparent distinction between the practice of faith between Turks and Kurds, the majority of whom in both cases are Sunni Muslims, Kurds I spoke to wanted to demonstrate that 'their' Islam was open, tolerant and willing to countenance diversity in kind and degree of religious observance. This was particularly the case in light of the advance of ISIS, proponents of a violent interpretation of Islam and a force that many Kurds considered to be supported vicariously or, as some alleged, directly by Turks and the AKP government. In highlighting their acceptance of religious diversity, Kurds were denouncing the Islam of ISIS, and by extension of Turkey. This may be a reflection of what has been historically a more heterogeneous approach to religion, but it was also a way of marking distinction from conservative, conformist Islam, which many Kurds, rightly or wrongly, associated with Turks generally and Erdoğan and the AKP specifically. Here a *perception* of difference became important.

Kurds' evocation of the landscape were also a means of creating a distinction between themselves and the Turks. Many I spoke with were keen to highlight their prior occupancy, the fact that there has been a Kurdish presence in the lands of Mesopotamia dating back to antiquity, well prior to the arrival of the Turks in the eleventh century. The idea of *toprak* (soil) and a Kurdish link to it recurred among participants; this link was something that Turks could not claim in the south-eastern part of the country, thus something that marked Kurds as different. Kurds can claim to be 'native', in that their ancestors were present in Anatolia prior to the arrival of the Turks. In the same way, attempts to rebrand or reclassify the region as Mesopotamia, or Anatolia, or Kurdistan, and on a micro scale to reinstitute Kurdish, or other, names were an effort to repudiate the 'toponymic engineering' that had been imposed by the Turkish state apparatus in earlier decades. Meanwhile, recognising solidarity with Kurds living across borders – claiming closer relations with Kurds living in Syria than with Turks living in Izmir – was similarly a way of asserting Kurdish distinctiveness.

All of these markers of Kurdishness are also important for the reason that they are means of fostering internal cohesion. In using the language, celebrating Newroz despite disapproval or repressive measures, upholding a version and vision of Islam different to the Turkish norm, asserting their links to the landscape as natives, casting Diyarbakır as a capital city and acknowledging their ethnic and familial bonds with Kurds living in Iran, Iraq and Syria, Kurds are drawing close their own kin, providing the mechanisms with which to instil solidarity. These causes and issues become sources of camaraderie and the lynchpins of collective identification.

That so many of the aforementioned markers require struggles – to be able to speak the language, to celebrate Newroz, to repudiate Turkish re-annotation of the map – in turn points to the important role that resistance plays as a pole for Kurdish identification. Resistance need not mean military struggle, and it is not automatically a signal of separatist intent; postures of resistance point to a broader inclination and aspiration among Kurds, a struggle to define their own political space within Turkey. In my observation, this takes place in many forms, even within everyday episodes and interactions – from small boys chanting in the street to standing in solidarity with those killed in terror attacks. Resisting in mundane circumstances is important because the Republic of Turkey has long pressured Kurds to conform, to subscribe to a top-down definition of what the standard citizen should look like. Under earlier Kemalist administrations this meant a secular, western-inclined, *Turkish* citizen. For a time, during the first few AKP terms, broader debate opened up about national identity, the idea that Turkey was a 'mosaic' gained some support, and legislative and legal reforms were undertaken in pursuit of EU membership. Here Kurds had more room to assert a distinct identity. But this was a briefly opened window. The arena has again contracted, with Erdoğan becoming the dominant force in all matters political, apparently intent on imposing his own will and vision on the public sphere.

Yet Turkey's status as a democracy, troubled though it may be, allows space to push back against this. In June 2015, Kurds saw the HDP as the instrument that could apply the brakes to the AKP enterprise, and the associated project of Recep Tayyip Erdoğan's 'Turkish-style' presidency, both of which had gathered considerable momentum and stood to significantly alter Turkey's political terrain if left unchecked. In supporting the HDP, Kurds were asserting their Kurdishness but also endeavouring to ensure that Kurdish voices are heard in Turkey's parliament. That the HDP convincingly passed the electoral threshold on 7 June 2015 prompted raucous celebrations, as

I witnessed in a whirl of whistles, fireworks, wandering humanity and cars cruising outside the walls of Diyarbakır.

Such elation resulted from winning a record number of seats in the assembly and, into the bargain, depriving the AKP of its majority and – temporarily – Erdoğan of the opportunity to introduce his presidential model. Kurds had made their presence felt and, best of all, won representation in parliament – they had carved out a political space, despite the risk of failing to pass the threshold and losing all representation, and in the face of considerable hurdles, including harassment and terror attacks. The election results meant that they were in a position to have a say in the running of the country, to be able to shape and contribute to debates and policies that would determine the political trajectory that Turkey pursued. This suggests that while the Kurdish struggle is one for a political *identity* – the freedom to participate within politics, within the 'daily plebiscite', on equal terms, on their own terms – it is at the same time a struggle for political *input*. Rather than a struggle that is carried out in its entirety under the banner of Kurdishness, it is a struggle carried out to have a say in the running of the country, to participate in its reshaping and redefinition.

Figure C.1   Kurds dance the *govend* in Eminönü, Istanbul, following the HDP's electoral success in June 2015. © William Gourlay.

This harks back to Doğu Ergil's findings of 1995. He found that the PKK won support among Kurds not because it advocated an independent Kurdistan, but because it brought the issue of Kurdish identity onto the agenda and it fought to improve the circumstances of Kurds living in Turkey. Currently the HDP wins support for similar reasons: it is a vehicle for Kurdish identity (among others), but it is primarily a vehicle for participation in Turkey's political arena, one with which many Kurds and other under-represented groups (e.g. Armenians, leftists, et al.) identify. In my observation, Kurds want representation in Turkey's parliament because through the weight of circumstance, living alongside Turks, being educated in Turkish, supporting Turkish football teams in international leagues, they have become a part of Turkey's socio-political fabric.

Donald Horowitz argues that in divided societies ethnic conflict is at the centre of politics.[4] We might invert this and argue that in a united society, one that is free, open, pluralist and allows all to contribute, ethnic conflict is avoided, indeed, is non-existent, because all regardless of ethnicity are able to participate equally. The sentiments of the Kurds I spoke with echo that. Their gripe was not with their being a part of Turkey's political system but with the restrictions placed upon their participation in it. As Doğu Ergil noted, they did not want out, they wanted in. Kurdish ethnic identity would not spur conflict if Kurds were able to live in a truly democratic political entity. They could and would accept citizenship in such a polity, they would fully subscribe to the 'ideal' of Turkey if that ideal did not centre on a vision of homogenous Turkishness, or one imagined by Erdoğan and propagated by his henchmen, but on a just, free, tolerant, pluralist and democratic society. Kurds are critical of Turkey, not because it is Turkish, but because it does not live up to such ideals.

Whither the Kurds?

During the period, between May 2013 and June 2015, that I made visits to Istanbul and Diyarbakır to gather material for this book, it appeared that politics in Turkey was on the cusp of change for the better. The Gezi protests, at first, seemed to be a corrective to Erdoğan's domination of the public sphere. It looked like Kurdish concerns and demands in Turkey could be addressed through peaceful, democratic mechanisms. It was a period when Kurds could speak their language and celebrate Newroz more freely than they had been able to in earlier decades. That I found 'Kurdistan' T-shirts and Kurdish literature on sale in Diyarbakır and met Turkish schoolgirls visiting the Armenian cathedral of Surp Giragos is evidence of the greater acknowledgement and acceptance of ethnic diversity in Turkey. This was a more secure and confident Turkey, one that was willing to embark on a peace process, to move beyond the securitised vision of Kurdish politics that had long prevailed, to make concessions in pursuit of the greater good. Discussions of ethnicity were normalised, viewed as just another facet of political negotiation, rather than as precursors to separatism. There can be little doubt that this peaceful political milieu – these contingent events – contributed to the specific contours of the portrait of Kurdish identity that I observed.

The situation, however, was to unravel rapidly. As detailed earlier, since that time Turkey has endured a consistent escalation of political tensions, multiple elections, ongoing conflict with the PKK and a coup attempt. Turkey's Kurds have seen cities destroyed, politicians accused of terrorism and arrested, elected officials removed and Turkish invasions of Afrin and Rojava, Kurdish-controlled territory in Syria. It is difficult to imagine that the residents of Diyarbakır, so optimistic and politically engaged in June 2015, still harbour hope and optimism in the wake of these developments and the razing and expropriation of large parts of their city in early 2016.

Kurds interviewed in several south-eastern cities, including Diyarbakır, in late 2015, amid surging violence, largely attributed the collapse of the peace process and ensuing problems to the actions of the government. They blamed the AKP for catalysing the resumption of violence as a means to win the nationalist vote in order to win back their parliamentary majority.[5] Many of those interviewed thought the situation in the south-east was similar to that of the 1990s, an era of terrorism and violence – many thought it was now worse![6] There is certainly an echo of the 1990s apparent in government rhetoric directed at the HDP, Erdoğan repeatedly attempting to tar the HDP politicians with the same brush as the PKK.[7] Concurrently there were instances of mob violence directed at Kurds and other oppositional voices.[8] Such is the resurgent nationalist mood that in summer 2019 Kurdish tourists from northern Iraq were set upon by a mob when they tried to take a photograph of a Kurdistan scarf in Uzungöl.[9]

It must be pointed out that such instances are the exception rather than the rule. Broadly speaking there is greater acceptance of a Kurdish presence in Turkey. And Turkey now pays lip service to its multicultural foundations, although the AKP ensures that identity politics does not gather sufficient momentum that it catalyses divergence from the government agenda or undermines government authority.[10] At times Erdoğan goes to lengths to win over Kurds, attempting to rally all 'who revere the flag' ('*kim bu bayrak sahip çıkıyorsa*'),[11] and, as noted, often refers to his 'Kurdish brothers'. At the same time, he now rarely misses an opportunity to undermine Kurdish political entities, chiefly the HDP, attempting to sway public sentiment against it in alleging an HDP–PKK–terror nexus.

Yet the very fact that Erdoğan feels the need to evoke his 'Kurdish brothers' demonstrates a realisation that the Kurdish demographic is of considerable import within Turkey's political architecture. The general election of 7 June 2015 made that point emphatically. That said, the Kurds were acknowledged as a sizeable constituency from the early days of the Republic of Turkey, but at that time their difference was seen as something to be either subdued, assimilated or denied. Since such measures proved unsuccessful, and are seen as unconscionable in modern-day politics, Kurds now represent a constituency that must be won to achieve an electoral majority. In this sense, while Kurds have long had to endure injustices, inequalities and lack of economic development, they have not been without agency and have, since 1923, had an impact on Turkey's political landscape. This is something that they have long recognised and that the state has too, albeit adopting different measures through history to either smother it, during the 1980s and 1990s, or co-opt it, during the AKP era.

The alacrity with which Erdoğan has fallen back on a refrain conflating Kurdish political groups and terrorist organisations raises the question of whether the AKP was ever sincere in its attempt to instigate a peace process with the PKK and a 'resolution process' that would address Kurdish concerns. It is true that in recent years other significant political events – the Gezi protests, the rise of the Syrian Kurds, war with the PKK, the 2016 coup attempt – have presented challenges to Erdoğan and shifted Turkey's geopolitical moorings. Some wariness to challenges, whether from terror groups or geopolitical shifts, on Erdoğan's part is understandable. But that he now incessantly evokes the PKK as public enemy number one makes one wonder why he thought it an organisation worth negotiating with in the first place. In essence, Erdoğan appears to have subdued any progressive instincts he may once have harboured and sought recourse in the tried-and-tested nationalist posture of blaming the usual suspects – both internal and external – for attempting to upset Turkey's apple cart. Chief among those usual suspects is the PKK and the spectre of its intentions and reach among the broader Kurdish population, including in Syria. Broadly speaking, this is a chorus that many within the Turkish populace respond to, and with Erdoğan's dominance of the political arena, the media and the national conversation there are few voices to disabuse them of the idea.

Therein lies a conundrum for Erdoğan, and indeed all political actors at the national level. Discourses that link Kurdish political activity with the PKK and its terrorist designation win favour in some parts of the electorate, yet such a discourse is sure to marginalise Kurds who form a significant constituency. That is not to say that Kurds all share the same political opinions and vote as a bloc – this is clearly not true. Yet politicians evoking the spectre of PKK terrorism and alleging HDP complicity as a ploy to win the nationalist vote, always a sizeable constituency, risk losing the support of many Kurds, another sizeable constituency. This is less an issue for CHP or MHP politicians, who win relatively few Kurdish votes, but the AKP, which has historically enjoyed some Kurdish support, is caught between the stools of a pluralist posture that will retain Kurdish votes and a hard-line posture that will appeal to the nationalist cohort.

These dynamics were apparent in the municipal elections of 2019, when the AKP, having aligned with the hard-line MHP, won a majority of the vote nationwide but lost the major cities of Istanbul, Ankara and Antalya to the CHP, in some measure, it is assumed, because the HDP did not run candidates and Kurds voted against the AKP. Prior to the polls, perhaps worried at wider cooperation between opposition parties, Erdoğan had broadened his accusations of PKK complicity to include the CHP and the IYI Party, and threatened to dismiss any eventual victors who he alleged were fronts for the PKK.[12] In view of such threats, any gestures Erdoğan made to Kurds were unsuccessful. HDP co-leader Pervin Buldan noted that Erdoğan had made a habit of 'winking' at Kurds during electoral campaigns but Kurds were no longer falling for it.[13] Erdoğan made good on his threats, with the Supreme Electoral Board moving to disallow several HDP mayors-elect from taking up their posts in the south-east on the grounds that they had previously been removed for alleged wrongdoings and replaced by 'trustees'.[14] Somewhat paradoxically, it appears that pro-government circles attempted to enlist jailed PKK leader Abdullah Öcalan to buttress AKP interests in the Istanbul municipal election rerun, with state-run Anadolu Agency claiming that Öcalan suggested Kurds remain independent. Jailed HDP leader Selahattin Demirtaş argued to the contrary and urged Kurds to vote against AKP candidate Binali Yıldırım. Since the HDP emerged as an electoral power, and as it wins votes from Turks and Kurds, the AKP has accused it of being a front for the PKK, but here the ostensible leaders of the two parties, Öcalan and Demirtaş, sent different messages to Kurds. This undercuts the AKP's claims that the HDP operates at the behest of the PKK, but also reveals a level of cynicism on the part of the AKP, which merrily vilifies the PKK to ingratiate itself in the eyes of Turkish nationalists while simultaneously seeking to enlist the PKK leader to curry favour with Kurdish voters.

Such circumstances illustrate the ongoing difficulties facing Kurdish politicians and constituents, left at the mercy of Erdoğan's whims and official manipulations. Yet the result of the do-over election in Istanbul, when Ekrem Imamoğlu convincingly defeated the AKP candidate with the enthusiastic support of Kurdish voters, demonstrates that even if Kurdish voters and candidates may operate in straitened circumstances, at the ballot box they still follow their own trajectory and refuse to concede to official machinations.

Imamoğlu's win is significant for several other reasons. It demonstrated that Kurds can have a significant impact on election results, not only in the south-east where they are the majority, but also in Turkey's big cities where they make up large minorities. It also indicated that a new form of politics, that does not follow the Erdoğan template, may be successful. Indeed, Turkey may be ripe for it. Campaigning in Istanbul, Imamoğlu sought to engage directly with the electorate, delivering a message of inclusiveness intended to bridge divides, in stark contrast to Erdoğan's stage-managed rallies which are big on heated rhetoric and hectoring of opponents and purported enemies but allow no space for interaction. Thus although Erdoğan has determinedly led Turkey along a trajectory of his own definition, progressively dominating the political space and driving a discourse that has polarised the electorate, after so long in power and with a weakening economy, room may be opening for alternative voices. While campaigning from prison for the 2018 presidential election, Selahattin Demirtaş opined on the divisiveness of Erdoğan's rhetoric and the oppressive measures he doled out to opponents of all ilk, writing, 'What was limited to the Kurds has become the norm for Mr Erdogan's opponents elsewhere too. The only hope for a liberal, democratic future lies in our coming together to defeat the authoritarian regime.'[15]

The result of the rerun municipal election in Istanbul indicates that such a future may be possible. Imamoğlu maintained his determination to engage with Kurds by meeting with and offering encouragement to Kurdish mayors in August 2019, even after they – like others before them – had been removed from office on grounds of supporting 'terrorism'.[16] Nonetheless, Erdoğan still has tricks up his sleeve, such as evoking the spectre of Kurdish 'terrorism', which he used as a pretext for the invasion of Rojava two months later. This won him wide acclaim from Turks of all stripes, his popularity rebounding instantaneously, and saw all parties except the HDP rallying around the flag. How this will play out in the long term for Turkey is more difficult to determine, as international criticism mounts and Kurds in Turkey are further frustrated.

All of this suggests that although Kurdish identity and political positions have long been shaped by the 'contingent events' that unfurl in Turkey's sociopolitical arenas, it is not that Kurds have always been helplessly passive, conceding to and being subdued by the forces of nation building and currents of national politics. Indeed, as active players in political affairs, Kurds have in various ways shaped the trajectory of the Turkish polity: as such, Kurds have themselves constituted a series of 'contingent events' that have influenced Turkey's identity and socio-political development. This is as true of the early years of the Republic, when Kurdish rebellions temporarily disrupted the smooth implementation of the modernisation project, as of the PKK insurgency that peaked in the 1990s and the electoral emergence of the HDP in 2015 that stalled the AKP's hitherto unstoppable rise. Even now, when Erdoğan has amassed so much power he must still pay heed to the Kurdish factor, whether that be courting the Kurdish vote or vilifying Kurdish actors to appeal to the nationalist rump. Accordingly, Kurds seem to be subconsciously aware of their own political clout. As so many Kurds related to me, they feel that, by dint of going to school with Turks, marrying Turks, befriending Turks, they belong in Turkey. At the same time they are determined to defend their identity and political spaces and to have their say. They may rail at injustices in the Turkish system, but this demonstrates that they expect justice from that very system. Kurdish agitation is not a rejection of Turkey, but a desire for a better Turkey, one where Kurds can confidently assert their identity alongside that of the Turks.

Although Kurdish identity is no longer regarded in Turkey as something to be denied or erased, in the tense political circumstances that prevail it is still deemed threatening in many quarters. Yet the actions of the fans of the oft-maligned – assertively Kurdish – Amedspor football team demonstrate another current that has flowed in Kurdish politics and society, one that has often been entirely overlooked or discounted – that the majority of Kurds just want to get ahead and in so doing contribute to a more vibrant Turkey. In March 2019, a rare occasion when they were allowed to travel outside of Diyarbakır to see their team play, the fan group fetched up in Istanbul as Amedspor took on Eyüpspor. At an away stadium, under the watchful eye of a prominent police presence, Amedspor's Kurdish supporters set up a chant: 'Amedspor! Eyüpspor! Hand in hand, arm in arm, both teams unite! Peace in the stadium! Hey, pro-government media, do you hear us? Do you see us chanting for peace?'[17]

Notes

1. Although, in my experience, No Smoking signs are more routinely ignore in Diyarbakır.
2. Barth, *Ethnic Groups and Boundaries*, p. 15.
3. Van Bruinessen, 'The ethnic identity of Kurds in Turkey', pp. 613–21.
4. Horowitz, *Ethnic Groups in Conflict*, p. 12.
5. Yanmış, 'Resurgence of the Kurdish conflict in Turkey', pp. 11–12.
6. Ibid., p. 31.
7. *Yeni Şafak*, 'Erdoğan of HDP deputies', 16 March 2016.
8. Saymaz, 'Kırşehir'deki Madımak'ın görüntüleri', 19 October 2015.
9. *Gazete Duvar*, 'Trabzon'da Kürdistan atkısıyla fotoğraf çektiren turistlere saldırı', 19 July 2019.
10. Danforth, 'In Turkey, obedience to the state trumps multiculturalism', 2 February 2016.

11. *HaberTürk*, 'Yenikapı'da Teröre Karşı Tek Ses', 20 September 2015.
12. Mortimer, 'Erdogan threatens to dismiss mayors', 26 February 2019.
13. *BBC*, 'Erdoğan Kürt seçmene göz kırpıyor ama Kürtler artık bunu yemez', 2 November 2018.
14. *Reuters*, 'Pro-Kurdish elected mayors stripped of mandates', 12 April 2019.
15. Demirtaş, 'I am running for president in Turkey', 20 June 2018.
16. *Ortadoğu News*, 'İmamoğlu, Ahmet Türk ve Selçuk Mızraklı'yı ziyaret etti', 31 August 2019.
17. Kasapoğlu, 'Turkey Kurds', 15 May 2019.

BIBLIOGRAPHY

Abbas, Tahir and Ismail Yiğit (2015), 'Scenes from Gezi Park: Localisation, nationalism and globalisation in Turkey', *City*, 19(1), pp. 61–76.

Abdulla, N. (2016), 'How ISIL advanced Kurdish nationalism', *Turkish Policy Quarterly*, 14(4), pp. 89–97.

Aghajanian, Liana (2015), 'Copenhagen to Kobani, Berlin to Erbil', *Foreign Policy*, http://foreignpolicy.com/2015/01/06/copenhagen-to-kobani-berlin-to-erbil-kurds-peshmerga-isis/, accessed 13 December 2015.

Agirdir, Bekir (2008), 'Kürtler ve Kürt Sorunu', Konda, Istanbul, pp. 4–5. Available at http://konda.com.tr/wp-content/uploads/2017/02/2008_11_KONDA_Kurtler_ve_Kurt_Sorunu.pdf.

Agos (2016), 'Expropriation means closing down of Surp Giragos', 28 April, http://www.agos.com.tr/en/article/15164/expropriation-means-closing-down-of-surp-giragos.

Ahmed, Khani (2008), *Mem and Zin*, trans. Salah Saadalla (Istanbul: Avesta).

Akbarzadeh, Shahram, Costas Laoutides, William Gourlay and Zahid Ahmed (2019), 'The Iranian Kurds' transnational links: impacts on mobilization and political ambitions', *Ethnic and Racial Studies*, DOI: 10.1080/01419870.2019.1689280.

Akkaya, Ahmet Hamdi and Joost Jongerden (2010), 'The PKK in the 2000s: Continuity through breaks?', in Joost Jongerden and Marlies Casier (eds), *Nationalisms and Politics in Turkey* (London: Taylor & Francis), pp. 143–62.

Akkoyunlu, Karabekir (2014), 'Opinion: Soma disaster threatens Turkey's fragile social contract', *CNN*, 16 May, http://edition.cnn.com/2014/05/16/opinion/turkey-social-contract/index.html?hpt=hp_c1.

Akyol, Mustafa (2009), 'From Turkish people to the people of Turkey', *Hürriyet Daily News*, 17 April, http://www.hurriyet.com.tr/from-turkish-people-to-people-of-turkey-11457366.

Al Jazeera (2014), '"Neden Alevi bakan olmasın" [Why can't there be an Alevi minister?]', 4 April, http://www.aljazeera.com.tr/haber/neden-alevi-bakan-olmasin.

Al Jazeera (2016), 'Turkey deploys tanks in Syria, warns Kurdish YPG', 26 August, https://www.aljazeera.com/news/2016/08/turkey-deploys-tanks-syria-warns-kurdish-ypg-160825131652728.html.

Al Monitor (2019), 'New Diyarbakir mayor backs opposition candidate in Istanbul election rerun', 4 June, https://www.al-monitor.com/pulse/originals/2019/06/diyarbakir-mayor-adnan-selcuk-mizrakli-kurds-turkey.html#ixzz5tutlcTvP.

Alpman, Polat (2018), 'Working on communities under political domination: Subaltern Kurds in Turkey', in Bahar Başer et al. (eds), *Methodological Approaches in Kurdish Studies: Theoretical and Practical Insights from the Field* (Lanham, MD: Lexington Books), pp. 85–100.

Alptekin, Hüseyin (2018), 'Kurdish votes in the June 24, 2018 elections: An analysis of electoral results in Turkey's eastern cities', *Insight Turkey*, 20(4), pp. 211–30.

Amnesty International (1991), 'Vedat Aydın, President of People's Labour Party in Diyarbakir, member of the Turkish Human Rights Association', AI Index: EUR 44/92/911.

Anadolu Agency (2015), 'Erdogan: There is no Kurdish problem in Turkey', 23 March, https://aa.com.tr/en/turkey/erdogan-there-is-no-kurdish-problem-in-turkey/64407.

Andrews, Peter Alford (ed.) (1989), *Ethnic Groups in the Republic of Turkey* (Wiesbaden: Dr Ludwig Reichert Verlag).

ANF News (2018), 'Thousands of Kurds protest Afrin Invasion in European cities', 11 March, https://anfenglish.com/rojava/thousands-of-kurds-protest-afrin-invasion-in-european-cities-25401.

Anonymous (2000), 'Proverbs of Kurdistan', *International Journal of Kurdish Studies*, 14(1/2), pp. 41–119.

Aras, Ramazan (2015), *The Formation of Kurdishness in Turkey: Political violence, fear and pain* (London: Routledge).

Arparcık, Demet (2018), 'Feeling solidarity in an estranged city: Ethnography in postwar Diyarbakır under surveillance', in Bahar Başer et al. (eds), *Methodological Approaches in Kurdish Studies: Theoretical and practical insights from the field* (Lanham, MD: Lexington Books), pp. 101–19.

Asatrian, Garnik (2009), 'Prolegomena to the study of the Kurds', *Iran & the Caucasus*, 13(1), pp. 1–57.

Ashdown, Nick (2015), 'This is what being a Kurd is about', *Al Jazeera*, 10 January, http://www.aljazeera.com/news/middleeast/2015/01/what-being-kurd-about-2015165576342191.html.

Aslan, Senem (2009), 'Incoherent state: The controversy over Kurdish naming in Turkey', *European Journal of Turkish Studies*, 10, https://journals.openedition.org/ejts/4142.

Assénat, Martine (2016), 'Diyarbakır: aperçu de l'après-guerre', *Dipnot*, 3 May, https://dipnot.hypotheses.org/1896.

Associated Press (2014), 'Turkey's largest city is rattled by growing signs of ISIS support', 14 October, http://www.businessinsider.com/turkeys-capital-is-rattled-by-growing-signs-of-isis-support-2014-10?IR=T.

Atkinson, Rowland and John Flint (2001), 'Accessing hidden and hard-to-reach populations: Snowball research strategies', *Social Research Update*, 33, pp. 1–3.

Aydın, Delal (2014), 'Mobilising the Kurds in Turkey: Newroz as myth', in Cengiz Güneş and Welat Zeydanlıoğlu (eds), *The Kurdish Question in Turkey: New perspectives on violence, representation and reconciliation* (Abingdon: Routledge), pp. 68–88.

Aykan, Bahar (2014), 'Whose tradition, whose identity? The politics of constructing "Nevruz" as intangible heritage in Turkey', *European Journal of Turkish Studies*, 19, http://ejts.revues.org/5000.

Aziz, Mahir (2015), *The Kurds of Iraq: Nationalism and identity in Iraqi Kurdistan* (London: I. B. Tauris).

Bahcheli, Tozun and Sid Noel (2010), 'The Justice and Development Party and the Kurdish question', in Marlies Casier and Joost Jongerden (eds), *Nationalisms and Politics in Turkey* (London: Taylor & Francis), pp. 101–20.

Bajalan, Djene Rhys (2012), 'Şeref Xan's Şerefname: Kurdish ethno-politics in the early modern world, its meaning and its legacy', *Iranian Studies*, 45(6), pp. 795–818.

Barbalet, J. M. (1988), *Citizenship: Rights, struggle and class inequality* (Minneapolis: University of Minnesota Press).

Barkey, Henri J. and Graham E. Fuller (1998), *Turkey's Kurdish Question* (Lanham, MD: Rowman & Littlefield).

Barkey, Henri (2014), 'Turkish democracy: Two steps forward, two steps backward', *Harvard International Review*, Spring, pp. 75–8.

Barth, Frederik (1969), *Ethnic Groups and Boundaries: The social organisation of cultural difference* (London: Allen & Unwin).

Başaran, Ezgi (2012), 'Çözüm için Kürtleri tatmin, Türkleri de ikna etmek lazım', *Radikal*, 6 February, http://www.radikal.com.tr/yazarlar/ezgi-basaran/cozum-icin-kurtleri-tatmin-turkleri-de-ikna-etmek-lazim-1077830/.

Başaran, Ezgi (2017), *Frontline Turkey: The conflict at the heart of the Middle East* (London: I. B. Tauris).

Başer, Bahar and Mari Toivanen (2018), 'Politicized and depoliticized ethnicities, power relations and temporality: Insights to outsider research from comparative and transnational fieldwork', *Ethnic and Racial Studies*, 41(1), pp. 2067–84.

Başer, Bahar, Samim Akgönül and Ahmet Erdi Öztürk (2017), '"Academics for Peace" in Turkey: A case of criminalising dissent and critical thought via counterterrorism policy', *Critical Studies on Terrorism*, 10(2), pp. 274–96.

Başer, Bahar (2015), *Diasporas and Homeland Conflicts: A comparative perspective* (Farnham: Ashgate).

Başer, Kumru (2011), 'Diyarbakır'da Sivil Cuma' [Civilian Friday in Diyarbakır], *BBC Turkçe*, 3 June, http://www.bbc.co.uk/turkce/haberler/2011/06/110603_election_baser_blogs10.shtml.

Bayat, Asef (2007), *Making Islam Democratic: Social movements and the post-Islamist turn* (Stanford, CA: Stanford University Press).

Bayat, Asef (2010), *Life as Politics: How ordinary people change the Middle East* (Stanford, CA: Stanford University Press).

Baydar, Yavuz (2013), 'Turkey and the Kurds: The era of mass hypnosis is over', *The Guardian*, 7 March, https://www.theguardian.com/commentisfree/2013/mar/07/turkey-kurds-recep-tayyip-erdogan.

Bayir, Derya (2013), 'Representation of the Kurds by the Turkish judiciary', *Human Rights Quarterly*, 31(1), pp. 116–42.

BBC (2013), 'Turkey Kurds: PKK chief Ocalan calls for ceasefire', 21 March, https://www.bbc.com/news/world-europe-21874427.

BBC (2014), 'Turkey clamps down on Syria border after Kurdish unrest', 22 September, https://www.bbc.com/news/world-middle-east-29306088.

BBC (2015), 'Erdoğan: PYD de bir terör örgütüdür' [Erdoğan: PYD is also a terror organisation], 5 October, http://www.bbc.com/turkce/haberler/2015/10/151005_erdogan_tusk.

BBC (2016), 'Diyarbakır Büyükşehir Belediyesi'ne kayyum atandı', 1 November, https://www.bbc.com/turkce/haberler-turkiye-37836887.

BBC (2018a), 'Turkey arrests hundreds for criticising Afrin offensive', 29 January, https://www.bbc.com/news/world-europe-42863531.

BBC (2018b), 'Afrin looted by Turkish-backed rebels', 19 March, https://www.bbc.com/news/world-middle-east-43457214.

BBC (2018c), 'Erdoğan Kürt seçmene göz kırpıyor ama Kürtler artık bunu yemez', 2 November, https://www.bbc.com/turkce/haberler-turkiye-46070469?.

BBC (2018d), 'Witness: Kurdish singer Ahmet Kaya', November, https://www.bbc.co.uk/sounds/play/p04f319d.

Belge, Ceren (2011), 'State building and the limits of legibility: Kinship networks and Kurdish resistance in Turkey', *International Journal of Middle East Studies*, 43(1), pp. 95–114.

Bengio, Ofra (2012), *The Kurds of Iraq: Building a state within a state* (Boulder, CO: Lynne Rienner).

Bengio, Ofra (2014), 'The Kurdish momentum', in Ofra Bengio (ed.), *Kurdish Awakening: Nation building in a fragmented homeland* (Austin: University of Texas Press), pp. 269–81.

Berberoğlu, Enis (1999), 'Diyarbakır kazandı', *Hürriyet*, 21 March, http://www.hurriyet.com.tr/enis-berberoglu-diyarbakir-kazandi-39069148.

Bezci, Egemen and N. Borroz (2016), 'ISIS helps forge the Kurdish nation', *The National Interest*, 5 February, http://nationalinterest.org/feature/isis-helps-forge-the-kurdish-nation-15116, accessed 12 December 2016.

Bianet (2011), 'Sivil Cuma Namazı Kılındı' [Civilian Friday prayers performed], 8 April, http://bianet.org/bianet/siyaset/129155-sivil-cuma-namazi-kilindi.

Bianet (2014), 'Diyarbakır municipality FC adopts a Kurdish name', 29 October, http://bianet.org/english/sports/159552-diyarbakir-municipality-fc-adopts-a-kurdish-name.

Bianet (2017), 'Mığırdıç Margosyan couldn't recognize his street amidst ruins', 25 April, https://bianet.org/english/politics/185871-migirdic-margosyan-couldn-t-find-his-street-in-ruins.

Bianet (2019a), 'Closure case for parties which have "Kurdistan" in their names', 11 February, http://m.bianet.org/english/politics/205383-closure-case-for-parties-which-have-kurdistan-in-their-names.

Bianet (2019b), 'We are the own children of this country', 15 March, https://bianet.org/english/freedom-of-expression/206064-hdp-we-are-the-own-children-of-this-country.

Blaser, Noah (2019), 'Why Turkey's PKK conflict looms larger than ever in local election aftermath', *Foreign Policy Research Institute*, 9 April, https://www.fpri.

org/article/2019/04/why-turkeys-pkk-conflict-looms-larger-than-ever-in-local-election-aftermath/.

Bocheńska, Joanna et al. (2018), 'Introduction', in Joanna Bocheńska (ed.), *Rediscovering Kurdistan's Cultures and Identities: The call of the cricket* (Cham, Switzerland: Palgrave Macmillan), pp. 1–34.

Book of Dede Korkut, The (1974), (London: Penguin).

Bozarslan, Hamit (2008), 'Kurds and the Turkish state', in Reşat Kasaba (ed.), *The Cambridge History of Turkey*, Vol. 4 (Cambridge: Cambridge University Press), pp. 333–56.

Bozarslan, Mahmut (2019), 'Turkish judiciary toughens stance on "Kurdistan" groups', *Al Monitor*, 22 February, https://www.al-monitor.com/pulse/originals/2019/02/turkey-kurds-turkish-judiciary-in-kurdistan-onslaught.html.

Bozarslan, Mahmut (2019), 'Erdogan's threats to replace elected mayors could backfire', *Al Monitor*, 1 March, https://www.al-monitor.com/pulse/originals/2019/02/turkey-erdogans-threats-replacing-elected-mayors-backfires.html.

Brubaker, Rogers (2004), *Ethnicity without Groups* (Cambridge, MA: Harvard University Press).

Bullock, John and Harvey Morris (1993), *No Friends but the Mountains: The tragic history of the Kurds* (London: Penguin).

Butler, Daren (2019), 'Syria offensive feeds disenchantment among Turkey's Kurds', *Reuters*, 23 October, https://www.reuters.com/article/us-syria-security-turkey-kurds-idUSKBN1X21N7?.

Cağaptay, Soner (2017), *The New Sultan: Erdoğan and the crisis of modern Turkey* (London: I. B. Tauris).

Çarkoğlu, Ali, and Binnaz Toprak (2000), *Turkiye'de Din, Toplum ve Siyaset* (İstanbul: TESEV).

Çarkoğlu, Ali and Ersin Kalaycıoğlu (2015), *Türkiye'de ve Dünya'da Milliyetçilik*, Istanbul Policy Center, http://ipc.sabanciuniv.edu/wp-content/uploads/2015/12/T%C3%BCrkiyede-ve-Dunyada-Vatandaslik-2014-1.pdf.

Carter, Nick (1996), 'Nation, nationality, nationalism and internationalism in Italy, from Cavour to Mussolini', *The Historical Journal*, 39(2), pp. 545–51.

Casier, Marlies (2010), 'The politics of solidarity: The Kurdish question in the European Parliament', in Joost Jongerden and Marlies Casier (eds), *Nationalisms and Politics in Turkey* (London: Taylor & Francis), pp. 197–217.

Casier, Marlies (2011), 'Beyond Kurdistan? The Mesopotamia social forum and the appropriation and re-imagination of Mesopotamia by the Kurdish movement', *Journal of Balkan and Near Eastern Studies*, 13(4), pp. 417–32.

Celep, Ödül (2004), 'Can the Kurdish left contribute to Turkey's democratization?', *Insight Turkey*, 16(3), pp. 165–80.

Çelik, Ayşe Betül (2000), 'Alevis, Kurds and *Hemşehris*: Alevi Kurdish revival in the nineties', in Paul White and Joost Jongerden (eds), *Turkey's Alevi Enigma: A comprehensive overview* (Leiden: Brill), pp. 141–57.

Çetin, Fethiye (2008), *My Grandmother: A memoir* (London: Verso).

Christie-Miller, Alex (2013), 'Occupy Gezi: From the fringes to the centre, and back again', *The White Review*, July, http://www.thewhitereview.org/feature/occupy-gezi-from-the-fringes-to-the-centre-and-back-again/.

Chudacoff, Danya and Noah Blaser (2014), 'I do not want to be called a Turkish Kurd', 12 October, http://www.aljazeera.com/news/middleeast/2014/10/do-not-want-be-called-turkish-kurd-2014101253147924127.html.

Çiçek, Cuma (2016a), 'Kurdish identity and political Islam under AKP rule', *Research and Policy on Turkey*, 1(2), pp. 147–63.

Çiçek, Cuma (2016b), *The Kurds of Turkey: National, religious and economic identities* (London: I. B. Tauris).

Çınar, Alev (2001), 'National history as a contested site: The conquest of Istanbul and Islamist negotiations of the nation', *Comparative Studies in Society and History*, 43(2), pp. 364–91.

Çırakman, Aslı (2011), 'Flags and traitors: The advance of ethno-nationalism in the Turkish self-image', *Ethnic and Racial Studies*, 34(11), pp. 1894–912.

Cizre, Ümit (2001), 'Turkey's Kurdish problem: Borders, identity, and hegemony', in Brendan O'Leary, Ian Lustick and Thomas Callaghy (eds), *Right-sizing the State: The politics of moving borders* (Oxford: Oxford University Press), pp. 222–52.

Cizre, Ümit (ed.) (2016), *The Turkish AK Party and its Leader: Criticism, opposition and dissent* (London: Routledge).

CNN (2019), 'Kurdish politician and 10 others killed by "Turkish-backed militia" in Syria, SDF claims', 13 October, https://edition.cnn.com/2019/10/13/middleeast/syria-turkey-kurdish-politician-intl/index.html.

CNN Türk (2018), 'Cumhurbaşkanı Erdoğan: Şimdi sıra Kandil'de sıra Sincar'da' [President Erdoğan: Now it is Qandil's, it is Sinjar's turn], 5 June, https://www.cnnturk.com/turkiye/cumhurbaskani-erdogan-simdi-sira-kandilde-sira-sincarda.

Connor, Walker (1995), *Ethnonationalism: The quest for understanding* (Princeton, NJ: Princeton University Press).

Crabapple, Molly (2018), 'How Turkey's campaign in Afrin is stoking Syrian hatreds', *New York Review of Books*, 11 April, https://www.nybooks.com/daily/2018/04/11/how-turkeys-campaign-in-afrin-is-stoking-syrian-hatreds/.

Cumberland, Roger (1926), 'The Kurds', *The Muslim World*, 16(1), pp. 150–7.
Cumhuriyet (2009), 'Başbuğ'dan 'Türkiye halkı' vurgusu', 14 April, http://www.cumhuriyet.com.tr/haber/diger/55270/Basbug_dan__Turkiye_halki__vurgusu.html.
Cumhuriyet (2014a), 'Davutoğlu'ndan cani IŞİD'i meşrulaştıran sözler' [From Davutoğlu legitimising words for villainous ISIS], 8 August, http://www.cumhuriyet.com.tr/haber/turkiye/103123/Davutoglu_ndan_cani_ISiD_i_mesrulastiran_sozler.html.
Cumhuriyet (2014b), 'Erdoğan: Şu an Kobani düştü düşüyor', 7 October, http://www.cumhuriyet.com.tr/haber/siyaset/127825/Erdogan__Su_an_Kobani_dustu_dusuyor.html, accessed 2 December 2016.
Cumhuriyet (2016a), '12 TV, 11 radyo kanalı kapatıldı', 29 September, http://www.cumhuriyet.com.tr/haber/turkiye/607682/12_TV__11_radyo_kanali_kapa-tildi.html.
Cumhuriyet (2016b), 'Demirtaş da katılmıştı', 7 December, http://www.cumhuriyet.com.tr/haber/turkiye/641747/Demirtas_da_katilmisti..._HDP_milletvekiline__cuma_namazi__davasi.html.
Dağ, Rahman (2014), 'Democratic Islam Congress and the Middle East', *Open Democracy*, 13 June, https://www.opendemocracy.net/north-africa-west-asia/rahman-dag/democratic-islam-congress-and-middle-east.
Dağı, Ihsan (2012), 'Good for the Kurds, bad for the Turks?', *Today's Zaman*, 29 July, http://ihsandagi.blogspot.com/2012/07/good-for-kurds-bad-for-turks.html.
Dahrendorf, Ralf (1994), 'The changing quality of citizenship', in Bart Van Steenbergen (ed.), *The Condition of Citizenship* (London: Sage), pp. 10–19.
Daily Sabah (2015a), 'Turkey's President Erdoğan releases message for Nevruz, hopes it will bring peace', 21 March, https://www.dailysabah.com/politics/2015/03/21/turkeys-president-erdogan-releases-message-for-nevruz-hopes-it-will-bring-peace.
Daily Sabah (2015b), 'Fighting ISIS does not legitimize YPG terrorists', 27 September, http://www.dailysabah.com/diplomacy/2015/09/28/fighting-isis-does-not-legitimize-ypg-terrorists-pm-davutoglu-tells-us.
Daily Sabah (2019), 'Every citizen regardless of ethnic roots part of nation', 12 March, https://www.dailysabah.com/politics/2019/03/12/erdogan-every-citizen-regardless-of-their-ethnic-roots-part-of-turkish-nation.
Danforth, Nick (2016), 'In Turkey, obedience to the state trumps multiculturalism', *Muftah*, 2 February, http://muftah.org/turkey-obedience-multiculturalism/#.VrExz0102Uk.
Darıcı, Haydar (2013), '"Adults See Politics as a Game": Politics of Kurdish children in urban Turkey', *International Journal of Middle East Studies*, 45, pp. 775–90.

Darweish, Marwan and Andrew Rigby (2015), *Popular Protest in Palestine: The uncertain future of unarmed resistance* (London: Pluto Press).

Dawod, Hosham (2006), 'Ethnicity and power: Some reflections on ethnic definitions and boundaries', in Faley Jabar and Hosham Dawod (eds), *The Kurds: Nationalism and politics* (London: Saqi), pp. 79–89.

Dayak, Sevgi (2017), 'Turkish secularism revisited', *The Middle East in London*, 13(5), pp. 11–12.

Demirtaş, Selahattin (2018), 'I am running for president in Turkey. From my prison cell', *New York Times*, 20 June, https://www.nytimes.com/2018/06/20/opinion/president-turkey-elections-demirtas.html?.

Demirtaş, Serkan (2015), 'HDP not to return "ethnic politics" after polls: Demirtaş', *Hürriyet Daily News*, 1 June, http://www.hurriyetdailynews.com/hdp-not-to-return-ethnic-politics-after-polls-demirtas-.aspx?pageID=238&nID=83252&NewsCatID=338.

Demirtaş, Serkan (2019), 'No Kurdish opening likely after local polls', *Hürriyet Daily News*, 9 February, http://www.hurriyetdailynews.com/opinion/serkan-demirtas/no-kurdish-opening-likely-after-local-polls-in-turkey-141110.

DIHA (2015a), 'Halk Mardin'de Erdoğan'a sırtını döndü', 7 May, https://www.youtube.com/watch?v=Uubl4YoEYtg.

Diken (2015b), 'Ak Trol' değil profesör: Her şehide karşılık bir HDP milletvekili indirilmeli', 10 August, http://www.diken.com.tr/ak-trol-degil-profesor-her-sehide-karsilik-bir-hdp-milletvekili-indirilmeli/.

Diken (2015c), 'HDP'nin Seçim Videosu Yayında: İnadına Barış, İnadına Umut' [HDP's live election video: Determinedly peace, determinedly hope], 16 October, http://www.diken.com.tr/hdpnin-secim-videosu-yayinda-inadina-baris-inadina-umut/.

Diken (2015d), 'Erdoğan'ın 'Amed ne ya?' sorusuna yanıt Davutoğlu'nun 'Amed'li seçim afişinden', 30 October, http://www.diken.com.tr/erdoganin-amed-ne-ya-sorusuna-yanit-davutoglunun-amedli-secim-afisinden/.

Diken (2017), 'HDP'nin referandum şarkısı 'Bejin Na'ya bir yasak da Diyarbakır'dan', 1 April, http://www.diken.com.tr/hdpnin-referandum-sarkisi-bejin-naya-bir-yasak-da-diyarbakirdan/.

Diken (2019), 'AKP'li Göktaş'tan 'ilahi' vaat: Erdoğan'a oy verin, cennetin anahtarını alın', 16 March, http://www.diken.com.tr/akpli-goktastan-ilahi-vaat-erdogana-oy-verin-cennetin-anahtarini-alin/.

Dorleijn, Margreet (2006), 'Turkish–Kurdish language contact', in Hendrik Boeschoten and Lars Johanson (eds), *Turkic Languages in Contact* (Wiesbaden: Harrassowitz Verlag), pp. 74–94.

Düzel, Neşe (2003), 'Basın General Emri Dinlememeli', *Radikal*, 26 May, http://www.radikal.com.tr/turkiye/basin-general-emri-dinlememeli-670956/.

Economist, The (2005), 'Peace be unto you: Turkey and the Kurds', 20 August.

E-Kurd Daily (2014), 'Syrian Kurdistan's Kobani defense minister: Everyone needs to support the resistance', 15 November, http://ekurd.net/mismas/articles/misc2014/11/syriakurd1682.htm, accessed 13 December 2016.

Elekdağ, Şükrü (1992), 'Güneydoğu sorununda yeni eğilimler anketi', *Milliyet*, 6 September, p. 17.

Ensaroğlu, Yilmaz (2013), 'Turkey's Kurdish question and the peace process', *Insight Turkey*, 15 (2).

Entessar, Nader (1989), 'The Kurdish mosaic of discord', *Third World Quarterly*, 11(4), p. 87.

Erdem, Tarhan (2013), 'Türkiye'de Kürtler ne kadardır? (2)', *Radikal*, 25 April, http://www.radikal.com.tr/yazarlar/tarhan-erdem/turkiyede-kurtler-ne-kadardir-2-1130993/.

Erdoğan, Recep Tayyip (2019), 'Trump is right on Syria. Turkey can get the job done', *New York Times*, 7 January, https://www.nytimes.com/2019/01/07/opinion/erdogan-turkey-syria.html.

Ergil, Doğu (2000), 'The Kurdish question in Turkey', *Journal of Democracy*, 11(3), pp. 122–35.

Ergil, Doğu (2004), 'Reframing the problem: An approach to the Kurdish question in Turkey', in *NGOs at the Table: strategies for influencing policies in areas of conflict* (Lanham, MD: Rowman & Littlefield Publishers), pp. 147–64.

Ergil, Doğu (2006), '"Knowledge is a potent instrument for change": Interview with Doğu Ergil', *European Journal of Turkish Studies*, 5, https://journals.openedition.org/ejts/762.

Ergil, Doğu (2008), *Doğu Sorunu: Teşhisler ve Tesbitler 1995* (Istanbul: Akademi Kültür Yayincilik).

Ergül, Aslı (2012), 'The Ottoman identity: Turkish, Muslim or Rum?', *Middle Eastern Studies*, 48(4), pp. 629–45.

Eriksen, Thomas Hylland (1995), 'We and us: Two modes of group identification', *Journal of Peace Research*, 32(4), pp. 427–36.

Eriksen, Thomas Hylland (2004), *What is Anthropology?* (London: Pluto Press).

Eriksen, Thomas Hylland (2010), *Ethnicity and Nationalism: Anthropological perspectives* (London: Pluto Press).

Evrensel (2015), '15 Mayıs Kürt Dil Bayramı: 'En güzel dil ana dili'', 15 May, https://www.evrensel.net/haber/112867/15-mayis-kurt-dil-bayrami-en-guzel-dil-ana-dili.

Evrensel (2016), 'Diyarbakırlı işçi yakılarak öldürüldü', 1 September, https://www.evrensel.net/haber/289132/diyarbakirli-isci-yakilarak-olduruldu.

Ferdowsi, Abolqasem (2006), *Shahnameh: The Persian book of kings*, trans. Dick Davis (New York: Viking).

Findley, Carter Vaughn (2010), *Turkey, Islam, Nationalism and Modernity* (New Haven, CT: Yale University Press).

Firat News Agency (2015a), 'YPG/YPJ fighters at the border to Jarablus', 11 February, http://www.kurdishinfo.com/ypgypj-fighters-border-jarablus , accessed 13 December 2016.

Firat News Agency (2015b), 'Demirtaş: We will present the oppressed of Turkey with a great victory', 19 March.

Galip, Özlem (2015), *Imagining Kurdistan: Identity, culture and society* (London: I. B. Tauris).

Gambetti, Zeynep (2010), 'Decolonizing Diyarbakır: culture, identity and the struggle to appropriate urban space', in Kamran Asdar Ali and Martina Rieker (eds), *Comparing Cities: The Middle East and South Asia* (Karachi: Oxford University Press), pp. 95–127.

Gauthier-Villars, David (2019), 'Turkish leader's political star rebounds', *Wall Street Journal*, 29 October, https://www.wsj.com/articles/turkish-leaders-political-star-rebounds-with-syria-invasion-11572372751?.

Gazete Duvar (2019), 'Trabzon'da Kürdistan atkısıyla fotoğraf çektiren turistlere saldırı', 19 July, https://www.gazeteduvar.com.tr/gundem/2019/07/18/kurdistan-yazili-atkiyla-fotograf-cektiren-turistlere-sinir-disi/.

Gellner, Ernest (2006), *Nations and Nationalism*, 2nd edition (Maldon: Blackwell).

Gençoğlu Onbaşi, Funda (2016), 'Gezi Park protests in Turkey: From "enough is enough" to counter-hegemony?', *Turkish Studies*, 17(2), pp. 272–94.

Ghazaryan, Gayane (2019), 'The Kurdish voice of Radio Yerevan', *EVN Report*, 24 January, https://www.evnreport.com/evn-youth-report0/the-kurdish-voice-of-radio-yerevan?.

Göle, Nilufer (2012), 'Post-secular Turkey', *New Perspectives Quarterly*, 29(1), pp. 7–11.

Grabolle-Çeliker, Anna (2013), *Kurdish Life in Contemporary Turkey: Migration, gender and ethnic identity* (London: I. B. Tauris).

Gramsci, Antonio (1971), *Selections from the Prison Notebooks of Antonio Gramsci* (New York: International Publishers).

Grigoriadis, Ioannis and Esra Dilek (2018), 'Struggling for the Kurdish vote: Religion, ethnicity and victimhood in AKP and BDP/HDP rally speeches', *Middle Eastern Studies*, 54(2), pp. 289–303.

Guardian, The (2015), 'A language family tree in pictures', 23 January, https://www.theguardian.com/education/gallery/2015/jan/23/a-language-family-tree-in-pictures.

Guiton, Barney (2014), '"ISIS sees Turkey as its ally": Former Islamic State member reveals Turkish army cooperation', *Newsweek*, 7 November, http://www.newsweek.com/isis-and-turkey-cooperate-destroy-kurds-former-isis-member-reveals-turkish-282920.

Güneş, Cengiz (2007), 'Kurdish politics in Turkey: A question of identity', *International Journal of Kurdish Studies*, 21(1/2), pp. 17–36.

Güneş, Cengiz (2012), *The Kurdish National Movement in Turkey: From protest to resistance* (London: Routledge).

Güneş, Cengiz (2013), 'Explaining the PKK's mobilization of the Kurds in Turkey: Hegemony, myth and violence', *Ethnopolitics*, 12(3), pp. 247–67.

Gunter, Michael (2005), 'The Kurdish minority identity in Iraq', in Maya Shatzmiller (ed.), *Nationalism and Minority Identities in Islamic Societies* (Montreal: McGill-Queen's University Press), pp. 263–82.

Gunter, Michael (2007), 'The modern origins of Kurdish nationalism', in M. Ahmed and M. Gunter (eds), *The Evolution of Kurdish Nationalism* (Costa Mesa, CA: Mazda), pp. 2–17.

Gunter, Michael (2011a), 'Turgut Özal and the Kurdish question', in Marlies Casier and Joost Jongerden (eds), *Nationalisms and Politics in Turkey: Political Islam, Kemalism and the Kurdish issue* (London: Routledge), pp. 85–100.

Gunter, Michael (2011b), *Historical Dictionary of the Kurds* (Lanham, MD: Scarecrow Press).

Gunter, Michael (2014), 'The Turkish–Kurdish peace process stalled in neutral', *Insight Turkey*, 16(1), pp. 19–26.

Gürbüz, Mustafa (2016), *Rival Kurdish Movements in Turkey: Transforming ethnic conflict* (Amsterdam: Amsterdam University Press).

Gurses, Mehmet (2015), 'Is Islam a cure for ethnic conflict?', *Politics and Religion*, 8, pp. 135–54.

Gurses, Mehmet (2018), *Anatomy of a Civil War: Sociopolitical impacts of the Kurdish conflict in Turkey* (Ann Arbor: University of Michigan Press).

Güvenç, Muna (2011), 'Constructing narratives of Kurdish nationalism in the urban space of Diyarbakır, Turkey', *Traditional Dwellings and Settlements Review*, 23(1), pp. 25–40.

Haberler (2013), 'Erdoğan: Mustafa Kemal de Kürdistan Dedi Oda mı Bölücüydü', 19 November, https://www.haberler.com/erdogan-parti-grubunda-konusuyor-5325113-haberi/.

HaberTürk (2015), 'Yenikapı'da Teröre Karşı Tek Ses', 20 September, https://www.haberturk.com/gundem/haber/1130700-terore-karsi-yenikapiya.

HaberTürk (2018), 'Muharrem İnce'den Diyarbakır'da Kürt sorunu mesajı' [Muharrem İnce's Kurdish issue pledge in Diyarbakır], 11 June, https://www.haberturk.com/ince-diyarbakir-da-konusuyor-2011483.

Hakyemez, Serra (2018), 'Sur', *Middle East Report*, 287, https://merip.org/2018/10/sur/.

Hall, Stuart (1996), 'Who needs "identity"?', in Stuart Hall and Paul du Gay (eds), *Questions of Cultural Identity* (London: Sage).

Halstead, Narmala (2001), 'Ethnographic encounters: Positionings within and outside the insider frame', *Social Anthropology*, 9(3), pp. 307–21.

Harb, Mona and Reinoud Leenders (2005), 'Know thy enemy: Hizbullah, "terrorism" and the politics of perception', *Third World Quarterly*, 26(1), pp. 173–97.

Hart, Kimberly (2013), *And Then We Work for God: Rural Sunni Islam in western Turkey* (Stanford: Stanford University Press).

Hashimoto, C. and E. Bezci (2016), 'Do the Kurds have "No Friends but the Mountains"? Turkey's secret war against Communists, Soviets and the Kurds', *Middle Eastern Studies*, 52(4), pp. 640–55.

Hassanpour, Amir (1992), *Nationalism and Language in Kurdistan, 1918–1985* (Mellen Research University Press).

Hebdige, Dick (1979), *Subculture: The meaning of style* (London: Routledge).

Herbst, Jeffrey (2014), *States and Power in Africa: Comparative Lessons in Authority and Control* (Princeton, NJ: Princeton University Press).

Hobsbawm, Eric (1990), *Nations and Nationalism since 1780: Programme, myth, reality* (Cambridge: Cambridge University Press).

Hobsbawm, Eric (2005), 'Introduction: Inventing traditions', in Eric Hobsbawm and Terence Ranger (eds), *The Invention of Tradition* (Cambridge: Cambridge University Press), pp. 1–14.

Hoffman, Bruce (2017), *Inside Terrorism* (New York: Columbia University Press).

Holmes, Leslie (1993), 'On Communism, Post-Communism, Modernity and Post-Modernity', in Janina Frentzel-Zagórska (ed.), *From a One-party State to Democracy: Transition in Eastern Europe* (Amsterdam: Editions Rodopi), pp. 21–44.

Horowitz, Donald (1985), *Ethnic Groups in Conflict* (Berkeley: University of California Press).

Hosseinioun, M. (2015), 'Reconceptualising resistance and reform in the Middle East', in F. Gerges (ed.), *Contentious Politics in the Middle East: Popular resistance and marginalised activism beyond the Arab Uprisings* (New York: Palgrave Macmillan), pp. 52–73.

Houston, Christopher (2008), *Kurdistan: Crafting National Selves* (Bloomington: Indiana University Press).

Hrant Dink Foundation, http://turkiyekulturvarliklari.hrantdink.org/en/.

Human Rights Watch (1991), 'Whatever happened to the Iraqi Kurds?', 11 March, https://www.hrw.org/reports/1991/IRAQ913.htm.

Human Rights Watch (2015), 'Turkey: Mounting security operation deaths', 22 December, https://www.hrw.org/news/2015/12/22/turkey-mounting-security-operation-deaths.

Hürriyet (2000), '45 Ay Hapis' [45 months in prison], 11 March, http://www.hurriyet.com.tr/45-ay-hapis-39139251.

Hürriyet (2005), 'Kürt sorunu benim sorunum', 12 August, http://www.hurriyet.com.tr/gundem/kurt-sorunu-benim-sorunum-341847.

Hürriyet (2012), 'Dindar gençlik yetiştireceğiz' [We will raise a religious youth], 2 February, http://www.hurriyet.com.tr/dindar-genclik-yetistirecegiz-19825231.

Hürriyet (2015a), 'Erdoğan: 'Bunların dinle işi yok' [Erdoğan: 'They have nothing to do with religion'], 3 May, http://www.hurriyet.com.tr/erdogan-bunlarin-dinle-isi-yok-28901358.

Hürriyet (2015b), 'Cumhurbaşkanı Erdoğan: '1 Kasım'da 550 tane yerli ve milli milletvekili istiyorum'', 21 September, http://www.hurriyet.com.tr/cumhurbaskani-erdogan-1-kasimda-550-tane-yerli-ve-milli-milletvekili-istiyorum-30124611.

Hurriyet (2017), 'TBMM'de bir ilk ... HDP'li Osman Baydemir'e 'Kürdistan' cezası', 13 December, http://www.hurriyet.com.tr/gundem/hdpli-osman-baydemire-kurdistan-cezasi-40677021.

Hürriyet (2019), 'Erdoğan'dan manifesto sonrası bir ilk ...', 3 February, http://www.hurriyet.com.tr/gundem/erdogandan-manifesto-sonrasi-bir-ilk-iste-1994-ruhunun-sifreleri-41104270.

Hürriyet Daily News (1999), 'Yilmaz: Road to EU passes through Diyarbakir', 17 December, http://www.hurriyetdailynews.com/yilmaz-road-to-eu-passes-through-diyarbakir.aspx?pageID=438&n=yilmaz-road-to-eu-passes-through-diyarbakir-1999-12-17 [cited in *Yearbook of Muslims in Europe*, Vol. 1, edited by Jorgen Nielsen, Samim Akgönül, Ahmet Alibašic, Brigitte Maréchal and Christian Moe (Brill: Leiden, 2009), p. 393].

Hürriyet Daily News (2011), 'Syriacs send their first deputy to Parliament', 14 June, http://www.soc-wus.org/2011News/6152011125418.htm.

Hürriyet Daily News (2012), 'All to blame for lost sons: Police chief', 8 October, http://www.hurriyetdailynews.com/all-to-blame-for-lost-sons-police-chief.aspx?pageID=238&nID=31892&NewsCatID=338.

Hürriyet Daily News (2013a), 'Öcalan calls on Kurdish militants to bid farewell to arms for a "new" Turkey', 21 March, http://www.hurriyetdailynews.com/pkk-leader-tells-militants-to-leave-turkey-in-nevruz-message.aspx?pageID=238&nID=43373&NewsCatID=338.

Hürriyet Daily News (2013b), 'Nationalist party gathers huge crowds in İzmir in reaction to peace process', 20 April, http://www.hurriyetdailynews.com/nationalist-party-gathers-huge-crowds-in-izmir-in-reaction-to-peace-process.aspx?pageID=238&nID=45298&NewsCatID=338.

Hürriyet Daily News (2013c), 'No winner in dirty war, Turkish PM says', 1 May, http://www.hurriyetdailynews.com/no-winner-in-dirty-war-turkish-pm-says-45979.

Hürriyet Daily News (2013d), 'PKK leader praises protests as "meaningful", warns against manipulation', 7 June, http://www.hurriyetdailynews.com/pkk-leader-praises-protests-as-meaningful-warns-against-manipulation-48443.

Hürriyet Daily News (2013e), 'I did not see anyone consume alcohol', 27 June, http://www.hurriyetdailynews.com/i-did-not-see-anyone-consume-alcohol-in-mosque-during-gezi-protests-muezzin-says-49573.

Hürriyet Daily News (2013f), 'Öcalan calls for democratic Islam congress', 15 October, http://www.hurriyetdailynews.com/ocalan-calls-for-democratic-islam-congress-56274.

Hürriyet Daily News (2014a), 'Released footage shows no attacks', 14 February, http://www.hurriyetdailynews.com/released-footage-shows-no-physical-attack-on-headscarf-wearing-woman-during-gezi-protests-62479.

Hürriyet Daily News (2014b), 'Turkish PM cites 19th-century Britain to prove mine accidents are "typical"', 14 May, http://www.hurriyetdailynews.com/turkish-pm-cites-19th-century-britain-to-prove-mine-accidents-are-typical.aspx?pageID=238&nID=66472&NewsCatID=338.

Hürriyet Daily News (2015a), 'PM Davutoğlu wants a new Middle East for Turks, Kurds, Arabs', 25 January, http://www.hurriyetdailynews.com/pm-davutoglu-wants-a-new-middle-east-for-turks-kurds-arabs.aspx?pageID=238&nID=77427&NewsCatID=338.

Hürriyet Daily News (2015b), 'We will not make you the president, HDP co-chair tells Erdoğan', 17 March, http://www.hurriyetdailynews.com/we-will-not-make-you-the-president-hdp-co-chair-tells-erdogan.aspx?pageID=238&nID=79792&NewsCatID=338.

Hürriyet Daily News (2015c), 'Inclusive HDP candidate list aspires to pass 10 pct election threshold', 7 April, http://www.hurriyetdailynews.com/inclusive-hdp-candidate-list-aspires-to-pass-10-pct-election-threshold.aspx?pageID=238&nID=80731&NewsCatID=338.

Hürriyet Daily News (2015d), 'YPG not a terrorist organisation for US', 22 September, http://www.hurriyetdailynews.com/ypg-not-a-terrorist-organization-for-us-spokesman-says.aspx?PageID=238&NID=88832&NewsCatID=359.

Hürriyet Daily News (2016a), 'Diyarbakır's ruined Sur to be rebuilt "like Spain's Toledo", vows Turkish PM', 1 February, http://www.hurriyetdailynews.com/diyarbakirs-ruined-sur-to-be-rebuilt-like-spains-toledo-vows-turkish-pm-94615.

Hürriyet Daily News (2016b), 'Amedspor holds Fenerbahce to draw in Cup quarterfinal', 9 February, http://www.hurriyetdailynews.com/amedspor-holds-fenerbahce-to-draw-in-cup-quarterfinal-94952.

Hürriyet Daily News (2016c), 'Restricted celebrations mark Nevruz day across Turkey', 20 March, http://www.hurriyetdailynews.com/restricted-celebrations-mark-nevruz-day-across-turkey-.aspx?pageID=238&nID=96692&NewsCatID=341.

Hürriyet Daily News (2017a), 'Turkey won't allow establishment of a state in northern Syria: President Erdoğan', 24 June, http://www.hurriyetdailynews.com/turkey-wont-allow-establishment-of-a-state-in-northern-syria-president-erdogan-114706.

Hürriyet Daily News (2017b), 'Police detain five for making victory sign', 24 July, http://www.hurriyetdailynews.com/police-detain-five-for-making-victory-sign-in-istanbul-.aspx?pageID=238&nID=115900&NewsCatID=509.

Hürriyet Daily News (2018), 'Deputies brawl in Turkish parliament over Afrin operation', 8 March, http://www.hurriyetdailynews.com/deputies-brawl-in-turkish-parliament-over-afrin-operation-128439.

Hürriyet Daily News (undated), 'Pictures released by the armed forces depict destruction in southeastern Sur amid clashes, curfew', http://www.hurriyetdailynews.com/Default.aspx?pageID=447&GalleryID=2688.

Içduygu, Ahmet, David Romano and Ibrahim Sirkeci (1999), 'The ethnic question in an environment of insecurity: The Kurds in Turkey', *Ethnic and Racial Studies*, 22(6), pp. 991–1010.

Içduygu, Ahmet and Özlem Kaygusuz (2004), 'The politics of citizenship by drawing borders: Foreign policy and the construction of national citizenship identity in Turkey', *Middle East Studies*, 40(6), pp. 26–50.

Imber, Colin (2002), *The Ottoman Empire, 1300–1650* (London: Palgrave Macmillan).

İnce, Başak (2012), *Citizenship and Identity in Turkey: From Atatürk's republic to the present day* (London: I. B. Tauris).

Index on Censorship (2018), 'War abroad, repression at home: Turkey's academics caught up in wave of arrests', 10 April, https://www.indexoncensorship.org/2018/04/war-abroad-repression-at-home-turkeys-academics-and-students-caught-up-in-new-wave-of-arrests/.

Insel, Ahmet (2003), 'The AKP and normalising democracy in Turkey', *South Atlantic Quarterly* 102(2/3), pp. 293–308.

International Crisis Group (2011), 'Turkey: Ending the PKK insurgency', Europe Report 213.

International Crisis Group (2017), 'Managing Turkey's PKK conflict: The case of Nusaybin', Europe Report 243, 2 May.

International Crisis Group (2018), 'Turkey's election reinvigorates debate over Kurdish demands', Briefing 88, 5 June, https://www.crisisgroup.org/europe-central-asia/western-europemediterranean/turkey/b88-turkeys-election-reinvigorates-debate-over-kurdish-demands.

Isaacs, Harold (1979), 'Basic group identity: The idols of the tribe', in Nathan Glazer and Daniel Moynihan, *Ethnicity: Theory and experience* (Cambridge, MA: Harvard University Press), pp. 29–52.

Isin, Engin and Patricia Wood (1999), *Citizenship and Identity* (London: Sage).

Izady, Mehrdad (1992), *The Kurds: A concise handbook* (Washington, DC: Crane Russak).

Jacinto, Leela (2016), 'Destruction of Kurdish sites continues as Turkey hosts UNESCO', *France 24*, 20 July, http://www.france24.com/en/20160714-turkey-unesco-heritage-sites-damage-kurdish-diyarbakir-sur.

Jamison, Kelda (2016), 'Hefty dictionaries in incomprehensible tongues: Commensurating code and language community in Turkey', *Anthropological Quarterly*, 89(1), pp. 31–62.

Jenkins, Gareth (2008), *Political Islam in Turkey: Running west, heading east?* (New York: Palgrave Macmillan).

Jones, Dorian (2002), 'Kurdish students accused of undermining Turkey', *Times Higher Education*, 22 March, http://www.timeshighereducation.co.uk/story.asp?storyCode=167975&sectioncode=26.

Jones, Dorian (2013a), 'Jail is occupational hazard for Kurdish mayor', *Deutsche Welle*, 16 January, http://www.dw.com/en/jail-is-occupational-hazard-for-kurdish-mayor/a-16494351.

Jones, Dorian (2013b), 'Turkey: Armenian church catalyst for change in Kurdish region', *EurasiaNet*, 17 December, http://www.eurasianet.org/node/67879.

Joppke, Christian (2007), 'Transformation of citizenship: Status, rights, identity', *Citizenship Studies*, 11(1), pp. 37–48.

Jwaideh, Wadie (2006), *The Kurdish National Movement: Its origins and development* (New York: Syracuse University Press).

Kadıoğlu, Ayşe (2007), 'Denationalization of citizenship? The Turkish experience', *Citizenship Studies*, 11(3), pp. 283–99.

Kadıoğlu, Ayşe and Fuat Keyman (2011), *Symbiotic Antagonisms: Competing nationalisms in Turkey* (Salt Lake City: University of Utah Press).

Kahraman, Ahmet (2003), *Kürt Isyanları: Tedip ve Tenkil* (Istanbul: Evrensel Basın Yayın).

Karakoç, Ekrem and Zeki Sarıgil (2019), 'Why religious people support ethnic insurgency? Kurds, religion and support for the PKK', *Politics and Religion*, doi:10.1017/S1755048319000312.

Karaman, Hayrettin (2017), 'Neyi Oyluyoruz?', *Yeni Safak*, 13 April, https://www.yenisafak.com/yazarlar/hayrettinkaraman/neyi-oyluyoruz-2037309.

Karpat, Kemal (1972), 'The transformation of the Ottoman State, 1789–1908', *International Journal of Middle East Studies*, 3(3), pp. 243–81.

Kasapoğlu, Cağıl (2019), 'Turkey Kurds: The bitter politics of the football pitch', *BBC*, 15 May, https://www.bbc.com/sport/football/48035673.

Kaya, Ayhan (2013), *Europeanisation and Tolerance in Turkey: The myth of toleration* (Basingstoke: Palgrave Macmillan).

Kaya, Ayhan (2015), 'Islamisation of Turkey under the AKP rule: Empowering family, faith and charity', *South European Society and Politics*, 20(1), pp. 47–69.

Kaya, Zeynep and Matthew Whiting (2017), 'Sowing division: Kurds in the Syrian War', *Middle East Policy*, 24(1), p. 82.

Kaya, Zeynep and Robert Lowe (2017), 'The curious question of the PYD–PKK relationship', in Gareth Stansfield and Mohammed Shareef (eds), *The Kurdish Question Revisited* (Oxford: Oxford University Press), pp. 275–88.

Keles, Janroj Yilmaz (2014), 'The European Kurds rallying to fight IS', *Open Democracy*, 10 December, https://www.opendemocracy.net/opensecurity/janroj-yilmaz-keles/european-kurds-rallying-to-fight-is.

Kellas, James (1998), *The Politics of Nationalism and Ethnicity* (Houndsmill: Macmillan Press).

Kemahlıoğlu, Özge (2015), 'Winds of change? The June 2015 parliamentary election in Turkey', *South European Society and Politics*, 20(4), pp. 445–64.

Keskin, Adnan (2005), 'Erdoğan: Kürt sorunu demokrasiyle çözülür' [Erdoğan: The Kurdish problem is solved with democracy], *Radikal*, 11 August, http://www.radikal.com.tr/politika/erdogan-kurt-sorunu-demokrasiyle-cozulur-754439/.

Khani, Ahmed (2008), *Mem and Zin*, trans. Salah Saadalla (Istanbul: Avesta).

King, Charles and Neil Melvin (1999), 'Diaspora politics: Ethnic linkages, foreign policy, and security in Eurasia', *International Security*, 24(3), pp. 108–38.

Koç, İsmet and Mehmet Ali Eryut (2010), 'Demographic integration through intermarriage of Turks and Kurds in Turkey', Paper presented at the European Population Conference 2010, Vienna, Austria, 1–4 September 2010, http://epc2010.princeton.edu/abstracts/100371.

Krajeski, Jenna (2014), 'What Kobani means for Turkey's Kurds', *The New Yorker*, 8 November, http://www.newyorker.com/news/news-desk/kobani-means-turkeys-kurds.

Kurdish Info (2013), 'Mother tongue education is an indispensable right', 26 August, http://www.kurdishinfo.com/tzp-kurdi-conference-mother-tongue-education-is-an-indispensable-right.

Kurdistan 24 (2017a), 'Ankara's rejection of Kurdistan referendum unites Iraq and Turkey Kurds', 26 September, https://www.kurdistan24.net/en/news/66b2f8a5-739b-42b0-b4b7-12866e4ef639.

Kurdistan 24 (2017b), 'Teacher bans kids from speaking Kurdish in Turkey school', 24 October, http://www.kurdistan24.net/en/news/fc1bf92d-212f-445e-9375-42f4eb1964b2.

Kurdistan 24 (2017c), 'Turkey teacher reports students to police for listening to Kurdish music', https://www.kurdistan24.net/en/news/3cbf262a-d0ea-4693-aacd-9ea8b6960b41/Turkey-teacher-reports-students-to-police-for-listening-to-Kurdish-music.

Kymlicka, Will (2001), *Politics in the Vernacular: Nationalism, multiculturalism and citizenship* (Oxford: Oxford University Press).

Laiser, Sheri (1996), *Martyrs, Traitors and Patriots: Kurdistan after the Gulf War* (London: Zed Books).

Latif, Alaa (2015), 'Thanks To extremism, Iraqis revive ancient religion', *Niqash*, 28 May, http://www.niqash.org/en/articles/society/5014/Thanks-To-Extremism-Iraqis-Revive-Ancient-Religion.htm.

Leezenberg, Michiel (2006), 'Political Islam among the Kurds', in Faley Jabar and Hosham Dawod (eds), *The Kurds: Nationalism and politics* (London: Saqi, 2006), pp. 203–27.

Leezenberg, Michiel (2016), 'The ambiguities of democratic autonomy: The Kurdish movement in Turkey and Rojava', *South East European and Black Sea Studies*, 16(4), pp. 671–90.

Letsch, Constanze (2015), 'Turkey election: Ruling party loses majority as pro-Kurdish HDP gains seats', *The Guardian*, 8 June, https://www.theguardian.com/world/2015/jun/07/turkey-election-preliminary-results-erdogan-akp-party.

Lewis, Bernard (1961), *The Emergence of Modern Turkey* (London: Oxford University Press).

Lowe, Robert (2010), 'The Serhildan and the Kurdish national story in Syria', in R. Lowe and G. Stansfield (eds), *The Kurdish Policy Imperative* (London: Royal Institute of International Affairs), pp. 161–79.

Lyon, David (2009), *Identifying Citizens: ID cards as surveillance* (Cambridge: Polity Press).

Mardin, Şerif (2006), 'Playing games with names', in Deniz Kandiyoti and Ayse Saktanber (eds), *Fragments of Culture* (London: I. B. Tauris), pp. 115–27.

Margosyan, Mıgırdiç (2017), *Gâvur Mahallesi* [Infidel Neighbourhood] (Istanbul: Aras).

Marilungo, Francesco (2016), 'The city of terrorism or a city for breakfast: Diyarbakir's sense of place in the TV series *Sultan*', *Middle East Journal of Culture and Communication*, 9(3), pp. 275–93.

Martin, Guy (2015), 'Go inside an ISIS giftshop', *Time*, 26 February, http://time.com/3722759/isis-gift-shop/.

Massicard, Elise (2006), 'Claiming difference in a unitarist frame: The case of Alevism', in Hans-Lukas Kieser (ed.), *Turkey beyond Nationalism: Towards post-nationalist identities* (London: I. B. Tauris), pp. 74–82.

Massicard, Elise (2012), *The Alevis in Turkey and Europe* (London: Routledge).

Mazower, Mark (2000), *The Balkans: A short history from the end of Byzantium to the present day* (London: Phoenix Press).

McDowall, David (1992), *The Kurds: A nation denied* (London: Minority Rights Group).

McDowall, David (2004), *A Modern History of the Kurds* (London: I. B. Tauris).

Meleagrou-Hitchens, Alexander and Ranj Alaaldin (2016), 'The Kurds of ISIS', *Foreign Affairs*, 8 August, https://www.foreignaffairs.com/articles/syria/2016-08-08/kurds-isis.

Mesopotamia Social Forum (2009), http://www.transform-network.net/blog/blog-2009/news/detail/Blog/mesopotamia-social-forum-msf-in-diyarbakir.html.

Milliyet (1994), 27 November, cited in Yavuz (2003), p. 232.

Milliyet (2011), 'Sivil Itaatsizlike Camide' [Civil disobedience in the mosque], 6 April, http://www.milliyet.com.tr/sivil-itaatsizlik-camide-siyaset-1373814/.

Milliyet (2014), 'IŞİD korkusu imaj değiştiriyor' [Fear of ISIS is changing images], 13 October, http://www.milliyet.com.tr/isid-korkusu-imaj-degistirtiyor-gundem-1953885/.

Milliyet (2015a), 'Hülya Avşar: Adım Malakan' [Hülya Avşar: My name is Malakan], 26 February, http://www.milliyet.com.tr/hulya-avsar-adim-malakan-magazin-2019654/.

Milliyet (2015b), 'Türkiye'nin IŞİD ile PKK çatışması', 27 July, http://www.milliyet.com.tr/turkiye-isid-ve-pkk-yi-vuruyor--gundem-2092419/.

Ministry of Foreign Affairs (n.d.), 'Policy of zero problems with our neighbors', http://www.mfa.gov.tr/policy-of-zero-problems-with-our-neighbors.en.mfa.

Mortimer, Jasper (2019), 'Erdogan threatens to dismiss mayors seen as PKK-linked', *Al Monitor*, 26 February, https://www.al-monitor.com/pulse/originals/2019/02/erdogan-threat-dismiss-mayors-pkk-turkey.html.

Mutlu, Servet (1996), 'Ethnic Kurds in Turkey: A demographic study', *International Journal of Middle East Studies*, 28(4), pp. 517–41.

Nash, Manning (1989), *The Cauldron of Ethnicity in the Modern World* (Chicago: University of Chicago Press).

Natali, Denise (2001), 'Manufacturing identity and managing Kurds in Iraq', in B. O'Leary, I. Lustick and T. Callaghy (eds), *Right-sizing the State: The politics of moving borders* (Oxford: Oxford University Press), pp. 253–88.

Natali, Denise (2005), *The Kurds and the State: Evolving national identity in Iraq, Turkey and Iran* (Syracuse: Syracuse University Press).

Navaro-Yashin, Yael (2002), *Faces of the State: Secularism and public life in Turkey* (Princeton, NJ: Princeton University Press).

New York Times (2005), 'Popular Turkish novelist on trial for speaking of Armenian genocide', 16 December.

Nezan, Kendal (1996), 'The Kurds: Current position and historical background', in Philip Kreyenbroek and Christine Allison (eds), *Kurdish Culture and Identity* (London: Zed Books), pp. 7–19.

Norwich, John Julius (1997), *A Short History of Byzantium* (London: Penguin).

O'Connor, Francis and Semih Çelik (2019), 'Outsiders twice over in Kurdistan', in Başer et al. (eds), *Methodological Approaches in Kurdish Studies* (Lanham, MD: Lexington Books), pp. 123–44.

O'Shea, Maria (2004), *Trapped Between the Map and Reality: Geography and perceptions of Kurdistan* (London: Routledge).

Oda TV (2016), 'HDP'nin Cuma namazı buluşmasında neler yaşandı', 4 March, http://odatv.com/hdpnin-cuma-namazi-bulusmasinda-neler-yasandi-0403161200.html.

Öktem, Kerem (2008), 'The nation's imprint: Demographic engineering and the change of toponymes in republican Turkey', *European Journal of Turkish Studies*, 7, https://journals.openedition.org/ejts/2243.

Önderoğlu, Erol (2009), 'Mayor defends child prosecuted for teaching Kurdish at home', *Bianet*, 1 September, http://bianet.org/english/minorities/116778-mayor-defends-child-prosecuted-for-teaching-kurdish-at-home.

Onuş, Sinan (2015), 'Erdoğan'ın kastettiği, "yerli ve milli" vekiller kim?', *BBC*, 21 September, https://www.bbc.com/turkce/haberler/2015/09/150921_sinan_akp_milli.

Oomen, T. K. (1997), *Citizenship, Nationality and Ethnicity* (Cambridge: Polity Press).

Ortadoğu News (2019), 'İmamoğlu, Ahmet Türk ve Selçuk Mızraklı'yı ziyaret etti: Size güç olmak için buradayız', 31 August, http://www.ortadogunews.com/gundem/imamoglu-ahmet-turk-ve-selcuk-mizrakli-yi-ziyaret-etti-h275.html.

Özbudun, Ergun (2014), 'AKP at the crossroads: Erdoğan's majoritarian drift', *South European Society and Politics*, 19(2), pp. 155–67.

Özcan, Nihat Ali and Hakan Yavuz (2006), 'The Kurdish question and Turkey's Justice and Development Party', *Middle Eastern Policy*, 13(1), pp. 102–19.

Özen, H. (2014), 'Latent dynamics of movement formation: The Kurdish case in Turkey (1940s–1960s)', *Current Sociology*, 63(1), pp. 57–74.

Özsöy, Hisyar (2013), 'The missing grave of Sheikh Said: Kurdish formations of memory, place, and sovereignty in Turkey', in Kamala Visweswaran (ed.), *Everyday Occupations: Experiencing militarism in South Asia and the Middle East* (University of Pennsylvania Press), pp. 191–220.

Özyurt, Ahu (2014), 'Sympathy for the devil that is ISIS', *Hürriyet Daily News*, 26 September, http://www.hurriyetdailynews.com/Default.aspx?PageID=238&NID=72179&NewsCatID=515.

Paasche, T. F. (2015), 'Syrian and Iraqi Kurds: Conflict and cooperation', *Middle East Policy*, 22(1), pp. 77–88.

Pakulski, Jan (1997), 'Cultural citizenship', *Citizenship Studies*, 1(1), pp. 73–86.

Pamuk, Humeyra (2015), 'Turkey's Erdogan sees Syrian and Kurdish hands in Ankara attack', *Reuters*, 22 October, https://www.reuters.com/article/us-turkey-explosion-erdogan/turkeys-erdogan-sees-syrian-and-kurdish-hands-inankara-attack-idUSKCN0SG13F20151022?

Pamuk, Orhan (2005), *Istanbul: Memories of a city* (London: Faber & Faber).

Poole, Ross (1999), *Nation and Identity* (London: Routledge).

Pope, Hugh (2013), 'Turkey and the democratic opening for the Kurds', in Fevzi Bilgin and Ali Sarihan, *Understanding Turkey's Kurdish Question* (Lanham, MA: Lexington Books), pp. 117–40.

Posta (2018), 'Cumhurbaşkanı Erdoğan: CHP'nin bakışı yerli ve milli değil', 21 April, https://www.posta.com.tr/cumhurbaskani-erdogan-chp-nin-bakisi-yerli-ve-milli-degil-1408728.

Poyrazlar, Elçin (2013), 'What do Turkey's Kurds really want', *Vocativ*, 27 December, http://www.vocativ.com/world/turkey-world/turkey-kurds-really-want/.

Presidency of the Republic of Turkey (2015), 23 March, https://www.tccb.gov.tr/en/news/542/29848/president-erdogan-meets-with-mukhtars-at-the-presidential-palace.

Radikal (2009), 'Hani farklılıklar zenginliğimizdi' [Weren't our differences our greatest wealth?], 12 August, http://www.radikal.com.tr/turkiye/hani-farkliliklar-zenginligimizdi-949371/.

Radikal (2012), 'Kuzu: Kürtçe eğitim şeytana uymaktır', 19 October, http://www.radikal.com.tr/Radikal.aspx?aType=RadikalDetayV3&ArticleID=1104662&CategoryID=78.

Radikal (2013a), 'Erdoğan: AKM yıkılacak, Taksim'e cami de yapılacak' [Erdoğan: The AKM will be demolished, and a mosque will be built in Taksim], 2 June, http://www.radikal.com.tr/politika/erdogan-akm-yikilacak-taksime-cami-de-yapilacak-1135947.

Radikal (2013b), 'Biz birkaç çapulcunun yaptıklarını yapmayız', 9 June, http://www.radikal.com.tr/politika/basbakan-erdogan-biz-birkac-capulcunun-yaptiklarini-yapmayiz-1136875/.

Rénan, Ernst (1996 [1882]), 'What is a nation?' (translated by Martin Thom), in Geoff Ely and Ronald Grigor Suny (eds), *Becoming National: a reader* (New York: Oxford University Press), pp. 42–56.

Reuters (2014a), 'Turkey vows support for besieged Syrian town, but no military pledge', 3 October, https://www.reuters.com/article/us-mideast-crisis-turkey/turkey-vows-support-for-besieged-syrian-town-but-no-military-pledge-idUSKCN0HS0ET20141003.

Reuters (2014b), 'Iraqi peshmerga fighters approach Kobani, ready for battle', 29 October, http://www.reuters.com/video/2014/10/29/iraqi-peshmerga-fighters-approach-kobani?videoId=346738382.

Reuters (2016), 'Turkey removes two dozen elected mayors in Kurdish militant crackdown', 11 September, https://www.reuters.com/article/us-turkey-security-kurds-idUSKCN11H065.

Reuters (2017), 'Erdogan calls Kurdish referendum illegitimate', 29 September, https://www.reuters.com/article/us-mideast-crisis-kurds-referendum-erdog/turkeys-erdogan-calls-iraqi-kurdish-referendum-illegitimate-idUSKCN1C32YG, accessed 2 July 2019.

Reuters (2018), 'Turkey-backed forces pull down Kurdish statue', 18 March, https://www.reuters.com/article/us-mideast-crisis-syria-afrin-statue/turkey-backed-forces-pull-down-kurdish-statue-in-afrin-town-center-statement-idUSKBN-1GU0CU.

Reuters (2019), 'Pro-Kurdish elected mayors stripped of mandates in Turkey over dismissals: Party', 12 April, https://www.reuters.com/article/us-turkey-election-kurds-idUSKCN1RN1XB.

Rudaw (2016), 'Why is Spanish Toledo not good enough for Diyarbakir?', 9 April, http://www.rudaw.net/english/middleeast/turkey/09042016.

Rudaw (2019a), 'Jailed Demirtas calls for strategic voting in Sunday's municipal elections', 29 March, http://www.rudaw.net/english/middleeast/turkey/290320191.

Rudaw (2019b), 'Yıldırım: Kürdistan mebusu da vardı', 6 June, https://www.rudaw.net/turkish/kurdistan/060620196.

Rumelili, Bahar and Didem Çakmaklı (2017), 'Civic participation and citizenship in Turkey: A comparative study of five cities', *South European Society and Politics*, 22(3), pp. 365–84.

Sabah (2007), 'Kart-kurt'tan eyalete', 28 February, http://arsiv.sabah.com.tr/2007/02/28/gnd120.html.

Sabah (2015), 'More Turks interested in Kurdish', 1 February, https://www.dailysabah.com/feature/2015/02/01/more-turks-interested-in-kurdish.

Sabah (2018), 'Cumhurbaşkanı Erdoğan'dan "Dünya Nevruz Günü" mesajı', 21 March, https://www.sabah.com.tr/gundem/2018/03/21/cumhurbaskani-erdogandan-dunya-nevruz-gunu-mesaji.

Sakallıoğlu, Ümit Cizre (1996), 'Historicizing the present and problematizing the future of the Kurdish question: A critique of the TOBB report on the eastern question', *New Perspectives on Turkey*, 14(1), pp. 1–22.

Sakallıoğlu, Ümit Cizre (1998), 'Kurdish nationalism from an Islamist perspective: The discourses of Turkish Islamist writers', *Journal of Muslim Minority Affairs*, 18(1), pp. 73–89.

Saraçoğlu, Cenk (2011), *Kurds of Modern Turkey: Migration, Neoliberalism and Exclusion in Turkish Society* (London: I. B. Tauris).

Sarıgil, Zeki (2010), 'Curbing Kurdish ethnonationalism in Turkey: An empirical assessment of pro-Islamic and socio-economic approaches', *Ethnic and Racial Studies*, 33(3), pp. 533–53.

Sarıgil, Zeki and Omer Fazlıoglu (2013), 'Religion and ethno-nationalism: Turkey's Kurdish issue', *Nations & Nationalism*, 19(3), pp. 551–71.
Sarıkaya, Muharrem (2015), 'Demirtaş'ın Bilinmeyenleri!', *Haber Turk*, 8 February, http://www.haberturk.com/gundem/haber/1040409-demirtasin-bilinmeyenleri.
Saymaz, İsmail (2015), 'Kırşehir'deki Madımak'ın görüntüleri', *Radikal*, 19 October, http://www.radikal.com.tr/turkiye/kirsehirdeki-madimakin-goruntuleri-1454096/.
Scott, James C. (1998), *Seeing Like a State: How certain schemes to improve the human condition have failed* (New Haven, CT: Yale University Press).
Scott, James. C. (1985), *Weapons of the Weak: Everyday forms of peasant resistance* (New Haven, CT: Yale University Press).
Şengül, Serap Ruken (2013), 'Qırıx: An "Inverted Rhapsody" of Kurdish national struggle, gender, and everyday life in Diyarbakır', in Kamala Visweswaran (ed.), *Everyday Occupations: Experiencing militarism in South Asia and the Middle East* (University of Pennsylvania Press), pp. 29–59.
SETA (The Foundation for Political, Social and Economic Research) (2009), *Public Perceptions of the Kurdish Question in Turkey* (Istanbul: SETA).
Shankland, David (2003), *The Alevis in Turkey: The emergence of a secular Islamic tradition* (London: Routledge).
Siaband, Samande (1988), 'Mountains, my home', *Kurdish Times* 2(2), pp. 7–12.
Smith, Anthony (1991), *National Identity* (London: Penguin).
Sofos, Spyros and Umit Özkirimli (2008), *Tormented by History: Nationalism in Greece and Turkey* (London: Hurst).
Soleimani, Kamal (2016), *Islam and Competing Nationalisms in the Middle East, 1876–1926* (London: Palgrave Macmillan).
Somer, Murat (2011), 'Democratization, clashing narratives and "Twin Tolerations" between Islamic-Conservative and pro-secular actors', in Marlies Casier and Joost Jongerden (eds), *Nationalisms and Politics in Turkey: Political Islam, Kemalism and the Kurdish Issue* (Abingdon: Routledge), pp. 28–47.
Soner, Ali (2010), 'The Justice and Development Party's policies towards non-Muslim minorities in Turkey', *Journal of Balkan and Near Eastern Studies*, 12(1), pp. 23–40.
Sönmez, Mustafa (2013), 'Kurds still migrating to western Turkish cities', *Hürriyet Daily News*, 4 May, http://www.hurriyetdailynews.com/kurds-still-migrating-to-western-turkish-cities.aspx?pageID=238&nID=46198&NewsCatID=344.
Stansfield, Gareth (2014), 'Kurds, Persian nationalism and Shi'I rule: Surviving dominant nationhood in Iran', in David Romano and Mehmet Gurses (eds),

Conflict, Democratisation and the Kurds in the Middle East: Turkey, Iran, Iraq, Syria (New York: Palgrave Macmillan), pp. 59–84.

Stockholm Center for Freedom (2017), 'Monument of Kurdish philosopher and poet Ahmad-i Khani demolished by Turkish government', 28 June, https://stockholmcf.org/monument-of-kurdish-philospher-and-poet-ahmad-i-khani-demolished-by-turkish-government/.

Syrian Observatory for Human Rights (2018), 20 September, http://www.syriahr.com/en/?p=102951.

Syrian Observatory for Human Rights (2019), 13 October, http://www.syriahr.com/en/?p=144674.

Szanto, Edith (2018), '"Zoroaster was a Kurd!": Neo-Zoroastrianism among the Iraqi Kurds', *Iran and the Caucasus*, 22(1), pp. 96–110.

T24 (2018), 'Erdoğan: Ey HDP, sokağa çıkarsanız biliniz ki güvenlik güçlerimiz sizin boynunuzdadır!', 21 January, https://t24.com.tr/haber/erdogan-ey-hdp-sokaga-cikarsaniz-biliniz-ki-guvenlik-guclerimiz-sizin-boynunuzdadir,540958.

Taş, Hakkı (2015), 'Turkey – from Tutelary to Delegative Democracy', *Third World Quarterly*, 36(4), pp. 776–91.

Taşpınar, Ömer (2005), *Kurdish Nationalism and Political Islam in Turkey: Kemalist identity in transition* (New York and London: Routledge).

Taşpınar, Ömer (2012), 'Turkey: The new model?', in Robin Wright (ed.), *The Islamists Are Coming: Who they really are* (Washington, DC: Woodrow Wilson Center Press), pp. 127–36.

Taştekin, Fehim (2014), 'Politics strain Turkey's first Kurdish-language institute', *Al Monitor*, 13 November, http://www.al-monitor.com/pulse/originals/2014/11/turkey-kurdish-universities-unites-four-pieces-kurdistan.html.

Taştekin, Fehim (2019), 'Kurds in Turkey unite to take aim at Ankara in elections', *Al Monitor*, 15 January, https://www.al-monitor.com/pulse/originals/2019/01/turkey-kurds-do-the-impossible-and-set-up-alliance.html.

Taylor, Charles (1985), *Human Agency and Language* (Cambridge: Cambridge University Press).

Tekdemir, Ömer (2018), 'The reappearance of Kurdish Muslims in Turkey: The articulation of religious identity in a national narrative', *British Journal of Middle Eastern Studies*, DOI: 10.1080/13530194.2018.1430534.

Temelkuran, Ece (2014), 'Revolutionary Nice', *Guernica*, 2 February, https://www.guernicamag.com/ece-temelkuran-revolutionary-nice/.

Temelkuran, Ece (2016), *Turkey: The insane and the melancholy* (London: Zed Books).

Tezcür, Güneş Murat (2009), 'Kurdish nationalism and identity in Turkey: A conceptual reinterpretation', *European Journal of Turkish Studies*, 10, https://journals.openedition.org/ejts/4008.

Today's Zaman (2013), 'Erdoğan: "Past mistakes in fighting terrorism helped PKK"', 22 January, retrieved from https://web.archive.org/web/20130122172829/http://todayszaman.com/news-304769-.html.

Toumani, Meline (2008), 'Minority rules', *New York Times Magazine*, 17 February, http://www.nytimes.com/2008/02/17/magazine/17turkey-t.html?_r=0.

Toumani, Meline (2014), *There Was and There Was Not* (New York: Picador).

Tripp, Charles (2013), *The Power and the People: Paths of resistance in the Middle East* (Cambridge: Cambridge University Press).

Tuncel, Sebahat (2018), 'Arab Spring, Kurdish Summer', *New York Times*, 11 June, http://www.nytimes.com/2011/06/18/opinion/18tuncel.html.

Twain, Mark (1910), *Mark Twain's Speeches* (New York: Harper & Brothers).

Ulgen, Sinan (2013), 'Erdoğan's fetishism of the "National Will"', *Politico*, 6 June, http://www.politico.eu/article/erdogans-fetishism-of-the-national-will/.

Üngör, Uğur Ümit (2012a), *The Making of Modern Turkey: Nation and state in eastern Anatolia, 1913–50* (Oxford: Oxford University Press).

Üngör, Ümit (2012b), 'Untying the tongue-tied: Ethnocide and language politics', *International Journal of Sociology of Language*, 217(133), pp. 127–50.

Unver, Akin (2016), 'Schrödinger's Kurds: Transnational Kurdish geopolitics in the age of shifting borders', *Journal of International Affairs*, 69(2), pp. 65–98.

Uslu, Emrullah (2016), 'Jihadist highway to Jihadist haven: Turkey's Jihadi policies and western security', *Studies in Conflict and Terrorism*, 39(9), pp. 781–802.

Van Bruinessen, Martin (1989), 'The ethnic identity of Kurds in Turkey', in Peter Andrews (ed.), *Ethnic Groups in the Republic of Turkey* (Wiesbaden: Reichert Verlag), pp. 613–21.

Van Bruinessen, Martin (1992a), 'Kurdish society, ethnicity, nationalism and refugee problems', in Philip G. Kreyenbroek and Stefan Sperl (eds), *The Kurds: A contemporary overview* (London: Routledge), pp. 33–67.

Van Bruinessen, Martin (1992b), *Agha, Shaikh and State: The social and political structures of Kurdistan* (London: Zed Books).

Van Bruinessen, Martin (1994), 'Genocide in Kurdistan? The suppression of the Dersim rebellion in Turkey (1937–38) and the chemical war against the Iraqi Kurds (1988)', in G. J. Andreopoulos (ed.), *Conceptual and Historical Dimensions of Genocide* (Philadelphia: University of Pennsylvania Press), pp. 141–70.

Van Bruinessen, Martin (1998), 'Shifting national and ethnic identities: The Kurds in Turkey and the European diaspora', *Journal of Muslim Minority Affairs*, 18(1), pp. 39–52.
Van Bruinessen, Martin (1999), 'The Kurds and Islam', Working Paper 13, Islamic Area Studies Project, Tokyo, Japan.
Van Bruinessen, Martin (2000), *Mullas, Sufis and Heretics: The role of religion in Kurdish society* (Istanbul: ISIS).
Van Bruinessen, Martin (2003), 'Ehmedî Xanî's *Mem û Zîn* and its role in the emergence of Kurdish nationalism', in Abbas Vali (ed.), *Essays on the Origins of Kurdish Nationalism* (Costa Mesa, CA: Mazda), pp. 40–57.
Van Bruinessen, Martin (2009), 'Turkey's AKP government and its engagement with the Alevis and Kurds', conference paper presented at 'Otherness and beyond: dynamism between group formation and identity in modern Muslim societies', Tokyo University of Foreign Studies.
Van Bruinessen, Martin (2016), 'The Kurds as objects and subjects of historiography: Turkish and Kurdish nationalists struggling over identity', in Fabian Richter (ed.), *Identität Ethnizität und Nationalismus in Kurdistan. Festschrift zum 65. Geburtstag von Prof. Dr. Ferhad Ibrahim Seyder* (Münster: Lit Verlag), pp. 13–61.
Voloder, Lejla (2012), 'Secular citizenship and Muslim belonging in Turkey: Migrant perspectives', *Ethnic and Racial Studies*, 36(5), pp. 838–56.
Voloder, Lejla (2014), 'Introduction: Insiderness in migration and mobility research, conceptual considerations', in Lejla Voloder and Liudmila Kirpitchenko (eds), *Insider Research on Migration and Mobility: International perspectives on researcher positioning* (London: Routledge), pp. 1–17.
Waldman, Simon and Emre Calışkan (2017), *The New Turkey and its Discontents* (Oxford University Press).
Watts, Nicole (2004), 'Institutionalising virtual Kurdistan West: Transnational networks and ethnic contention in international affairs', in Joel Migdal (ed.), *Boundaries and Belonging: States and societies in the struggle to shape identities and local practices* (Cambridge: Cambridge University Press), pp. 121–47.
Watts, Nicole (2006), 'Activists in office: Pro-Kurdish contentious politics in Turkey', *Ethnopolitics*, 5(2), pp. 125–44.
Watts, Nicole (2010), *Activists in Office: Kurdish Politics and Protest in Turkey* (Seattle: University of Washington Press).
Westrheim, Kariane (2014), 'Taking to the streets! Kurdish collective action in Turkey', in Cengiz Güneş and Welat Zeydanlıoğlu (eds), *The Kurdish Question in Turkey: New perspectives on violence, representation and reconciliation* (Abingdon: Routledge), pp. 137–61.

White, Jenny (2013), *Muslim Nationalism and the New Turks* (Princeton, NJ: Princeton University Press).
White, Paul (2003), 'The debate on the identity of "Alevi Kurds"', in Paul White and Joost Jongerden (eds), *Turkey's Alevi Enigma* (Leiden: Brill), pp. 17–29.
Yackley, Ayla Jean (2013), 'Kurd rebel leader orders fighters to halt hostilities', *Reuters*, 21 March, http://www.reuters.com/article/us-turkey-kurds-idUSBRE-92J0OF20130321.
Yackley, Ayla Jean (2016), 'Turkish parliament speaker provokes row with call for religious constitution', *Reuters*, 26 April, https://www.reuters.com/article/us-turkey-politics-constitution/turkish-parliament-speaker-provokes-row-with-call-for-religious-constitution-idUSKCN0XN0MD.
Yackley, Ayla-Jean (2019), 'Jailed militant leader enters Istanbul election fray', *Al Monitor*, 21 June, https://www.al-monitor.com/pulse/originals/2019/06/abdullah-ocalan-urges-neutral-kurdish-vote-istanbul-election.html.
Yalçın-Heckmann, Lale (1989), 'On kinship, tribalism and ethnicity in eastern Turkey', in Peter Alford Andrews (ed.), *Ethnic Groups in the Republic of Turkey* (Wiesbaden: Dr Ludwig Reichert Verlag), pp. 622–31.
Yalçın-Heckmann, Lale (1991), 'Ethnicity, Islam and nationalism among Kurds in Turkey', in Richard Tapper (ed.), *Islam in Modern Turkey: Religion, politics and literature in a secular state* (London: I. B. Tauris), pp. 114–18.
Yanik, Lerna (2006), '"Nevruz" or "Newroz"? Deconstructing the "Invention" of a contested tradition in contemporary Turkey', *Middle East Studies*, 42(2), pp. 286–302.
Yanmış, Mehmet and Ahmet Aktaş (2015), *Kürtlerde Dinî Yaşam: Diyarbakır Örneği* [Religious life among Kurds: Diyarbakır examples] (Istanbul: Ukam Yayınları).
Yanmış, Mehmet (2016), 'Resurgence of the Kurdish conflict in Turkey: How the Kurds view it', Rethink Paper 25 (Washington, DC: Rethink Institute).
Yavuz, Hakan (1998), 'A preamble to the Kurdish question: The politics of Kurdish identity', *Journal of Muslim Minority Affairs*, 18(1), pp. 9–18.
Yavuz, Hakan (2001), 'Five stages in the construction of Kurdish nationalism in Turkey', *Nationalism and Ethnic Politics*, 7(3), pp. 1–24.
Yavuz, Hakan (2003), *Islamic Political Identity in Turkey* (Oxford: Oxford University Press).
Yavuz, Hakan (2005), 'Kurdish nationalism in Turkey', in Maya Shatzmiller (ed.), *Nationalism and Minority Identities in Islamic Societies* (Montreal: McGill-Queen's University Press), pp. 229–62.
Yavuz, Hakan (2009), *Secularism and Muslim Democracy in Turkey* (Cambridge: Cambridge University Press).

Yeğen, Mesut (2006), *Müstakbel-Türk'ten Sözde-Vatandaş'a*. (Istanbul: İletişim).

Yeğen, Mesut (2007), 'Turkish nationalism and the Kurdish question', *Ethnic and Racial Studies*, 30(1), pp. 119–51.

Yeğen, Mesut (2016), 'Armed struggle to peace negotiations: Independent Kurdistan to democratic autonomy, or the PKK in context', *Middle East Critique*, 25(4), pp. 365–83.

Yeni Akit (2015), 'Davutoğlu: Her Müslüman için cihad farz-ı ayndır', 2 January, http://m.yeniakit.com.tr/haber/davutoglu-her-musluman-icin-cihad-farz-i-ayndir-50176.html.

Yeni Şafak (2002), 'Olağanüstü Hal 30 Kasımda Bitiyor', 28 November, https://www.yenisafak.com/arsiv/2002/kasim/28/gundem.html

Yeni Şafak (2016), 'Erdoğan of HDP deputies: They are terrorists, not politicians', 16 March, http://www.yenisafak.com/en/news/erdogan-of-hdp-deputies-they-are-terrorists-not-politicians-2434601.

Yeni Şafak (2018), 'Postmodern Haçlı Seferi', 25 January, https://www.yenisafak.com/gundem/postmodern-hacli-seferi-3026594.

Yıldız, Ahmet (2016), *Ne Mutlu Türküm Diyebilene* (Istanbul: İletişim).

Yılmaz, Hakan (2014), *Turkiye'de Kimlikler, Kurt Sorunu, ve Cozum Sureci: Kamuoyundaki Algilar ve Tutumlar [Identities, Kurdish Question and the Solution Process in Turkey: public perceptions and attitudes]* (Istanbul: Açık Toplum Vakfı).

Yüksel, Ayşe Seda (2011), 'Rescaled localities and redefined class relations: neoliberal experience in south-east Turkey', *Journal of Balkan and Near Eastern Studies*, 13(4), pp. 433–55.

Zaman, Amberin (2013), 'Salih Müslim: Çetelere mermi veriliyor' [Salih Müslim: Bullets are given to gangs], *Taraf*, 18 September, available at http://www.yonelishaber.com/salih-muslim-cetelere-mermi-veriliyor-3435yd.html.

Zaman, Amberin (2018), 'Electoral noose tightens in Turkey's critical southeast', *Al Monitor*, 4 June, https://www.al-monitor.com/pulse/originals/2018/06/turkey-elections-pressure-kurds.html.

Zeydanlioglu, Welat (2012), 'Turkey's Kurdish language policy', *International Journal of Sociology of Language*, 21(7), pp. 99–125.

Zeydanlioğlu, Welat (2014), 'Repression or reform? An analysis of the AKP's Kurdish language policy', in Cengiz Günes and Welat Zeydanlioğlu (eds), *The Kurdish Question in Turkey: New perspectives on violence, representation and reconciliation* (Abingdon: Routledge), pp. 162–85.

Ziflioğlu, Vercihan (2012), 'Syriac weaver says mutual respect the answer', *Hürriyet Daily News*, 10 March, http://www.hurriyetdailynews.com/syriac-weaver-says-mutual-respect-the-answer.aspx?pageID=238&nid=15664.

Zubaida, Sami (2006), 'Religion and ethnicity as politicized boundaries', in Faley Jabar and Hosham Dawod (eds), *The Kurds: Nationalism and politics* (London: Saqi), pp. 93–102.

Zürcher, Erik J. (2010), *The Young Turk Legacy and Nation Building: From the Ottoman Empire to Atatürk's Turkey* (London: I. B. Tauris).

INDEX

AKP (Adalet ve Kalkınma Partisi; Justice and Development Party), 2, 3, 36, 93
   authoritarianism and hegemony of, 19, 33, 35, 39, 92, 105, 183, 185, 186, 210
   economy under, 33, 36, 37, 212, 213, 232
   and Islam, 30, 33, 85–6, 88, 90–2, 98, 105
   and Kurds, 12, 68, 69, 77, 96, 104, 105, 187, 206, 214–15, 225, 228
   and peace process with PKK, 7, 11, 133
   and political reform, 7, 28–30, 32, 198
   'trustees' replacing HDP mayors, 126, 212, 213, 231
Alevis, 44, 50, 72, 102, 106n, 107n, 108n, 113, 210
Amed *see* Diyarbakır
Amedspor, 187, 233
Anatolia, 130–1
Armenians, 6, 18, 20, 23, 80, 89, 102–3, 113, 122–4, 131, 135, 174, 190, 210, 227
assimilation, 21, 22, 26, 52, 54, 59, 99, 114, 120, 127, 170, 209
Assyrians, 29, 113, 119, 122–4, 135, 210

Atatürk, Mustafa Kemal, 4, 21, 34, 39n, 52, 62, 113, 121, 133
authoritarianism, 19, 35, 39, 92, 105, 186, 210, 232
Aydın, Vedat, 174–5, 178

Bahçeli, Devlet, 32, 77
Başaran, Ezgi, 35, 177
Başer, Bahar, 47, 133, 146
BDP (Barış ve Demokrasi Partisi, Peace and Democracy Party), 34, 94–5
Brubaker, Rogers, 7, 17n, 54, 56, 147

Çetin, Fethiye, 6, 7, 41n, 103
CHP (Cumhuriyet Halk Partisi, Republican People's Party), 34, 116, 212–14, 230
citizenship, 4, 51, 193–220
   definition(s) of, 194, 196, 209
   and ethnic identity, 10, 195
   Turks' and Kurds' conceptualisation of, 194, 196, 199
collective identification, 7, 50–1, 147, 149, 151, 169, 172–5, 223; *see also* ethnic identity
coup of 1980, 22, 25, 36, 37, 66, 88, 149, 194, 223
coup attempt of July 2016, 36, 70, 159, 211, 228, 229

Index

Da'esh *see* ISIS
Davutoğlu, Ahmet, 68, 93, 98, 121, 125, 126, 155, 157
Demirbaş, Abdullah, 122, 208
Demirtaş, Selahattin, 2, 94, 97, 146, 186, 203, 204, 209–10, 213, 231
   arrest and imprisonment of, 212
   opposition to Erdogan and AKP, 182–3, 214–15, 232
democracy
   under AKP rule, 88–91
   Kurdish struggle for, 105, 133, 208–11, 215, 226, 227, 232, 233
   in Turkey, 20, 30, 31, 38, 69, 125, 208, 225
dengbêj, 32, 87
Diyanet (Religious Affairs Directorate), 86, 88, 91, 95, 96
Diyarbakır, 1–3, 8, 9, 12–13, 21, 31, 32, 38, 43–50, 87, 95, 106, 113–15, 146, 148, 167, 172–5, 183–5, 198–9, 215, 221
   as Amed, 46, 114, 120, 121, 137n, 138n
   as capital and symbolic city, 1, 12, 44, 48, 115, 117–21, 135
   daily life in, 221
   destruction in 2015–16, 38, 126, 228
   Erdoğan in, 30, 90, 99
   as multicultural city, 113, 119, 121–4, 137n
   Turkish presence in, 121, 122, 123, 136n
   Ulu Cami, 8, 44, 45, 87, 117, 121
DTP (Demokratik Toplum Partisi, Democratic Society Party), 93–4, 208

economy in Turkey, 33, 36, 37, 198, 212, 213, 232
education in Turkey, 10, 21, 22, 64, 65, 81n, 86, 87, 130
   Kurdish language education, 67, 68, 69, 96, 223
   Kurds' suspicion of, 63, 65
Elçi, Şerafettin, 32, 177

elections, 2–3, 29, 33, 93, 95, 212–15
   general election of 7 June 2015, 2, 36, 98, 102, 116, 123, 182–3, 203–8, 211, 229
   Kurdish participation in, 182–9, 203, 215–16, 225–6, 231, 232
   municipal elections of 2019, 213–15, 231
   parliamentary threshold, 2–3, 182–3, 203, 205–6, 213, 225–6
Erdoğan, Recep Tayyip, 3, 7, 31, 85–6, 101, 116, 121, 126, 162, 198, 211, 218n, 229
   domination of political sphere, 33, 35, 37–9, 92, 168, 185, 188, 212, 227, 231–2
   and Islam, 90–2, 105
   and Kurds, 12, 30, 36, 38, 77, 90, 97, 98–9, 125, 133, 134, 154, 158, 176, 187, 229
   and *milli irade* (national will), 35, 169, 181
   and peace process, 31, 36, 37, 77, 133, 171, 229
   political alliances, 116, 186
   presidency, 3, 7, 36–7, 182, 185, 212, 213, 225–6
   redefinition of national identity by, 29
Ergil, Doğu, 9–10, 17n, 28, 48–9, 195, 211, 227
Eriksen, Thomas Hyllel, 26, 56, 144, 145, 173
ethnic identity, 19, 50–54
   and boundaries, 26, 55, 96
   consolidation in social interactions, 53–4, 169, 175
   definition against the Other, 26–7
   elements of, 6, 52, 114, 144, 169
   internal and external identification, 56
   in the Ottoman Empire, 19
   political nature of, 53
   subjective nature of, 6, 17n

Gezi Park protests, 32–36, 43, 91–2, 186, 227, 229
govend, 2, 70, 205, 219n

Halabja, 146, 148, 152, 155, 161
HDP (Halkların Demokratik Partisi, Peoples' Democratic Party), 2–3, 36, 55–6, 58n, 90, 99, 106, 116, 134, 190, 203–8, 211, 227
  allegations of terrorism against, 126, 159, 186–7, 228, 229–31
  multicultural appeal and candidates, 209–10
  opposition to Erdogan and AKP, 70, 182–7, 212, 213–15, 225–6
  removal of mayors, 126, 212, 231
homeland(s), 112, 132, 134–5
  as element of identity, 114–16, 127, 224

identity *see* ethnic identity
Imamoğlu, Ekrem, 214–15, 231, 232
Iranian Kurds, 40n, 144, 147, 164n
Iraqi Kurds, 72, 74, 101, 146, 161–2
  peshmerga, 142, 152, 155–6, 164n
  as refugees in Turkey, 148, 164n
ISIS, 43, 85–6, 92–3, 99–102, 105, 118, 150–7, 184, 205, 224
  opposition by Kurds, 99–102, 155–7, 161–2
  Turkey's relations with, 92–3, 100–1, 142–3, 153–5
Islam, 84–106
  association with ISIS, 99
  as element of Kurdishness, 84–111
  Islamic brotherhood (*kardeşlik*), 90–1, 94–5, 96–7, 105–6, 107n
  practice amongst Kurds, 86–8
  in Turkey, 84–5, 89, 91
Istanbul, 4, 12–14, 18, 20, 21, 35, 43, 46, 55, 68, 70, 84, 92, 117, 134, 167, 186, 200, 212, 214, 215, 218n, 221, 227, 230, 231, 232, 233
Izmir, 8, 23, 27, 47, 65, 82n, 179, 214

Kemalism, 21, 22, 29–30, 37, 59, 84, 88, 91
Khani, Ahmad, 24, 143, 179
Kobanî, 99, 100, 102, 150–6, 162, 164n
Kurdayetî, 141–66
Kurdish Hizbullah, 95, 108n

Kurdish identity, 12, 24–7, 38, 50–7, 59–61, 106, 114–15, 127, 129, 132, 149, 157, 162, 172, 180, 215, 222
  and citizenship, 195, 199, 227
  contested nature of, 4, 5, 7, 55–6, 143
  denial and belittling of, 11, 22, 23, 54, 58n, 196–7
  elements of, 24, 98, 205
  Islam as element of, 84–111
  language as element of, 61–70
  and religious diversity, 102–3, 107n, 110n, 224
  transnational nature of, 141–62, 224–5
Kurdish issue, 10, 11, 18, 23, 27, 30–1, 38, 169
Kurdish language, 24, 26, 48, 61–70, 78, 79n, 80n, 145, 179–80, 200, 221, 223
  banning and belittling of, 62, 63, 64, 66, 67, 70, 197
Kurdish political parties, 28, 41n, 93–4, 119, 121, 206; *see also* BDP; HDP
Kurdistan, 127, 131–4, 135, 140n, 224
  as historical region, 132
  Kurds' aspirations to, 9–10
  Turkish disdain towards, 131–2, 133
Kurdistan Workers' Party *see* PKK
Kurds
  daily life, 14, 55, 60, 87–8, 180, 188, 221
  history of, 4, 23–5, 104, 130, 132
  narrative of political division, 141
  population in Turkey, 5, 12, 16n, 17n, 79n
  resistance to state, 22, 24–6, 73, 74–5, 170, 178–82, 232
Kurmanji *see* Kurdish language

language
  as element of identity, 61–2, 179–80
  see also Kurdish language; Turkish language

Mardin, 9, 31, 44, 67, 69, 125, 183
Margosyan, Mıgırdıç, 123, 126, 138n
Mem û Zin, 24, 32, 71–2, 141, 143, 168
Mesopotamia, 128–30, 224

MHP (Milliyetçi Hareket Partisi, Nationalist Action Party), 32, 77, 116, 186, 187, 212–13, 230
minorities, 5, 16n, 20, 29, 48, 102, 113, 121–4, 135n, 136n, 208
multiculturalism
  in Ottoman Empire, 20
  in Republic of Turkey, 29–30, 31, 69, 78–9, 126, 130, 208, 228, 229

national identity, 39n, 127
  in Turkey, 10–11, 28–30, 32, 38, 56–7, 225
nationalism, 20, 52, 72, 145
  Kurdish, 23–4, 25, 52, 94, 106, 119, 142, 143, 172, 205
  Turkish, 12, 14, 23, 25, 29, 31–2, 37–8, 42n, 52, 76, 88, 90, 106, 169, 185, 187, 194, 197, 207, 210, 212
Newroz, 31, 70–8, 81n, 82n, 125, 172, 222–3, 224–5
  restrictions and outlawing of, 72–4
  Turkish claim on, 75–6
'New Turkey', 36–8

Öcalan, Abdullah, 1, 28, 31, 35, 80n, 125, 167, 177, 180, 214
  capture, 11, 28, 149–50
  and Islam, 94
  and peace process, 21, 77
  see also PKK
oppression
  and forging of identity, 25, 172–5
  Kurdish experiences of, 119–20, 153, 168–72
Ottoman Empire, 4, 16n, 19–20, 21, 24, 59, 132, 193
  ethnic identity in, 28, 32, 56, 58n, 113, 131
  millet system, 19, 20
Özal, Turgut, 27, 66, 88

Pamuk, Orhan, 18–19, 32, 39n
pan-Kurdish identity *see* Kurdayetî
peace process, 11, 12, 30, 32, 36, 37, 77, 133, 154, 157, 178, 228, 229

PKK (Partiya Karkerên Kurdistanê, Kurdistan Workers' Party), 1–2, 7, 8, 11, 12, 28, 31, 37, 40n, 65–6, 69, 72–4, 80n, 120, 124, 133, 155, 167–71, 175–9, 203, 213, 229–30
  alleged links with HDP, 159, 186–7, 228, 229–31
  evocation of Kurdistan, 1, 22, 131
  as Kurdish political vehicle, 9–10, 17n, 28, 227
  links with PYD, 108n, 110n, 143, 157–8, 165n, 187
  military campaigns and tactics, 22–23, 27, 125
  Turkey's campaign against, 10, 11, 125–6
political violence in Turkey, 10–11, 23, 35
PYD (Partiya Yekîtiya Demokrat, Democratic Union Party), 100–1, 152, 157–9
  allegations of terrorism, 101, 158
  links with PKK, 108n, 110n, 143, 157–8, 165n, 187

Refah Party, 89–90, 93
religion *see* Islam
Republic of Turkey, 193
  establishment of, 4, 10, 21, 59, 70, 81n, 84, 170, 193
  and Islam, 86, 88, 90
  Kurds in, 1, 4, 12, 13, 21–2, 24–5, 32, 51, 54, 97, 120, 124, 170, 185, 196, 199, 217n, 222, 225, 229, 232
  national identity in, 18, 19–20, 24–5, 29, 39n, 52, 56–7, 62, 113, 121, 127, 131, 188, 195, 216
Republican People's Party *see* CHP
resistance, 22, 73, 74–5, 78, 119–20, 167, 175–89, 222–3, 225; *see also* PKK; *serhildan*
Rojava, 146, 150–60

Said, Sheikh, 1, 21, 32, 95, 97, 120, 155, 168
SDF (Syrian Democratic Forces), 142, 158–60, 163n; *see also* PYD
secularism, 88, 89

separatism, 9, 28
  fear of in Turkey, 8, 23, 27
  link with Kurdish identity, 8–9, 22–3, 66, 72, 81n, 228
Şerefname, 24, 86, 104, 168
serhildan, 168–9, 178–82, 184, 189
Simmel's rule, 147, 151, 162, 172, 173, 185, 188
Syria
  civil war, 92
  Turkey's interventions in, 110n, 116, 158–60, 212, 228
  see also Kobanî
Syriacs see Assyrians
Syrian Kurds, 38, 43, 101, 142–3, 152, 156–7, 158, 161–2

Temelkuran, Ece, 22, 33–4, 173
terrorism, 23, 25, 27, 30, 40n, 73, 120, 157–8, 160, 176, 185, 186, 232
Turkification see assimilation
Turkish constitution, 4, 36, 66, 89, 92, 193–4

Turkish identity, 4, 6, 18–21, 24–5, 39n, 52, 56, 58n, 59, 70–1, 102–4, 195
  creation of, 20, 39n
Turkish–Kurdish relations, 5, 6, 31, 47, 90, 94–5, 200–3, 211, 215, 227, 233
  idea of kardeşlik (brotherhood), 90, 96–7, 105–6, 107n
Turkish language, 61–2, 63, 78, 200
Turkish police and military forces, 10, 29, 30, 50, 73, 170–1, 175, 210
Turkish Republic see Republic of Turkey

Van Bruinessen, Martin, 4, 5, 6, 24, 55, 56, 72, 85–6, 94, 102, 106, 148, 153, 176, 222

Yezidis, 102–4, 107n, 110n, 122, 150, 210
Yıldırım, Binali, 68, 77, 214, 231
Yüksekdağ, Figen, 2, 212

Zoroastrianism, 104

EU representative:
Easy Access System Europe
Mustamäe tee 50, 10621 Tallinn, Estonia
Gpsr.requests@easproject.com